PEASE & CHITTY'S

Law of Markets and Fairs

PEASE & CHITTY'S

Law of Markets and Fairs

EDWARD F COUSINS BA, LL M
of Lincoln's Inn, Barrister

ROBERT ANTHONY LL B, M SocSc
Consultant Solicitor with
Robert Hanratty, Anthony & Co

Fifth Edition

Butterworths
London
1998

United Kingdom	Butterworths, a Division of Reed Elsevier (UK) Ltd, Halsbury House, 35 Chancery Lane, LONDON WC2A 1EL and 4 Hill Street, EDINBURGH EH2 3JZ
Australia	Butterworths, a Division of Reed International Books Australia Pty Ltd, CHATSWOOD, New South Wales
Canada	Butterworths Canada Ltd, MARKHAM, Ontario
Hong Kong	Butterworths Asia (Hong Kong), HONG KONG
India	Butterworths India, NEW DELHI
Ireland	Butterworth (Ireland) Ltd, DUBLIN
Malaysia	Malayan Law Journal Sdn Bhd, KUALA LUMPUR
New Zealand	Butterworths of New Zealand Ltd, WELLINGTON
Singapore	Butterworths Asia, SINGAPORE
South Africa	Butterworths Publishers (Pty) Ltd, DURBAN
USA	Lexis Law Publishing, CHARLOTTESVILLE, Virginia

A CIP Catalogue record for this book is available from the British Library.

ISBN 0 406 90008 6

Visit us at our website: http://www.butterworths.co.uk

Typeset by Letterpart Limited, Reigate, Surrey
Printed and bound by Bookcraft (Bath) Limited, Somerset

Preface to the Fifth Edition

Reference is made in the preface to the Fourth Edition to the then government's consultation paper on market franchise rights which was produced by the Department of the Environment on 16 August 1993. This proposed, inter alia, the modification of market rights in this country. In particular it proposed that the concept of the common law distance should be abolished insofar as the rights held by local authorities were concerned. This formed part of the government's initiative in relation to de-regulation.

However, on 10 May 1994 the government withdrew these clauses from the De-regulation and Contracting Out Bill with a view to further discussion with all interested parties as to how best to remove the effects of market franchise and monopoly rights perceived by some to be adverse in the current climate. In fact no further proposals have been made in relation to the modification of market rights in this country.

Market law therefore still continues to be of considerable relevance to buyers and sellers of commodities in markets throughout the country. Further, there have been a number of changes in the law, including the abolition of the Sunday trading legislation, the effect of which has enabled local authorities to operate markets on Sundays. There have also been a number of important decisions which this Edition analyses, such as the case of *South Pembrokeshire District Council v Wendy Fair Markets Ltd* and *In Shops Centres Plc v Derby City Council*. Also the alleged anti-competitive nature of market rights insofar as the Treaty of Rome is concerned still is of considerable interest and is explored in Chapter 11.

Finally the authors wish to express their thanks to all those who have assisted in the production of this Fifth Edition. We hope that this work will still continue to be seen as a concise treatise on this branch of the law and a practical handbook for all those involved in the operation of markets in this country.

Edward F Cousins
Lincoln's Inn, London WC2

Robert Anthony
Welshpool, Powys

April 1998

Preface to the Fourth Edition

In the Preface to the Third Edition of Pease and Chitty (published in March 1984) we referred to the need to publish a new edition having been prompted by a continuing and unfulfilled demand for the then Second Edition. This position has not changed and in fact the relevance of market law has increased substantially over the last few years.

There are many reasons for this, based principally upon changing social and economic circumstances. The social factors include a perceived demand for local markets, not only in the search for bargain goods, but also to provide a means for family outings. Economically, markets are increasingly providing an alternative method of shopping to conventional shops, a somewhat ironic situation, having regard to the history of retailing. Private market operators have proliferated over recent years. These developments have led to increasing challenges to the established legal rights under market law deriving from Charter and Statute.

In this context mention should be made of the Government's Consultation Paper on market franchise rights which was produced by the Department of the Environment on 16 August 1993. It proposes, inter alia, that the concept of the common law distance should be abolished in so far as the rights held by local authorities are concerned. Further, on 16 November 1993 judgment was handed down in the case of *South Pembrokeshire District Council* v *Wendy Fair Markets Ltd.* in which Jacob J. rejected a number of substantive arguments, raised for the first time, seeking to utilise Articles of the Treaty of Rome in support of the alleged anti-competitive nature of market rights in this country. An injunction restraining the defendant company from breaching the Council's market rights was accordingly granted. Both these developments occurred too late for inclusion in the text.

Finally, the authors express their thanks to all those who have assisted in the production of this Fourth Edition. We trust it will be of benefit for years to come.

Edward F Cousins
Lincoln's Inn, London WC2

Robert Anthony
Welshpool, Powys

December 1993

Preface to the Third Edition

In their preface to the original edition of this book, dated December 1898, Messrs Pease and Chitty expressed the hope that it would prove to be both a concise treatise on a branch of law about which little had been written in recent years, and a practical handbook for clerks of urban authorities and other persons concerned in the management of markets. Eighty six years (and two editions) later, the publishers trust that those original aspirations continue to be met by this new version, now in looseleaf form.

The decision to republish *Pease & Chitty* was prompted by a continuing, unfulfilled demand for the most recent (1958) edition. In view of that demand, and the fact that much of the 1958 edition remains of value, albeit somewhat out of date, it was decided in the first instance to retain as much of the original work as possible in preparing the first looseleaf version of the book.

The work is in three main parts.

First is the principal, descriptive text. The nine basic chapters of *Pease & Chitty* are now preceded by a number of sections of modern text, reviewing the changes in the law since 1958 on topics of current interest and importance which are cross-referenced to relevant decisions of the courts. The second part of the book contains Statutes or parts thereof relating to the establishment and operation of markets and fairs. Three pre-1953 Acts have been included which were not incorporated in the 1958 edition, and seven post-1955 Statutes have been added to bring this section up to date. Further, marginal notes against earlier Statutes described the currency of the legislation. The third and final part of the new edition is a series of new appendices containing principally model byelaws, model regulations and model agreements, all information which it is hoped should be of assistance to market owners and those who have to administer the affairs of a market authority.

Pages in the first two parts which are substantially the same as those in the 1958 edition have a grey tint at the top outer corner. The book, now re-established and in looseleaf form, will be updated completely by about March 1985, by which time a proportion of the older pages will have been replaced.

As part of the proposed revision it is intended to expand the text and to insert extracts from some of the reports of older cases which still have a high degree of significance (being cases to which practitioners do not always have ready access).

The authors jointly express their thanks to all those who have given help or encouragement in the preparation of this new version of *Pease & Chitty*, and particularly wish to thank Margaret Anthony; Susan Cohen; Canterbury City Council (per Mr T L Horton), without whose initial spur this project might not have been conceived (at least, not by us!); and all those other officers of local authorities throughout England and Wales who supplied information about unreported cases.

Finally, any suggestions which would widen the scope of the work and increase its utility will be welcomed.

Edward Cousins
Lincoln's Inn, London WC2

Robert Anthony
Welshpool, Powys

March 1984

Preface to the First Edition

Our aim has been to state in a book of moderate size the whole of the English law of markets and fairs.

Most of the materials were collected by one of us more than ten years ago, but their arrangement for the press was postponed upon the appointment of the Royal Commission on Market Rights and Tolls.

he first Report of the Commissioners was published in 1889. It contains materials for a history of markets and fairs, prepared by Mr Elton, QC, and Mr. B F C Costelloe, from which we have derived assistance. In the final Report, published in 1891, considerable alterations in the law were recommended; but Parliament has shown no inclination to carry them out.

This book consists of an Introduction and two Parts, with an Appendix. Part I contains the common law of markets and fairs, and shows how it has been modified by statute.

In Part II we have set out and commented on the enactments under which in recent times markets have usually been established. The common law seems to be applicable to markets established under statutory powers, except in so far as it is inconsistent with those powers. Part II, therefore, does not contain the whole law of statutory markets, but only such additions and modifications as are contained in the Markets and Fairs Clauses Act, 1847, and the general enactments conferring on local authorities power to establish or regulate markets. It is hoped that the cross-references and explanations will be sufficient to enable the reader to discover to what classes of markets the various provisions of the law apply.

The Appendix consists of the principal Acts whereby the common law has been modified other than those set out in Part II.

We have endeavoured to refer to every reported case on the law of markets decided in the English Courts since the seventeenth century. Earlier cases, including those in the Year Books, have been utilised somewhat more sparingly, but all have been noticed which seem to be still useful to lawyers. The printed volumes of early records, such as the Placita de Quo Warranto and the Abbrevatio Placitorum, contain many cases upon markets and fairs, but most of these are only summaries of the pleadings and the findings of juries, and are of little importance as legal authorities, however valuable they may be to the antiquary or to the historian of particular franchises. From these records we have only cited typical cases to illustrate the law as understood in the thirteenth and fourteenth centuries.

After the Introduction had been printed our attention was drawn to the passages in Professor Maitland's 'Domesday Book and Beyond', in which the origin of market-rights is explained. We are glad to find that the views we have adopted do not differ widely from those of Professor Maitland, and we refer our readers to his learned discussion of the subject.

We hope that this work will prove to be both a concise treatise on a branch of the law about which but little has been written in recent years, and a practical handbook for clerks of urban authorities and other persons concerned in the management of markets.

We desire to acknowledge our indebtedness to Mr. Stuart Moore, of the Inner Temple, for advice and information readily given to us.

J G P
H C

December, 1898.

Contents

Table of Statutes

References in this table to *Statutes* are to Halsbury's Statutes of England (Fourth Edition) showing the volume and page at which the annotated text of the Act will be found.

References in the right-hand column are to page number. Where a page number is set in **bold** this indicates that the Statute is set out in part or in full.

Table of Cases

PAGE

A

B

C

D

E

F

G

H

L

M

N

S

W

Y

CHAPTER 1

Introduction

1 NATURE OF MARKETS AND FAIRS

A Origins

A market[1] at common law is the franchise[2] right of having a concourse of buyers and sellers to dispose of commodities in respect of which the franchise is given[3]. No one can have, in law, a franchise of market, or 'a free market', as it is sometimes called[4], without a grant from the Crown or the authority of Parliament[5]. The franchise gives the holder the sole and exclusive right of holding markets within certain limits[6]; and although any person, provided he does not interfere with existing market rights, may make provision for a concourse of buyers and sellers upon his land, such a concourse, if not held under franchise or statute, is not a market in law and will not enjoy the privileges of a franchise market[7].

Markets and fairs, although probably of different origins[8], have always been treated in law as possessing almost the same incidents. Indeed, the word 'market'[9] is sometimes employed to include 'fair'[10]. Coke said that whilst every fair is a market, not every

1 From the Latin *mercatus*: buying and selling, trade.

2 See p 13, *below*.

3 *Downshire (Marquis) v O'Brien* (1887) 19 LR Ir 380, 390 per Chatterton VC. This is perhaps the happiest definition of a market to come from the Bench, but see also per Bruce J in *Collins v Cooper* (1893) 9 TLR 250. Although properly applicable to the right itself, the term is also often applied to the concourse of buyers or sellers, or to the place or day of holding the market. For example, in *Scottish Co-operative Wholesale Society Ltd v Ulster Farmers' Mart Co Ltd* [1960] AC 63 at 86, Lord Somervell defined a market as a place to which sellers who have not found buyers take their goods in the hope of finding buyers and to which buyers resort in the hope of finding the goods they want. See also p 79, *below* and *R v Bungay Justices, ex p Long* (1959) 123 JP 315 (where it was held that a meeting of people in public houses could not constitute a market). It is not essential that the owner of the franchise should own the land on which the market or fair is held except that without ownership or exclusive occupation of the soil he cannot charge stallage: see pp 51, 58, *below*. However, it is essential for there to be a concourse of buyers and sellers, see *In Shops Centres plc v Derby City Council* (1996) 95 LGR 161.

4 A 'free market' appears to mean, not a market free to the public, or free of toll, but a franchise-market, a market belonging entirely to the lord, free from the control of other persons; compare the terms 'free court', 'free fishery', 'freehold', 'free warren', and the other comprehensive expressions 'liberties' and 'franchises'.

5 See pp 13, 14, 19, *below*. The distinction between a Crown grant and a statute was not always clear in early days: see p 19, *below*.

6 See pp 69–71, *below*.

7 See p 69, *below*. The so-called street markets in London are not franchise markets: see p 6, *below*.

8 Suggestions concerning their origins may be found in the First Report of the Royal Commission on Market-Rights & Tolls (1889), by C I Elton, QC and B F C Costello; see also the judgment of Bruce J in *Collins v Cooper* (1893) 9 TLR 250, and footnote 10, *below*.

9 See footnote 1, *above*.

10 From the Latin *feria*, holiday; also an ecclesiastical term for a saint's day. The earliest fair charters are to abbeys and priories; that of St Bartholomew to the prior in 1133; and that of Stourbridge granted by King John in 1211 to the lepers of the Hospital of St Mary. Where tolls are mentioned in the charters, they are granted for the purposes of religion and charity. The gatherings at such festivals were not only for religious purposes, but also for pleasure

market is a fair[11]. The chief distinction between markets and fairs at common law appears to be connected with frequency and duration and the type of commodity offered for sale. Markets were essentially local and provided an outlet for the surrounding countryside for mainly agricultural produce; they were held once or twice a week and were normally of a day's duration. Fairs were seasonal, held two or three times a year and each was usually of several days' duration. Fairs attracted merchants and traders from further afield who brought goods and services not available locally; rural — often isolated — communities were thereby provided with an important link with the outside world. A fair has been described as great sort of market[12]; the two franchises are, however, historically separate and distinct although of equal dignity, and often exist together in the same locality[13].

A further, lesser, historical distinction concerns the ancillary activities found in a fair. Amusements have a recognised place in a fair[14]; but a market is given over entirely to business. Amusements appear not, however, to constitute a legal incident of a fair and there cannot be any franchise for a fair devoted merely to amusements. Consequently, there is no right or obligation under a franchise to hold a fair of this nature[15].

A 'mart' seems to be the same as a fair; Coke called it 'a great fair holden every year'[16]. The term is commonly applied today to a livestock market. A 'wake' was a concourse for the purposes of pleasure held usually on a feast day following after a vigil connected with the local patron saint or some religious purpose[17]. No marketing took place and its origin lies not in a franchise but in customary law[18]. 'Statute sessions' were formerly held in the spring and autumn and were called hiring fairs or statute fairs, or sometimes hiring mops. At these gatherings labourers were hired for the ensuing season and they owed their origins to the Statutes of Labourers, the first of which was passed in the reign of Edward III, and which regulated the rate of wages of labourers. The last statute on the subject was 5 Eliz I c 4 which repealed all previous enactments and provided that it should be lawful

> 'for the high constables in every shire to hold and continue petty sessions, otherwise called statute sessions, in all shires wherein such sessions have been used to be kept in such manner as heretofore accustomed'.

---

and business. They were often held in churchyards until forbidden by Statute of Winchester 1285 (13 Edw I, c 1) (repealed). The word 'nundinae' is sometimes used to describe a fair: originally it signified a weekly market; in later times it was used to describe any periodical trading assembly.

11 2 Inst 406; construing Stat Westm II 1285 (13 Edw I, c 24) (repealed). See also Stat Westm I 1275 (3 Edw I, c 31) (repealed): 'marche: this word doth here include a fair, as well as a market' (2 Inst 221).

12 See 15 Vin Abr 244, Market (A3); *Collins v Cooper* (1893) 68 LT 450.

13 *Newcastle (Duke) v Worksop UDC* [1902] 2 Ch 145 at 155, 156; and see *Gloucestershire County Council v Farrow* [1984] 1 WLR 262 at 269 per Goulding J (at first instance).

14 The existence of amusements accompanying a fair is recognised in the Metropolitan Police Act 1839, s 38. In *Wyld v Silver* [1962] Ch 561 at 570 Lloyd-Jacobs J held that the word 'fair' is a term of art and connotes a concourse of buyers and sellers for the purchase and sale of commodities pursuant to a franchise with an optional addition of provision for amusement. See also on appeal: [1963] Ch 243 at 261.

15 See *Walker v Murphy* [1914] 2 Ch 293 at 302 (affd [1915] 1 Ch 71) where the dissenting judgment of Bruce J in *Collins v Cooper* (1893) 68 LT 450, that the word 'fair' signified more than an event devoted solely to amusements, was preferred.

16 2 Inst 221.

17 *Wyld v Silver* [1963] Ch 243 at 261, 262 per Harman LJ.

18 *Ibid* at 269, per Russell LJ.

Stalls from which goods were sold were frequently found at statute sessions but this did not make them franchise markets or fairs[19].

A market or fair created solely by statute may have the incidents of a franchise market or fair, except so far as the incidents are inconsistent with the statute[20].

As mentioned above, the incident which constitutes the chief distinction between a franchise market and a mere concourse of buyers and sellers is that the owner of the former enjoys protection, and has, within certain limits, something akin to a monopoly, that is to say, the sole and exclusive right in law of holding markets[21]. He has the right to prevent the establishment, within 6⅔ miles of his own market, of any rival market which will draw customers away from his own. However a franchise market was originally much more than a right to provide for a concourse of buyers and sellers and to prevent others from doing the same; and the principle that no one can hold a market without the authority of the Crown is more fundamental than the principle that when the Crown has granted a market to one subject it cannot afterwards derogate from its grant by authorising the establishment of a rival. The monopoly is the consequence of the grant.

Many markets originated, or were established, in the Anglo-Saxon period but numbers grew impressively in the two hundred and fifty years following the Norman Conquest, a period during which population and agricultural output increased as more land was taken into cultivation. The granting of a market charter in itself stimulated agricultural production by providing an outlet for surplus produce, and the upsurge of trade during the Middle Ages encouraged the transformation of communities from the semi-rural to the wholly urban. New towns began to develop. The sale of wood and grain was vital to this process and the high cost of transport of bulk products like grain gave an added impetus to the development of those local markets not enjoying the advantages of easy access to sea or river routes.

The creation, or recognition, of markets by the king, coupled with the granting of borough status (the two not infrequently went together), were, therefore, crucial elements in the process of urbanisation; and the existence of trade and the presence of craftsmen were factors more significant than size in determining whether a settlement was a town or a village[22]. Furthermore, the development of centres for the sale of surplus produce and supply of specialised services probably was more responsible than anything else for breaking down the isolation of rural communities in the thirteenth century.

But these newly acquired rights and privileges had to be protected. A town expanded with its market, drawing in settlers from the surrounding countryside who developed specialist skills which contributed enormously to the economy of the town. By the late thirteenth century, stimulated by the grant of borough status, towns were often self governing, and could implement and enforce economic policies and their own rules and regulations. The new rights were jealously guarded against the lord, and against rival towns. Each town's economic objectives were to protect the flow of trade to its own market; ensure a regular supply and a fair distribution of foodstuffs and raw materials within the town through prevention of the manipulation of food prices (forestalling, engrossing, regrating), and uphold the privileges in buying and selling enjoyed by townspeople or burgesses over strangers. The grant of a market franchise could,

---

19 See per Blackburn J in *Simpson v Wells* (1872) LR 7 QB 214.

20 See pp 21, 22, *below*. 'Statute' or 'hiring' fairs are not legal fairs: see p 2, *above*.

21 See p 69, *below*.

22 See, for example, Platt, *The English Medieval Town* (1976), c 3; Lloyd, *The Making of English Towns* (1984), c 4; Girouard, *The English Town* (1990), c 1.

therefore, be very profitable to the grantee, and to the town burgesses who often regulated the buying and selling. It was a coveted privilege, and one which gave rise to frequent disputes[23].

This process of urbanisation continued until the middle of the fourteenth century when plague and (particularly in Wales) insurrection checked both population growth and agricultural output. Many markets without the natural advantage of location on coast or river or main traffic route declined during this period, some to disappear entirely. Others more favourably sited survived, grew and flourished, and flourish to this day.

It is probable that the operation of a legal market was made dependent on a grant to secure revenue to the Crown and to ensure control and good order in the market place. It was important that trade should be carried on only in places where it could be conducted under proper regulations, where law and order could be enforced, and where publicity of sales (which was considered essential to their validity) could be secured. Anglo-Saxon laws confined buying and selling to cities and towns, and required the presence of witnesses[24]. The laws of William I showed a similar concern:

> 'We forbid also that any live cattle be sold or bought except within cities, and then before three faithful witnesses. Likewise let no market or fair be, or be permitted to arise, except in the cities of our kingdom, and in boroughs enclosed and walled, and in castles and in very secure places where the customs of our kingdom and our common law and the dignities of our Crown, which have been constituted by our good predecessors, cannot perish, or be defrauded or violated; and all things ought to be done regularly and openly and by judgment and justice'[25].

To permit or encourage irregular buying and selling of commodities was in direct violation of such a system, and accordingly it was necessary to obtain the king's licence before promoting concourses of buyers and sellers — at any rate where they were to be held outside established towns. The grantees of such licences became market owners, charged with ensuring due observance of the law. The witnessing of sales would be one of the matters for which the lord would have to provide; and disputes arising out of such sales would, not unnaturally, be referred to him or his deputy. To this may be ascribed the origin of courts of pie powder (see below); and there would thus be most intimately connected with the holding of a market the exercise in it of civil jurisdiction.

By the thirteenth century the mere gathering together of buyers and sellers had ceased to be unlawful; but by this time the holding of a court had become incident to every market or fair. The assumption of civil jurisdiction without a grant from the Crown was unlawful: no one could hold a court except by virtue of a franchise or the tenure of lands[26]. Hence, at this period also, a grant from the king was necessary for the holding

---

23 For a lively account of the 13th century dispute between the towns of Welshpool and Montgomery over their respective markets see R Morgan, *The Montgomeryshire Collections* Vol 65, pp 7–23.

24 See Laws of Edward the Elder (901–924); Laws of Athelstan (circ 925); Laws of Edgar (959–975); Laws of Canute (circ 1017); Laws of Edward the Confessor (1043–1066); printed in *The Ancient Laws and Institutes of England* (1840), pp 68, 88, 90, 117, 167.

25 See *The Ancient Laws and Institutes of England*, p 212. Cf *ibid*, p 209.

26 See Prof Maitland's introduction to *Select Pleas in Manorial and other Seignorial Courts*, Selden Soc, vol i, where the difference between feudal or manorial jurisdictions and those which were regarded as regalities or franchises is discussed. The lord of the manor, as such, had no right to market jurisdiction. He only obtained it by charter; so that the market jurisdiction belongs rather to the class of franchise jurisdictions than to that of manorial or feudal jurisdictions. See also footnote 51, p 7.

of a market or fair, and these franchises were thenceforth treated on the same footing as the many other liberties the possession of which entitled the holder to a definite jurisdiction. It was laid down that where there was no attempt to exercise such jurisdiction the promotion of a gathering of buyers and sellers was not to be regarded as the assumption of a franchise. There are several cases in the Placita de Quo Warranto[27] which show that such gatherings at stated times were not necessarily considered to be markets. They were sometimes called wakes[28], and were not usurpations of franchise, at any rate when no toll was taken.

These cases were followed in the eighteenth century in *R v Marsden*[29], where it was held that the mere promotion or encouragement of a concourse of buyers and sellers at stated times was not the usurpation of a franchise, there being no holding of a court of pie powder, nor taking of toll. In this case Wilmot J said that

> 'the reason why a fair or market cannot be otherwise claimed [than by grant or prescription] is not merely for the sake of promoting traffic and commerce, but also for the like reason as in Roman law, for the preservation of order and prevention of irregular behaviour: *ubi est multitudo, ibi debet esse rector*'.

It was, and is, an essential condition of holding a market or fair that it should be open for all persons to frequent it for the purpose of buying and selling[30]. In consideration of the provision of land for the benefit of the public the Crown frequently granted to lords of markets and fairs the right to take toll upon goods sold in them. However, no toll could be taken without a grant. Toll was not incident to a market or fair, and many of them were toll-free. To take a toll in a toll-free market, or to take an excessive toll in any market, is unlawful and a ground of forfeiture of the franchise. The market must be kept open to all to buy and sell there freely, subject only to the payment of such tolls as have been duly authorised by the Crown or Parliament[31].

Where there is no market or fair there is nothing illegal in demanding payments resembling toll from persons admitted to buy and sell upon one's land. A person may, as a rule, throw open a building or make available a piece of land to buyers and sellers, and may stipulate whatever payment he pleases. If, however, he holds a market or fair, he must admit the public free of charge unless he has also a grant of toll. Such payments, when demanded without any franchise, cannot be recovered as toll, nor can they be distrained for or, in the absence of a contract, be recovered by action[32].

The taking of toll has been treated either as indicating that a gathering was in fact a market, or evidence of usurpation of a franchise[33]. Probably it should be regarded only as evidence that the person who takes the toll is purporting to do so under a franchise.

---

27 See pp 115 (Crosthwaite), 801 (Ramesbury), 212 (Emmeseye), 321 (Canterbury). In the last case the place seems to have been open, not to the public, but only to the tenants of the manor. The judges said that this is '*non regale, nec libertas: immo potius debet dici liberum tenementum*.' See also *Abbot of Abingdon's case* (Trin 14 John), Abb Plac, p 54.

28 See p 2, *above*.

29 (1765) 3 Burr 1812; see also *R v* ——— (1682) 2 Show 201.

30 See p 13, *below*.

31 See p 51, *below*.

32 See pp 63, 64, *below*.

33 Lord Mansfield, in *R v Marsden* (1765) 3 Burr 1812, said: 'There are no marks of a fair or market, no toll taken.' See also *R v* ——— (1682) 2 Show 201; and the cases from the Plac Quo Warr, cited in footnote 27, *above*.

B Street markets

In some towns, usually those without a market charter, there are streets in which traders are accustomed to put up stalls and sell their goods. This activity may be regulated under the Local Government (Miscellaneous Provisions) Act 1982 and the London Local Authorities Act 1990, each of which introduced a code which may be adopted by a local authority[34]. Many of the provisions were found previously in local Acts

There are many so-called street markets in London. No tolls are taken and they are not franchise markets. It is possible that in some cases they are held where markets formerly existed, but they appear to be simply gatherings of sellers at places chosen by them for their own convenience.

In the metropolis, costermongers may carry on business in the streets provided that they comply with the regulations from time to time made by the Commissioner of Police with the approval of the Home Secretary and are licensed or registered[35].

C Courts of pie powder

Courts of pie powder (or pie poudre[36]) were formerly incident to every market and fair granted by the Crown[37], and might exist by grant, prescription or custom independently of any market or fair[38]. The law administered derived from the custom of merchants so that the existence of these courts was of prime importance to the development of English mercantile law. The statute 17 Edward IV recites that

> 'Divers fairs be holden and kept in this Realm, some by prescription allowed before the Justices in eyre, and some by grant of our lord the King that now is, and some by the grant of his noble progenitors and predecessors, and to every of the same fairs is of right pertaining a Court of Pypowders, to minister in the same due justice in this behalf; in which court it hath been at all times accustomed that every person coming to the said fairs should have lawful remedy of all manner of contracts, trespasses, covenants, debts and other deeds under or done within any of the same fairs, and within the jurisdiction of the same, and to be tried by merchants being of the same fair . . .'

The court was a court of record, held before the steward (seneschal) appointed by the lord[39], or (by special custom) before the mayor or his deputy and two bailiffs of the borough or citizens[40]. In some boroughs, merchants sat also as assessors. At Stourbridge fair, which belonged to the Corporation of Cambridge, the court was held before the mayor and bailiffs of Cambridge[41].

In earlier times, the court had jurisdiction in matters arising both within and outside the limits of the fair or market and this jurisdiction extended to pleas in respect of

---

34 See pp 114 and 232 *below*.

35 See p 40, footnote 121, *below*.

36 'Court of Pepoudres, vulgarly piepowders'; 4 Inst 272. A corruption of OF 'pied pouldre', Lat '*curia pedis pulverisati*'; so called from the dusty feet of the suitors; see Shorter Oxford Eng Dict. In *Wilkinson v Nethersol* (1596) Cro Eliz 530, Anderson CJ said that these courts had this name 'because they are there to hold pleas only of things *parvi pouderis*'.

37 Stat 17 Edw IV, c 2, preamble, and I Rich III, c 6 (both repealed with savings by SLR Act 1948); 4 Inst 272; *Howel v Johns* (1600) Cro Eliz 773; *Goodson v Duffield* (1612) Cro Jac 313, 2 Bulst 21; YB 8 Hen VII, 4b, 12 Hen VII, 16b.

38 *Goodson v Duffield, above*; YB 13 Edw IV, 8b; 4 Inst 272.

39 YB 6 Edw IV, 3b; 3 Black Comm 32.

40 *Goodson v Duffield, above*; see also Com Dig, Market, G 1; Bac Abr, Court of Pipowders; 4 Inst 272.

41 Dyer, 132b, pl 80.

contracts, covenants, debts, deeds, trespasses, batteries or disturbances made, done or arising in the fair or market[42]. The court, perhaps, dealt with slanders spoken in the fair or market concerning goods exposed there[43], but not with slanders of the person which did not touch any matters of contract made there, nor with any actions concerning land. The court had no jurisdiction in penal matters[44]. The jurisdiction was contemporaneous with the holding of the fair or market, and a court held at one fair could not decide questions arising on a contract made at a preceding fair[45]. Procedure was simple and expeditious: pleas were begun without a writ and an answer had to be made within a day and in many cases within an hour. Cases could be adjourned from hour to hour and were often concluded on the same day as they had begun although judgment might be deferred to the time of another fair or market[46].

From the middle of the fifteenth century the common law began to secure a hold over the further development of mercantile law and the influence of merchants in the settlement of their disputes declined. A statute of 1477[47] restricted the jurisdiction of the courts to matters arising in the fair or market and which occurred during the time the fair or market was held. Defendants were thus enabled to escape the jurisdiction of the local court by removing themselves outside the borough limits. This, coupled with the possibility of appeal to the common law courts, and the expense that that implied, resulted in a decline in the popularity of the courts, a decline hastened by a general decrease in itinerant trading as roads and communications improved[48]. The necessity for immediate hearing of disputes was thereby rendered nugatory.

By the seventeenth century, the local courts were in a condition of terminal decline and, in the following century, Blackstone remarked that they were 'in a manner forgotten'[49]. Their demise, however, proved to be surprisingly protracted.

The County Courts Act 1888[50] enabled the lord of any hundred, honour, manor or liberty, having any court in right thereof in which debts or demands might be recovered, to surrender to the Crown the right of holding such court for any such purpose, and provided that such surrender should not be deemed to imply the surrender or loss of any other franchise incident to the lordship[51]. The same Act enabled the Crown, by order in council, to exclude from the jurisdiction of a court of local jurisdiction causes of which a county court had cognisance, if a petition, praying for such order, were presented to the Crown by the council of any city or borough, or a majority of the ratepayers of any

---

42 *Goodson v Duffield* (1613) Cro Jac 313, 2 Bulst 21; *Howel v Johns* (1600) Cro Eliz 773, 774; Statutes 17 Edw IV, c 2, and I Rich III, c 6 (repealed with savings by SLR Act 1948).

43 *Howel v Johns, above*; see 10 Cro 73b.

44 *Wilkinson v Nethersol* (1596) Cro Eliz 530. The Record of the Court of the Fair of St Ives (1275), extracts from which have been published by the Selden Society in vol ii of *Select Pleas in Manorial Courts*, presents a vivid picture of the procedure in the court of a fair. It is not clear, however, that all the matters dealt with by the steward of the fair came before him in the exercise of his jurisdiction as judge of a Court of Pie Powder. (See Prof Maitland's introduction.)

45 *Goodson v Duffield, above*; Dyer, 132b, pl 80.

46 Selden Soc, vol xxiii, pp xxv–xxvi.

47 17 Edw IV, c 2.

48 See Potter: *Historical Introduction to English Law* (1962) p 189.

49 See 8 Co Rep 383.

50 51 & 52 Vict, c 43.

51 Section 6 (repealed). The repealed 9 & 10 Vict, c 95, s 14 was to the like effect. See Law of Property Act 1922, Sch 12, para 5, preserving the rights of the lord of the manor to franchise rights in respect of fairs and markets on the abolition of copyholds, and see ss 128(1)(2), 138(12) and Sch 12, paras 4 and 6. The relevant parts of the 1922 Act were repealed by the Statute Law (Repeals) Act 1969.

parish, within which the local court was established[52]. The jurisdiction was finally abolished in 1971[53].

2 CORRECTION OF THE MARKET

Lords of markets and fairs, as such, appear not to have enjoyed any general jurisdiction over matters of a criminal nature. Market offences such as the sale of unwholesome meat, or the use of false weights and measures, mentioned in the *Judicium Pillorie*[54], came more properly within the jurisdiction known as view of frankpledge (*visus franci plegii*) or court leet, or that of sheriff's tourn; and the records of courts leet provide many examples of the punishment of offences of this nature[55]. The right to punish forestallers was either a separate franchise[56], or part of the jurisdiction of frankpledge[57].

Very often the lord of the market or fair possessed also the view of frankpledge, and in such cases the same authority which had the market jurisdiction had also criminal jurisdiction over market offences. In some places, the town burgesses were able to exercise control through the enforcement of regulations. For example, the burgesses of Newport were authorised by Earl Hugh of Stafford on 14 April 1535 to form a gild which was to determine weights and measures, set standards for victuallers and craftsmen, control all borough ordinances and regulations and hold the annual fifteen day fair to which was attached a pie powder court under the presidency of the Reeve of Newport. The burgesses of Newport were thus empowered to maintain firm control of the economic, legal and political life of the town[58].

Whilst the lord of a market, as such, had no general criminal jurisdiction, it nevertheless seems fairly clear that he had the right and duty of enforcing the Assize of Bread and Ale on market and fair days within the market, and that this right was incident to a market or fair, and followed from the grant[59].

The Assize of Bread and Ale[60] fixed the price of bread in relation to that of wheat, and the price of beer or ale in relation to those of wheat, barley and oats. Bakers and brewers convicted of not observing the assize were to be fined for the first three offences, but if the offence was 'grievous and often' they were to be sentenced, the baker to the pillory, and the brewer to the tumbrel. For the punishment of offenders against the assize, the market owner was bound to have in the market place his pillory and tumbrel, and to use them[61]. Many markets were forfeited because the lord took fines when he

---

52 Section 7 (repealed).

53 By the Courts Act 1971, s 43, as from 1 January 1972. The Report of the Royal Commission, vol iii, p 102, referred to a pie powder court as still held at Hemel Hempstead. And, until abolition, such a court still existed at Bristol (the Bristol Tolzey and Pie Poudre Courts). With regard to the latter court see the Orders in Council, dated 16 May 1871, 26 June 1873, 19 July 1883, and the orders and rules for that court, dated 20 June 1878.

54 51 Hen III, st 6, Ruff (repealed SLR Act 1863).

55 See, for instance, the Court-Leet Jurisdiction in Norwich, Selden Soc, vol v.

56 See Plac Quo Warr, Northolm, p 556.

57 For the statute for View of Frankpledge, see 18 Edw II, Ruff (repealed by 50 & 51 Vict, c 55, but without prejudice to any court-leet, &c, then still held; see s 40).

58 See Griffiths (ed), *Boroughs of Medieval Wales* (1978) pp 208–209.

59 See Plac Quo Warr, Ormskirk (p 370), Wigan (p 371), Hovingham (p 219).

60 *Assiza Panis et Cervisiae* (51 Hen III, st I, Ruff); see also *Judicium Pillorie* (51 Hen III, st 6, Ruff). These statutes were repealed by the Statute Law Revision Act 1863.

61 Stat *Judicium Pillorie* (*above*); see also Plac Quo Warr, Northolm (pp 551–557), Seton (p 123), Wahull (p 36), Ireby (p 124), Ilkeston (p 137), Suthyevele (p 75).

ought to have had recourse to these devices. This administration was referred to as the correction of the assize or the correction of the market[62], and the lord's officers for enforcing it were called correctors. So far as the lord of the market or fair was concerned, this right did not, it seems, carry with it any general right of correcting the Assize of Bread and Ale, but extended only to breaches in the market or fair.

Apart from the foregoing, there appears not to have been any general right in a market owner to exercise criminal jurisdiction. No safe conclusion can be drawn from a reading of the records of the fair courts as to the extent of market jurisdiction, except, perhaps, that the market owner did not also possess view of frankpledge. Moreover, it cannot be assumed that jurisdiction in fact exercised in any such court was always rightfully exercised, but nor should it be forgotten that a town had a reputation to maintain and that reputation could be damaged and traders coming to the market deterred if the quality of goods and services was not upheld. It was thus in a town's interests that ordinances regulating the conduct of, or correcting, the market be enforced.

3 EXTRAORDINARY JURISDICTION

In some cases lords of fairs claimed very extensive jurisdiction by special grant or prescription. An example of this claim can be found in the case of St Giles' Fair at Winchester. There a charter of Edward III[63] (confirming and enlarging previous charters) granted to the Bishop, who was the lord of the fair, that the keys of the city should be given up to him before the fair:

> '. . . and the Bishop from the time that the keys and custody of the gates have been delivered to him shall, by his justicaries and other ministers, have the custody of the whole city and cognisance of all pleas between the men and tenants of the city, and all other persons within a circuit of seven leagues round the fair, regarding breaches of law, debts, and all contracts whatsoever . . . And the said justicaries shall hold all the pleas of the Crown, whether by appeals or by indictments arising out of the facts, within the aforesaid precinct, shall pass judgment thereon, and take execution during the fair, as our justicaries do in like cases elsewhere in our realm of England.'

Similarly, the Archbishop of York had a fair there by prescription, and at the time of the fair the city bailiffs handed their staves over to the Archbishop's bailiffs, 'who shall during the fair keep the peace of the city, and collect the tolls, and take all other profits, as the city bailiffs do at other times'[64]. Again, at Hereford, the Bishop claimed by charter 'the whole care and custody of the city at the time of the fair,' and 'to have all attachments and power over all merchandise, as well, in houses as without; and that all plaints of all manner of forfeitures are to come before the bailiffs of the Bishop, and they are to do justice to all complainants, and are to receive the amercements thereon during the fair'[65].

---

62 YB II Hen VI, f 19; see also per Littledale J in *R v Starkey* (1837) 7 Ad & El 95, 107.

63 Edited by G W Kitchin DD, formerly Dean of Winchester, and printed in the Report of Royal Commission, vol i, p 91. The citizens of Winchester were granted a separate annual fair by the Crown in the fifteenth century.

64 Plac Quo Warr, 222–223; Drake's *History of the City of York* (1736), pp 218, 256.

65 Abb Plac, p 113; Duncombe's *History of Hereford* (1804), p 293.

4 THE CLERK OF THE MARKET

The franchise of a market or fair did not carry with it the right to keep standards and hold assizes of weights and measures. Where the lord of a market possessed this right, he had it as a separate and independent franchise[66]. Any general history of the law of weights and measures would be out of place here[67], but it seems proper, on account of his name and office, to make some reference to the Clerk of the Market of the King's Household (*Clericus mercati hospitii regis*).

It has been said that the duties of this ancient officer of the Crown originally consisted in the regulation of a continual market kept at the gate of the king's court[68]. But in the time of Edward I and afterwards, when this method of supplying the royal table had been abandoned, his duties were somewhat different. He was entrusted with standards and samples of the king's weights and measures; and with these he travelled from place to place and held his courts at all markets within the verge[69]. He examined the weights and measures used in the market, burned such as were false, and fined offenders[70]. The refusal of the bailiff of a market to submit to his jurisdiction was a ground for seizure of the franchise into the king's hands[71]. In some cases he may have had power to inquire into the jurisdiction of the lord of the market, and to ascertain whether the Assize of Bread and Ale had been duly kept[72].

By the retention of fines which ought to have been paid into the Exchequer[73] and the exaction of bribes and illegal fees, the office was made very profitable; and in 1389 and 1392 the abuses of the office attracted the attention of Parliament[74]. Another matter of complaint about the same period was that the officer acted outside his jurisdiction, and refused to recognise the charters which the Crown from time to time granted to cities and other places excmpting them from his control[75]. Such exemptions seem to have been granted freely down to the reign of Henry VIII. At any rate, two of his statutes provided that, notwithstanding any grant to the contrary, the King's Clerk of the Market, and

66 See, for example, Plac Quo Warr, Standford (p 395), Catthorp (p 395), Stanewyg (p 70).

67 The present law on the subject, so far as it relates particularly to markets and fairs, is dealt with at p 119 *et seq, below*.

68 4 Inst 273; 2 Inst 543.

69 The verge extended to within 12 miles from the place where the king was keeping his court.

70 Fleta, bk 2, c 20; Britton, bk I, c 31, ff 75b, *et seq*; 4 Inst 273.

71 See Britton, *loc cit, above*; cf per Brian CJ, YB 2 Hen VII, f II.

72 *Ibid.* In 1406 the clerk of the market was ordered 'to do his office as in the time of Edward I ordained and used'; see Rot Parl 8 Hen IV, No 82. The extent of his jurisdiction must have depended in each case upon the terms and validity of the letters patent appointing him; see *Burdett's Case* (1709) 1 Salk 327, which seems to be the latest reported case in which this officer's powers were considered in a court of law. This royal officer must not be confused with the clerk or bailiff of a market appointed by the lord to regulate it on the lord's behalf.

73 The accounts of the clerks of the market from 25 Edw I to 36 Eliz appear to be kept at the Record Office; see 19th Report of the Deputy Keeper of the Public Records, p 7 (1858), and 20th Report, p xiii (1859).

74 See 15 Rich II, st I, c 4, and 16 Rich II, c 3 (repealed SLR Act 1863). See also Rot Parl 18 Edw III, No 12(4), and 50 Edw III, Nos 87 and 152.

75 See Rot Parl 51 Edw III, No 53; 1 Rich II, Nos 75 and 128. Under the charters of 1327, 1462 and 1550, the exclusive right of performing all that appertained to the office within the City of London and the Borough of Southwark was conferred upon the Lord Mayors and their deputies, who thus acquired authority to regulate the weights and measures used in the London markets (see Birch, *Hist Charters of London* (1887) pp 55, 82, 122; Royal Commisson, 1893, City of London, Statement by the Corporation, p 272). In the Duchy of Lancaster the Duke acquired by charter the like exclusive right (see Hardy's *Charters of the Duchy* (1845)).

none other, should exercise the office within the verge in places where the king from time to time tarried in person[76].

'The Description of England' in Holinshed's Chronicles contains an interesting chapter on fairs and markets[77]. The 'covetousness' of the clerks of the market is there lamented, and it is stated that at each view of measures they had a trick of providing business for the next. By 1640 further abuses had arisen. The clerks had assumed jurisdiction both within and without the verge[78], and the office was usually farmed out in each county at a sum which the lessee could make up only by extortion. To remedy this, the 16 Cha I c 19, was passed, which again confined the jurisdiction of the Crown official within the verge of the king's court, and entrusted the execution of the office outside, in cities and boroughs to the mayor or other head officer, and in liberties and franchises to the lord or his deputy. All these persons were subsequently empowered and required to seal or mark measures of corn and salt when brought to them for that purpose[79]; and it was further provided[80] that in places where there was no clerk of the market this duty should be performed by 'the person having the benefit of the market'. These seem to be the latest statutes in which the Clerk of the Market of the King's Household is referred to by name[81].

Blackstone says that 'the court of the clerk of the market is incident to every fair and market in the kingdom, to punish misdemeanours therein'[82]; but at the time when he wrote the court of this officer of the king's household was, in all probability, almost obsolete[83]. Indeed, even in Coke's day there was 'no great need for him, for the justices of assize, the justices of oyer and terminer, the justices of the peace, the sheriffs in their tourns, and the lord in their leets, may so inquire of false weights and measures'[84]. It has been stated that one of the recorded instances of a clerk of the market exercising powers as a king's officer was in Middlesex, in 1738, when such an officer was authorised by letters patent to inspect all weights and measures within the 'little verge'.

---

76 27 Hen VIII, c 24, s 10; 32 Hen VIII, c 20, s 7. The franchise rights of London and certain other places were preserved.

77 Bk 2, ch 18 (2nd ed, 1587).

78 Relying, possibly, on the 14 Edw III, st 1, c 12; 'And it is not the king's mind but that the clerk of the market shall do his office where he will, according as he was wont to do in times past'.

79 22 Cha II, c 8, s 4.

80 22 & 23 Cha II, c 12, s 4.

81 The repeal of these statutes by the Statute Law Revision Act 1863 was without prejudice to established jurisdictions or existing franchises or offices, although derived from those statutes. The Weights and Measures Act 1878, s 69 (repealed), preserved existing franchises to examine, and verify or destroy, weights and measures; and the Weights and Measures (Purchase) Act 1892 (repealed) authorised county and borough councils to purchase such franchises by agreement.

82 4 Bl Com 275.

83 Blackstone was misled by a passage in Nathaniel Bacon's *Law of English Government* (bk I, c 8) into stating that the court derived its jurisdiction from the bishop.

84 See 4 Inst 273. The sheriff's tourn was abolished by 50 & 51 Vict, c 55, s 18.

CHAPTER 2

Creation and Acquisition of Markets and Fairs

1 TITLE TO THE FRANCHISE

A Nature

The right of holding a market or fair is well known to the common law. It is an incorporeal hereditament, and is one of those incorporeal hereditaments which are called franchises[1]. A franchise is usually defined as a royal privilege or branch of the Crown's prerogative subsisting in the hands of a subject[2], either by virtue of a grant or by prescription. A franchise not only authorises something to be done, but gives the owner the right of preventing others from interfering with it[3]. The right of creating a franchise to hold a market or fair has, from time immemorial, been annexed to the Crown as part of the prerogative[4]; and no market or fair in the hands of a subject can have a legal origin or legal existence unless established by the royal prerogative[5], or by the authority of an Act of Parliament[6].

The Crown, indeed, may create a market or fair 'by ordinance without granting it unto any'[7]. In other words, the Crown may, by virtue of the prerogative, establish a market or fair to subsist in the hands of the Crown, and the formal instrument providing for its establishment is called an ordinance. The early records contain several references to markets and fairs subsisting in the hands of the Crown[8], and also examples

---

1 Finch, L 164; 2 Bl Com 36–38; 3 Cru Dig, 4th ed, vol xxvii 267.

2 *Ibid.*

3 See *below* p 69; *A-G v Horner* (1885) 11 App Cas 66 at 80.

4 Bracton, bk 3, tract 2, c 1, s 3, f 117; Bac Abr, Fairs and Markets (A 1); notes to 2 Wms Saund 501n(b).

5 As to the rare case of the valid creation of a franchise by a subject having jura regalia, see *Grant on Corporations*, 11. Durham market seems to have originated in a grant in 1180 to the Corporation of Durham by the then Bishop of Durham: see Report of Royal Commission, vol xiii, part ii, p 176; vol iv, p 384. For a claim by a lord of Powys (Gruffydd ap Gwenwynwyn) in the thirteenth century that every lord having a town in the Welshry was permitted by Welsh law to hold a market and fair in his land, see the Welsh Assizes Roll, 1277–84 ed JC Davies, PRO, pp 148–149, 235–236. Richard Morgan gives a vivid account in the Montgomeryshire Collections, Vol 65, pp 7–23 of the dispute between Gruffydd and Henry III over their respective markets at Welshpool and Montgomery.

6 In *New Windsor Corpn v Taylor* [1899] AC 41, Watson LJ was of the opinion (at 48) that the legislature alone cannot create a franchise. This was doubted by Megarry VC in *Leicester City Council v Oxford and Bristol Stores Ltd* (21 December 1978, unreported), who could not see why, if the statute were clear, it should be said that Parliament has no power to create a franchise or any other common law right by Act of Parliament. Compare also the observations of Bowen LJ in *Manchester Corpn v Lyons* (1882) 22 Ch D 287 at 310. See also *below* p 21.

7 Hob 15, the source of the statements to the same effect in 2 Roll Abr 197; 17 Vin Abr 145; Chitty's *Prerogatives of the Crown*, p 193.

8 See, for example, Rot Hundred, vol i, p ii (Sallingford fair), p 13 (Wycombe fair), p 18 (Windsor fair), p 70 (Exeter fair, a moiety of which was in the hands of the king and the citizens); Abb Plac, p 206b (Hereford fair), p 246 (Marlborough market); Plac Quo Warr, p 185 (Bridport market).

of ordinances for their creation[9]; but few, if any, remain in the ownership of the Crown[10]. The 'King's markets' and the 'King's fairs' of former times have been either granted away to subjects[11], or discontinued.

In early times the franchise of holding markets and fairs was normally granted to the lord of the manor within which they were to be held, or, where they were to be held within a city or borough, to the city or borough corporation. Charters incorporating inhabitants of towns often contained grants of markets and fairs to the new corporations; and, indeed, sometimes the inhabitants were incorporated for no other purpose than that the body incorporate might hold a market or fair. This was the case at Hemel Hempstead under a Charter of 1539[12]. Sometimes the inhabitants were not incorporated, but a body corporate was created to hold fairs in trust for them. Thus at Hungerford the franchise was granted in 1432 to the then lords of the manor, and the grant incorporated them and made them trustees of the franchise for the inhabitants[13]. In the reign of Queen Anne there were instances of grants to individual persons in fee in trust for the inhabitants, in which neither the inhabitants nor their trustees were incorporated[14]; and in one case the trust was for the poor of the parish[15]. Markets and fairs at one time existed at Skipsea and Withernsea under grants simply 'to the men of the vill their heirs and successors'[16]. The difficulties, both legal and practical, in the way of the franchise being exercised by the inhabitants of a place when not incorporated were probably met, in these cases, by the fact that the manors were in the hands of the king, whose bailiffs seem to have regulated these markets and fairs[17]; and accordingly grants of this kind should, perhaps, be described as ordinances. There is authority, however, for the view that a grant by the Crown to the inhabitants of a particular parish or vill for such a specific purpose as the holding of a market has the effect of incorporating them so as to facilitate the carrying into effect of that purpose[18].

In more recent times, markets and fairs have generally been established by special or general Acts of Parliament, and in many cases old markets have been modified by statute[19]. How far a statutory market has the incidents of a common law market and

---

9 See, for example, Rot Chart, p 77 (2 John, Portsmouth), p 135 (6 John, Marlborough).

10 See the Parliamentary Return on Market Rights and Tolls, 1886; 74th Report of the Commissioners of Woods 1896; and the Final Report of the Royal Commission on Market Rights & Tolls, pp 18 *et seq.*

11 Thus, the Crown sold Romford Market in 1829: see Report of Royal Commission, vol iii, p 53; and see *ibid* as to Hitchin.

12 See Report of Royal Commission, vol iii, p 102.

13 *Ibid*, vol iv, p 173.

14 Pat 8 Anne, p 5, No 13 (Chagford); Pat 5 Anne, p 2, No 18 (Wincalton). See Report of Royal Commission (1888), vol i, pp 133, 134.

15 Pat 4 Anne, p 3, No 9 (St Udy). See Report of Royal Commission, vol i, p 132.

16 See Cal Rot Chart, p 174, 12 Edw III, Nos 29, 30. Poulson (*Hist of Holderness*, vol i, p 445) sets out the grant to the men of Skipsea.

17 See Poulson, *Hist of Holderness*, vol i, p 398, vol ii, p 458.

18 See *Rivers (Lord) v Adams* (1878) 3 Ex D 361, 366, per Kelly CB, who cites the early authorities; and *Willingale v Maitland* (1866) LR 3 Eq 103, 109. But in *Wyld v Silver* [1963] Ch 243 (see *below*, pp 100–101), a prescriptive right to hold a fair or wake was held to be vested in the inhabitants of a parish: '. . . the present right . . . is a right in each member of the fluctuating body of inhabitants from time to time to offer goods for sale or to disport himself in manner consistent with the law. It seems to me that it is quite incapable of resting in anyone except the inhabitants. How could the sum of their rights vest in the churchwardens and overseers (or in any trustee)?' (per Russell LJ at 271).

19 *Below*, pp 19, 20

how far an old market modified by a statute retains such incidents depends on the terms of the statute[20].

B The owner as market authority

An individual grantee of a market or fair is generally called the lord or the owner of the market or fair. But this is, perhaps, not an altogether convenient expression where a market or fair is in the hands of a body of persons, such as trustees or a district council. 'The market authority' is a term which is generally used to include every kind of market owner.

2 CREATION OR ACQUISITION OF MARKET RIGHTS

A Acquisition by charter and letters patent

(1) Nature

The instruments by which the Crown grants rights and privileges to subjects are known as charters, letters patent and letters close[21]. From the end of the twelfth century to the year 1516, all grants of markets and fairs were made by charter[22]. After that date, grants were made by letters patent[23]. Since 1846 very few grants of market rights have been made by the Crown[24].

The difference between charters and letters patent is mainly one of form, charters being documents of a more strictly formal nature[25]. If the charter or letters patent is expressed as having been granted by the Crown 'with Parliament's assent', or similar words, strictly this is in the nature of a grant of a private or local and personal Act of Parliament, and should be construed and receive effect according to its nature[26].

(2) Crown cannot derogate from grant

The essential feature of a market franchise is that the holder has the sole and exclusive right of holding markets within the common law distance of 6⅔ miles[27], the

20 *Below*, p 21.

21 As to proof of grants, see the section on 'Grants', in 'Evidence of Market Rights', Ch 11, *below*. 'Charters are donations of the sovereign; and not laws, but exemption from law' (Hobbes).

22 Introduction to *Rotuli Chartarum*, by Sir Thos Duffus Hardy, vol i, pt i, pp 1, 11.

23 Introduction to *Rotuli Litterarum Patentium*, vol i, p 11. Grants have generally been made in perpetuity but occasionally have been limited in time, eg for a term of 40 or 95 years or with a clause determining the grant upon a certain event: see Pat 6 Anne, p 4, No 8; 9 Anne, p 3, No 7; 4 Anne, p 4, No 21; Report of Royal Commission, vol i, pp 132–134.

24 Walton J in *Kingston-Upon-Thames Royal Borough Council v Sherman and Waterman Associates Ltd* (6 July 1976, unreported) said that he was not aware of any suggestion that the power of the Crown to grant franchises of markets is any the less exercisable now than it ever was. His remarks were, however, *obiter* and the charter in question (granted by Elizabeth II on 10 March 1964) was, in effect, confirmatory of earlier charters on the occasion of the reorganisation of London government.

25 Many examples of grants of markets and fairs may be found in the *Rotuli Chartarum*. See, for example, the grant by Edward I dated 16 January 1280 in respect of Newtown, Powys in Rot Chart 8 Edw 1, m 11 no 73 (translation in *Mont Colls* vol 32, p 188).

26 *Great Eastern Rly Co v Goldsmid* (1884) 9 App Cas 927 per Selborne LC at 934 and 936. See p 128, *below*.

27 See pp 69–71, *below*.

justification for which, it has been said, is the benefit of the public[28]. This exclusive right is, however, private in nature and the market owner does not act on behalf of the Crown in the exercise of the latter's prerogative, notwithstanding the duties towards members of the public imposed on the market owner by the grant of the franchise[29]. Many of the rules which have grown up under the common law for the purpose of regulating rights and duties of market franchises were formulated with the public interest in mind[30]. This principle affects the power of the Crown to grant market rights: the Crown may not, except with the consent of the owner of the existing market rights[31], grant new market rights which would be injurious to the earlier grant[32]. An Act of Parliament is the only instrument which can infringe or detract from a previous grant. The rule is recognised by the common inclusion in a grant of a clause to the effect that the grant is made unless it is to the injury of neighbouring markets and fairs[33]. But the omission of such a clause from a grant will not benefit the grantee since it is implied by law[34].

It has been said, however, that a prior grantee loses the benefit of his priority by not making use of his grant[35], but not by merely failing to provide proper accommodation for the public[36]. Failure by a grantee to provide proper accommodation will not entitle the Crown to derogate from the grant previously made by granting a new charter whilst the old remains unrepealed[37]. A new grant may, nevertheless, be justified where the prior grant is so limited by metes and bounds or by the district that accommodation sufficient for the needs of the public cannot be provided. The new market must, however, provide sufficient additional accommodation to remedy the inconvenience, without affecting the existing market[38].

If a grant by the Crown of market rights purports to give greater protection than that given by the common law, the grant is void[39].

(3) Inquisition under writ of ad quod damnum

In order to guard against the making of improper grants, it was the practice of the Crown not to make a grant until an inquisition had been held under a writ of *ad quod*

---

28 'The justification for the grant of a monopoly of market is that the existence of the market is for the benefit of the public. If the market keeper is not to get his outlay back and something more, he will give up the market, and where will the public be then?' per Hamilton LJ in *A-G v Horner (No 2)* [1913] 2 Ch 140 at 198 (referring also to the observations of Lord Macnaghten in *Simpson v A-G* [1904] AC 476 at 483). See also the remarks of Slade LJ in *Sevenoaks District Council v Pattullo and Vinson Ltd* [1984] 1 All ER 544 at 551.

29 *Spook Erection Ltd v Secretary of State for the Environment* [1989] QB 300, 86 LGR 736; and see pp 128, 129, *below*.

30 *Ibid.*

31 Consent may be presumed from long user without objection: *Holcroft v Heel* (1799) 1 Bos & P 400; *Campbell v Wilson* (1803) 3 East 294; *Great Eastern Rly Co v Goldsmid* (1884) 9 App Cas 927. See also p 17, *below*. For a modern case involving the construction of old charters, see *Crown Estate Comrs v City of London Corpn* (1992) Times, 11 May.

32 Such grant would be void as against the owner of the existing market rights. See Bracton, lib ii, c 24, f 56b; Vin Abr 'Franchise' (G)9; *Re Islington Market Bill* (1835) 3 Cl & Fin 513.

33 'Ita ut non sit ad nocumentum vicinorum mercatorum'.

34 *R v Butler* (1685) 3 Lev 220.

35 Bracton, lib ii, c 24, ff 56b, 57.

36 The remedy is to sell out of the market; see pp 31, 84–86, *below*.

37 *Re Islington Market Bill* (1835) 3 Cl & Fin 513.

38 *Ibid*, and see pp 81, 82, *below*.

39 *Re Islington Market Bill* (1835) 3 Cl & Fin 513.

damnum and a jury had found, by their return to the writ, that the proposed market or fair would not be to the damage of the Crown or any subject[40]. But an invalid grant derives no validity from the fact that such inquisition was held. If it should appear, after the grant has been made, that it caused an injury to the earlier grant, or that the Crown was otherwise deceived in making it[41], that is a ground for its repeal by *scire facias*[42]. Moreover, the grantee of a market or fair injured by a later grant may bring an action for damages at once and without waiting until the later grant has been repealed[43].

B Acquisition by prescription or usage

A claim to hold a market or fair, or to take tolls, as of right, can be supported at common law only on the ground that the Crown has granted a franchise to the claimant or his predecessors in title[44]; but it by no means follows that inability to produce such a grant is fatal to the claim. 'Prescription and antiquity of time fortifies all titles, and supposeth the best beginnings the law can give them'[45].

(1) Immemorial user

A market or fair is said to have been held from time immemorial or, to use the traditional phrase, from time 'whereof the memory of man runneth not to the contrary', whenever it has been held from before legal memory, that is, the beginning of the reign of Richard I in 1189[46]. If the possessor of a market or fair can show that he and his predecessors in title held it openly, uninterruptedly and as of right[47] from time immemorial, the law will presume that the market or fair had a lawful origin in an ancient grant, which, owing to the vicissitudes of history[48], has been lost forever[49]. In such circumstances, the owner of the market or fair is said to have a title by prescription to the franchise.

(2) Long user

Positive evidence that the market or fair has been held ever since the commencement of legal memory is not, however, essential to secure a title by prescription. It would seldom be possible in practice to produce such evidence. Thus, whenever evidence is given of uninterrupted modern user, a presumption is raised of enjoyment from time

---

40 FNB 225F. In 1252, Henry III ordered the Sheriff of Shropshire to investigate 'by proof of oath and of lawful men of his county, if the market of Griffin son of Wenunwin of la Pole [see footnote 5, *above*] is to the damage of the . . . King's market of Montgomery' and that, if so, it should be forbidden: Close Rolls, VII, m 23, p 55. For a more recent example (1683), see *Great Eastern Rly Co v Goldsmid* (1884) 9 App Cas 927 at 939, 940. The writ has now fallen into disuse.

41 17 Vin Abr 102, 'Prerogative' (Ob) 14.

42 *R v Aires* (1717) 10 Mod 258, 354, sub nom *R v Eyre* 1 Stra 43; *R v Butler* (1685) 3 Lev 220; *Re Islington Market Bill* (1835) 3 Cl & Fin 513; and see *Great Eastern Railway Co v Goldsmid* (1884) 9 App Cas 927 and p 139, *below*.

43 2 Inst 406; and see pp 139, 140, *below*.

44 See p 13, *above*.

45 *Slade v Drake* (1618) Hob 295. See under 'Evidence of Market Rights', Ch 11, *below*.

46 Co Litt 114b, 215a; 2 Roll Abr 268, 269; *Chapman v Smith* (1754) 2 Ves Sen 506 at 514.

47 . . . and not by violence, stealth, or entreaty (*nec vi, nec clam, nec precario*).

48 Not excluding, thought Walton J, the depredations of rats and mice: *Kingston-upon-Thames Royal Borough Council v Sherman and Waterman Associates Ltd* (6 July 1976, unreported).

49 Co Litt 114b; *Wyld v Silver* [1963] Ch 243.

immemorial which may be rebutted by evidence to the contrary[50]; and a user for 20 years, if uncontradicted and unexplained, is sufficient to raise such a presumption[51]. If, however, it is shown that the user arose within legal memory, then, however long the modern user, a claim to a title by prescription will fail[52].

(3) Lost modern grant

The doctrine of lost modern grant developed[53] as a result of the ease with which claims to prescription could be defeated by showing that the right did not exist at some time subsequent to the commencement of legal memory. Accordingly, even if it is shown that there was a time within legal memory at which the market or fair did not exist, the court will presume a legal origin in a grant, now lost, if a user for any considerable length of time has been open, uninterrupted and as of right[54], and such legal origin is possible.

The court will not, however, infer an origin which involves illegality or impossibility. Thus, the court will not presume a lost modern grant which, had it existed, would have contravened a public statute[55]; nor will the court make a presumption not in accordance with the right claimed[56].

ILLUSTRATIONS

In *A-G v Horner*[57], it was considered that a long usage to hold markets on certain week days arose out of a grant from James II which was subsequently made void by statute. And, in *Benjamin v Andrews*[58], no legal origin could be presumed for a market held on a Saturday for 25 years since it was considered to be an abuse of an existing grant to hold one on Fridays. In both these cases, therefore, the claim failed.

---

50 *Jenkins v Harvey* (1835) 1 Cr M & R 877 at 894, per Parke, B; *Shephard v Payne* (1864) 16 CBNS 132 at 135, per Blackburn J; *Penryn Corpn v Best* (1878) 3 Ex D 292; *A-G v Horner (No 2)* [1913] 2 Ch 140.

51 *R v Joliffe* (1823) 2 B & C 54; *Bealey v Shaw* (1805) 6 East 208, per Lord Ellenborough CJ. The period of 20 years is, however, merely a convenient guide and not a fixed rule; but obviously the longer the period the harder it ought to be to rebut the presumption of immemorial user. Market franchises are not easements or profits à prendre within the Prescription Act 1832, and must still be prescribed for at common law: *Benjamin v Andrews* (1858) 5 CBNS 299; and see p 89, *below*.

52 Co Litt 115a; *Kingston-upon-Hull Corpn v Horner* (1774) 1 Cowp 102, 108.

53 The earliest reported decision is *Lewis v Price* (1761) 2 Wms Saund 175a.

54 'It is a maxim of the law of England to give effect to everything which appears to have been established for a considerable time, and to presume that what has been done has been done of right and not of wrong': per Pollock CB, *Gibson v Doeg* (1857) 2 H & N 615. 'It is a most convenient thing that every supposition not wholly irrational, should be made in favour of long continued enjoyment': per Bramwell B, *Penryn Corpn v Best* (1878) 3 Ex D 292. See also: *Kingston-upon-Hull Corpn v Horner* (1774) 1 Cowp 102; *Holcroft v Heel* (1799) 1 Bos & P 400; *Campbell v Wilson* (1803) 3 East 294; *Halliday v Phillips* (1889) 23 QBD 48; affd sub nom *Phillips v Halliday* [1891] AC 228; *A-G v Horner* (1884) 14 QBD 245; affd (1885) 11 App Cas 66; *A-G v Horner (No 2)* [1913] 2 Ch 140 at 176–177, per Buckley LJ; *Hammerton v Earl of Dysart* [1916] 1 AC 57.

55 *Neaverson v Peterborough RDC* [1902] 1 Ch 557 at p 573; *A-G v Horner* (1884) 14 QBD 245.

56 *Benjamin v Andrews* (1858) 5 CBNS 299; *Campbell v Wilson* (1803) 3 East 294; *A-G v Horner (No 2)* [1913] 2 Ch 140 at 169–170, per Cozens-Hardy MR.

57 (1884) 14 QBD 245. In *A-G v Horner (No 2)* [1913] 2 Ch 140, the Court of Appeal was not prepared to presume a legal origin for a 'private market' held on days other than the charter days, which was a usage inconsistent with the rights claimed.

58 (1858) 5 CBNS 299.

(4) Nature of user

To establish a claim to a market or fair by prescription, or under a lost grant, it is necessary to show a usage which, as regards such details as time and place, is in accordance with the right claimed. If the claim is to hold a market on Saturdays, it is useless to prove that it is sometimes held on Saturdays, and sometimes on Wednesdays; and if it is to hold a fair in one place, it is useless to give evidence that it has sometimes been held elsewhere. Such evidence, as a rule, tends to defeat the claim set up. But a claim may be established by proving a larger right which includes the lesser right claimed[59]. A claim to hold a market at a particular spot within a manor will be sustained by proving a right to hold it anywhere within the manor; and proof of a right to hold a market on Wednesdays and Saturdays is sufficient to establish a claim to hold a market on Saturdays.

C Acquisition by statute

(1) General

The privilege of holding a market or fair may be created by statute, and rights so acquired are much less likely to be called into question than franchise rights created by charter[60]. The Crown has no power to grant a market to the disturbance of another market previously granted[61], nor can it authorise unreasonable tolls[62]; but Parliament is not bound to respect existing rights[63], and the reasonableness of tolls specifically authorised by Parliament cannot be questioned. Further, a statutory market is not liable to forfeiture to the Crown, nor can it be repealed by writ of *scire facias*[64].

In early times, there was often no very great difference, as regards the general form of the instrument, between an Act of Parliament and a charter; and it may be difficult to establish to which category a particular document belongs. If, however, the charter conferring market rights is expressed as having been made with the authority of Parliament, or words to that effect, then it has the force of an Act of Parliament[65]. Nevertheless, clear and express words are necessary to authorise the establishment of a statutory market[66].

(2) Local or special Acts

Many Acts of Parliament have been passed for the establishment or regulation of markets and fairs; and these frequently incorporate the whole or part of the Markets and Fairs Clauses Act 1847[67] which was passed to reduce repetition and ensure greater uniformity by consolidating in one Act provisions frequently found in earlier local Acts

---

59 Per Coleridge J, *Bailey v Appleyard* (1838) 8 Ad & El 161.
60 *New Windsor Corpn v Taylor* [1899] AC 41 at 50, per Lord Davey.
61 See pp 15, 16, *above*.
62 See p 53, *below*.
63 A statute may 'cross and change the common law, which a charter alone cannot do': *Prince's Case* (1606) 8 Co Rep 1a.
64 *New Windsor Corpn v Taylor* [1899] AC 41 at 45, 48, 50.
65 *Prince's Case* (1606) 8 Co Rep 1a, 20a; *Great Eastern Rly Co v Goldsmid* (1884) 9 App Cas 927; and see pp 127–128, *below*.
66 Per Templeman LJ in *R v Basildon District Council, ex p Brown* (1981) 79 LGR 655 at 666 and also at 673 per Dunn LJ. *Quaere* whether a statutory market can be created by estoppel: *ibid*. (Compare the remarks of Dunn LJ at *ibid* p 674, and Lord Denning MR at 662–663.)
67 The Act is set out on pp 179 *et seq*, *below*. See also pp 109 and 110, *below*.

for constructing or regulating markets and fairs. The 1847 Act now affects all markets and fairs the construction or regulation of which is authorised by a local Act[68] ('the special Act'[69]) which declares that the 1847 Act is to be incorporated with it[70].

The special Act may incorporate the whole of the 1847 Act. Alternatively, it may incorporate a portion of it either by incorporating the Act with the exception of specified clauses, or by incorporating specified clauses of it. The 1847 Act, or the specified portion incorporated, forms part of the special Act as if it were set out at length, subject to any express variations or exceptions in the special Act[71].

At the date of the passing of the 1847 Act, it was probably thought that it would provide a complete code for market authorities. Experience has shown, however, that the code is incomplete and in practice special Acts for the establishment of markets usually contain more ample provision for regulating markets and keeping order in them. Many authorities include provisions relating to markets in their General Powers Act.

(3) Public Acts[72]

(a) *The Food Act 1984*[73]. A council of a local authority may either establish a market within its area[74] or acquire by agreement (but not otherwise), by purchase or on lease, the whole or part of an existing market undertaking within its area, and any rights enjoyed by any person within its area in respect of a market and of tolls[75]. In either case, a local authority may provide a market place with convenient approaches to it, and a market house and other buildings convenient for the holding of a market[76]. A market cannot, however, be established under this Act which would interfere with any market rights, powers or privileges enjoyed within the area by any person without that person's consent[77]. But a grant of planning permission will not confer on the owner of land a market right sufficient to create a fetter on the market authority from setting up a rival market, or otherwise.[78] And note that a local authority[79] which has already *established* a market under this Act, or under the Acts preceding and replaced by this Act[80], is not protected as against another local authority seeking to establish a market[81]; although a franchise market *acquired* by a local authority under these powers would enjoy protection.

---

68 And not only local Acts: see the Animal Health Act 1981, pp 111 and 214 to 231, *below*.
69 1847 Act, s 2, p 180, *below*.
70 *Ibid*, ss 1, 2. As to the power of a municipal corporation to oppose a bill for establishing a market in a borough, see *A-G v Brecon Corpn* (1878) 10 Ch D 204.
71 1847 Act, s 1, p 180, *below*. For an example of an express variation in a special Act, see *Rutherford v Straker* (1887) 42 Ch D 85n, and paragraph E on p 92, *below*, and the cases there cited.
72 See p 171, *below*.
73 The Act is set out on pp 243 *et seq*, *below*.
74 1984 Act, s 50(1)(a), p 243, *below*.
75 *Ibid*, s 50(1)(b).
76 1984 Act, s 50(1)(b)(i) and (ii). For these purposes, land may be acquired compulsorily: *ibid*, s 110.
77 1984 Act, s 50(2). For a discussion of the interpretation of this subsection, see *Stoke-on-Trent City Council v WJ Wass Ltd* (4 March 1997, unreported) at first instance, (1989) 87 LGR 129, CA. For disturbance, see Chapter 6, *below*.
78 *Delyn Borough Council v Solitaire (Liverpool) Ltd* (1995) 93 LGR 614; and p 129, *below*.
79 'Local authority' means a district council, a London borough council or a parish or community council: 1984 Act, s 61; Food Safety Act 1990, Sch 2, paras 2, 11.
80 That is, the Food and Drugs Acts 1955 and 1938 and the Public Health Act 1875: see 1984 Act, s 50(3).
81 *Ibid*.

A local authority which has established or acquired a market under this Act, or preceding legislation, is a market authority[82].

(b) *The Animal Health Act 1981*[83]. Certain local authorities are empowered under the Animal Health Act 1981[84] to provide, erect and fit up wharves, stations, lairs, sheds and other places for the landing, reception, sale, etc of imported or other animals, carcases, fodder, etc[85]; and a wharf or other place so provided is a market within the Markets and Fairs Clauses Act 1847[86] and that Act is incorporated, with certain exceptions, with the 1981 Act[87].

(4) Statutory markets and the common law incidents

When a statutory market has been established under a local or public Act, the question may arise as to whether the whole law of the market must be sought for in the Act and any Acts incorporated with it, or whether the statutory market can have any incidents of a common law market in addition to the rights expressly attached to it by such Acts. It now appears to be settled that all the incidents of a common law market are incidents of a statutory market except in so far as they are varied or taken away by the statutes[88]. There is no reason to suppose that when, as a matter of historical constitutional development, the grant of a market franchise passed from one authority to another, namely, from the Crown to Parliament, the nature of the rights incidental to the franchise should have altered[89].

How will a new enactment affect an existing franchise market? A franchise market is subject to the common law rights and duties[90], but when a special Act is passed for its regulation, the question may arise as to whether rights formerly enjoyed in connection with the market remain intact. In *Manchester Corpn v Lyons*[91], Bowen LJ said:

> 'When there is a franchise created by charter, and the legislature afterwards operates upon it, it is obvious that the legislature can do exactly what it pleases. It can either leave the old franchise standing, and place a new parliamentary right beside it, or it may leave the old franchise standing and incorporate certain statutory incidents into the old franchise, provided it makes its intention clear; or it may extinguish the old franchise, expressly or by implication, and substitute in its place, not a franchise properly so called, but parliamentary rights and obligations as distinct from a franchise . . .'

It is necessary in each case to look at the Act itself to ascertain what the legislature has chosen to do; and the whole Act must be considered in determining whether the rights given by that Act are intended to supersede those which previously existed[92].

---

82 1984 Act, s 61.
83 The Act is set out on pp 214 *et seq*, *below*.
84 See 1981 Act, s 50.
85 *Ibid*, s 54(1).
86 1981 Act, s 54(3).
87 *Ibid*, s 54(2); and see footnote 68, *above*.
88 *Manchester City Council v Walsh* (1985) 84 LGR 1 and see pp 90, 91, *below*, in relation to disturbance, and the cases there cited.
89 *Manchester City Council v Walsh* (1985) 84 LGR 1 at 10, per Griffiths LJ. In *New Windsor Corpn v Taylor* [1899] AC 41, Watson LJ expressed the view (at 48) that it was beyond the powers of the legislature to create a franchise. This was doubted by Sir Robert Megarry VC in *Leicester City Council v Oxford and Bristol Stores Ltd* (21 December 1978, unreported).
90 See p 13, *above*, and pp 27, 46, 52, 69, 95 and 103, *below*.
91 (1882) 22 Ch D 287 at 310.
92 *Manchester Corpn v Lyons* (1882) 22 Ch D 287 at 307, per Cotton LJ; *Birmingham Corpn v Foster* (1894) 70 LT 371; *Taylor v New Windsor Corpn* [1898] 1 QB 186; affd sub nom *New*

3 TRANSFER AND DEVOLUTION OF MARKET RIGHTS

A Market franchise and market place

A market franchise must be distinguished from the place where the market is held. A conveyance or lease of the market place will not normally transfer the franchise, for market place and franchise are distinct properties[93]. The owner of the franchise need not even own the land upon which the market is held[94]; and if he owns both franchise and market place, he may convey the former to one person and the latter to another.

A franchise owner may also validly sever the rights of market by conveying the rights to hold a general market whilst reserving the right to hold a livestock market[95]; but he is not entitled to sever the right of market for a particular locality so as to enable the holding, in that locality, of two or more markets dealing wholly or in part in the same commodity in different places on the same day[96]. A reservation or retention which purported to have this effect would be a legal impossibility[97].

B Mode of transfer

(1) Conveyance and lease

The transfer of market franchises is governed by the law relating to incorporeal hereditaments. Accordingly, a conveyance of the franchise can be made only by deed[98]; and a deed is necessary to create a valid lease of the franchise for any term, however short[99]. This general rule may, however, be modified in particular instances by Act of Parliament.

Windsor Corpn v Talor [1899] AC 41. In the case of a new statutory market, an intention may more readily be implied to negative or limit the monopoly that would otherwise attach to the franchise than in the case where a statute continues an existing market: *Hailsham Cattle Market Co v Tolman* [1915] 1 Ch 360 at 367–368, per Sargant J; affd [1915] 2 Ch 1.

93 *A-G v Horner* (1884) 14 QBD 245 at 254, per Brett MR; affd (1885) 11 App Cas 66.

94 *Ibid.* But a market owner may lose the right to hold a market in a particular locality, even if he owns the soil of the market place: see *Gloucestershire County Council v Farrow* [1983] 2 All ER 1031; affd [1985] 1 All ER 878 (see pp 99, 100, *below*), where it was held that use by the public of the market square as a highway for a period of 20 years continuously and without interruption gave rise to a re-dedication, under the Highways Act 1980, s 31, of the square as a highway freed from the right to hold a market on it. This would not have the effect, however, of preventing proper exercise of the franchise rights on other land within the market area albeit subject to the need to obtain planning permission in appropriate circumstances: see pp 127 to 129, *below*.

95 As in *Sevenoaks District Council v Pattullo and Vinson Ltd* [1984] 1 All ER 544 (see case illustration, p 74, *below*). Also, it was suggested in *Tamworth Borough Council v Fazeley Town Council* (1979) 77 LGR 238 at 266 that concurrent market rights may be granted to two separate grantees by the Crown, or by statute.

96 *Sevenoaks District Council v Pattullo and Vinson Ltd* [1984] 1 All ER 544 at 550, 551. The court distinguished the right of a market owner to transfer the market itself, or part of the market dealing in one commodity, from one place to another within the manor or the market area for the convenience of the public (see *Curwen v Salkeld* (1803) 3 East 538; *Wortley v Nottingham Local Board* (1869) 21 LT 582; and pp 33, 34 *et seq, below*). The court declined to decide, however, whether a franchise of market is capable in law of being severed by reference to market days, so as to allow conduct of a market in one place on one day of the week and in another place on another day; and this must await judicial consideration.

97 *Ibid* at p 551, per Slade LJ.

98 Co Litt 9a, 49a, 169a.

99 *Ibid*; *Somerset (Duke) v Fogwell* (1826) 5 B & C 875, 882.

ILLUSTRATION

By a private Act of Parliament, the market of Devonport belonging to A was enlarged into a market for sheep and cattle, etc and A was empowered to let the building, etc on the market site and to take tolls from any persons bringing goods or articles to the market. There was also a clause providing that if the owner should demise or lease the market, the lessee would be entitled to the tolls authorised by the Act, as the owner would have been entitled if the lease had not been made. *Held* that a lessee of the market, under a parol demise, was entitled to demand and receive tolls: *Bridgland v Shapter*[100].

Generally, where rent is reserved upon a lease of a market franchise for a term of years, arrears of rent cannot be recovered by distress but only by action[101]. But upon a lease by the Crown the arrears may be distrained for upon any lands belonging to the lessee[102]. If the lease is a lease of lands as well as of the franchise, and one entire rent is reserved, it may be that the whole of the rent is recoverable by distress upon the land; but if the lease is invalid as regards the franchise, a distress for the entire rent would be wholly unlawful[103].

A covenant by a lessee to pay the rent reserved upon a lease of the tolls of a market or fair runs with the land and binds an assignee of the lessee, whether named in the covenant[104], or not[105].

(2) Mortgage

Incorporeal hereditaments, such as a market franchise, may be the subject of a mortgage. The mortgage is in the same form, so far as applicable, as in the case of other hereditaments, and if it is a legal mortgage it must be by deed[106].

The power of a local authority to borrow and the mode of borrowing are controlled by the Local Government Act 1972[107], but express power is given to a local authority to borrow for the purpose of the Animal Health Act 1981[108]. Such purposes include the provision of wharves, stations, lairs, sheds and other places for the landing, reception, keeping, sale, etc of imported or other animals, etc[109] which are constituted markets under that Act[110].

If the undertakers of a statutory market have power under their statutes to mortgage the undertaking or the tolls, the High Court has jursidiction, unless expressly taken away by the statutes, to appoint, at the instance of the mortgagee, a receiver of the rents and profits, or the tolls, and will do so whenever it is necessary or proper for the protection of the mortgagee's security[111]. The court will not, however, appoint a

---

100 (1839) 5 M & W 375.

101 Co Litt 47a; 7 Bac Abr, Rent (B); *Jewel's Case* (1588) 5 Co Rep 3a; *Gardiner v Williamson* (1831) 2 B & Ad 336.

102 *Mountjoy (Lord) and Huntington's (Earle) Case* (1589) 5 Co Rep 3b at 4a, b; *Knight's case* (1588) 5 Co Rep 54b at 56a; Chitty's *Prerogatives of the Crown*, 208, 209.

103 2 Roll Abr 451; *Gardiner v Williamson* (1831) 2 B & Ad 336.

104 *Lucan (Earl) v Gildea* (1831) 2 Hud & B 635.

105 *Egremont (Earl) v Keene* (1837) 2 Jo Ex Ir 307.

106 It is subject to the general law of mortgages.

107 Section 172 and Sch 13, Pt I.

108 See s 53(1).

109 Animal Health Act 1981, s 54(1).

110 *Ibid*, s 54(3).

111 *De Winton v Brecon Corpn* (1859) 26 Beav 533; *Hopkins v Worcester and Birmingham Canal Properties* (1868) LR 6 Eq 437, 447; see also *Drewry v Barnes* (1826) 3 Russ 94, 104; *Fripp v Chard Rly Co* (1854) 11 Hare 241.

manager of an undertaking, the management of which has been entrusted by Parliament to the undertakers above[112].

(3) Death of the owner

On the death of the owner, a franchise market or fair passes to his personal representatives as real estate[113]; but if the owner dies intestate and without leaving any person entitled as next of kin under the statutory trusts, the franchise passes as *bona vacantia* to the Crown[114].

The franchise is not, however, extinguished, but continues *in esse* in the Crown, so that the Crown can either hold the market or fair on its own behalf or again grant it out to a subject[115].

C Power to transfer

(1) Market owner

A market owner (not being a public body) may sell or lease market rights generally without impediment, and such disposal will be governed by the law of incorporeal hereditaments as mentioned above.

(2) Public body

Where market rights, whether at common law or statutory, are vested in a public body, not for its own benefit but for the benefit of the public, the question arises as to whether that body has power to dispose of such rights.

A public body, such as a local authority, is a creature of statute, and may do only such things as are expressly or impliedly authorised by statute or by subordinate legislation. Further, a local authority cannot disable itself from fulfilling its obligations to exercise its powers and duties for the benefit of the public; and any attempt to do so would be *ultra vires* and void[116].

The Local Government Act 1972, s 111(1), does, however, give wide powers[117] to local authorities to do anything, including the disposal of any property or rights, which is calculated to facilitate, or is conducive or incidental to, the discharge of any of their functions. Further, s 123 of the 1972 Act empowers principal councils[118], subject to

---

112 *Gardner v London, Chatham and Dover Rly Co* (1867) 2 Ch App 201, 212; *Blaker v Herts and Essex Waterworks Co* (1889) 41 Ch D 399; *De Winton v Brecon Corpn* (1859) 26 Beav 533, 542.

113 Administration of Estates Act 1925, ss 1(1), (3), 3(1).

114 *Ibid*, s 46(1)(vi) (but as restricted by the Inheritance (Provision for Family and Dependants) Act 1975, s 24). Before the Intestates' Estates Act 1884, s 4, the franchise became extinct (3 Inst 21; Chitty's *Prerogatives of the Crown*, 233) and after the Act it escheated to the Crown. It now passes as stated in the text.

115 *Heddy v Wheelhouse* (1597) Cro Eliz 591; *Strata Mercella (Abbot of) Case* (1591) 9 Co Rep 24a; *Whistler's Case* (1613) 10 Co Rep 63a.

116 See *Gardner v London, Chatham and Dover Rly Co* (1867) 2 Ch App 201 at 212, per Cairns LJ; *A-G v Great Eastern Rly Co* (1880) 5 App Cas 473 at 478, per Selborne LJ; *Haynes v Ford* [1911] 1 Ch 375 at 385, per Neville J; affd [1911] 2 Ch 237; *Re Salisbury Rly and Market House Co Ltd* [1969] 1 Ch 349. See also *Staffordshire and Worcester Canal Co v Birmingham Canal Co* (1866) LR 1 HL 254; *Mulliner v Midland Rly Co* (1879) 11 Ch D 611; *Hobbs v Midland Rly Co* (1882) 20 Ch D 418; *Associated Provincial Picture Houses Ltd v Wednesbury Corpn* [1948] 1 KB 223.

117 And which renders in statutory form the common law rule established in earlier cases such as *A-G v Leeds Corpn* [1929] 2 Ch 291; *A-G v Smethwick Corpn* [1932] 1 Ch 562.

118 Which includes district councils: Local Government Act 1972, s 270(1).

certain limitations not material here, to dispose of land held by them in any manner they wish. For the purpose of the 1972 Act, it is clear that 'land'[119] includes incorporeal hereditaments such as market rights[120]; and it is suggested, therefore, that a local authority in which market rights are vested[121] would not be acting outside its powers in seeking to transfer or delegate such rights[122]. The question which arises, if a local authority seeks to transfer its market rights, is whether it can continue to restrain rival markets given that a third party would have day to day control of the market operation. In *Stoke-on-Trent City Council v Wass*,[123] Nicholls LJ commented that as long as the owner of market rights is currently not exercising or seeking to exercise those rights, and is not holding a market at all, he has no cause of action against a person holding an unauthorised market since there is no disturbance in the enjoyment of the owner's rights. The tort of disturbance of market rights is a possessory action and a council must, therefore, try to ensure that on a disposal of a right to hold a market it retains the right to suppress rival operations. If market rights were transferred absolutely, it seems clear that a council would lose this ability. If, on the other hand, the market rights were leased or licensed (with or without the market place), with the council explicitly retaining the ownership of the rights and a degree of control (eg by way of byelaws) over the market place, coupled, perhaps, with the establishment of a new market under s 50 of the Food Act 1984 in some other location within its district, the right to take action against a rival should be preserved. Careful drafting of the documentation is, however, essential particularly since there is no judicial authority on this point.

A local authority may not dispose of land in breach of any trust, covenant or agreement which is binding upon it[124].

(3) Other statutory powers

(a) *The Municipal Corporations Act 1882*. There remains in force power under the 1882 Act, s 136[125], for trustees[126] appointed or acting under any local Act of Parliament for

---

119 Defined in *ibid* as including 'any interest in land and any easement or right in, to or over land'.

120 By the Interpretation Act 1978, s 22(1) and para 5(b) of Sch 2, 'land' includes 'messuages tenements and hereditaments, houses and buildings of any tenure'; and by *ibid*, Sch 1, 'land' includes 'buildings and other structures, land covered with water, and any estate, interest, easement, servitude or right in or over land'. 'Land' thus encompasses incorporeal as well as corporeal hereditaments (cf the definition in the Limitation Act 1980 and see p 89, *below*) and will, therefore, include market rights: see, for example, *Great Western Rly Co v Swindon and Cheltenham Rly Co* (1884) 9 App Cas 787 at 802, per Watson LJ and *Wyld v Silver* [1963] Ch 243 at 264–265, per Harman LJ. In Megarry and Wade's *Law of Real Property* (4th ed at p 790), franchises are included in the list of principal incorporeal hereditaments, together with such other rights as easements, profits and tithes.

121 Whether at common law, or established or acquired under the Food Act 1984, the Animal Health Act 1981, or a local Act.

122 *Quaere* whether a local authority which established or acquired a market under the Food Act 1984, s 50, or preceding legislation, would remain the market authority within the meaning of *ibid*, s 61; and whether it would remain entitled to enforce byelaws made under *ibid*, s 60 prior to transfer and at a time when it maintained the market. It is suggested that both questions should be answered in the affirmative.

123 *Stoke-on-Trent City Council v W & J Wass Ltd* (1989) 87 LGR 129, CA.

124 Local Government Act 1972, s 131(1)(a).

125 Although municipal corporations no longer exist: see the Local Government Act 1972, ss 1(11), 20(6) and 245(5).

126 'Trustees' means trustees, commissioners or directors, or the persons charged with the execution of a trust or public duty, however designated: Municipal Corporations Act 1882, s 7(1).

the providing or maintaining of a market in or for any place (whether or not their powers under the Act extend beyond that place) to transfer to a local authority (with its consent) all the rights, powers, estates, property and liabilities vested in or imposed on the trustees under the local Act[127]. On transfer (which must be in writing or by deed[128]) the local authority assumes, as trustee, the powers and responsibilities under the Act formerly vested in the trustees[129].

(b) *The Local Government Act 1972.* Under the 1972 Act, s 253(1) and (2), functions of a public body[130] empowered to provide or maintain a market for public purposes and not for profit may be transferred by order[131] of the Secretary of State to the local authority[132] whose area comprises the district of that public body[133]. The approval of the public body to the transfer is required[134].

(c) *The Food Act 1984.* By s 51(1) of the 1984 Act[135], the owner of a market undertaking, or of any rights in respect of a market and of tolls, whether established or enjoyed by virtue of statutory powers or not, may sell or lease to a local authority[136] the whole or any part of his market undertaking or rights, but subject to all attached liabilities. The power applies, therefore, to owners of a franchise market, or a franchise of tolls, or of a statutory market; and the object of the subsection is, it appears, to give a power of sale or lease to owners who would otherwise have no such power. In the case of a company wishing to dispose of market rights, the provisions of the 1984 Act, s 51(2), must be observed[137].

---

127 *Ibid*, s 136(1).

128 1882 Act, s 136(2).

129 *Ibid*, s 136(3).

130 Specified as any trustees, commissioners or other persons empowered as stated in the text: 1972 Act, s 253(2). The definition of 'public body' in *ibid*, s 270(1) is wider.

131 The order may contain such incidental, consequential, transitional and supplementary provisions as the Secretary of State considers necessary or proper; and it may be subject to annulment by resolution of either House of Parliament: 1972 Act, s 253(3).

132 'Local authority' here means a county council, the Greater London Council, a district council, a London borough council, a parish or community council or the Common Council of the City of London: *ibid*, ss 253(4), 270(1).

133 The transfer may be made jointly to two or more local authorities whose areas together comprise the district of the public body: 1972 Act, s 253(1).

134 *Ibid.*

135 See p 245, *below*, replacing similar provisions in the previous legislation.

136 'Local authority' means a district council, a London borough council or a parish or community council: 1984 Act, s 61.

137 See p 245, *below*.

CHAPTER 3

The Market Place and the Place for Holding Fairs

1 THE RIGHTS OF THE PUBLIC IN THE MARKET PLACE

A To frequent the market place, and bring goods for sale

Wherever a market or fair is held, every member of the public has, of common right, the liberty of coming into the place and frequenting it for the purpose of buying and selling, and also the liberty of bringing there and exposing for sale his goods[1] and the goods of others[2]. The sole limitations on this public right appear to be that it may be exercised only whilst the market or fair is open, and that if the market or fair is not a general one the goods brought or exposed for sale there must be goods of the kind or kinds for which the market or fair is held. With regard to the former limitation, it may be observed that the approaches to a market or fair, and the ways over it, may be highways (in which case the public may use them as such at all times), but they are not necessarily so[3].

ILLUSTRATION

A trader has the same right on paying the proper tolls to sell by auction in a market the marketable goods of others as he has to use the market for selling his own goods by private treaty and there is the same obligation on the market owner to provide him with accommodation. Where therefore the owners of a market refused for reasons other than lack of room to allow a trader to use the market for sales by auction of the marketable goods of others, they could not maintain an action to restrain the trader from carrying on auctions in premises close to but outside the market, in a manner which did not amount to the setting up of a rival market, on the ground that he was causing a disturbance of the market. So *held* by the Court of Appeal in *London Corporation v Lyons, Son & Co (Fruit Brokers) Ltd*[2].

Whilst the market or fair is proceeding, goods brought into the place for sale[4], or goods in course of removal from the place after sale[5], are not liable to distress damage feasant[6]; and this is so, even though some toll is due in respect of the goods and payment of the toll is refused[7].

---

1 *Austin v Whittred* (1746) Willes 623.

2 *London Corpn v Lyons Son & Co (Fruit Brokers) Ltd* [1936] Ch 78 approving *Nicholls v Tavistock UDC* [1923] 2 Ch 18, and see p 86.

3 *A-G v Horner* (1885) 11 App Cas 66 at 80. Also see *Gloucestershire County Council v Farrow* [1984] 1 WLR 262; affd [1985] 1 WLR 741 (see pp 99, 100, *below*).

4 *Austin v Whittred* (1746) Willes 623; *Wigley v Peachy* (1732) 2 Ld Raym 1589; *Lawnson's (Mayor) Case* (1587) Cro Eliz 75. As to the protection of goods etc, on the way to the market, see p 29, *below*.

5 *Sawyer v Wilkinson* (1598) Cro Eliz 627.

6 The right to seize and detain *any animal* was in any event abolished by s 7 of the Animals Act 1971; but the common law remedy still applies with regard to other goods.

7 *Wigley v Peachy*, *above*, footnote 4. Non-payment does not constitute a trespass; *Six Carpenters' Case* (1610) 8 Co Rep 146a.

B Mode of sale

The persons using the markets have a right on payment of the dues to fix the conditions on which they will sell their goods and the persons to whom they will sell[8], except so far as the market or a particular part thereof is restricted in the form of sale[9]. So they may sell their goods by public auction[10] or they may sell by private auction except so far as the particular part of the market where the sale is held is set aside for sale by public auction[11]. The users cannot, however, be restrained from selling by public auction in the market in places other than the part of the market set aside for sale by public auction[12].

C Right to fixed place — stalls

Although every person has the right of frequenting the market or fair, and of bringing his goods there, no one has, of common right, the liberty of occupying exclusively any particular part of the soil on which it is held[13]. A member of the public has no general right to erect a stall[14], or to place a table, chair, basket, or other article, or his goods[15], upon the soil, in such a manner as to occupy the land to the exclusion of other persons. He may only do that if he has obtained the leave of the owner of the soil, or has in some way acquired a special right so to do[16]. If he does such an act without any such leave or right, he is a trespasser, and he is liable to an action to trespass at the suit of the owner of the soil[17]. Moreover, the latter is probably entitled to pursue after notice all the usual summary remedies in case of a trespass, and to pull down the stall[18], put out the offender[19], and remove the offending article or goods[20], using and doing no unnecessary force and damage.

It is proper to add, however, that the mere placing upon the soil for some temporary purpose of goods, or of a basket or sack which contains goods, does not necessarily amount to an exclusive occupation; whether it does so or not is a question of fact, depending upon all the circumstances of the case[21].

A person who erects a stall, or anything in the nature of a stall, with the express or implied consent of the owner of the soil, is liable for stallage[22].

---

8 *Scott v Glasgow Corpn* [1899] AC 470 at 475; *Nicholls v Tavistock UDC* [1923] 2 Ch 18 at 27.

9 *Scott v Glasgow Corpn, above*, footnote 8. As to the power to impose restrictions, see *below*, pp 111 to 113.

10 *Nicholls v Tavistock UDC, above,* footnote 8 (applying *Scott v Glasgow Corpn, above*, footnote 8 and *Wortley v Nottingham Local Board* (1869) 21 LT 582) and not following *Collins v Wells Corpn* (1885) 1 TLR 328. The right to sell goods by auction includes a right to sell the goods of other persons: see *London Corpn v Lyons Son & Co (Fruit Brokers) Ltd* [1936] Ch 78 at 125, 126, 131.

11 See footnote 9, *above*.

12 *London Corpn v Lyons, Son & Co (Fruit Brokers) Ltd* [1936] Ch 78.

13 See cases cited in footnotes 5 and 7 *above.*

14 *Northampton Corpn v Ward* (1746) 2 Stra 1238.

15 *Yarmouth Corpn v Groom* (1862) 1 H & C 102; *Norwich Corpn v Swann* (1777) 2 Wm Bl 1116.

16 For example, by custom; see *below*, pp 57 to 58.

17 See cases cited in notes 5 and 7 *above.*

18 Compare *Davies v Williams* (1851) 16 QB 546.

19 *Stourbridge Market Case*, 11 Hen VI, fo 23, pl 20.

20 The cases against distress damage feasant (*above*, footnotes 4, 5 and 7) are scarcely authorities against removal for misfeasance. The distinction between nonfeasance and misfeasance is recognised in *Northampton v Ward, above*, footnote 14.

21 *Yarmouth Corpn v Groom* (1862) 1 H & C 102; *Townend v Woodruff* (1850) 5 Exch 506.

22 *Yarmouth Corpn v Groom, above*, footnote 21. For stallage see pp 57 *et seq*, *below*.

2 PROTECTION OF GOODS, CATTLE, ETC, ON WAY TO MARKET

A Badgering and engrossing, forestalling and re-grating

It was formerly an offence at common law to prevent or endeavour to prevent by force or threats any goods, wares or merchandise being brought to any fair or market. Other offences included buying mechandise on its way to market, or buying hay and straw in the market and selling it again in the same place in order to raise its price.

By an Act of 1844[23] these offences of badgering, engrossing, forestalling and re-grating were abolished as were certain statutes passed in relation to these offences, as being pernicious and in restraint of trade. Although s 2 of that Act provided for the continuance of certain offences relating to spreading false rumours and preventing or attempting to prevent by force or threats merchandise being brought to any market or fair, in 1892 these offences were finally abolished[24].

B Distress for rent of cattle on the way to market

It may be mentioned here that cattle on their way to a market or fair, which are put into a ground with the consent of the occupier to graze for only one night, are not liable to the distress of the landlord of the ground for arrears of rent[25]. This privilege is apparently for the encouragement of persons frequenting markets and fairs from distances which their cattle cannot travel without being fed on the way. This is of little significance today.

3 THE RIGHTS AND DUTIES OF THE OWNER IN PROVIDING A PLACE

A Site

A grant of a market or fair usually specifies, more or less definitely, some area or district within which the market or fair is to be held; and whenever that is the case the market or fair must be held within the area or district specified, and not elsewhere.

ILLUSTRATION

The burgesses of Andover being the grantees of a right to hold a fair at Weyhill claimed that they could keep their fair at any one place where they pleased. *Held*, that if the place is not limited by the grant, the grantees 'may keep it where they please, or rather where they can most conveniently': *Dixon v Robinson*[26].

It would be incorrect, however, to suppose that in this case the area was not limited by the grant then before the court. The grantees were merely claiming to keep their fair at Weyhill and their grant in fact limited this fair to Weyhill[27]. There does not appear to be

---

23 7 & 8 Vict, c 24, s 1. See also per Fry LJ in *Mogul Steamship Co v McGregor, Gow & Co* (1889) 23 QBD 598 at 629; affd [1892] AC 25 at 58. As to the protection of goods, etc, in the market, see *above*, pp 27 to 28.

24 By the Statute Law Revision Act 1892.

25 *Nugent v Kirwan* (1838) 1 Jebb & S 97; see per Parke B, *Muspratt v Gregory* (1836) 1 M & W 633 at 647; *Fowkes v Joyce* (1689) 3 Lev 260, 2 Lut 1161.

26 (1687) 3 Mod Rep 107 per Herbert CJ.

27 See Patent Roll 41 Eliz, Pt 12.

any instance of a grant imposing no limits whatever as to space; and it is difficult to see how, with a view to such a grant, any proper return could have been made to a writ of *ad quod damnum*, or in what locality the inquisition could have been held[28].

In *A-G v Horner*[29] the question arose as to the effect of a charter which granted a market to be held *in sive juxta* Spital Square. It was decided that the grant permitted the extension of the market, if the owner thought fit and had the means of extending it, beyond Spital Square into the surrounding area[30]. Lord Blackburn, however, was not prepared to accept the view that the grant permitted any and every extension, however great[31], and it is submitted that a grant of a market to be held 'in or near' a specified place would not authorise an extension to a point which could not reasonably be said to be 'near' that place.

Grants have generally been for the holding of a market or fair in some city, borough, township, manor, or other like district. But they have sometimes required it to be held in a particular place in such district[32]. As an instance of a grant limiting a market to a fixed spot, defined by metes and bounds and containing a precise quantity of land, the grant may be mentioned which Charles II made of Covent Garden Market[33].

Where the grant merely specifies a district, such as a borough or manor, for the holding of the market or fair, the grantee has a general right, as between himself and the public, to hold it anywhere within that district[34], and to determine in what place or places within that district it is to be held[35]. This general right is limited, however, by the rule that an obligation is cast upon the grantee by his acceptance of the grant to provide convenient accommodation for all who wish to buy and sell in his market or fair[36]. The grant is made for the benefit of the public as well as for the benefit of the grantee, and if he confines his market or fair to particular places within the district he must fix it in such places as will from time to time yield to the public a reasonable accommodation[37].

The grantee of a market to be held in a fixed spot defined by metes and bounds has a similar general right, limited by similar considerations of public convenience. If the space allotted by the grant is more than is necessary for the purposes of the market in ordinary times, he may lawfully appropriate a part of that space to other purposes, and he is not bound to extend the market over the whole of the soil[38]. But he is bound to leave sufficient room for the purposes for which the franchise was granted to him, and whenever the convenience of the public requires that the whole of the allotted space shall be devoted to the use of the market there is an obligation on the part of the grantee so to devote it[39].

---

28 As to such writs, see pp 16, 17, *above*. Such writs have now fallen into disuse.
29 (1886) 11 App Cas 66; (1884) 14 QBD 245.
30 But the right to extend will only apply with respect to the market days in the grant; *A-G v Horner (No 2)* [1913] 2 Ch 140.
31 *A-G v Horner* (1885) 11 App Cas 66 at 81. See also per Cotton LJ (1884) 14 QBD 261.
32 See, for example, the grant to Charles Hore and Richard Hore of markets to be held 'within a place inclosed with brick walls, called Vinegar Ground', in the parish of St James, Clerkenwell, Middlesex; Patent Roll 6 Anne, part 4, No 8.
33 See *Prince v Lewis* (1826) 5 B & C 363 at 365.
34 *Islington Market Bill* (1835) 3 Cl & Fin 513, 12 M & W 20n; and see *below*, pp 32, 33, as to the extent of a market place.
35 *Mosley v Walker* (1827) 7 B & C 40 at 54, per Bayley J. For the effect of this power on the Local Government (Miscellaneous Provisions) Act 1982, s 3, Sch 4, para 1(2)(b), see *Jones v Lewis*, Times, 14 June (1989) and p 114, footnote 54, *below*.
36 *Islington Market Bill* (1835) 3 Cl & Fin 518, 12 M & W 20n.
37 *Mosley v Walker* (1827) 7 B & C 40 at 54, per Bayley J.
38 *Prince v Lewis* (1826) 5 B & C 363.
39 *Ibid.*

B Failure to provide sufficient accommodation

If the owner of a market fails in his duty by not providing sufficient space accommodation for the public there would be a good defence to an action brought by him against any person for selling out of the market to the prejudice of his right, provided such person had been prevented from selling in the market by the want of convenient room[40].

In the case of a market held under a grant which confines it to a fixed place, limited by metes and bounds, the grantee fulfils his duty to the public of providing them with accommodation if he properly devotes the whole of that place to the purposes of the market; for the grant does not permit him to do more. If the accommodation is insufficient for the wants of the public, that can be no ground for the repeal of the grant or for any proceedings against the grantee. It might be a sufficient ground for a new grant of a new market to be held elsewhere in the same neighbourhood; but such a new grant would not be valid if it injuriously affected the existing grant, and the new market would not be legal if it did more than provide merely for the surplus wants of the public which the existing market was unable to meet[41].

A like case to which the same principles would be applicable might possibly arise with regard to a market not confined to a fixed place, but granted to be held anywhere in a district. The district might be so narrow, and the residue of the district not appropriated to the market might be so occupied, that the grantee could not be held responsible for not providing all the accommodation required by the public[42].

It must be observed that the owner of a market does not fail in his duty to the public merely because the market is sometimes very full. 'The very idea of a market is that it is a place which will on market days be crowded'[43].

ILLUSTRATIONS

Charles II granted to William, Earl of Bedford, that he, his heirs and assigns, should have and hold and keep a market in a place called the Piazza, near the church of St Paul, Covent Garden, and within certain specified limits for the buying and selling of all kinds of vegetables, fruits, flowers, roots and herbs. This grant was later confirmed by Act of Parliament and the grantee was authorised to take tolls. But the grantee had for his own profit permitted part of the space, within the limits described, to be used for other purposes than those specified in the grant. The remaining part of the space, within which the market was to be held by the terms of the grant, became insufficient for the public accommodation, and there was not, on ordinary occasions, space within the market for carts and waggons, resorting thither with vegetables, &c.

Held, that the lord of the market could not maintain an action against an individual for selling vegetables in the neighbourhood of his market, and thereby depriving him of toll, even at a time when there was room in the market, without showing that on the day when the sale took place he gave notice to the seller that there was room within the market.

Prince v Lewis[44].

In answer to a number of questions propounded by counsel to the House of Lords in connection with the introduction of a Bill in Parliament for the purpose of establishing a

---

40 *Prince v Lewis* (1826) 5 B & C 363; *Mosley v Walker* (1827) 7 B & C 40. *Islington Market Bill* (1835) 3 Cl & Fin 513, 12 M & W 20n at 23: and see *below*, p 86.

41 *Islington Market Bill* (1835) 3 Cl & F 513, 12 M & W 20n; see further *below*, pp 83 to 85.

42 *Ibid.*

43 *Goldsmid v Great Eastern Rly Co* (1883) 25 Ch D 511 at 543, per Cotton LJ.

44 (1826) 5 B & C 363 at 365.

cattle market in Islington, *inter alia*, the following answers were given by Lord Littledale on behalf of the House—

'. . . These questions evidently apply to the grant of a market, not to be held in a certain spot defined or known by metes and bounds, but generally in the vill or district of Blackacre. There is no doubt but that the grantee of such a market may hold it anywhere within that vill or district, or in more places than one, and may change the place in which it is held; and an obligation is cast upon him by his acceptance of the grant, to provide convenient accommodation for all who are ready to buy and sell in the public market. If he does not do so, or if, after having once appropriated a particular site for the use of the public as a market place, he afterwards employs or permits it, or part of it, to be employed for other purposes without providing as convenient a place for the public to buy and sell elsewhere, within the limits of his grant, the consequence would be first, that there would be a good defence to an action brought by the grantee of the franchise against any person for selling out of the market to the prejudice of his right, provided such person had been prevented from selling in the market by the want of convenient room. This point was decided in the case of *Prince v Lewis*[45], and confirmed by that of *Mosley v Walker*[46]. A second consequence would be, that this breach of a public duty on the part of the grantee of the franchise might, unless those inconveniences were removed, and a sufficient space restored for the accommodation of the public, operate as a forfeiture, and furnish a ground for a *scire facias* to repeal the patent by which the market was granted. And thirdly, we are not prepared to say that such misconduct of the grantee would not render him liable to an indictment for a misdemeanour, in like manner as the grantee of a ferry is punishable for a default in providing proper boats and ferrymen, though we are not aware of any instance in which such a proceeding against the owner of a market has been adopted; and if an indictment would lie against him for his default, an action would also lie at the suit of any private individual who should have received any special injury thereby.'

Per Lord Littledale, *Islington Market Bill*[47].

C Extent of a market place

In *Mosley v Walker*[48] Bayley J observed that, generally speaking, the grantee of a market may 'permit every place within the specified limits of the market to be the place where articles may be sold'; and on other occasions judges have recognised that the owner of a market or fair, granted to be held in a district, generally has a right, and sometimes owes a duty, to allow it to be held throughout the district[49]. It is a question of fact, whether there has been an appropriation to a particular place[50].

If the market is not limited by metes and bounds the owner may enlarge the market place so as to extend it into the surrounding area. Instances in which whole cities have been given over to fairs are supplied by St Giles' Fair at Winchester and Lammas Fair at York; and in this connection, perhaps, mention may be made of the custom which prevailed in the City of London, whereby every shop open to the public was market overt[51]. In early times, when a very great part of the trade of the country was conducted at markets and fairs, their extension over so large a district as a city or town was, no

---

45 *Ibid.*

46 (1827) 7 B & C 40 at 54, per Bayley J.

47 (1835) 3 Cl & Fin 513, 12 M & W 20n.

48 (1827) 7 B & C 40 at 54.

49 See the *Islington Market Bill* (1835) 3 Cl & Fin 513, 12 M & W 20n. In *Kerby v Whichelow* (1700) 2 Lut 1498, Powell J said, apparently with regard to the pleadings, that 'the vill in this case shall be taken to be the market place'.

50 *London Corpn v Lyons Son & Co (Fruit Brokers) Ltd* [1936] Ch 78 at 106, citing Bayley J in *Mosley v Walker* (1827) 7 B & C 40 at 54.

51 Market overt was repealed by the Sale of Goods (Amendment) Act 1994. See p 95, *below*.

doubt, justified by the wants of the public; and there may be cases in which it is, or would be, still quite justifiable. It is submitted, however, that if the owner of a market or fair were to extend it so unreasonably that the public lost the benefit of the concourse of buyers and sellers which the grant was intended to bring about, and other substantial inconveniences ensued, that would constitute a ground for the repeal of the grant by *scire facias*. The question, however, does not appear ever to have arisen, and it is hardly likely that it ever will arise.

ILLUSTRATION

The lord of an ancient market may, by law, have a right to prevent other persons from selling goods in their private houses situated within the limits of his franchise.

Where such a market had been from ancient times held in a public street, but in consequence of the increased population and traffic, persons frequenting the market place were subjected to inconvenience and danger, and the lord had permitted part of the market place to be used for other puposes than for the sale of articles usually sold there. An action brought by the lord against the owner of a house adjoining to the market place for there opening a shop and selling goods, but who, at the time when he sold the goods, had a stall in the market place which he might have occupied.

Held, that it was properly submitted to the jury to find whether, from the state of the market place, the defendant had a reasonable cause for selling in his private house; and a verdict having been found for the plaintiff, the court refused to grant a new trial. *Mosley v Walker*[52].

4 THE RIGHT OF REMOVAL

A Within the area

Whenever a market or fair is granted to be held within an area, such as a city, borough, township, or manor, there is incident to such grant a right to remove the fair or market from time to time from one convenient place to another within that area; and the right continues, although the fair or market has always been held in one particular place[53]. The right may be exercised not only with regard to the whole market or fair, but also with regard to particular parts of it[54].

This right of removal is incident to every grant, unless the grantee is tied down by its terms to some particular spot[55], and it may be established even in the case of a prescriptive fair or market. Where a market has always been owned, or was originally owned, by the corporation of a borough, or the lord of a manor, a jury may infer that it was originally granted to be held anywhere within the borough, or manor, and if such an inference be drawn the right of removal within the limits of the borough or manor follows as incident to the grant[56].

---

52 (1827) 7 B & C 40 at 54, per Bayley J.

53 *Curwen v Salkeld* (1803) 3 East 538.

54 *Wortley v Nottingham Local Board* (1869) 21 LT 582; cf per Bayley J *Mosley v Walker* (1827) 7 B & C 40 at 54. For consideration of the question of severance of market rights, see p 22, *above*, and *Sevenoaks District Council v Pattullo and Vinson Ltd* [1984] 1 All ER 544.

55 *Curwen v Salkeld*, *above*, but he may remove the market within that limited area; see *Prince v Lewis* (1826) 5 B & C 363 and *above*, pp 29 to 31.

56 *R v Cotterill* (1817) 1 B and Ald 67, *De Rutzen v Lloyd* (1836) 5 Ad & El 456; and see *Gingell, Son and Foskett Ltd v Stepney Borough Council* [1908] 1 KB 115; affd sub nom *Stepney Corpn v Gingell, Son and Foskett Ltd* [1909] AC 245 (right to hold market extended over new streets).

B Outside the area

A removal to a situation outside the area defined by the grant is generally illegal, and it constitutes a ground of forfeiture[57]. But such a removal may be made legal by statute. In the case of an extension of boundaries by special Act or order, or by existing statutory provisions, a market which might have been held, either by grant or prescription, in any part of the ancient borough or town may now be held in any place within the extended boundaries, whether within or beyond the limits of the ancient place[58].

C Other requisites of good removal

In exercising his power of removal, the owner of a fair or market must take care to accommodate the public[59]. The power must not be exercised to the prejudice of the object of the grant which is said to be for the benefit of the public; and a removal to an inconvenient place would lay the foundation of a *scire facias* to repeal the grant[60]. An illegal removal is no defence to an action for disturbance by setting up a rival market[61], but it would probably be a defence to an action for disturbance by selling outside the market[62], and it would certainly justify selling in the old market place, for if a removal is bad the market continues in point of law in the old market place[63].

D Bad removal

A removal is not good unless the new market place is as unrestricted and free as the old[64]. Where a market in which no toll or stallage had ever been taken was removed to a close which belonged to the owner of the market, but which he had leased on terms which allowed the lessee to take stallage, it was held that the removal was illegal, and that no nuisance was committed by resorting to the old market place[65].

Where any persons other than the owner of the market possess prescriptive rights therein, a removal without their consent is bad, if it injuriously affects such rights[66]. Thus, where the occupiers of shops adjoining a market place had a prescriptive right to erect stalls in the market place opposite their shops, it was held that the market owner could not remove the market to a place where this right would become worthless[67]. Where the owner of a market does not own the soil on which it is held, a removal might deprive the owner of the soil of the right to stallage; but it seems that a removal which did so would not generally be bad on that account[68].

---

57 For an early case of an illegal removal, see Abb Plac, p 72, temp. John (Hoiland, Linc). As to forfeiture, see *below*, pp 97 to 99.

58 *Dorchester Corpn v Ensor* (1869) LR 4 Exch 335, *quaere*, whether this principle can be said to apply to the various extensions of local government boundaries by the Local Government Act 1972 and the London Government Act 1963.

59 *Curwen v Salkeld* (1803) 3 East 538.

60 *R v Cotterill* (1817) 1 B & Ald 67 at 75, per Lord Ellenborough; as to *scire facias*, see p 139, *below*.

61 *Middleton v Power* (1886) 19 LR Ir 1. As to disturbance, see Ch 6, *below*.

62 See *Prince v Lewis* (1826) 5 B & C 363; *Mosley v Walker* (1827) 7 B & C 40 at 53; and cf *Aiton v Stephen* (1875) 1 App Cas 456.

63 *R v Starkey* (1837) 7 Ad & El 95; *Ellis v Bridgnorth Corpn* (1863) 15 CBNS 52 at 79.

64 *R v Starkey, above.*

65 *Ibid.*

66 *Ellis v Bridgnorth Corpn* (1863) 15 CBNS 52.

67 *Ellis v Bridgnorth Corpn* (1863) 15 CBNS 52.

68 *De Rutzen v Lloyd* (1836) 5 Ad & El 456 at 458n.

E Duty to remove

It may become the duty of the owner if he has power to remove a market[69] to remove it for the better accommodation of the public. 'I take it to be implied in the terms in which the market[70] is granted that the grantee, if he confines it to the particular parts within a town, shall fix it in such parts as will from time to time yield to the public reasonable accommodation, and that if the place once allotted ceases to give reasonable accommodation he is bound, if he had land of his own, to appropriate land on which to hold it; or, if not, to get land from other persons, in order that the market, which was originally granted for the benefit of the public, as well as for the benefit of the grantee, may be effectually held; and that the public may have the benefit which it was originally intended they should derive from it[71].'

The consequences which follow upon the owner of a market failing in his duty to provide reasonable accommodation for the public are stated elsewhere[72].

F Consequences of removal

After the market has been lawfully removed, the public have no longer a right to go into the old market place as such[73], but it appears that the owner of a market who removes it ought to give a reasonable public notice of the removal[74]. Probably, public notices ought to be placed at the entrance or entrances to the old market place.

5 UPON WHAT LANDS A MARKET OR FAIR MAY BE HELD

A Ownership not essential

A market or fair must be held on land on which the lord of the market can properly perform his duties of correcting the market and protecting the rights of the public[75]. Such duties can be most readily performed where the lord owns both the market or fair and the land on which it is held.

At no time, however, does it seem to have been thought necessary that the market owner should own the fee of the market place. In 1433, the Corporation of Cambridge pleaded[76] that they had, by prescription, a fair at Stourbridge as part of the fee of the town of Cambridge; and the court held that they might so have it, although the land on which the fair was held was the fee of the Prior of Barnwell, because, as Paston J said[77], the Corporation might 'prescribe to have a fair in another's freehold well enough'. The case, however, shows that the Corporation had sufficient control over the soil to have the regulation of the stalls in the market. The case of Stourbridge Fair came up again in 1746[78], and then the plea was that the Corporation were seised in fee of the fair, and 'of the sole and separate use of the ground and soil of the places at Barnwell and Stourbridge' where the fair was held, during the times of holding it, 'for

69 See *above*, pp 33, 34.
70 That is, a market granted to be held in a town or other like district.
71 *Mosley v Walker* (1827) 7 B & C 40 at 55, per Bayley J.
72 *Above*, pp 31, 32 and *below*, p 85.
73 *Curwen v Salkeld* (1803) 3 East 538.
74 *Ibid.*
75 See *above*, p 27 and *below*, p 109.
76 YB II Hen VI, fol 23, pl 20.
77 *Ibid.*
78 *Austin v Whittred* (1746) Willes 623.

pickage, stallage, and groundage there, and all other uses and purposes of the said fair'.

ILLUSTRATION

The owner of a market removed it on to land held by his tenant under a lease which did not demise the franchise, but empowered the tenant to exact from vendors in the market certain novel tolls. To these tolls the market owner himself had no right. The court held that the removal was illegal because 'when the lord removes, the new market must be unrestricted and free as the old'. Littledale J, however, was of opinion that the removal was also illegal because 'the market must be held on the soil of the lord': 'the lord is to have the correction of the market, and how can he have that when he has not the soil?' *R v Starkey*[79].

But an opinion contrary to that of Littledale J was expressed in *Lockwood v Wood*[80]. There one of the questions was whether any right to stallage could exist under a grant of a market to be held in lands in which neither the Crown nor the grantee had any rights at the date of the grant. Lord Denman CJ, in delivering the judgment of the Queen's Bench, laid it down that the grantee could not claim stallage unless he possessed land in which to hold the market, but could claim it at whatever time after the grant he became interested in the land. His lordship added that 'if he never was so interested, he might, nevertheless, hold the fairs and markets on land belonging to other persons by their mere sufferance and permission; but unless he had the actual possession of it he could not claim stallage'. This judgment was afterwards affirmed in general terms in the Exchequer Chamber[81].

The question whether a grant of a market could be made otherwise than in respect of lands held by the grantee at the date of the grant was fully considered in the case of *A-G v Horner*[82], and there the Court of Appeal (overruling Stephen J) held that it could. 'A grant', said Lord Esher MR, 'of a franchise of a market has nothing to do with ownership of the land by the person to whom it is granted[83].' The judgment of the Court was affirmed in the House of Lords[84].

From the above cases it seems clear that, apart from questions as to the right to stallage, the owner of a market need not own, or even have the possession of, the land upon which his market is held; he may hold the market on any land on which he has obtained a right or licence to hold it. All that is necessary is that he holds it upon land in which he can exercise his duties of correcting the market and can secure to the public their rights and immunities.

It is perhaps hardly necessary to add that if he holds the market upon another's land under a mere licence from the landowner his power to hold it there may be determined at any time by the withdrawal of the licence.

'As against the owner of land the Crown cannot by its grant enable anyone to take that land and use it, either for the purposes of a market or anything else[85].'

---

79 (1837) 7 Ad & El 95.
80 (1841) 6 QB 31.
81 (1841) 6 QB 47.
82 (1884) 14 QBD 245.
83 *Ibid*, p 254.
84 (1886) 11 App Cas 66.
85 Per Cotton LJ, *A-G v Horner* (1884) 14 QBD 245 at 260. There may, however, be an inference drawn from the evidence that the owner has exercised the right of holding the market with the consent of the owner of the soil of the highway; *ibid*, and see pp 37 *et seq*, *below*.

B Churchyards as place of holding

Prior to 1285 it was a common practice to hold fairs in churchyards and the fair was usually held on the day of the festival of the saint to whom the church was dedicated. But the Statute of Winchester[86] (now repealed) enacted that 'henceforth neither fairs nor markets to be kept in churchyards, for the honour of the church'.

C Highways as place of holding

It was also a common practice in early times to hold a market or fair either wholly or in part in public streets leaving a sufficient portion of the streets open for public passage[87]. The prevalence of this practice has been recognised by the judicial statement that, 'formerly all markets were holden in the public streets[88],' and in one case, in which it was held that a removal of a market from a public street to a private close was bad, the right to hold the market in the street was, apparently, not disputed[89]. There are many instances in which the practice still obtains[90].

Where the origin of both the highway and the market or fair is immemorial, the practice, if shown to be ancient, is justifiable, although it somewhat abridges the right of the public in the use of the highway as such. For the proper inference is that the grant of the market or fair preceded the dedication of the highway and that the highway was dedicated subject to the right to hold the market or fair on the soil. The law recognises that a highway may be dedicated subject to a right of partial interruption during a certain limited and not unreasonable period of time for the purposes of a market or fair as often as it may be lawfully held[91]. Accordingly an immemorial custom for victuallers to erect stalls in the highway during a fair, sufficent room being left for public passage, has been upheld as reasonable and valid[92].

The practice may also be justified although the market or fair was granted, and the highway was dedicated, within the time of legal memory. Upon proof that the market is older than the highway, and that, going as far back as living memory can go, the practice has always obtained, the proper inference, in the absence of evidence to the contrary, is that the highway was dedicated subject to the right to hold the market or fair therein[93]. The burden of proving that he is entitled to hold his market in the highway lies upon the market owner, but, in considering whether he has discharged that burden, regard must be paid to the principle on which presumptions from usage are made[94], and 'all reasonable presumptions should be made in support, and not in destruction, of long enjoyment'[95]. Evidence that the market owner did not own the soil of the highway at the date of its dedication does not of itself make the practice unlawful, as the inference may reasonably be drawn, until the contrary be shown, that at that date he was exercising a

---

86 Now repealed by the Statute Law (Repeals) Act 1969, s 1, Sch, Pt II.

87 Cheapside seems to have been used as a market place until *circa* 1667, when Honey Lane Market was opened; and Newgate Street until *circa* 1681 when the market was removed to Newgate Market (replaced *circa* 1866 by the meat and poultry market in Smithfield).

88 Per Lord Tenterden, *Mosley v Walker* (1827) 7 B & C 40 at 52.

89 *R v Starkey* (1837) 7 Ad & El 95; see pp 33 to 35, *above*.

90 For a definition of 'street' under the Control of Pollution Act 1974, s 62, see *Tower Hamlets London Borough Council v Creitzman* (1984) 83 LGR 72.

91 *Elwood v Bullock* (1844) 6 QB 383. See also *Brandon v Barnes* [1966] 1 WLR 1505 (the obstruction of an 'access way' to Romford Market), and generally later in this Chapter.

92 *Elwood v Bullock* (1844) 6 QB 383.

93 *A-G v Horner* (1884) 14 QBD 245, (1885) 11 App Cas 66; on appeal.

94 *Ibid*, per Lord Selborne, 11 App Cas 77 at 78.

95 Per Lord Selborne, *Great Eastern Railway Co v Goldsmid* (1884) 9 App Cas 927 at 939.

right of holding the market on the soil with some consent or other from the landowner[96].

It has been suggested by high authority that the practice might be upheld even though the market were shown to be of later origin than the highway, and that after proper inquiry the Crown might grant a valid franchise to hold a market in public streets[97]. However, there seem to be great difficulties in the way of accepting the latter proposition. During argument in *Elwood v Bullock*[98] Lord Denman observed that 'if the way was first, no grant of a fair could control it'; and the safer view, probably, is that where the market is of later origin than the highway the right to hold it there, so as to obstruct any part of the thoroughfare, could be created only by an Act of Parliament.

Cases may, perhaps, be found in which markets or fairs are known to have been held from a very early date in public streets, whilst those streets are known to be older than the grants of the markets or fairs. It may be that such markets or fairs were originally held on narrow strips of land at the side of the highway, which have subsequently become part of the highway; and perhaps a presumption to this effect ought to be made, whenever necessary and possible, in order to support an ancient usage.

In *Gloucestershire County Council v Farrow*[99], however, it was held that once the provisions of s 31 of the Highways Act 1980 (relating to the presumptions of dedication) were satisfied so as to deem a public right of way to have been dedicated as a highway, the effect of the section, on its proper construction, was to prevent the exercise of other rights over the land which were inconsistent with its user as a highway if those other rights had not been exercised during 20 years' uninterrupted public enjoyment. Accordingly, since the market franchise had not been exercised in the market square at Stow on the Wold in the 20 years prior to the commencement of the action, during which period the public had enjoyed continuous and uninterrupted user of the whole of the market square as a public right of way, and since there was no evidence of any intention not to dedicate the land as a highway, the market square was to be deemed to have been dedicated as such free of any restriction on the public use of the square as a highway which would result from the holding of the weekly market thereon.

As Goulding J stated at first instance[100]:

> 'On the whole I am of the opinion that Parliament enacted section 31 . . ., and its statutory predecessor, in order to avoid the need for lengthy and expensive antiquarian investigations when highway rights are called in question . . . Accordingly, I must hold that the manorial right to have a weekly market in the market place has been lost by the lapse of a twenty-year period without such market being held.'

However, as Fox LJ indicated[101] in the Court of Appeal, the right to hold a Thursday market in Stow on the Wold was not being extinguished[102]. The right still existed. It was

---

96 *A-G v Horner*, footnote 93, *above*; see also *A-G v Horner (No 2)* [1913] 2 Ch 140 CA; *Gingell, Son and Foskett Ltd v Stepney Borough Council* [1908] 1 KB 115; affd sub nom *Stepney Corporation v Gingell, Son and Foskett Ltd* [1909] AC 245.

97 Per Lord Esher, *A-G v Horner* (1884) 14 QBD 245. Lindley LJ, at 265, however, expressed doubt upon the point.

98 (1844) 6 QB 383 at 407.

99 [1984] 1 WLR 262; affd [1985] 1 WLR 741. See also *Brandon v Barnes* [1966] 1 WLR 1505, and p 38, *below*.

100 [1984] 1 WLR 262 at 270.

101 [1985] 1 WLR 741 at 747.

102 See also pp 99, 100, *below*. For a recent discussion of this case and the effect of the Highways Act 1980, see G Holgate, (1985) JPL 92, 'Loss of Rights to Hold Markets and Fairs; Effect of the Highways Act 1980'. *Quaere* whether these rights could be revised in the

not a right which is annexed simply to the market place. It could be exercised over any land in Stow within the boundaries which may be limited by the proper construction of the franchise. The judge's decision only prevented it being exercised in the market place.

D Effect of statutes regulating the use of the highway

A highway is a way which is open at all times to the public at large, as of right, for the purpose of passing and repassing from one place to another. Thus the right of free passage must not be obstructed or impeded, save for those restrictions, interruptions and obstructions which are lawfully authorised. But, as we have seen, the use of the highway as a lawful venue for holding a market or fair may constitute such an obstruction or interruption to free passage, in which case the highway is said to be dedicated subject to the existing obstruction.

The law relating to obstruction of the highway is of ancient origin, and has reflected changing social and economic conditions of the times. Both in 1530, and in 1835, new statutes were passed defining the limitations to the right of free passage, and providing for penalties in the event of transgression. Nevertheless, market rights in public streets are not taken away or affected by Acts of Parliament which prohibit the exposure for sale of marketable articles, or the placing of stalls in the streets, so as to incommode the passage thereof, if the statutes ought to be construed as being aimed merely against nuisances; for no acts lawfully done in the exercise of market rights can be treated as nuisances[103]. For this reason it appears that valid rights and customs relating to markets and fairs lawfully held in highways are not affected by the provisions of the Highways Act 1980[104], which prohibit, *inter alia*, obstructions by pitching booths or stalls in highways[105] provided, of course, that those rights continue to be exercised[106]. However, it was said that a custom to set up stalls on a highway at statute sessions could not be immemorial, and therefore afforded no justification for obstructing an ancient highway[107].

In this context it must be remembered that once a highway has been vested in the highway authority as a highway maintainable at the public expense[108] the effect is to bestow upon the authority an interest in land. This interest is in the nature of a determinable legal estate in fee simple in the surface of the land restricted to highway use[109]. If, and when, the land ceases to be used as a highway it will revert to the owner in fee simple of the underlying soil[110] who is presumed to be the owner of the land through which the highway passes. Where the highway abuts land belonging to different owners it is presumed that each owner owns the underlying soil to the centre line of the highway.

---

market place if and when it ceased to be a highway and the surface reverted to owners of the sub-soil.

103 *Goldsmid v Great Eastern Rly Co* (1883) 25 Ch D 511, sub nom *Great Eastern Rly Co v Goldsmid* (1884) 9 App Cas 927, (1883) 25 Ch D 511; *A-G v Horner* (1885) 11 App Cas 66; (1884) 14 QBD 245; where the effect of the Paving Acts (12 Geo I, c xxxviii, 28 Geo III c ix and 57 Geo III, c ccix) was considered.

104 See Highways Act 1980, ss 137, 148 and its statutory predecessors; and pp 42, 43, *below*.

105 For decisions under previous statutes see *Elwood v Bullock* (1844) 6 QB 383; *Gerring v Barfield* (1864) 16 CBNS 597; *Mercer v Woodgate* (1869) LR 5 QB 26; *R (Kennedy) v County Cork Justices* (1911) 45 ILT 217. See also *Brandon v Barnes* [1977] 1 WLR 1505, p 42, *below*.

106 See *Gloucestershire County Council v Farrow* [1985] 1 WLR 741.

107 *Simpson v Wells* (1872) LR 7 QB 214, where the origin of statute sessions for hiring servants was considered. *R v Smith* (1802) 4 Esp 111, seems of doubtful authority.

108 Highways Act 1980, s 41.

109 *Tithe Redemption Committee v Runcorn UDC* [1954] Ch 383.

110 *Rolls v St George the Martyr, Southwark, Vestry* (1880) 14 Ch D 785.

Thus a market formerly held on a highway which had been rededicated free from such market rights could be revived if the highway ceased to be vested in the highway authority.

The Metropolitan Police Act 1839[111] prohibits the commission of a variety of acts in any thoroughfare or public place within the limits of the Metropolitan Police District[112]. And the Town Police Clauses Act 1847[113] contains like prohibitions with regard to any street[114] within the towns and districts to which the Act applies. In prohibiting the exposure for show or sale of any horse or other animal, these statutes expressly except from the prohibition such an exposure in a market lawfully appointed for that purpose[115]. No such express exception is made with regard to certain other prohibited acts which, apart from the statutes, might be justified in some cases by some valid right or custom in connection with a market or fair, such as the causing of an obstruction in a public footpath or thoroughfare, or the placing of a stool or stall on a footway. It seems, however, that the statutes do not affect such acts if it can be proved that the thoroughfare or street, or the portion thereof upon which the acts are committed, was dedicated subject to the right to commit them[116].

An auctioneer who sells in an open market place situated by the side of a street cannot be convicted under s 28 of the Town Police Clauses Act of causing an obstruction in the street because a crowd collects in the street to listen to him[117].

The Metropolitan Streets Act 1867[118] provides that no goods or other articles shall be allowed to rest on any footway or other part of a street within the general limits of the Act[119] or be otherwise allowed to cause obstruction or inconvenience to the passage of the public for a longer time than may be absolutely necessary for loading or unloading such goods or other articles. But, by reason of the Metropolitan Streets Amendment Act 1867[120], the above provision, prohibiting the deposit of goods in streets, does not apply to costermongers, street hawkers, or itinerant traders, so long as they carry on their business in accordance with the regulations from time to time made by the Commissioner of Police with the approval of the Home Secretary[121].

---

111 Sections 54, 60; and see *Hinchon v Briggs* (1963) 61 LGR 315, [1963] Crim LR 357; *Brandon v Barnes* [1966] 1 WLR 1505.

112 As from 1 April 1965 the Metropolitan Police District comprises Greater London (excluding the City, Inner and Middle Temples) and adjacent small parts of Essex, Herts and Surrey: London Government Act 1963, s 76(1)(a)–(d); Police Act 1964, s 62(4), Sch 8.

113 Section 28. That section is incorporated in the Public Health Act 1875 (as amended), by *ibid*, s 171 and applies throughout England and Wales outside Greater London which means the administration area comprising the areas of the London boroughs, the City of London and the Inner and Middle Temples (London Government Act 1963, s 2(1)). For a case under s 28 see *Wolverton UDC v Willis (trading as SG Willis & Sons)* [1962] 1 WLR 205.

114 Street here includes any road, square, court, alley and thoroughfare, or public passage (s 3); see *Curtis v Embery* (1872) LR 7 Exch 369.

115 The exception in s 28, is 'in fair lawfully appointed for that purpose'.

116 See *Spice v Peacock* (1875) 39 JP 581; *Jones v Matthews* (1885) 1 TLR 482; *Leicester Urban Sanitary Authority v Holland* (1888) 57 LJMC 75; see also *Curtis v Embery* (1872) LR 7 Exch 369; and cf *Whittaker v Rhodes* (1881) 46 JP 182, *R v Young* (1883) 52 LJMC 55, *Hitchman v Watt* (1894) 58 JP 720.

117 *Ball v Ward* (1875) 33 LT 170.

118 Section 6.

119 Namely, within six miles from Charing Cross; *ibid*, s 4 as amended by Metropolitan Streets Act 1885, s 2.

120 Section 1.

121 If the costermongers, etc, comply with the regulations they cannot be proceeded against either under the Amending Act or the Metropolitan Paving Act 1817, s 65 restricting sales in streets, but if they violate the regulations they may be proceeded against under either of

Under the original Act[122] the surface of any space over which the public have the right of way that intervenes in any street between the footway and the carriageway was deemed to be part of the footway, notwithstanding any claim of any person by prescription or otherwise to the deposit or exposure for sale of any goods or other articles on such surface; but the amending Act[123] repealed this definition. It would seem that the provisions of the original Act, as now amended, cannot be construed as taking away actual market rights in streets. This view appears to be supported by the speedy repeal, as already mentioned, of the definition given by the original Act to footways, which might certainly have been considered to interfere with rights subject to which streets had been dedicated.

E Obstruction — the inapplicability of the *de minimis* principle

Important current provisions are also contained in the Highways Act 1980 which, by s 137(1)[124], provides that:

> 'If a person, without lawful authority or excuse in any way wilfully obstructs the free passage along a highway he is guilty of an offence. . .'

Decisions under these provisions have constantly reaffirmed the principle of unrestricted access by the public to the whole of the highway, and the only exceptions which have been made relate to those obstructions which are lawful such as lawfully held markets, or of such a temporary nature that they cannot be considered to be obstructions at all. The various attempts by stall holders to raise issues based on the definition of 'lawful authority or excuse', such as acquiescence by the local authority in the stall holder's conduct, have been consistently rejected, as have arguments based on the *de minimis* principle.

ILLUSTRATION

A tradesman encroached on a footway, in that bookshelves were set out together with a sunblind and side panels which projected over the pavement, and it was held by the justices that this encroachment did not constitute an offence, apparently on the basis of the *de minimis* rule.

Held on appeal to the Divisional Court, that the case should be remitted back to the justices on the basis that the offence had been proved.

'It is perfectly clear that anything which substantially prevents the public having free access over the whole of the highway which is not purely temporary in nature is an unlawful obstruction . . . In my judgment, however, in this case, it is quite impossible to say that the principle of *de minimis* applies. Here was a substantial projection into the footway whereby

---

those Acts; see *Keep v Vestry of St Mary Newington* [1894] 2 QB 524, where *Summers v Holborn District Board of Works* [1893] 1 QB 612 was considered. They may also require to be licensed under the London Local Authorities Act 1990, Part III. The London Local Authorities Act 1990, Pt III was amended by the London Local Authorities Act 1994, s 6, Sch, see pp 270. See pp 115, 116, *below*. Apart from Greater London, street trading is regulated in many districts by local enactments. Such districts also may be prompted to adopt the street trading code pursuant to the Local Government (Miscellaneous Provisions) Act 1982, Sch 4. See pp 232 *et seq*, *below*. See also Street Trading, pp 114 *et seq*, and Pedlars, p 133, and the cases of *Watson v Molloy* [1935] 3 All ER 459 and *Stevenage Borough Council v Wright* (1996) 95 LGR 404.

122 Section 6.

123 Section 1.

124 This section is virtually identical to its statutory predecessor, Highways Act 1959, s 121(1).

the public were prevented from having free access over the whole of the footway.' *Seekings v Clarke*[125] (per Lord Parker[126]).

Again, the *de minimis* principle was also held inapplicable in *Wolverton UDC v Willis (trading as SG Willis and Sons)*[127], *Hinchon v Briggs*[128] and *Hertfordshire County Council v Bolden*[129].

F What constitutes an obstruction?

There have been several decisions on what constitutes an obstruction under s 121(1) of the Highways Act 1959,[130] most of which relate to the parking of vans or the erection of stalls on the highway.

ILLUSTRATION

A defendant had parked his motor van on the highway for the purpose of selling hotdogs from it. He was seen to park and five minutes later was asked several times by the prosecutor to move on. He refused to do so and was arrested. In giving the court's judgment, Lord Parker CJ *held*: 'It is really difficult to think of any argument that could be used in the present case to the effect that the appellant had lawful authority to obstruct the highway if what happened was an obstruction. Whether or not the user amounting to an obstruction is or is not an unreasonable use of the highway is a question of fact. It depends on all the circumstances, including the length of time the obstruction continues, the place where it occurs, the purpose for which it is done, and, of course, whether it does in fact cause an actual obstruction as opposed to a potential obstruction.' *Nagy v Weston*[131].

In the case of *Pitcher v Lockett*[132] reported in the following year it was again held that the selling of hotdogs from a stationary van was an unreasonable use of the highway and was unlawful[133].

G Obstruction — pitching a stall

Similarly, there have been a number of actions pursuant to s 148 of the 1980 Act (formerly s 127 of the 1959 Act)[134].

H Obstruction — whether land is a highway

In *Brandon v Barnes*[135] (a case under the Metropolitan Police Act 1839), the defendant was charged with wilfully obstructing the thoroughfare by means of a barrow contrary to s 54(6). The land obstructed was an access way for pedestrians and vehicles to

---

125 (1961) 59 LGR 268.
126 *Ibid* at 269.
127 [1962] 1 WLR 205. This was a case under s 28 of the Town Police Clauses Act 1847 under which a prosecution may be brought for placing or exposing for sale any goods so that they project into or over any footway or beyond the line of any house, shop or building at which they are so exposed 'so as to obstruct or incommode the passage of any person or along such footway'.
128 (1963) 61 LGR 315, a case under s 60 of the Metropolitan Police Act 1839.
129 (1986) 151 JP 252.
130 Now s 137(1), Highways Act 1980.
131 [1965] 1 WLR 280, at 284.
132 (1966) 64 LGR 477.
133 See also *Redbridge London Borough v Jaques* [1970] 1 WLR 1604.
134 *Divito v Stickings* [1948] 1 All ER 207; *Cambridgeshire and Isle of Ely County Council v Rust* [1972] 2 QB 426; *Waltham Forest London Borough Council v Mills* (1980) 78 LGR 248.
135 [1966] 3 All ER 296.

Romford Market. In support of the contention that the access way was a thoroughfare within the meaning of the 1839 Act, the court was referred to s 34(1) of the Highways Act 1959 (a provision now replaced by s 31(1) of the Highways Act 1980)[136].

It was found as a fact that no circumstances existed from which the intention not to dedicate could be inferred, and thus the access road was a highway; and it was held that, if an obstacle to passage is placed on the highway otherwise than in accordance with (i) the franchise rights and (ii) the authority of the owner of the soil, it is an obstruction of the highway if it materially interferes with the use of the highway[137]. Since the defendant could derive the right to obstruct only from the owner's authority (which he did not have) and not from the franchise, he was held wilfully to have caused an obstruction.

I Liability for statutory nuisance

The owner of a market held in a street may be answerable for a nuisance arising in the market place. Thus, in *Draper v Sperring*[138] it was held that the owner of such a market in which sheep were penned so that their droppings caused a nuisance was a person by whose 'act, default, permission or sufferance' the nuisance arose, and was therefore liable to an order to remove the nuisance under the Nuisances Removal Act 1855[139]. Such a case can now be dealt with under the provisions of the Public Health Act 1936[140] or the Public Health (London) Act 1936[141].

For a case concerning the deposit of a thing on the highway so as to constitute a nuisance contrary to the Highways Act 1980, s 149 see *Scott v Westminster City Council.*[142]

6 PROVISION OF STALLS, PENS, ETC

The owner of a market is under no obligation to provide pens for animals brought into the market, but if he provides them and charges a toll therefor he owes a duty to the stall holders or users of the pens to provide them in a reasonably safe condition for their purpose[143].

The owner of the market is not, however, liable to members of the public at large for injury caused by the escape of animals from any pen provided by him[144], nor is he so

---

136 *Ibid* at 303.
137 *Ibid* at 304.
138 (1861) 10 CBNS 113.
139 Now repealed.
140 Sections 92, 93; see now the Environmental Protection Act 1990 ss 80, 80A, 81, 82, Sch 3. See also the Public Health (Recurring Nuisance) Act 1969 (repealed by the EPA 1990, s 162(2), Sch 16, Pt III); Statutory Nuisance (Appeals) Regulations SI 1990 No 2276, as amended by SI 1990 No 2483.
141 Section 82.
142 (1995) 93 LGR 370. Braziers mounted on four-wheeled barrows used for the sale of chestnuts held to be unlawfully 'deposited' on the highway entitling the highway authority forthwith to remove them as a danger to the public.
143 *Draper v Sperring* (1861) 10 CBNS 113 at 123, per Willis J; *Brackenborough v Spalding UDC* [1942] AC 310 at 314, 322, 328.
144 *Lax v Darlington Corpn* (1879) 5 Ex D 28; *Brackenborough v Spalding UDC,* footnote 143, *above*.

liable, it seems, to members of the public resorting to the market[145]. It seems that he would, however, be liable to the users of the market in respect of a structure dangerous in itself[146] and he may be liable for a public nuisance in the street[147].

---

145 *Ibid* at 330, per Lord Porter: 'Where no duty is imposed a defendant who takes inadequate steps to attain a particular result which he is authorised but under no legal obligation to bring about incurs no legal liability if those steps do not effect the desired result provided they do not increase the danger.'

146 *Lax v Darlington Corpn* (1879) 5 Ex D 28, per Lush J.

147 See footnotes 138–141, *above*.

CHAPTER 4

The Days and Hours for Holding Markets and Fairs

1 THE DAYS

A Franchise markets and fairs

In grants of markets and fairs, the days on which they are to be held are usually specified. Where a market or fair is held under a prescriptive title, it is presumed that it is held under a lost grant, and that such grant specified as the days for holding it the days upon which the evidence shows that it has in fact been held[1].

In most grants of fairs the specified days have reference to a Saint's day, usually the day of the patron Saint of the place where the fair is to be held[2]. For a three days' fair the grant generally provides for its being held on the eve, the day, and the morrow of such a Saint. Grants allotting three days to a fair are common. But in some cases a greater number of days have been allotted. Thus, Westminster Fair was granted to be held from the eve of St Edward for 15 days[3].

Markets are usually granted to be held upon a particular day or particular days in every week[4]. Instances can be found, however, of monthly and fortnightly[5] markets. A grant of markets to be held on two days in the week is often treated as a grant of two separate franchises.

As a general rule, the grantee is bound to hold his fair or market upon the days for which it has been granted, and it is unlawful for him to hold it on other days. Holding a market or fair upon days other than those specified in the grant was, at one time, a common cause of forfeiture[6].

Formerly, there was a distinction in this respect between fairs and markets. An entire change of day, whether for a fair or a market, being illegal, was a cause of forfeiture[7]. But whereas illegally to extend the time of holding a fair was a cause of forfeiture of the whole fair[8], yet if a market was held on the proper day, and also on an additional and improper day, that did not lead to a forfeiture of the whole market, but only to a forfeiture of the market held on the improper day[9]. For the market held on the additional day was treated as an entire and separable market, wrongfully usurped, and not as a mere extension of the lawful market.

---

1 See p 18, *above*.
2 The Latin *feria* (fair) was the proper ecclesiastical term for a Saint's day.
3 See Chart 29, Hen 1, part 1, memb 3; and *Plac Quo Warr*, p 480.
4 For example, at Chester, Okehampton, Aberdare, Lechlade, etc.
5 For example at Cranbrook, Axminster, Gillingham, Stallbridge, etc. At Llangattock there is a market every third Tuesday.
6 15 Vin Abr, tit Market (F); Com Dig tit Market (I); *Newcastle (Duke) v Worksop UDC* [1902] 2 Ch 145 at 158. Also see Abb Plac, p 36 (4 John, Luton), p 43 (5 John, Lichfield and Wolverhampton); *Plac Quo Warr*, p 384 (temp Edw I, Lancaster): *Select Pleas of Crown* (Seldon Society) Vol i, pl 22, 44, 50.
7 *Ibid.* See YB 22 Ass f 93, pl 34.
8 Statute of Northampton, 1328, repealed by the Statute Law (Repeals) Act 1969, s 1, Sch, Pt VII.
9 YB 22 Ass f 93, pl 34; Com Dig Market (1); *A-G v Horner* (1884) 14 QBD 245.

B Statutory markets and fairs

In the case of a market or fair held under a statute incorporating the Markets and Fairs Clauses Act 1847[10], s 14, the days of holding are the prescribed days (if any) and such other days as the undertakers may appoint from time to time by any byelaw made under the statute establishing the market or fair or under the incorporated Markets and Fairs Clauses Act 1847[11]; and a local authority providing a market under the Animal Health Act 1981 has the same power by virtue of the incorporation of the Markets and Fairs Clauses Act 1847[12], s 14.

In the case of a market established under the Food Act 1984 or to which that Act applies[13], the market authority may appoint the days on which the market is to be held[14]. However, it seems that there would be no power to hold a market or fair on prohibited days[15] although, recently, a number of local authorities have permitted car boot sales and markets on Sundays.

C The holding of markets and fairs on Sundays and feast days[16]

In early times any change of the market day was unlawful including a change from Sunday to a weekday[17]. But in the thirteenth century it appears that the opinion began to prevail that Sunday marketing was wrong, and consequently changes of market days from Sunday to weekdays were often allowed without payment of a fine[18], and at last they came to be regarded as lawful[19]. Finally, in 1448 the Sunday Fairs Act[20] was passed which made it illegal to show or expose any goods or merchandise (except necessary victuals) for sale in any fair or market held upon any Sunday[21], or upon Good Friday[22], or upon certain 'principal feasts'; and permitted persons who had no day for holding their fair or markets other than these days to hold it within three days later or three days earlier, after making proclamation of the change of day. The feast days mentioned in the statute are Ascension Day[23], Corpus Christi Day[24], Assumption

---

10 As to incorporation see *below*, pp 179, 180. But any provision of a local Act which confers powers on a local authority to make byelaws appointing days on which or hours during which markets or fairs are to be or may be held must be construed as conferring on the authority a power to appoint such days or hours by resolution: Local Government (Miscellaneous Provisions) Act 1976, s 36(1).

11 See *ibid*, s 42, p 186, *below*.

12 Animal Health Act 1981, s 54(2) incorporates s 14 of the Markets and Fairs Clauses Act 1847.

13 As to such markets see pp 243 *et seq*, *below*.

14 1984 Act, s 52: see p 246, *below*. For meaning of 'market authority' and 'local authority' see 1984 Act, s 61.

15 Compare *Clifton v Holborn Borough Council* (1929) 27 LGR 658.

16 So-called street markets in the City of London are not markets (see p 6, *above*).

17 *Plac Quo Warr*, p 710 (temp Edw I, Eccleshall); Abb Plac, p 43 (5 John, Lichfield and Newcastle-under-Lyme).

18 Abb Plac, p 71 (temp John, Edenham and Lafford); Maitland, *Pleas of the Crown for Gloucester*, p 12, and p 171.

19 Bracton, fol 117.

20 Stat 27 Hen VI, c 5, 'considering the abominable injuries and offences done to Almighty God, and to his Saints, always aiders and singular assisters in our necessities'.

21 At a much earlier date, Sunday markets had been forbidden; see the Laws of Athelstan (*circa* AD 925) and of Aethelred, Witan of 1014.

22 'Accustomably and miserably holden and used in the realm of England'.

23 A moveable feast, falling on the Thursday which comes forty days after Easter and a holy day under 5 & 6 Edw VI, c 3, and a feast day according to the calendar of 1750 (24 Geo II, c 23).

24 Thursday next after Trinity Sunday. It is not a holy day under 5 & 6 Edw VI, c 3, nor is it recognised as a feast day in the calendar of 1750.

Day[25] and All Saints' Day[26]. With regard to Sundays, an exception was made of 'the four Sundays in harvest'[27], but this exception was abolished in 1850[28]. The penalty for exposing goods contrary to the statute is forfeiture of the exposed goods to the lord of the fair or market.

This statute did not in any event affect the prescriptive or charter rights of persons entitled to markets or fairs by making it unlawful to hold them on Sundays or the other specified days: it only imposed penalties on persons who exposed goods for sale in markets and fairs held on such days[29].

The Sunday Fairs Act was finally repealed in 1969 by the provisions of the Statute Law (Repeals) Act 1969[30], and the remaining Sunday trading legislation relating to shops has now been the subject of further repealing legislation.[31]

When the calendar was reformed by the Calendar (New Style) Act 1750, the nominal days for keeping the fixed feasts and fasts remained the same[32] and accordingly all fairs and markets the dates for holding which depended upon the dates of such feasts and fasts continued to be holdable on the same nominal days; and the Act provided[32] that any market, fair, or mart which had been held at a moveable time depending upon the fall of Easter, or any other moveable feast, should continue so to be held, the fall of Easter or such other moveable feast being computed in accordance with the new tables.

But in the case of markets, fairs, and marts fixed to certain nominal days of a month, or depending upon the beginning or any certain day of a month, the nominal days for holding them were changed by the provisions of the Act[33], and such markets, fairs and marts are now held eleven days later than their old nominal days. So that, for example, Dunstable Fair, which was originally granted to be held on 1 August and 11 May, was afterwards properly held on 12 August and 22 May

2 CHANGE OF DAYS

A Franchise markets and fairs

As a general rule, the grantee is bound to hold his fair or market upon the days for which it has been granted, and it is unlawful for him to hold it on other days; if he does so change the day, the franchise is liable to forfeiture[34].

The present position appears to be that an unauthorised change of the market or fair day would constitute an abuse of the franchise rendering it liable to forfeiture, the effect

---

25 Assumption BVM, 15 August. It is not a holy day under 5 & 6 Edw VI, c 3, nor is it recognised as a feast day in the calendar of 1750.

26 The first of November and a holy day under 5 & 6 Edw VI, c 3, and a feast day according to the calendar of 1750.

27 '*In autumno*'.

28 By Stat 13 & 14 Vict, c 23 (repealed by the Statute Law Reform Act 1875).

29 *Comyns v Boyer* (1596) Cro Eliz 485; *Cork Corpn v Shinkwin* (1825) Sm and Bat 395 at 399.

30 Section 1, Sch, Pt IV. This repeal is not to have the effect of requiring any market or fair to be held on a Sunday or certain other holy days; and a market or fair may continue to be held on any day on which it might lawfully have been held if that Act had not been repealed, *ibid*, s 4(1).

31 See the Sunday Trading Act 1994, p 255, *below*.

32 Section 3.

33 Section 4. A 'mart' it has been said, is a great fair; see p 2, *above*. Today, the term is more usually applied to a livestock market.

34 See footnotes 6–9, *above*.

of which is to entitle the Crown to obtain a repeal of the grant by *scire facias*[35]. But the position with regard to fairs is somewhat obscure in the light of the repeal of the Statute of Northampton[36].

A right to change the day of holding may, however, be presumed and if a market or fair has been held for a long time past upon days other than the days specified in the grants which relate to the market or fair, it may sometimes be presumed from the long user that there was a further grant or licence, which has since been lost, authorising the change of day[37].

B Statutory markets and fairs

In the case of a market or fair held under a statute in which the Markets and Fairs Clauses Act 1847, s 14 is incorporated the days of holding may be changed under the powers to make byelaws (see s 36(1)) appointing other days for the holding of the market or fair[38] and in the case of a market established under the Food Act 1984, or to which that Act applies, the market authority may change the days of holding under its power to appoint such days[39].

C Power of Secretary of State to change any fair day

The Fairs Act 1873 (as amended) gives to a principal Secretary of State[40] power to alter or increase or abridge the days of holding fairs in England and Wales. He may order that a fair shall be held

(1) on some other day or days, or
(2) on the same day or days and any preceding or subsequent day or days, or
(3) on or during a lesser number of days than the fair is used to be held[41].

But he can only make such an order upon a representation duly made to him[42] that it would be 'for the convenience and advantage of the public' that the change should be made; and the representation can only be made to him[42] either

(1) by the owner of the fair, or
(2) by the district council of the district in which the fair is held, or if the fair is in London, by the appropriate London borough in which the fair is held[43].

Before the Secretary of State takes the representation into consideration, the Act requires a notice of the representation and of the time when the Secretary of State will take the representation into consideration, to be published.

Where the representation is made by the owner[44] of the fair, this notice must be given to the district council[45] or, if the fair is situate in London, to the appropriate London borough[45], and where the representation is made by the district council, or London

---

35 See pp 98 to 100, *below*.
36 See footnote 8, *above*.
37 See *Penryn Corpn v Best* (1878) 3 Ex D 292, as explained in *Manchester Corpn v Lyons* (1882) 22 Ch 287 at 300; *Middleton (Lord) v Power* (1886) 19 LR Ir 1 at 12; *Newcastle (Duke) v Worksop UDC* [1902] 2 Ch 145 at 158.
38 See p 46, *above*.
39 See p 46, *above*.
40 In practice, usually the Home Secretary.
41 1873 Act, s 6.
42 *Ibid.*
43 1873 Act, s 6, as amended by the Local Government Act 1894, ss 21(3), 27(1)(e), 32, 35; Local Government Act 1972, ss 1(10), 179(3); Local Government Order 1965, SI 1965 No 654, art 3(24), Sch 1.
44 1873 Act, s 3.
45 1873 Act, s 6, and see footnote 43, *above*.

borough, the notice must be given to the owner of the fair[45]. In every case, before the representation is considered the notice must be published:

(1) once in the *London Gazette*, and also
(2) in three successive weeks in some one and the same newspaper published in the county, city, or borough in which the fair is held, or if there is no newspaper published there, then in a newspaper of some county adjoining or near[46].

As soon as the order has been made, notice of the making of the order must be similarly published[47], and the order has apparently no force until such publication has been completed. When the requirements of the Act with regard to publication have been complied with, the fair may only be held on the day or days mentioned in the order[47]. The Act expressly preserves all the rights of the owner of the fair, with regard to toll or otherwise, notwithstanding the change of the day or days[47].

For the purposes of the Act, 'owner' means 'any person or persons, or body of commissioners or body corporate, entitled to hold any fair, whether in respect of the ownership of any lands or tenements or under any charter, letters patent, or otherwise howsoever'[48].

3 THE HOURS

A Franchise markets and fairs

With regard to the proper hours for holding fairs and markets, it has been said that *dies* in grants means *dies solaris* (ie from sunrise to sunset) and not *dies naturalis* (ie from midnight to midnight), so that fairs and markets can be lawfully held only by day[49]. It cannot be said that this doctrine has always been maintained in practice.

B Statutory markets and fairs

In the case of a market or fair held under a statute in which the Markets and Fairs Clauses Act 1847[50], s 42, is incorporated, the hours during each day on which the market or fair may be held may be fixed and changed by byelaws made by the undertakers[51], and the local authority providing a market under the Animal Health Act 1981 has the same power[52].

In the case of a market established under the Food Act 1984, or to which that Act applies[53], the hours may be appointed by the market authority for holding the market[54].

---

46 1873 Act, s 6.
47 1873 Act, s 7.
48 1873 Act, s 3.
49 2 Co Inst 714 (11th exception); *Reid v Metropolitan Police Comr* [1973] 1 QB 551 at 559–560; and see *Tutton v Drake* (1860) 5 H & N 647, and p 95, *below*, Sale of Goods in Market Overt.
50 As to incorporation, see pp 179, 180, *below*.
51 1847 Act, s 42, pp 185, 186, *below*.
52 By virtue of the incorporation with the Animal Health Act 1981, s 54(2), of the Markets and Fairs Clauses Act 1847, s 42. But any provision of a local Act which confers power on a local authority to make byelaws appointing days on which or hours during which markets or fairs are to be or may be held must be construed as conferring on the authority a power to appoint such days or hours by resolution: Local Government (Miscellaneous Provisions) Act 1976, s 36(1).
53 As to such markets, see pp 243 *et seq*, *below*.
54 Section 52, see p 246, *below*.

4 STATUTORY RESTRICTIONS OF HOURS

A Fairs in the Metropolitan Police District

The business and amusements of fairs held within the Metropolitan Police District[55] are required by the Metropolitan Police Act 1839[56] to cease at 11 pm and not to begin earlier than 6 am. If any house, room, booth, standing, tent, caravan, waggon, or other place, is 'open' between 11 pm and 6 am for any purpose of business or amusement, in the place where the fair is held, the person having the care or management of such and also every person being there who does not quit the same forthwith upon being asked to do so, will be liable to a penalty not exceeding level 1 on the standard scale upon summary conviction[57].

---

55 As from 1 April 1965 the Metropolitan Police District comprises Greater London (excluding the City, Inner and Middle Temples) and adjacent small parts of Essex, Herts and Surrey. London Government Act 1963, s 76(1)(a)–(d); Police Act 1964, s 62(4), Sch 8. The London Government Act 1963, s 76 may be amended (as to alteration of police areas) by orders made by the Secretary of State under the Police Act 1964, s 2, as substituted by the Police and Magistrates' Courts Act 1994, s 14.

56 And see p 173, *below*. This restriction seems to apply only to a fair in the strict meaning of the word as a market, and will not apply to a fair at which there is no exposure of goods for sale nor selling of goods but held for amusement only; cf *Collins v Cooper* (1893) 68 LT 450.

57 *Ibid*, s 54, as amended by the Criminal Law Act 1977, s 31(6), the Criminal Justice Act 1982, s 46 and the Police and Criminal Evidence Act 1984, ss 26(1), 119(2), Sch 7, Pt I.

CHAPTER 5

Toll and Stallage

1 NATURE

The usual payments made to the owners of markets and fairs are of toll and stallage[1]. The legal definition of toll (in connection with a fair or market) is 'a reasonable sum of money due to the owner of the fair or market upon the sale of things tollable within the fair or market, or for stallage, piccage or the like'[2]; and it has been held that in grants[3], Acts of Parliament[4] and pleadings[5], toll may include stallage as a general word for all such charges or payments. It is, however, usual to limit the word 'toll' to payments made on the sale within the market or fair, as distinguished from stallage and other payments which are made in respect of some user of the soil[6]:

> 'toll is a charge which can only be made by special grant prescription or statute, and there has to be found some power to levy it . . . stallage is something which the owner of the soil of the market place or market house is entitled to exact as a condition for allowing people to come on to his land'[7].

It is in this more limited sense that the word 'toll' will be used in this chapter[8].

---

1 Other dues, such as piccage or pennage, may be payable (see p 57, *below*).

2 2 Co Inst 220. There may also be variable and differential tolls: see p 60, *below*.

3 *Lockwood v Wood* (1841) 6 QB 31.

4 *Bedford (Duke) v Emmett* (1820) 3 B & Ald 366, 371.

5 *Bennington v Taylor* (1701) 2 Lut 1517.

6 Com Dig, Market (F1); *Bedford (Duke) v Overseers of St Pauls Covent Garden* (1881) 51 LJMC 41 at 45, per Bowen J. As to stallage, piccage and pennage, see p 57, *below*.

7 *Kearton v Robinson* (1965) 63 LGR 341 at 342–343, per Lord Parker CJ. See also *Oswestry Corpn v Hudd (Valuation Officer)* [1966] 1 WLR 363 and pp 136, 137, *below*.

8 It may be of interest to refer briefly to the nature of certain tolls — probably now obsolete — which were connected with markets and fairs. It is difficult to say what meanings are to be attached to some of the terms, but to the best of the authors' judgment the definitions given are fairly accurate. *Lastage* or *Lestage*: a toll paid for liberty for persons to carry their goods up and down to markets and fairs; see Birch's *Historical Charters, &c, of London* (1887), p 328. *Pesage* or *Poizage*: a duty for weighing commodities; *ibid*, 331. *Tronage*: a duty paid for weighing wool, and other heavy commodities; *ibid*, 336, Lat *'trutina'* (scales). *Scavage* or *Shewage*: toll paid for a licence to show or expose wares; *ibid*, 333; Jacob's Law Dictionary, the 'scavenger' collected it. *Sumage* or *Summage*: toll paid for carrying goods on horseback; Jacob's Law Dictionary (cf 'sumpter', a pack-horse). *Toll-turn*: toll paid for cattle or goods on their return from a fair or market; Com Dig Toll (D). *Toll-traverse*: toll paid for cattle or goods taken over private land; Com Dig Toll (D a); see *Brecon Market Co v Neath Rly Co* (1872) LR 7 CP 555. *Toll-through*: toll paid for passing through or into a town or over a public-way, bridge or ferry; Com Dig Toll (C). In particular markets or fairs, tolls of a special kind may be payable by custom or prescription. Thus, at Lichfield market there was payable to a bell-man for sweeping out the market a toll on all corn brought into the market, whether sold or not; *Hill v Hawkur* (1615) Moore KB 835; *SC Hill v Hank* (1614) 2 Bulst 201, 1 Roll Rep 44; and see Riley's *Memorials of London*, p 366: Ordinance for the cleansing of Smithfield, 46 Edw III.

2 THE RIGHT TO TOLL

A By grant, prescription or statute

The right of taking toll is not incident to a market or fair, and some markets and many fairs are toll-free. Everyone has, at common law, the right and liberty of buying and selling in a public market or fair, and toll is not payable in respect of sales there unless the market owner is entitled to it by special grant or prescription[9], or by statute[10]. In relation to a franchise market or fair, the right to take toll has been described as a subordinate franchise appurtenant to the market or fair[11].

A grant of a market or fair does not carry with it a grant of toll, unless there is wording specifically creating a right to toll. It is not sufficient for the grant to be 'with all profits, commodities, emoluments, liberties and free customs appertaining to such fair'[12] or any similar general words not peculiarly applicable to toll since toll is not incident to a market or fair.

There is a distinction, however, between an original grant of a new market or fair and a confirmatory grant of an ancient one, or a re-grant of the latter after it has passed by forfeiture or otherwise into the hands of the Crown. In the case of a confirmatory grant, or of a re-grant, general words may be sufficient to continue any right of toll, whether by grant or prescription, which had previously existed[13]. The grant or re-grant must, however, be of the ancient market or fair, and not merely a grant of a new franchise, as was the case in *Holloway v Smith*[14], where new fairs were granted, and where it was held that a custom to take toll in an old fair, although cited in the grant, did not justify taking toll in the new fairs.

A right to take toll may be founded on prescription and the court may find, if the evidence is adequate, either a lost grant of a reasonable toll or a lost grant of a toll of a reasonable amount[15].

---

9 *Heddy v Wheelhouse* (1597) Cro Eliz 558, 559. *R v Maidenhead Corpn* (1620) Palm 76; *Osbuston v James* (1688) 2 Lut 1377; *Holloway v Smith* (1742) 2 Stra 1171; *Austin v Whittred* (1747) Willes 623; *Lowden v Hierons* (1818) 2 Moore CP 102; *Wright v Bruister* (1832) 4 B & Ad 116; *Stamford Corpn v Pawlett* (1830) 1 Cr & J 57; *Egremont (Earl) v Saul* (1837) 6 Ad & El 924. According to Moore's report of *Heddy v Wheelhouse*, the judges there said that toll is payable of common right for live cattle but not for victuals or other wares, but this statement is not borne out by the decision in the case, which was that toll is not demandable for a heifer or a cow, unless by grant from the King or by prescription, and the case seems to be more correctly reported by Coke: (1597) Cro Eliz 558, 591. Also, toll is not due by common usage for hens or geese, or for many other things of such nature: per Clench J in *Escot v Lanreny* (1594) Owen 109; cf 1 Rot Hundred p 280b (Lafford, Lincs) p 239b (Lutterworth, Leics).

10 See the Markets and Fairs Clauses Act 1847, s 36, p 184, *below*.

11 *Newcastle (Duke) v Worksop UDC* [1902] 2 Ch 145 at 156, per Farwell J and see also pp 56, 101, 102, 104, *below*.

12 As in, for example, *Holloway v Smith* (1742) 2 Stra 1171; *Heddy v Wheelhouse* (1597) Cro Eliz 558, 591 ('*cum omnibus libertatibus, et liberis consuetudinibus ad hujusmodi feriam spectantibus vel pertinentibus*'); *Earl of Egremont v Saul* (1837) 6 Ad & El 924, 931; *Lightfoot v Lenet* (1617) Cro Jac 421.

13 *Heddy v Wheelhouse* (1597) Cro Eliz 591, per Popham J; *Earl of Egremont v Saul* (1837) 6 Ad & El 924, 931.

14 (1742) 2 Stra 1171.

15 *Wright v Bruister* (1832) 4 B & Ad 116 (where it was held that a toll of one penny for every pig brought into the market, which toll had been taken for many years, was reasonable); *Lawrence v Hitch* (1868) LR 3 QB 521 and see pp 53 to 55, *below*. As to evidence of a prescriptive right see 'Evidence of Market Rights', Ch 11, *below*.

B Toll-free markets

If the Crown grants a market or fair without a specific grant of toll, the market or fair is toll-free; and the Crown cannot later grant toll for such market or fair 'without *quid pro quo*, some proportionable benefit to the subject'[16]. The reason is that a market or fair, when once established, exists for the benefit of the public, as well as for the benefit of the owner. In *Lowden v Hierons*[17], however, it appeared that there had been a usage to take toll in Covent Garden for some 150 years before action was brought, but that the market had been free down to 1670, when a further grant[18] was obtained of the market *cum tolneris hujusmodi mercuturae aliquatinus spectantibus*. On these facts, the court seems to have thought that it was open to a jury to presume from the usage that a valid grant of toll had been made since the original charter[19].

C Toll must be reasonable; power to increase toll

If a grant of toll specifies the amount which may be taken, such amount must be reasonable. A grant of an unreasonable toll is wholly void, and no portion of it is payable[20].

A grant of toll which does not specify the amount to be taken is interpreted as a grant of a reasonable toll[21].

ILLUSTRATION

By grant of Queen Anne[22], the plaintiff Corporation enjoyed the right to hold two fairs or markets yearly for ever with all tolls and profits from the fair proceeding and arising. No toll was specified but in pursuance of the grant the Corporation was accustomed to receive a toll of 2d per beast from buyers in the market. The defendant refused to pay the toll arguing that the grant of a toll without specifying the amount was void since it would allow the grantee to take whatever may appear to him to be reasonable and expose the public to extortion. *Held* that the grant entitled the plaintiff Corporation to take a reasonable toll: *Corporation of Stamford v Pawlett*[23].

---

16 2 Co Inst 220; *R v London Corpn* (1682) 2 Show 263; *Lancum v Lovell* (1832) 6 C & P 437, 465.

17 (1818) 2 Moore CP 102.

18 22 Car II.

19 See per Dallas J in *Lowden v Hierons* (1818) 2 Moore CP 102; although Alexander CB in *Stamford Corpn v Pawlett* (1830) 1 Cr & J 57 at 79 thought that this case was sent to a new trial for lack of evidence that a reasonable sum, by way of toll, had been regularly paid.

20 2 Co Inst 220; *Heddy v Wheelhouse* (1597) Cro Eliz 558, 591; Moore 474.

21 *R v Maidenhead Corpn* (1620) Palm 76; *Stamford Corpn v Pawlett* (1830) 1 Cr & J 57, 400.

22 13 Anne

23 (1830) 1 Cr & J 57. In delivering the judgment of the Court of Exchequer Alexander CB said (at 81), on the question of a 'reasonable' toll: 'The grantee demands it at his peril, and at the hazard of a private as well as of a public prosecution: of a private, at the suit of the party injured; of a public, at the suit of the Attorney-General, in the name of his Majesty. The inconvenience of raising such questions cannot be avoided by specifying the sum. The King cannot grant an unreasonable toll; and it is competent to every subject of the realm, from whom the toll is demanded, to question its being reasonable, even when the exact sum is specified in the charter. This question may always be brought under discussion, in whatever terms the grant may be expressed.' The judgment was affirmed in the Exchequer Chamber, *ibid*, at 400.

If, however, the language of the grant is ambiguous it may be void for uncertainty, as was held in the case of a grant of 'such toll as is used to be taken *ibi et alibi infra regnum Angliae*'[24].

Where the right to take toll is founded on prescription, it seems that a court may find, if the evidence is adequate, either a lost grant of a reasonable toll, or a lost grant of a toll of a specified amount[25]. The former finding is the more favourable for the market owner as such a grant does not prevent his varying the amount of his toll, provided that the amount taken is always reasonable; and the toll is not liable to be invalidated on the ground of rankness[26].

Where the amount of toll is not fixed by charter[27], custom or prescription, or statute, it may be increased from time to time so long as it is reasonable. If the amount is so fixed, and there is no provision for increase in the charter or statute, it may only be increased by authority of an Act of Parliament, whether private or public[28].

D Reasonableness

Reasonableness is a question of law. If the sum demanded by way of toll is in accordance with an express grant, or prescription, the court will support its payment, unless it is shown to be unreasonable; and the onus of showing that the toll is unreasonable lies on the party disputing it[29].

A continuance of uniform payment and acquiescence in it is evidence of reasonableness[30]. The mere fact that a toll of a particular amount has been taken for a long period of time will not, in the absence of evidence, warrant the assumption that a toll of a larger amount is unreasonable[31].

ILLUSTRATION

The plaintiff was the lessee of markets and street tolls in Cheltenham. No specific toll was granted by the charter of Henry III or subsequent letters patent of Charles I, but, for as long as living witnesses could remember, a board had been displayed in the market place showing the market tolls including a toll of one shilling for every cartload of vegetables. These tolls had been collected regularly, and as of right, from at least 1810. The defendant refused to pay toll on a cartload of vegetables brought into the market arguing, in response to the plaintiff's claim to a prescriptive toll, that the amount of the toll although reasonable at the present time would have been unreasonable in 1189 (the commencement of legal memory), and for many years after and could not, therefore, have had a legal origin.

---

24 *Lightfoot v Lenet* (1618) Cro Jac 421.

25 See *Wright v Bruister* (1832) 4 B & Ad 116, *Gunning on Tolls*, 62; *Lawrence v Hitch* (1868) LR 3 QB 521. In the *Worksop market and fair case*, Plac Quo Warr p 627, the Crown alleged as an abuse, and proved, that the lord had taken twice as much for tolls as he and his predecessors from time immemorial had before taken, and the market and fair were forfeited. The tolls were prescriptive. It does not appear whether the lord's claim was to tolls of a specified or of reasonable amount; but the case is consistent with either view.

26 *Lawrence v Hitch* (1868) LR 3 QB 521. The doctrine of rankness had some place in the law of tithes, but has never been successfully applied to prescriptive tolls, although its application would have been fatal to many. See *below*.

27 *Lawrence v Hitch* (1868) LR 3 QB 521,

28 For power to increase charges in statutory markets, see pp 61 to 63, *below*.

29 *Wright v Bruister* (1832) 4 B & Ad 116, where a toll of one penny on every pig brought into a market was held to be not necessarily unreasonable.

30 *Gard v Callard* (1817) 6 M & S 69. As to slight variations from time to time, see *Beaufort (Duke) v Smith* (1849) 4 Exch 450.

31 See *Mills v Colchester Corpn* (1868) LR 3 CP 575.

Held: (1) that, on the facts, it ought to be presumed that the toll of one shilling had been taken from time immemorial and that if the doctrine of rankness[32] applied, the other facts showed that one shilling for a cartload of vegetables was not unreasonable in the time of Richard I; (2) that it may also be presumed that the grant was of a reasonable toll which may vary in amount from time to time with the value of money; and that such toll is valid in point of law[33]: *Lawrence v Hitch*[34].

If, however, a toll were claimed by charter granting a toll of a specified amount which, although reasonable now, must have been unreasonable at the time of the grant, it might be successfully contended on that ground that the grant of the toll was void[35]. Many tolls which are now taken in ancient charter and prescriptive markets would have been unreasonable at the time when the charter was granted, or in the first year of the reign of Richard I[36], and would be bad unless they could be supported as tolls varying in amount.

E Excessive toll

Statute[37] formerly provided that where an excessive or 'outrageous'[38] toll was taken by the lord, the Crown was entitled to seize the market or fair into its own hands[39]; and that if an officer of the market took outrageous toll without authority, he would be liable both to compensate the injured party and to forty days' imprisonment.

At common law, an abuse of franchise of toll, by taking excessive toll, renders that franchise (but not, it seems, the market or fair) to forfeiture[40] by *scire facias*[41].

F Persons liable to pay toll

At common law, toll for goods sold in markets and fairs is payable by buyers and not sellers[42]. It is, however, not difficult to envisage the practical difficulties involved in

---

32 See footnote 26, *above*.
33 See *R v Maidenhead Corpn* (1620) Palm 76 at 86; *Wright v Bruister* (1832) as reported in *Gunning on Tolls*, pp 62, 63. The point does not appear in the report in 4 B & Ad 116.
34 (1868) LR 3 QB 521.
35 *Ibid*; cf *Bryant v Foot* (1868) LR 3 QB 497.
36 Thus, in the time of Edward III, the following tolls were held to be unreasonable, viz one penny for each of the following when sold in market or fair: horse, ox, cow, eight sheep, four pigs over one year old, eight young pigs, and a cart laden with merchandise; for a horse's load one half-penny or farthing, and for a man's load one farthing. Plac Quo Warr, p 146 (Meysham), and p 140 (Bauquell). See also *ibid* p 627 (Worksop). In 1832, a toll of a penny for a pig sold in market was held to be reasonable: *Wright v Bruister* (1832) 4 B & Ad 116. See also *Heddy v Wheelhouse* (1597) Cro Eliz 558, Moore 474.
37 3 Edw I, c 31 (Statute of Westminster the First, 1275): repealed by the Theft Act 1968, s 33(3), Sch 3, Pt I (repeal not to extend to Northern Ireland, *ibid*, s 36).
38 2 Co Inst 220.
39 The franchise of toll was not extinguished, but continued to exist in the Crown's hands.
40 See Co Dig Market (1) citing Palmer, 82; Vin Abr Market (F) 7, to the contrary, cites 2 Show 265; but the passage in Shower is mere argument, on the false assumption that toll is incident to a market; and see *Newcastle (Duke) v Worksop UDC* [1902] 2 Ch 145 at 157, and pp 98, 99, 101, 102, *below*. In *Newcastle (Duke) v Worksop UDC*, *above*, at 158, Farwell J remarked (without deciding the point) that it was not easy to see how a subordinate franchise of toll, if surrendered or forfeited, could vest in the Crown, whilst the franchise of fair could remain in the lord; cf *R v Maidenhead Corpn* (1620) Palm 76 at 78, 82, where the court held that toll was neither incident nor subordinate to the market and could be forfeited and the market remain.
41 See p 99, *below*.
42 *Leight v Pym* (1687) 2 Lutw 1329; YB 9 Hen VI, f 45, pl 28; 2 Co Inst 221.

collecting toll from buyers[43] and in most modern statutory markets[44], and perhaps now even in many franchise and prescriptive markets, toll is, in practice, paid by sellers. The common law rule may be excluded by custom or prescription[45] and, in addition, any individual seller may contract with the market owners that his, the seller's, goods shall be sold in the market, toll-free, in consideration of an agreement by the seller to pay a sum equal in amount to the toll properly payable by the buyer[46].

In a very early case[47], the lord claimed a prescriptive right to take toll from both buyer and seller: the amount taken was held unreasonable but if the total amount taken were not excessive, perhaps such right might be successfully prescribed for.

G Articles and sales liable to toll

It has been questioned whether tolls are payable on articles not in use at the time of the grant, or not then known, which have subsequently become marketable articles. It is submitted that there can be no objection to taking tolls on such articles if the terms of the charter by which the tolls were granted are sufficiently wide[48]; and in the case of a prescriptive market, or a market with prescriptive tolls, there might be evidence from which it could be inferred that the lost grant contained a clause which provided for such articles, as by granting a reasonable toll on all chattels and things brought into the market and there sold.

Where statutory markets are concerned, the question of whether articles are subject to toll obviously depends upon the construction of the Act regulating the market; but nevertheless care is required in construing the relevant provisions and it may be necessary to apply the *ejusdem generis* rule to establish whether or not certain goods are subject to toll[49]. The rule is, however, to be applied with caution and prima facie words are to be given their natural meaning, unless that meaning is cut down by the context as a result of the operation of the rule[50].

Toll is usually payable only on tollable articles actually brought into the market and there sold[51]. By custom or statute, however, toll may be payable for goods brought into the market for sale and not sold[52].

---

43 See, for example, the remarks of Danckwerts J in *A-G v Colchester Corpn* [1952] Ch 586 at 594.

44 See *Hailsham Cattle Market Co v Tolman* [1915] 1 Ch 360; affd [1915] 2 Ch 1 and the Food Act 1984, s 54(3), p 247, *below*.

45 See *Leight v Pym* (1687) 2 Lut 1329; *Hill v Smith* (1809) 10 East 476, overruled on another point (1812) 4 Taunt 520.

46 *A-G v Horner (No 2)* [1913] 2 Ch 140 at 173.

47 *Case of Bauquell*, Plac Quo Warr, p 140.

48 See *R v Maidenhead Corpn* (1620) Palm 76 at 85; *Brune v Thompson* (1843) 4 QB 543, 552; *Carlisle Corpn v Wilson* (1804) 5 East 2; *Waterhouse v Keen* (1825) 4 B & C 200.

49 *Whittle (Hy) Ltd v Stalybridge Corpn* (1967) 65 LGR 344, where Buckley LJ held that the words 'other provisions' in a local Act had to be construed *ejusdem generis* with the preceding words 'meat, fish, poultry, vegetables, fruit . . .'. Since the latter were all natural products, manufacturered products such as bread and confectionery (sold by the plaintiff) did not attract toll. See also *Loftos v Gleave* (1891) 55 JP 149; *Kearton v Robinson* (1965) 63 LGR 341; and pp 60–61, *below*.

50 *Anderson v Anderson* [1895] 1 QB 749, cited in *Aberdare Markets and Town Hall Co v Bolwell & Hayward Ltd* (1992) 90 LGR 613, CA.

51 *Wells v Miles* (1821) 4 B & Ald 559; *Kerby v Whichelow* (1701) 2 Lut 1498; *Leight v Pym* (1687) 2 Lut 1329; *Bennington v Taylor* (1700) 2 Lut 1517; *Swindon Central Market Co Ltd v Panting* (1872) 27 LT 578; *Vines v Reading Corpn* (1826) 12 Moore CP 201; *Londonderry Corpn v Osborne* [1926] NI 58.

52 *Leight v Pym* (1687) 2 Lut 1329; *Hill v Hawkur* (1614) Moore KB 835; *Bedford (Duke) v Emmett* (1820) 3 B & Ald 366 at 371.

If goods are sold by sample in a market, but the bulk is not brought into the market, toll is not payable on the bulk[53]; and there cannot be a grant or prescription to take toll on goods not actually brought into the market and there sold[54]. In *Hill v Smith*[55], Lord Mansfield said:

> 'Fairs were invented that contracts might have good testimony and be made openly, and that the seller might know what to ask and the buyer what to give . . . The goods should be sold there publicly. This sale by sample is directly contrary to the origin and purpose of markets; and it would be a strange thing that toll should be taken by the owners of the market on that very transaction which is contrary to the intention of the market.'

3 THE RIGHT TO STALLAGE

A Nature of the right

Stallage is the sum which may be demanded by the owner of the soil on which a market or fair is held in return for the privilege of placing a stall upon it[56], or for standing room for cattle or goods within the market or fair. *Piccage* (the right to make holes in the ground for support[57]) and *pennage* (the right to erect pens[58]) are merely varieties of stallage, and are terms met less frequently today. The market owner need not, however, own the freehold of the soil, but he must be entitled in some way to actual possession or control of it[59].

Although the market owner is under no duty to erect stalls or pens[60], he does have a duty not to prevent the public from exercising its common law right of resorting freely to the market place. If he so covers the site of the market place with stalls that insufficient room remains for those who do not wish to take stalls, he will be in breach of that duty[61].

No one has a right, at common law, to erect or occupy stalls or pens in a market without the consent of the market owner[62], unless he has acquired a special right to do so. Nor, generally, may anyone take exclusive occupation of any part of the soil of the market without the consent of the owner of the soil: anyone so doing will be a trespasser[63]. Nevertheless, there may be a custom for a particular class of persons to

---

53 *Tewkesbury Corpn v Diston* (1805) 6 East 438; *Moseley v Pierson* (1790) 4 Term Rep 104. But an action lies for the injury done to the market: see *Tewkesbury (Bailiffs etc) v Bricknell* (1809) 2 Taunt 120 and pp 87, 88, *below*.

54 *Hill v Smith* (1812) 4 Taunt 520; *Wells v Miles* (1821) 4 B & Ald 559; *Kerby v Whichelow* (1700) 2 Lut 1498.

55 (1812) 4 Taunt 520 at 531.

56 See, for example, *Kearton v Robinson* (1965) 63 LGR 341 at 343.

57 *Northampton Corpn v Ward* (1746) 2 Stra 1238.

58 *R v Marsden* (1765) 3 Burr 1812.

59 *Austin v Whittred* (1747) Willes 623; *Lockwood v Wood* (1841) 6 QB 31; *A-G v Horner* (1885) 11 App Cas 66; and see pp 35, 36, *above*.

60 *Draper v Sperring* (1861) 10 CBNS 113 at 123; *Brackenborough v Spalding UDC* [1942] AC 310 at 314, 322, 328; and see p 43, *above*.

61 *R v Burdett* (1697) 1 Ld Raym 148; *A-G v Colchester Corpn* [1952] Ch 586 at 595. It appears that such action would be grounds for forfeiture of the market: 2 Co Inst 221. As to rights of the public, see p 27, *above*.

62 See p 28, *above*.

63 *Northampton Corpn v Ward* (1746) 2 Stra 1238; *Norwich Corpn v Swann* (1777) 2 Wm Bl 1116; but see footnote 67, *below*. A lease of stallage in a street market passes no interest in the soil of the market place to the lessee on non-market days: *Coleman v Howard* (1860) 2 LT 463.

erect stalls in a market or fair, paying a fixed or reasonable sum as stallage; and such custom will be an answer in an action for trespass[64].

ILLUSTRATION

In an action for trespass for entering onto the plaintiff's land and erecting a stall, the defendant claimed justification under a custom entitling victuallers to erect stalls and booths at fairs held at certain times of the year on the common in return for a payment to the lord of the manor of the sum of 2d. *Held*, affirming the judgment of the Queen's Bench: (1) that the custom was reasonable and an answer to an action for trespass brought by the owner of the soil; (2) that the word 'victualler' was to be understood in the sense which it bore at the time of the custom, that is, persons authorised by law to keep public houses: *Tyson v Smith*[65].

In essence, therefore, the right to stallage is different from the right to take tolls from the buyers of goods since it is dependent not on royal grant or prescription but arises by virtue of the ownership of the soil (which includes possession as lessee or licensee[66]). The only right enjoyed by the public over the soil of the market or fair is to enter to buy and sell[67]; stallage and like payments are made in respect of some user of the soil beyond mere entry into the market place.

B When stallage payable

Stallage is not payable unless there is some exclusive occupation of the soil by the person from whom it is demanded[68], as where stalls or tables are erected or baskets placed upon the ground. Whether or not occupation is exclusive is, however, a question of fact[69] and persons resting their goods or baskets on the ground for a short time will not be liable to stallage[70]. Similarly, where cattle are driven or stand in the market place, but are not penned, no stallage is payable[71].

---

64 *Tyson v Smith* (1838) 9 Ad & El 406; *Elwood v Bullock* (1844) 6 QB 383; *Chafin v Betsworth* (1684) 3 Lev 190; *A-G v Colchester Corpn* [1952] Ch 586 at 595.

65 (1838) 9 Ad & El 406. In this case, Tindal CJ said (at 425–426): 'At the early time at which this custom originated it may have been a profit to the lord, and at all events it may have been an object to him, with respect to the profits of his fair, to give encouragement to those who would erect booths and stalls for the entertainment of strangers coming to the fair . . . The custom, in fact, comes at last to an agreement, which has been evidenced by such repeated acts of assent on both sides from the earliest times, beginning before time of memory and continuing down to our own times, that it has become the law of the particular place.'

66 Thus, stallage may be demanded in the case of a newly constructed market: *Northampton Corpn v Ward* (1746) 2 Stra 1238, per Lee CJ; *Yarmouth Corpn v Groom* (1862) 1 H & C 102; and see per Lord Denman, *Lockwood v Wood* (1841) 6 QB 31.

67 *Ibid.* Although anyone erecting a stall without the authority of the market owner will be liable in trespass (see footnote 63, *above*), it seems that ejectment will not lie for a stall erected in a public street: *Doe d St Julian (Minister etc of) v Cowley* (1823) 1 C & P 123. Nor, probably, for a stall erected in a close to which the public has admission for market purposes: see *Northampton Corpn v Ward* (1746) 2 Stra 1238.

68 *A-G v Tynemouth Corpn* (1900) 17 TLR 77.

69 *Norwich Corpn v Swann* (1777) 2 Wm Bl 1116; *Yarmouth Corpn v Groom* (1862) 1 H & C 102. The construction of the stall is immaterial as is whether it is fixed into the ground or not: *ibid* at 112, per Wilde B.

70 *Townend v Woodruff* (1850) 5 Exch 506; and see *R v Bell* (1816) 5 M & S 221; *Wigley v Peachey* (1732) 2 Ld Raym 1589; *Lawnson's (Mayor) Case* (1587) Cro Eliz 75; *Sawyer v Wilkinson* (1598) Cro Eliz 627, where the owner of the soil was held not justified in distraining damage feasant goods brought into the market place and laid down for sale.

71 *Swindon Central Market Co Ltd v Panting* (1872) 27 LTNS 578.

It is sometimes difficult to distinguish stallages paid upon goods pitched in the market from tolls. For example, in the old Covent Garden market, in addition to rent paid for stalls, payments were made upon articles pitched for sale. Although called tolls, these payments were clearly stallages since they were charged on the space occupied by an article, and not upon the sale of the article[72]. Such stallages may be prescribed for[73].

Stallage may take the form of a rent payable weekly, or at other intervals, for the continuous hire of a stall; alternatively, a payment may be made for the use of a stall throughout the course of a single market day or fair day.

C Amount of stallage; power to increase stallage

The amount due for stallage may be fixed by charter[74], custom or prescription[75], or statute, and in such cases the amount so fixed may not be exceeded[76] and may be increased only by authority of an Act of Parliament, whether private or public[77]. If the amount is not so fixed, the market owner can charge what he pleases in a free bargain with the stall holder, and may increase the amount from time to time[78] subject to the decision to increase being susceptible to judicial review in the case of a local authority. Even if there is no express agreement on amount, or no special sum fixed by charter, custom, prescription or statute, a reasonable sum is recoverable in an action for use and occupation[79].

ILLUSTRATION

The defendant Corporation was the owner of an ancient market held in the High Street, the soil of which the Corporation also owned. Market charges had never been limited by charter, custom, prescription, or statute. In order to try to exclude undesirable elements from the market the Corporation adopted a new scale of charges for stallage (payable by

---

72 See *Bedford (Duke) v Overseers of St Paul's Covent Garden* (1881) 51 LJMC 41; *Bedford (Duke) v Emmett* (1820) 3 B & Ald 366.

73 See *Tyson v Smith* (1838) 9 Ad & El 406, per Tindal CJ at 425: 'It is clear that a prescription for a certain toll by way of stallage is good, notwithstanding toll and stallage are different things, . . . and, if the lord of the fair can justify distraining for such toll under a prescription, there seems no reason why the person who uses the stall on payment of the toll, and who cannot prescribe either in a que estate or in himself and his ancestors, being a stranger, should not justify under such a custom as the present.' See also *Bennington v Taylor* (1700) 2 Lut 1517.

74 *Lawrence v Hitch* (1868) LR 3 QB 521: and see p 52, *above*.

75 *Wright v Bruister* (1832) 4 B & Ad 116: and see p 52, *above*.

76 *Bennington v Taylor* (1700) 2 Lut 1517; *Hickman's Case* (1599) 2 Roll Abr 123 'Market' B 2. As to customary and prescriptive stallage, see footnote 73, *above*; as to the right of action for stallage, see pp 63, 64, *below*.

77 For power to increase tolls and stallages under statute, see pp 61 to 63, *below*, and *Ricketts v Havering London Borough Council* (1981) 79 LGR 146.

78 *Northampton Corpn v Ward* (1746) 2 Stra 1238; *A-G v Colchester Corpn* [1952] Ch 586 at 601, and see the case of *R v Birmingham City Council, ex p Dredger* (1993) 91 LGR 532, and footnote 100; see also Chap 9 pp 117, 118. A market owner who so covers the site of the market with stalls that insufficient room is left for the market to be enjoyed by those who do not wish to take stalls was formerly liable to be indicted for the offence of extortion, abolished by the Theft Act 1968: see *R v Burdett* (1697) 1 Lord Raym 148; *A-G v Colchester Corpn* [1952] Ch 586 at 595, 598, 600; and see pp 57, 58 and footnote 61, *above*; and footnote 80, *below*.

79 *Newport Corpn v Saunders* (1832) 3 B & Ad 411; *Taunton Market v Kimberley* (1777) 2 Wm Bl 1120; *A-G v Colchester Corpn* [1952] Ch 586. An action for stallage is analogous to an action for use and occupation of land: *ibid*, and 1 Roll Abr 106; but *quaere* whether an action for use and occupation will lie if the occupation is without the licence of the owner of the soil: see *Phillips v Homfray* (1883) 24 Ch D 439 at 461, per Bowen LJ.

virtue of the Corporation's ownership of the soil) whereby traders not resident in the borough were obliged to pay very much more than local traders and traders in comparable markets elsewhere. In an action brought at the relation of the General Secretary of the National Market Traders' Federation, it was claimed that the charges for stallage were excessive and unreasonable and that the Corporation was entitled by law to charge only a reasonable amount for stallage. The Corporation claimed to be able to make such charges for stallage as it thought fit. *Held*, dismissing the action, that where the right to occupy a space in a market, and the amount of stallage, are not regulated by charter, custom or otherwise, the charge for stallage is the result of a voluntary bargain between the owner of the soil and the stall holder and the owner may charge whatever he wishes: *A-G v Colchester Corpn*[80].

4 TOLLS AND STALLAGES IN KIND

Particularly in times past, tolls and stallages were, by custom or prescription, often paid in kind. A not infrequent due was a pint of wheat for every bushel exposed for sale[81].

Where a custom to take in kind exists, that custom must be closely observed.

ILLUSTRATION

At Cockermouth market the custom was for the collector to 'lift' a handful of corn out of every sack. He varied from the usual practice by 'sweeping' the corn out, and by so doing took more than a handful. *Held* he was liable in trover: *Norman v Bell*[82].

5 VARIABLE AND DIFFERENTIAL TOLLS AND STALLAGE

As described previously[83], toll is a payment on the sale of goods and is clearly distinguishable from stallage, which is a payment for the use of part of the soil and which is generally payable whether a sale is effected or not. The amount of toll payable on goods depends on the goods sold, not on the part of the market in which they are sold; and it is not possible to sustain at common law a different toll for the same article in different parts of the same market[84]. But payments in the nature of stallage, even though called toll, may vary according to the part of the market place in which the goods are pitched. For example, it may be very much more profitable to erect a stall in certain parts of the market and that will justify a higher stallage than in other parts.

---

80 [1952] 1 Ch 586. If, however, the market owner so covers the market place with stalls that there is no other accommodation, there will be no voluntary bargain: see *ibid* at 601 and footnote 78, *above*.

81 *Specot v Carpenter* (1682) T Jo 207; *Hill v Smith* (1812) 4 Taunt 520; *Norman v Bell* (1831) 2 B & Ad 190; *Hickman's Case* (1599) Noy 37; Roll Abr Market, B 2; *Hill v Hawkur* (1614) Moore KB 835; Abb Plac (4 John) p 41, (8 Edw 1) p 321; Plac Quo Warr p 569 (Twywell); Final Report of Royal Commission, p 101.

82 (1831) 2 B & Ad 190. Now wrongful interference with goods: see the Torts (Interference with Goods) Act 1977, s 1.

83 See p 51, *above*. For profits of statutory markets, see pp 61 to 63, *below*.

84 *Bedford (Duke) v Emmett* (1820) 3 B & Ald 366, but see pp 62, 63, *below*.

ILLUSTRATION

The preamble to an Act of Parliament recited the grant of a market, and that it was expedient that provision should be made for the better regulation of the market and for the more easy collection of tolls and dues payable in the market. It was enacted that it would be lawful for the market owner to take from all persons who should place, pitch or expose for sale in any part of the market any fruit, etc all such tolls as were usually collected in the market, or which were payable for or in respect of the same. *Held* that the market owner, although not entitled at common law to any toll, might under the Act recover such tolls as, at the time of the passing of the Act, were usually paid in any part of the market even though the tolls then usually paid in respect of some articles were different in different parts of the market: *Bedford (Duke) v Emmett*[85].

There is, however, nothing unlawful at common law in remitting the whole or any part of a toll taken in a market, provided the highest toll does not exceed that which may be lawfully demanded[86]. In some markets, a person of a particular class (for example, a freeman of the borough) may be entitled to be charged less for toll or stallage than outsiders[87].

6 CHARGES IN STATUTORY MARKETS

A The Markets and Fairs Clauses Act 1847

Local Acts authorising the holding of markets and fairs frequently incorporate the whole or part of the 1847 Act If the local (or 'special'[88]) Act authorises the taking of stallages, rents or tolls, such right will be regulated in accordance with the provisions of the 1847 Act, if the appropriate part of that Act[89] is incorporated in the special Act. The provisions of the 1847 Act relating to stallages, rents and tolls are dealt with in more detail elsewhere[90]; but it should be noted in particular that the market authority[91] may, from time to time, vary the stallage rents and tolls provided the amounts authorised by the special Act are not exceeded[92]. A local authority which maintains a market under a local Act may, however, make in connection with the market such charges as it determines from time to time, notwithstanding anything in the local Act[93]. This discretion should, however, be exercised in a reasonable manner[94].

---

85 (1820) 3 B & Ald 366.

86 *Newcastle (Duke) v Worksop UDC* [1902] 2 Ch 145 at 161 applying *Hungerford Market Co v City Steamboat Co* (1860) 3 E & E 365; and see *A-G v Colchester Corpn* [1952] Ch 586 at 597, 598 and 601. See also Plac Quo Warr p 158 (Derby); Rot Hund p 2 (Wallingford); Abb Plac p 140 (Faversham). As to the maximum in case of tolls, see pp 53 to 55, *above*, and in the case of stallage, see pp 59, 60, *above*.

87 See, for example, *Newcastle (Duke) v Worksop UDC* [1902] 2 Ch 145 and *A-G v Colchester Corpn* [1952] Ch 586.

88 See 1847 Act, s 2, p 180, *below*.

89 That is, ss 31–41, see p 184, *below*.

90 *Ibid.*

91 'The undertakers' under the 1847 Act: defined in *ibid*, s 2 as the persons authorised by the special Act to construct or regulate the market or fair.

92 1847 Act, s 36.

93 The Local Government (Miscellaneous Provisions) Act 1976, s 36(2): see p 209, *below*.

94 See next section, and the cases there cited, and in particular *R v Birmingham City Council, ex p Dredger* (1993) 91 LGR 532 for a case under s 36(2).

B The Food Act 1984

A market authority[95] may demand in respect of the market such charges as it may from time to time determine[96].

ILLUSTRATION

The defendant Council, concerned about the deficit on its market operation at Romford, and having ascertained that stallage charges at the market were less than at comparable markets, decided to increase charges by 120 per cent on the two weekdays on which the market operated, and by 270 per cent on Saturdays. Certain stall holders who considered that the increases were too great, and that the application of any profits to purposes unconnected with the market was not justified, sought a declaration from the High Court that the increased charges did not comply with the provisions of s 52(1) of the Food and Drugs Act 1955 (as amended)[97], and that the implementation of such increases was *ultra vires* the authority. *Held*, refusing the application, that the Council was right to take the view that the market was potentially a profit making operation and that it might be appropriate to operate it at an increased level of charges which would produce an income over and above the immediate needs of the market economy which could be devoted to the benefit of the borough generally, and that in the circumstances the proposed increases were not unreasonable: *Ricketts v Havering LBC*[98].

Although the discretion to increase charges under the 1984 Act is wide, care must nevertheless be taken to ensure that such discretion is not exercised unreasonably[99]. Furthermore, if a local authority market owner decides to raise charges for stalls to a level which makes it uneconomic to trade, it is open to the stall holder to argue that the resulting threat to his livelihood affects his common law rights, so removing into the realms of public law the relationship between local authority and stall holder. In these circumstances, the local authority decision is susceptible to challenge by way of judicial review[100].

Other provisions relating to charges under the 1984 Act include the requirement to display tables of the amounts payable[101], the time for payment[102], and recovery in the event of non-payment[103].

---

95 That is, a local authority which maintains a market established or acquired under the 1984 Act, s 50, or under corresponding provisions of preceding legislation: see 1984 Act, s 61.

96 *Ibid*, s 53(1): see p 246, *below*. 'Charges' includes stallage and tolls: 1984 Act, s 61.

97 Section 52(1) of the 1955 Act, as amended, was in almost identical terms to s 53(1) of the 1984 Act.

98 (1981) 79 LGR 146. See also *A-G v Colchester Corpn* [1952] Ch 586 at 601–603.

99 See the words of Lord Wrenbury in *Roberts v Hopwood* [1925] AC 578 at 613: 'A person in whom is vested a discretion must exercise his discretion on reasonable grounds. A discretion does not empower a man to do what he likes merely because he is minded to do so — he must in the exercise of his discretion do not what he likes but what he ought. In other words, he must, by use of his reason, ascertain and follow the course which reason directs. He must act reasonably.'

100 See *R v Barnsley Metropolitan Borough Council, ex p Hook* [1976] 1 WLR 1052; *R v Birmingham City Council, ex p Dredger and Paget* (1993) 91 LGR 532 and Chapter 9, footnote 19, *below* and p 113.

101 1984 Act, s 53(3).

102 *Ibid*, s 54.

103 1984 Act, s 55, and see p 248, *below*.

C The Animal Health Act 1981

A wharf or other place provided by a local authority under the 1981 Act is a market within the Markets and Fairs Clauses Act 1847[104] (which, with certain exceptions, is incorporated in the 1981 Act[105]), and a local authority[106] may charge for the use of the wharf or other place provided by it under the 1981 Act such sums (deemed to be tolls) as may be fixed by byelaws[107].

D The Local Government (Miscellaneous Provisions) Act 1982

A district council may[108], under the 1982 Act, charge such fees as it considers reasonable for the grant or renewal of a street trading licence or consent[109], and may determine different fees for different types of licence or consent[110]. In addition, a council may recover from a licence holder such reasonable charges as it may determine for the collection of refuse, the cleansing of streets and other services rendered by the council to him in his capacity as licence holder[111].

E Other Acts

Markets and fairs in which, for the time being, tolls are authorised to be taken and actually are taken in respect of cattle, are subject to the provisions of the Markets and Fairs (Weighing of Cattle) Acts 1887, 1891 and 1926[112].

7 RECOVERY OF TOLLS AND STALLAGE

A By action

Toll and stallage may be recovered by action without proof of an express contract[113].

In an action for recovery of toll, facts to be proved are usually as follows:

(1) that the plaintiff was in possession (as owner or lessee) of the market or fair and the tolls;

(2) the due holding of the market or fair at the time and place in question;

---

104 1981 Act, s 54(3).

105 *Ibid*, s 54(2).

106 Defined in the 1981 Act, s 50(2): see p 217, *below*.

107 *Ibid*, s 54(4).

108 Provided, of course, the council has resolved to apply the provisions of the 1982 Act to its district: see *ibid*, s 3 and pp 114 to 116 and 232, *below*.

109 1982 Act, s 3, Sch 4, para 9(1): p 240, *below*. A council is not, however, empowered to raise general revenue by way of street trading licences and consents: see *R v Manchester City Council ex p King* (1991) 89 LGR 696.

110 *Ibid*, para 9(2). The council may determine that fees may be paid by instalments: 1982 Act, Sch 4, para 9(4).

111 *Ibid*, para 9(6). A council must observe certain procedural steps before determining or varying charges: 1982 Act, Sch 4, paras 9(9), 9(10), 9(11). See para 9 also for provisions relating to deposit, recovery, remission and refund of fees and charges: pp 240, 241, *below*.

112 See pp 119, 121, *below*, and also pp 201 and 206, *below*. Sections 36–41 inclusive of the Markets and Fairs Clauses Act 1847 (which relate, *inter alia*, to the recovery of tolls by distress, disputes, and the exhibition of a list of tolls) are incorporated in the Markets & Fairs (Weighing of Cattle) Act 1887: *ibid*, s 8. These Acts are now of limited effect: see p 119, *below*.

113 See *Seward v Baker* (1787) 1 Term Rep 616; *Tewkesbury Corpn v Diston* (1805) 6 East 438; *Bedford (Duke) v Emmett* (1820) 3 B & Ald 366; *Reading Corpn v Clarke* (1821) 4 B & Ald 268; *Stamford Corpn v Pawlett* (1830) 1 Cr & J 57; *Newport Corpn v Saunders* (1832) 3 B & Ad 411; *Lockwood v Wood* (1844) 6 QB 31; *Yarmouth Corpn v Groom* (1862) 1 H & C 102.

(3) that the toll claimed is reasonable, and that it was payable (either by charter, prescription or otherwise by the buyer or seller as the case may be) on any sale in the market or fair of the articles in respect of which it is claimed;
(4) that tollable goods were brought into the market, and were then bought or sold (as the case may be) by the defendant;
(5) that the toll has not been paid.

In an action for stallage, or piccage, the facts to be proved are usually as follows:
(1) that the plaintiff was in possession (as owner or lessee) of the soil of the market or fair;
(2) the due holding of the market or fair at the time and place in question;
(3) that the defendant erected a stall in the market place, or took a standing and, if piccage is claimed, that in so doing he broke the soil;
(4) if the sum claimed is not fixed by custom, prescription or statute, and is not previously agreed, that the sum claimed is reasonable; and if it is claimed by express agreement, or by custom or prescription, that the agreement was made, or the custom or prescription exists[114];
(5) that the defendant has not paid the amount due.

Where there is no express agreement, or no special sum fixed by custom or prescription, a reasonable sum is recoverable for stallage as for use and occupation[115].

A county court has no jurisdiction to hear and determine any action in which the title to any toll, market, fair or franchise is in question[116].

B By distress

After demand and refusal of toll due in respect of goods, the owner of the market or fair may distrain upon those goods, or upon a reasonable part of them[117]. In some of the cases on this subject, the right to distrain was claimed by prescription[118]; and possibly the right cannot be claimed except by prescription, toll not being due of common right[119]. It has been said, however, that the right to distrain is incident to every toll[120] and need not be specially prescribed for and although the authorities are not clear, this is the sounder view. The distress must be made, it appears, while the goods are still in the market or fair[121]. The goods may not be sold under the distress[122], and the distrainor has no other power but to retain them until satisfaction is made[123]. No

---

114 See *A-G v Colchester Corpn* [1952] Ch 586 at 600; and see pp 59, 60, *above*.
115 See pp 59, 60, *above*.
116 County Courts Act 1984, s 15(2)(a). This is unaffected by the Courts and Legal Services Act 1990 and the High Court and County Courts Jurisdiction Order 1991 (SI 1991/724), and such actions continue to remain outside the county court jurisdiction although such actions can be transferred under the 1984 Act, s 40.
117 *Heddy v Wheelhouse* (1596) Cro Eliz 558; *Agar v Lisle* (1613) Hob 187; and see *Smith v Shepherd* (1599) Cro Eliz 710; *Hickman's Case* (1599) Noy 37; *Harris v Hawkins* (1662) 1 Keb 342; *Leight v Pym* (1687) 2 Lutw 1329.
118 See *Agar v Lisle* (1613) Hob 187; *Smith v Shepherd* (1599) Cro Eliz 710; *Bennington v Taylor* (1700) 2 Lut 1517.
119 See Com Dig Distress (A 1), citing 11 Co 44 b; *Harris v Hawkins* (1662) 1 Keb 342.
120 *Hickman's Case* (1599) Noy 37; Viner, Ab Toll (1); *Gunning on Tolls* 216. See also *Heddy v Wheelhouse* (1596) Cro Eliz 558, where the right apparently was not prescribed for; Gilbert's *Law and Practice of Distress and Replevin* (4th ed) 18, 19; and see *Whitstable Free Fishers and Dredgers Co v Gann* (1861) 11 CB NS 387 at 416.
121 *Hickman's Case* (1599) Noy 37; Viner, Ab Toll (1).
122 *Gunning on Tolls*, 217; Gilbert, *Distress*, 19.
123 3 Bl Com 10.

distress for toll can be made on goods sold outside the market even though there is a disturbance of the market[124]: the proper remedy is an action in damages for disturbance[125].

With regard to stallage, a claim to distrain after demand and refusal was upheld in *Bennington v Taylor*[126], when the owners of a fair prescribed for a reasonable stallage of an ascertainable amount, and also for the right to distrain for such stallage during the fair upon the goods exposed for sale in the stall.

8 REMEDIES FOR TOLL OR STALLAGE WRONGFULLY TAKEN

An action lies against anyone who takes toll when none is due, or takes from someone who is exempt[127]. If the toll-taker improperly takes too much by way of toll in kind, or wrongfully distrains for any toll, he is liable in an action for wrongful interference with goods[128]. Money improperly exacted as toll may be recovered as money had and received to the plaintiff's use[129], but not if paid merely to avoid litigation and because others in similar circumstances were paying toll[130].

9 EXEMPTIONS FROM TOLL

Exemptions from toll are of less importance than in former times. Nevertheless, it may be of interest to refer to the subject generally. Certain persons are entitled to exemptions by the common law[131]; others may be entitled by Crown grant, or by grant from the owner of the market or fair, or by prescription.

A Exemption at common law

(1) The Sovereign

The Sovereign and a queen consort are not liable to payment of toll[132]; but members of the royal family do not enjoy exemption from toll at common law, although they may be exempt from particular tolls by statute[133].

---

124 *Blakey v Dinsdale* (1777) 2 Cowp 661.

125 See Chapter 6, *below*.

126 (1700) 2 Lut 1517; see *Tyson v Smith* (1838) 9 Ad & El 406, 425.

127 Com Dig Toll (H 2), Market (F 1); *Wood v Haukshead* (1602) Yelv 14; FNB 94F. A remedy for the taking of 'outrageous' toll was formerly provided by the Statute of Westminster I (repealed by the Theft Act 1968): see p 55, *above*. As to persons exempt, see next section.

128 Formerly an action for trespass or trover: see *Leight v Pym* (1687) 2 Lut 1329; *Wigley v Peachey* (1732) 2 Ld Raym 1589; FNB 94F; *Norman v Bell* (1831) 2 B & Ad 190; the Torts (Interference with Goods) Act 1977, s 1.

129 *Waterhouse v Keen* (1825) 4 B & C 200; *Maskell v Horner* [1915] 3 KB 106, and see *Lewis v Hammond* (1818) 2 B & Ald 206.

130 *Maskell v Horner* [1915] 3 KB 106.

131 Thus, the commoners of the manor of Hungerford appear to claim exemption in Hungerford Market: see Report of Royal Commission, vol 4, p 173 (1888). The men of the Duchy of Lancaster appear to be free of toll under various charters: see Hardy's *Charters of the Duchy of Lancaster* (1845).

132 2 Inst 221; Co Litt 133b; Chitty, Prerog. 195, 377, 402.

133 Chitty, Prerog 405n(c).

(2) Ecclesiastical persons

Ecclesiastical persons, of whatever order or rank[134], are exempt from toll at common law for their ecclesiastical goods, and for goods bought by them for their sustenance; but not for merchandise[135].

(3) Lords of manors which are ancient demesne, and their tenants

Are exempt from toll in all markets and fairs by custom of the realm[136]. 'Ancient demesne' means those manors which were in possession of Edward the Confessor, and afterwards William the Conqueror, and which were described in Domesday as *terra regis*[137].

The exemption appears not to extend to every purchase or sale by tenants in ancient demesne[138]. It is clear that the exemption extends to sales by tenants of the produce of their tenements and to purchases by them of goods to maintain their tenements, or themselves or their households there[139]; and that consequently it includes the buying and selling of beasts bought to stock the land, or to be fatted[140]. It does not, however, apply to the purchase and sale of merchandise[141].

B Exemption by Crown grant

In early times, the Crown frequently gave charters of exemption from toll in one or more market towns in England to the corporations of favoured cities or boroughs. Thus, the Corporation of London obtained the liberty or privilege, granted and confirmed by various charters and statutes, that the citizens of London and all their goods should be quit and free of and from toll, and passage and lastage[142], and other customs, throughout the whole kingdom of England, and the ports of the seas, except only the

---

134 2 Inst 3. See Com Dig Ecclesiastical Persons, as to what persons are such; see also *Middleton (Lord) v Lambert* (1834) 1 Ad & El 401, 421.

135 FNB 227F; 2 Inst 4; Com Dig Ecclesiastical Persons (D), p 549 (5th ed); Rot Parl 8 Edw II m 4; YB 30 Edw III 15b.

136 *Savery v Smith* (1686) 2 Lut 1144; FNB 14E, 228 AD; YB 9 Hen VI f 25b; pl 20.

137 FNB 14D, 16D; Hob 118; *Hunt v Burn* (1701) 1 Salk 57. Tenants in ancient demesne have 'many and divers liberties, gifts and grants by law: as to be quit of toll and passage, and such impositions which men shall demand of them for the goods or chattels sold or bought by them in fairs or markets': FNB 14D. The reason for the exemption is stated by Coke to be, 'because at the beginning of their tenure they applied themselves to the manaurance and husbandry of the king's demesnes, and therefore, for the lands so holden, and all that came or renewed thereupon, they had the said privilege': 2 Inst 221. See also Stenton, *Anglo-Saxon England* (Oxford), p 483. This privilege of exemption still remains, and it may be claimed even though the tenants have been paying toll time out of mind: 2 Inst 654.

138 See *Ward v Knight* (1591) Cro Eliz 227, where it was expressly decided that 'tenants in ancient demesne should pay toll for their merchandises'.

139 YB 9 Hen VI, 256, pl 20; 19 Hen V1, 66b, pl 9.

140 YB 7 Hen IV, 44b, pl 11. These are transactions arising out of the cultivation of tenements, and are not merchandisings. Fitzherbert says (FNB 228 E citing YB 7 Hen IV): 'I concede that they shall be quit of toll generally, although they merchandise with their goods'. But Hale (FNB 228E, note b) and Coke (2 Inst 221) are of a different opinion; and Coke says: 'if such a tenant be a common merchant for buying and selling of wares or merchandise that rise not upon the manaurance or husbandry of those lands, he shall not have the privilege for them, because they are out of the privilege of ancient demesne, and the tenant in ancient demesne ought rather to be a husbandman than a merchant by his tenure, and so are the books to be intended'. See *Middleton (Lord) v Lambert* (1834) 1 Ad & El 401, for a discussion of the subject.

141 See footnote 138, *above*; and see also the *Leicester Town Case* (1586) 2 Leon 190; *Savery v Smith* (1687) 2 Lut 1144.

142 See p 51, footnote 8, *above*.

due and ancient customs of the Crown, and the prisage of wines[143]. And, to claim the exemption, a citizen of London need not reside in the city[144].

Grants of exemption by the Crown are either general or special, and are good except in so far as they derogate from previous grants[145]. A grant of exemption may exempt the grantees from payment of toll in a market or fair which belongs to the Crown at the date of the grant[146], or in which toll is claimed under a later grant. A grant of exemption will not, however, avail against a toll claimed under an earlier grant, for the former cannot detract from the latter; nor against a prescriptive toll, for that is presumed to have existed from time immemorial under a lost grant.

C Exemption by market owner, or by prescription

As a general rule, the grantee or owner of a market or fair can grant exemptions from toll, and, in this way, rights to exemption, founded upon grant or prescription, may arise after the market or fair has been established[147]. Exemption may be claimed by prescription or by long usage from which a lost grant will be presumed[148]. A grant of exemption from toll may include exemption from stallage[149]. If the franchise later comes into the hands of the Crown, it can only be regranted subject to the immunity[150].

A lord of the manor may prescribe that his tenants ought to be free of toll; and it has been said that if he can establish such a prescriptive right, he can maintain an action against any person who takes or claims toll from his tenants[151].

D Statutory abolition of exemptions

All exemptions from toll are liable to be taken away by Act of Parliament. Where a market or fair has been established, or is now regulated, by statute, the question as to whether any exemption from toll is abolished or preserved depends upon the construction of the statute.

The Municipal Corporations Act 1882[152] abolished the exemption enjoyed by inhabitants and freemen, etc from tolls levied in markets or fairs wholly or in part for the benefit of a borough[153] or body corporate. The Act does not, however, affect the rights of those claiming exemption from toll otherwise than as an inhabitant or freeman[154] or

---

143 A duty payable to the Crown on the importation of wines.

144 *London Corpn v Lynn Regis Corpn* (1796) 1 Bos & P 487; 7 Bro Par Cas 120; but the exemption does not exempt the citizens from tolls in the City of London; cf *Truro Corpn v Reynalds* (1832) 8 Bing 275.

145 The Crown cannot derogate from its own grant: see pp 15, 16, *above*.

146 See *Hill v Priour* (1679) 2 Show 34.

147 See FNB 226 I, 227 B, note c; 2 Inst 221; Bracton, lib 2, c 24, f 56b: Viner, 'Prerogative', I c 2, K c 1; *York's (Archbishop) Case* (1574) 4 Leon 168; *Lockwood v Wood* (1841) 6 QB 31. For other cases on the construction of grants of exemptions see *Hill v Priour* (1679) 2 Show 34.

148 See *Ellis v Bridgnorth Corpn* (1863) 15 CB NS 52 and see 'Evidence of Market Rights', Ch 11, *below*. As to the exemption of freeholders of the Duchy of Lancaster see *Osbuston v James* (1688) 2 Lut 1377. No prescriptive right to non-payment of tolls may be acquired, however, where the right to charge tolls is given by statute: see *Woolwich Corpn v Gibson* (1905) 3 LGR 961.

149 *Lockwood v Wood* (1841) 6 QB 31.

150 *Tewkesbury (Bailiffs etc) v Bricknell* (1809) 2 Taunt 120.

151 Viner, 'Actions' (case), NC8, C 2; YB 43 Edw III 30.

152 Section 208 (repealed).

153 That is, a city or town to which the Municipal Corporations Act 1882 applies: see *ibid*, s 7(1).

154 See 1882 Act, s 201 (repealed).

member of a municipal corporation[155], etc[156]. Accordingly, the Act would not affect any right of a person claiming exemption as tenant in ancient demesne, or as freeholder of the Duchy of Lancaster[157]; nor would it affect any right of a person claiming exemption as a citizen of London, for the City of London is not a municipal corporation within the meaning of the Act[158].

---

155 That is, the body corporate constituted by the incorporation of the inhabitants of a city or town to which the Act applies: *ibid*, ss 6, 7(1).
156 That is, the widow or kin of such an inhabitant, freeman or member: 1882 Act, s 208(3).
157 See footnote 148, *above*.
158 See footnote 155, *above*. The 1882 Act did not apply to London.

CHAPTER 6

Disturbance

1 RIGHT OF MARKET OWNER TO PEACEABLE ENJOYMENT

The owner of a market or fair is entitled to the peaceable enjoyment of his franchise, and to protection from disturbance. Disturbance is a tort in respect of which the owner has a right of action[1] and for which he may recover damages[2]. If the disturbance is likely to continue, restraint may be enforced by injunction[3].

Disturbance of a market may arise either out of the levying of a rival market or as a result of some other act which has the effect of depriving the market owner, either wholly or in part, of the benefit of his exclusive right to hold a market and to take profits[4].

2 DISTURBANCE BY LEVYING A RIVAL MARKET OR FAIR

The holder of a market franchise enjoys a right of protection from disturbance by a rival market or fair established within the common law distance of 6⅔ miles.

A The common law distance

In the Middle Ages, England was primarily an agricultural society, and the distribution of markets was determined to a great extent by the time it would take to travel to the market, dispose of the produce, and travel home again before dusk. An important factor in the foundation of local markets in medieval England, and in their survival and growth, was the captive trade maintained by the interdict on newer markets set up within a day's travelling distance[5]. Bracton[6] laid it down that the distance within which it may be a disturbance of an old market to set up a new one is 6⅔ miles[7]

1 See, for example, *Scottish Co-operative Wholesale Society Ltd v Ulster Farmers' Mart Co Ltd* [1960] AC 63; and p 89 *below*.

2 For measure of damages, see *Stoke-on-Trent City Council v W & J Wass Ltd* (1989) 87 LGR 129, CA and pp 75–77 *below*.

3 See, for example, *Birmingham Corpn v Perry Barr Stadium Ltd* [1972] 1 All ER 725 and pp 73, 74 *below*.

4 *Ibid* and see pp 85–89 *below*.

5 See, for example, Platt, *The English Medieval Town*, c 3; and see, for a modern example, the remarks of Johnstone J in *Loughrey v Doherty* [1928] IR 103 at 110.

6 Bk iv, c 46, f 235b; cf Britton, lib ii, c 32, c 8, f 159; Fleta, bk iv, c 28, s 13.

7 '*Infra sex leucas et dimidiam et tertiem partem dimidiae*'. Leuca, in this passage, has generally been translated by lawyers as 'mile'; see FNB 184n(a); 3 Bl Com 218; and cf 2 Inst 567. For a general inquiry into some of the various distances from time to time denoted by the word, and for a discussion and explanation of the rule given by Bracton, see (1916) 32 LQR 199–207.

'because every reasonable day's journey consists of 20 miles. The day's journey is divided into three parts. The first part, that of the morning, is to be given to those who are going to the market. The second is to be given to buying and selling, which ought to be sufficient to all, unless they be merchants who have stalls, who have deposited their goods and exposed them for sale, to whom a longer delay in the market may be necessary. But the third part is left for those returning from the market to their homes. And all these things it will be necessary[8] to do by day and not by night, on account of the snares and attacks of robbers[9], that all things may be in safety. When, therefore, a market has been obtained within such a limit, it will have to be levelled, since it is a nuisance, doing damage and injury because it is so near.'

Lord Parker of Waddington in *Hammerton v Earl of Dysart*[10] regarded the reasons given for this ruling as quite inadequate without questioning the validity of the rule; but its soundness is generally accepted despite, as Lord Parker pointed out, the varying facilities for travel in different cases[11].

There was formerly some doubt as to whether the distance is 6⅔ or 7 miles. The latter is the distance stated in the declaration in *Yard v Ford*[12] and the same distance is expressly mentioned in the charter granted by Edward III[13] to the Corporation of London, which contained a clause providing that no grant of markets should be made to others within 7 miles[14] of the city. Lord Parker (*above*) thought the distance to be 7 miles.

No doubt part of the explanation is that the mile as a unit of measurement has varied at different times and in different places[15]. The point was examined by Walton J in *Mayor, Aldermen and Burgesses of the Royal Borough of Kingston upon Thames v Sherman and Waterman Associates Ltd*[16]; and the learned judge concluded that a

---

8 Sir T Twiss translated this passage somewhat differently (ed 1880, vol iii, p 585); but cf the corresponding passage in Fleta, *loc cit above*.

9 The danger was so great that the Statute of Winchester, 13 Edw I, c 5 (repealed by 7 & 8 Geo IV, c 27) required the clearance of underwood and brush, whereby a man might lurk to do hurt, to be made for 200 feet on either side of highways leading from one market town to another.

10 [1916] 1 AC 57 at 88, 89. See also *Great Eastern Rly Co v Goldsmid* (1884) 9 App Cas 927 at 936.

11 Also, as Maddocks J remarked in *Newcastle-upon-Tyne City Council v Noble* (1990) 89 LGR 618, the reasoning is unsatisfactory since a rival market just outside the common law distance could attract persons living rather less than 6⅔ miles from either the rival or the lawful market.

12 (1670) 2 Saund 172. See 3 Bl Com 218. In the *Newton Case (Plac Quo Warr,* p 184), it was alleged for the Crown that every market ought to be distant from another five miles *(quinque miliaria)*. In the *Lyme Case* (*ibid*, p 185), however, Lyme market was held to be a nuisance to Bridport market, which was more than five (but under six) miles off.

13 1 Edw III, confirmed by the charter of 7 Rich II. Both charters were granted with the consent of Parliament.

14 *Leucae*, which is translated as 'miles' in *Great Eastern Rly Co v Goldsmid* (1884) 9 App Cas 927. The use of the word 'league' as an equivalent in *Re Islington Market Bill* (1835) 3 Cl & Fin 513, was probably due to the desire to avoid a definite translation. The judges there expressed the opinion (at 515) that such clause in a grant is void, if it adds, without any consideration therefor, 'any prohibition other than that which is attached by the common law to the grant of a market'. But they gave no opinion as to whether the distance of 7 miles mentioned was, or was not, greater than the common law distance.

15 See 32 LQR 199–207.

16 6 July 1976, unreported. In *Northampton Borough Council v Midland Development Group of Companies Ltd* (1978) 76 LGR 750, the same judge said (at 752): 'There is no doubt, I think, as a matter of law, that a person who has a market is entitled to prevent the levying of a rival market within 6⅔ miles of his own market.' See also *Tamworth Borough Council v Fazeley Town Council* (1978) 77 LGR 238 at 240, 241.

market was entitled to protection from rivals within a distance of 6⅔ miles. Subsequently, this distance was accepted by the Court of Appeal[17], albeit without any investigation of the rationale of the rule; and it is submitted that it is now settled that the shorter distance is the correct one.

It seems that a new market or fair levied more than the common law distance from an older cannot be injurious in law to the latter, even though it may cause loss. Bracton[18] and Blackstone[19] both say expressly that it cannot be; and there appears to be no modern reported case in which an action has been brought for disturbance by erecting a new market or fair more than 6⅔ miles from an old[20].

The usual form of grant is to hold a market in any place within a town or borough rather than at a fixed spot and the grantee has a power in these circumstances to move the market from place to place within the market limits[21]. The question arises as to whether the common law distance is to be measured from the place where an authorised market is actually established and conducted, or from the boundary of the area within which the market owner is entitled to establish a market. It might be thought that, if the former applied, uncertainty would arise in that the area of protection would not remain constant. For example, the owner of a 'market' established neither by franchise nor statute, but which had originally been set up perhaps many years previously more than the common law distance from a market so established, may suddenly find himself the subject of an action for disturbance by a market owner who had decided to set up a new market or move an existing market within the authorised area and to within the common law distance of his own, now rival, market[22]. Having regard, however, to the rationale of the common law distance, ie the protection of a market owner from competition for customers who would normally use his market, the distance is to be measured from the actual place where the authorised market is held and not from the edge of the area within which it might be held[23]. If the contrary applied there obviously would also be practical difficulties where the boundary of a market encompasses a wide area, which is frequently the case with modern local authority statutory markets.

ILLUSTRATION

A City Council was the owner of an exclusive statutory right to hold markets within the boundaries of the City The City Council also licensed many others to conduct markets at various places within the City The defendants conducted a rival unlicensed market at a site

17 In *Sevenoaks District Council v Pattullo and Vinson Ltd* [1984] 1 All ER 544, where Slade LJ, at 553, expressed the view that the law on the subject generally is 'recondite and confused' and 'might well benefit from the attention on the part of the legislature'.

18 Bk iv c 46, f 235b.

19 Bk iii, c 13, p 218, citing Hale on FNB 184. Blackstone also explains the reasons for the rule.

20 See, however, to the contrary, for what they are worth, the *Leominster Fair Case* (1285) Abb Plac 206, and the *Bath Market Case* (1377) Rot Parl 50 Edw III, vol ii, p 347. Both cases concerned fairs, and it is possible that the rule never applied to fairs: cf *R v Aires* (1717) 10 Mod Rep 354; and see also 32 LQR 206.

21 See *above*, pp 33, 34.

22 As occurred in *Stoke-on-Trent City Council v W & J Wass Ltd* (1989) 87 LGR 129: see p 75 *below*. See also the unreported decisions at first instance, 4 March 1987.

23 *Quaere*, however, in the case of a franchise market, whether the Crown would derogate from its own prior grant in granting new market rights at a place less than 6⅔ miles from the edge of the authorised area, albeit more than the common law distance of the actual market place. See pp 15, 16 *above* and p 83 *below*. Cf the position with regard to the establishment of local authority statutory markets under the Food Act 1984, s 50(2) and preceding legislation; see p 20 *above* and pp 243–245 *below*.

which was more than 6⅔ miles from the nearest authorised market, but less than 6⅔ miles from the boundary of the area within which the City Council had power to establish markets. On the City Council's claim that the defendant's market constituted an actionable disturbance of its own right of market, *Held* that the distance was to be measured from the place at which an authorised market was actually conducted and not from the boundary of the authorised area and, since the defendant's market was more than 6⅔ miles from any market conducted or licensed by the City Council, it did not constitute an actionable disturbance of the Council's right of market: *Birmingham City Council v Anvil Fairs*[24].

Until recently, there was no authority as to whether the 6⅔ miles should be measured by the nearest road or in a straight line. In view of the reason for fixing the distance at 6⅔ miles, i e. that it is one-third of a day's journey of 20 miles[25], it might be thought that the proper way to measure the distance is by the nearest road. At one time, measurement for the purposes of statutes was by the nearest and most usual way rather than 'as the crow flies'[26]; but by the Interpretation Act 1889, now replaced by the Interpretation Act 1978[27], measurement of any distance shall, unless a contrary intention appears, be measured in a straight line. In determining whether or not a reference in a document (other than a statute) to a measurement should be taken to be 'as the crow flies', regard must be had to the subject matter of the document and the object which the draftsman had in mind in mentioning the measure of distance[28].

The courts have, in analogous cases, generally favoured the distance 'as the crow flies'; and, in the market context, the distance should be measured in this way.

ILLUSTRATION

A City Council was the owner of an exclusive statutory right to hold public fairs and markets within the borough for the sale of a wide variety of items. The first defendant started holding car boot sales on a site owned by the second defendant in the area of a different local authority but within 6⅔ miles as the crow flies from the City Council's Quayside market. On the City Council's application for an injunction to restrain the defendants from holding further markets, *Held*, granting the injunction, that the correct method of measuring the distance under the common law rule was as the crow flies, that is,

---

24 (1989) 87 LGR 394. This point was previously undecided although there are *obiter dicta* to the contrary in *Great Eastern Rly Co v Goldsmid* (1884) 9 App Cas 927 (where Lord Selborne LC says at 936 that protection *prima facie* extends 'to a distance of nearly 7 miles from the places in which [the market rights] might be exercised') and in *Manchester City Council v Walsh* (1985) 84 LGR 1 (where Griffiths LJ says at 10: 'In our judgment the weight of authority must . . . establish that a statutory market, whether established under public or private Act, enjoys as part of the market rights protection from disturbance by a rival market set up within 6⅔ miles of the boundaries, unless the working of the relevant statutes modifies that right'). But cf *Re Islington Market Bill* (1835) 3 Cl & Fin 513 at 515 where the judges speak of the prohibition merely as being 'within the common law distance of an old market'. Browne-Wilkinson VC in *Anvil Fairs above* decided that nothing in these three cases turned on the point from which the distance should be measured and he could see no basis in principle why protection should be afforded to persons who could establish a market in a particular place but who have not done so. Unless and until the rival market is established, no customers are lost nor is there any actionable disturbance of the market owner's rights. See also *Stoke-on-Trent City Council v W & J Wass Ltd* (1988) 87 LGR 129, CA at 142 and at first instance (4 March 1987, unreported) p 75 *below*.

25 See Bracton, bk iv, c 46, f 235b; 3 Bl Com 219.

26 *Wing v Earle* (1591) Cro Eliz 212; (1592) Cro Eliz 267.

27 Section 8.

28 *Mouflet v Cole* (1872) LR 7 Exch 70, 8 id 32, and *Jewel v Stead* (1856) 6 E & B 350.

a direct radius, and not by measuring the shortest distance by road between the authorised market and its rival: *Newcastle-upon-Tyne City Council v Noble*[29].

B 'Same day' rival market presumed a nuisance

If a new market or fair is held[30] within the common law distance of the old, and on the same day, then there is an irrebuttable presumption that the new market is a nuisance to the old, and proof of damage is not required[31]. As Bracton says:

> 'when, therefore, a market has been obtained within such a limit it will have to be levelled, since it is a hurtful and tortious nuisance because it is so near'[32].

The cause of action is complete when the franchise owner establishes that there is a same-day market within the common-law distance; and nuisance is presumed unless the new market is itself licensed by the franchise holder, or is the subject of a concurrent right of market franchise either by Crown grant or pursuant to statute[33].

ILLUSTRATIONS

The plaintiff had a right, under a charter of Charles I, to hold markets in the borough every week on Wednesdays, Fridays, and Saturdays. The defendants conducted sheep and cattle auctions on Saturdays in a field within the limits of the borough. *Held* that the defendants' market was a disturbance of the plaintiff's by intendment of law: *Mayor of Dorchester v Ensor*[34].

The plaintiff Borough Council had held a Saturday market from time immemorial which, in 1663, had been confirmed by charter. In 1977, the defendant Town Council started to hold a Saturday market within 1½ miles of the plaintiff's market. *Held*, granting the injunction sought, that there was an irrebuttable presumption that the new market was a nuisance to the old: *Tamworth Borough Council v Fazeley Town Council*[35].

---

29 (1990) 89 LGR 618. The *dictum* of Sir Nicholas Browne-Wilkinson VC in *Birmingham City Council v Anvil Fairs* (1989) 87 LGR 394 at 396 applied.

30 See note 24, *above*.

31 *Yard v Ford* (1670) 2 Wms Saund 172 at 174, citing *Fitzherbert's Natura Brevium* 184a, note (b), where Hale cites *Weston's Case*, YB 11 Hen IV, f 5 in support of this proposition and also refers to *Clinton's Case*, YB Pasch, 13 Edw III, pl 20. See also to the same effect, *Dorchester Corpn v Ensor* (1869) LR 4 Exch 335 at 343; *Elwes v Payne* (1879) 12 Ch D 468 at 472, per Jessel MR; *Cork Corpn v Shinkwin* (1825) Sm & Bat 395 at 398, per Chatterton VC; *Winsford Entertainments Ltd v Winsford UDC* (1924) 23 LGR 254; *Hammerton v Earl of Dysart* [1916] 1 AC 57 at p 89, HL per Lord Parker of Waddington; *Morpeth Corpn v Northumberland Farmers' Auction Mart Co Ltd* [1921] 2 Ch 154 at 162, per Sargant J; *Tamworth Borough Council v Fazeley Town Council* (1978) 77 LGR 238, where the authorities from the earliest times are comprehensively reviewed; *Sevenoaks District Council v Pattullo and Vinson Ltd* [1984] 1 All ER 544; *Stoke-on-Trent City Council v W & J Wass Ltd* (1988) 87 LGR 129.

32 Bracton bk iv, c 46, f 235B; and to the same effect are Britton, ii, c 32, s 8, f 159; Fleta, iv, c 28, s 13.

33 *Tamworth Borough Council v Fazeley Town Council* (1978) 77 LGR 238 at 266. The nine judges in *Re Islington Market Bill* (1835) 3 Cl & Fin 513 at 520 were of the opinion that the establishment of a new market to be held at the same time within the common law distance of an old market *prima facie* is injurious to the old market, and therefore void. It appears that the phrase *prima facie* is used here not with reference to the burden of proof of damage but in view of the possibility of setting up a rival market authorised by grant in special circumstances: see *Tamworth Borough Council v Fazeley Town Council, above.*

34 (1869) LR 4 Exch 335.

35 (1979) 77 LGR 238.

The franchise owner is not entitled to sever the right of market for a particular locality so as to enable the holding, in that locality, of two or more markets dealing wholly or in part in the same commodity in different places on the same day.

ILLUSTRATION

The vendors, as predecessors in title to both the plaintiff District Council and the defendant, enjoyed a right by prescription to hold a market dealing in any commodity on Saturdays and other lawful days in the manor of Sevenoaks. In 1925 the vendors conveyed the market rights to the plaintiff's predecessors, excluding the right to sell livestock, this right being conveyed in 1927 to the defendant's predecessors. Thereafter, the plaintiff operated a general market on Saturdays and the defendant a livestock market on Mondays; but in 1981 the defendant started a general market on Saturdays on the site of the livestock market. *Held* (by CA) (1) that the vendor could not, by the 1925 conveyance, have reserved or retained valid and effective rights to hold a general market on the same day as the plaintiff's predecessor so that the 1925 conveyance had not severed the right to hold a general market so as to entitle the defendant to hold a general same-day market concurrently with that of the plaintiff; (2) since the defendant's market was held within the common law distance, the plaintiff was entitled to relief without proof of damage: *Sevenoaks District Council v Pattullo and Vinson Ltd*[36].

The levying of a rival market is therefore actionable *per se*, and is a ground for at least nominal damages (even though there is no right to take toll), and therefore for an injunction[37].

C 'Different day' rival market requires evidence of damage

If a new market or fair is held within the common law distance of the old, but on a different day or days, actual damage to the old market must be proved[38]. This is a question of fact; but, for the purposes of a motion for an interlocutory injunction, it is sufficient to show a likelihood of damage[39].

ILLUSTRATIONS

The plaintiffs were the owners of the tolls of an ancient cattle market held weekly on Thursdays. The defendants, who were auctioneers, fitted up with stalls and pens a

---

36 [1984] 1 All ER 544.

37 *Morpeth Corpn v Northumberland Farmers' Auction Mart Co* [1921] 2 Ch 154 at 162, per Sargant J (for a form of injunction, see *ibid* at 163); *Stoke-on-Trent City Council v W & J Wass Ltd* (1988) 87 LGR 129.

38 *Weston's Case,* YB 11 Hen IV, ff 5, 6; *Yard v Ford* (1670) 2 Saund 172; *R v Aires* (1761) 10 Mod 354; *Cork Corpn v Shinkwin* (1825) Sm & Bat 395; *Dorchester Corpn v Ensor* (1869) LR 4 Ex 335; *Elwes v Payne* (1879) 12 Ch D 468 at 472; *Great Eastern Rly Co v Goldsmid* (1884) 9 App Cas 927; *Marquis of Downshire v O'Brien* (1887) 19 LR Ir 380 at 387; *Morpeth Corpn v Northumberland Farmers' Auction Mart Co* [1921] 2 Ch 154; *Winsford Entertainments Ltd v Winsford UDC* (1924) 23 LGR 254.

39 *Birmingham Corpn v Perry Barr Stadium Ltd* [1972] 1 All ER 725; *Leicester Corpn v Maby* (1971) 70 LGR 209 at 215; *Kingston-upon-Thames Royal Borough Council v Sherman and Waterman Associates Ltd* (6 July 1976, unreported); *Northampton Borough Council v Midland Development Group of Companies Ltd* (1978) 76 LGR 750 at 754. For cases in which the market owner failed to obtain interlocutory relief in respect of different day markets, see *Warwick Corpn v Maby (No 2)* (1971) 116 Sol Jo 137; 136 LG Rev 463 and *Cirencester UDC v Cirencester Town AFC and Aketwise Merchants Ltd* (1973) 137 LGR 515.

neighbouring piece of ground and issued circulars stating that weekly sales of cattle would be held there on Mondays. The plaintiffs brought an action to restrain the defendants from holding sales as being an interference with the plaintiffs' market and applied for interlocutory relief. *Held* (at first instance, per Jessel MR) that having regard to modern facilities for traffic, a market on Monday was *prima facie* an injury to a market on Thursday, and an interlocutory injunction ought to be granted: *Elwes v Payne*[40].

The plaintiff Corporation enjoyed a statutory monopoly of holding markets within the boundary of the city. The defendant company purported to grant a licence to M to hold markets at its stadium within such boundary, and, despite protests from the plaintiff, M held a market there which attracted about 200 traders and 15,000 persons. The plaintiff issued a writ seeking to restrain M and the defendant from holding such markets, and moved for an interlocutory injunction. Before the hearing, M held a second market at which some 25,000 persons were present. *Held*, granting the injunction, that although at thc trial of the action the plaintiff must prove damage to its market rights, in order to justify the grant of an injunction on a motion it was sufficient to show only a likelihood of damage: *Birmingham Corpn v Perry Barr Stadium Ltd*[41].

The plaintiff Corporation claimed an ancient common law franchise to hold a market on Saturdays, such right being recited in four local Acts The defendants began to levy a rival market on Sundays, outside the plaintiff's franchise area, but within the common law distance. The plaintiff issued proceedings and sought interlocutory relief to restrain the defendant. *Held*, granting the injunction, that where the rival market was held on a day other than the market day, it was a question of fact whether damage was caused to the market owner and the levying of a rival market on the next day after a market day was evidence of apprehended damage sufficient to entitle the plaintiff to relief: *Leicester Corpn v Maby*[42].

Delay in seeking relief may be a bar to the grant of an interlocutory injunction[43].

D Measure of damages

The general rule in tort actions is that a successful plaintiff is entitled to receive damages equivalent to the loss he has suffered, no more or no less. A second general rule is that where the plaintiff has suffered loss to his property, or to some proprietary right, he is entitled to damages equivalent to the diminution in value of that property or right[44]. In

---

40 (1879) 12 Ch D 468. The decision was reversed unanimously in the Court of Appeal (*ibid* at 475), but on different grounds: see for example *Leicester Corpn v Maby* (1971) 70 LGR 209 at 215.

41 [1972] 1 All ER 725.

42 (1972) 70 LGR 209.

43 *Warwick Corpn v Maby (No 2)* (1971) 116 Sol Jo 137; 136 LG Rev 463, where a delay of 8 months without effective protest was held to be a bar to interlocutory relief. In an action, however, mere acquiescence or delay on the part of the market owner which has not continued long enough to satisfy the requirements of the Limitation Act 1980 will not constitute a bar to the enforcement of his legal rights (*Morpeth Corpn v Northumberland Farmers' Auction Mart Co* [1921] 2 Ch 154 at 163; and see 'Limitation of actions', p 89 *below*).

44 There are exceptions to the rules, ie trespass to land (eg *Whitwham v Westminster Brymbo Coal and Coke Co* [1896] 2 Ch 538); detinue (*Strand Electric and Engineering Co Ltd v Brisford Entertainments Ltd* [1952] 2 QB 246); patent infringement (eg *Meters Ltd v Metropolitan Gas Meters Ltd* (1911) 28 RPC 157). See also the decision of Brightman J in *Wrotham Park Estate Co v Parkside Houses Ltd* [1974] 1 WLR 798. In cases of trespass to land and patent infringement, and in some cases of detinue and nuisance, the court will award damages in accordance with what Nicholls LJ termed the 'user principle' in *Stoke-on-Trent City Council v W & J Wass Ltd* (1989) 87 LGR 129, CA at 140: see text *below*.

market cases, the owner of a market right is not entitled to more than nominal damages in respect of a same day rival market in the absence of evidence of actual loss.

ILLUSTRATION

In 1982 the defendant began to operate a Thursday market at L without the permission of the Council who operated statutory markets on Wednesday, Friday and Saturday. On 12 April 1984 the Council commenced a statutory market on Thursday at F within 6⅔ miles of the defendant's market at L Following unsuccessful attempts to prevent the defendant's market at L, the Council issued a writ in 1986 seeking an injunction and general damages, claiming that the Council's right to operate its market at F was being infringed. Peter Gibson J *held*, granting a permanent injunction to the Council that, although the Council had suffered no loss to its Thursday market, it was nevertheless entitled to damages calculated by reference to the licence fee that the Council could reasonably have required for the operation of the defendant's market between 12 April 1984 and the grant of the permanent injunction at trial. On appeal by the defendant on the question of damages: *Held*, allowing the appeal, that in cases of trespass to land, patent infringement and some cases of detinue and nuisance the 'user principle' applied to enable a plaintiff to recover as damages a reasonable sum for the wrongful use made of his property; that, whilst the owner of a market right was entitled to damages for disturbance of that right equivalent to the diminution in value through loss of stallage, tolls and so forth, the 'user principle' should not be extended to cover infringement of a market right by the holding of an unauthorised market where the plaintiff could not show any loss as a result of the infringement; and that, accordingly, since the Council had suffered no loss as a result of the defendant's unauthorised market, it was entitled to nominal damages only: *Stoke-on-Trent City Council v W & J Wass Ltd*, CA[45].

The market owner may prove damages by showing loss of tolls, stallage[46] or other profits. Alternatively, he may show damage to his stall holders especially if it is apparent that, should the rival market continue, the viability of marginal stalls would be seriously impaired[47]. Where a local authority owner of a charter market without tolls has subsequently acquired the right, by statute, to charge tolls, it may be sufficient in proving damage to rely on loss of those tolls[48]. It may not be easy to prove loss. If actual loss cannot be shown, no cause of action will lie in the case of an unauthorised different day market. In the case of a same day market it has been said that the grant of injunctive

---

45 (1989) 87 LGR 129. In this case the court drew a distinction between those trespass, detinue and patent cases where damages were awarded in accordance with the 'user principle' (see note 44, *above*) and market cases. In particular, an unlawful use of a plaintiff's right to hold his own market does not deprive him of the opportunity of holding one himself (*ibid* at 138); and, whilst a market right confers a monopoly in the same way as a patent, the protection afforded to the owner of a market right is limited to protecting him against disturbance of that right (*ibid* at 142).

46 *Cork Corpn v Shinkwin* (1825) Sm & Bat 395; *Morpeth Corpn v Northumberland Farmers' Auction Market Co Ltd* [1921] 2 Ch 154 at 162; *Wakefield City Council v Box* [1982] 3 All ER 506 at 509.

47 *Ibid*; *Northampton Borough Council v Midland Development Group of Companies Ltd* (1978) 76 LGR 750 at 754. Even though no pecuniary loss can be shown, it has been said that the exclusive privilege of holding a market, with the authority and jurisdiction incident thereto, may perhaps have a value which will render an encroachment upon the privilege the subject of an action for damages (*Cork Corpn v Shinkwin* (1825) Sm & Bat 395 at 402).

48 *Morpeth Corpn v Northumberland Farmers' Auction Mart Co* [1921] 2 Ch 154 at 162.

relief is peculiarly appropriate precisely because damages will not be an adequate remedy[49].

E What constitutes a rival market?

This is a question of fact[50], and the defendant's intention is immaterial[51].

To sustain an action for disturbance by levying a rival market, it is not necessary to show that the defendant has set up what purports to be a legal market. It is sufficient if he has erected stalls on his land and has taken rent in the nature of stallage from persons who have brought goods there to sell[52]; or has so used his land as to encourage and provide for a concourse of buyers and sellers: for example by establishing a depot with conveniences for the benefit of buyers and sellers[53], or by holding public auctions or sales whereby persons are provided with a means of selling their goods without bringing them to market[54]. It is not necessary for the defendant to have actually sold or conducted sales in the rival market. Any active interference by him in the conduct of the market, or participation in its profits or risks, is sufficient: for example, if he provides land for sale by auction and, in consequence of the use to which the land is put, takes an increased rent above that which would otherwise be obtainable[55].

ILLUSTRATIONS

The plaintiff was the holder of a market franchise for the sale of commodities on every day of the week except Sundays, and in respect of which stallage was taken. The defendant owned a piece of ground immediately contiguous to the plaintiff's market, and laid it out as a public market by filling it with stalls and letting those stalls to dealers in the same types of commodity already sold in the plaintiff's market. The defendant's market was held on some of the same days as the franchise market with the result that the plaintiff was deprived of stallage and other profits. *Held* that the defendant's operation constituted a rival market in respect of which a right of action lay: *Cork Corpn v Shinkwin*[56].

The defendant Railway Company set up a 'depot' or row of stalls in arches under a station 300 yards from the plaintiff's market, which it let to monthly tenants who were to sell not only their own commodities but also those of any member of the public which were sent via the defendant's railway. The defendant advertised widely, and invited the public both to send

---

49 *Sevenoaks District Council v Pattullo and Vinson Ltd* [1984] 1 All ER 544 at 553; *Stoke-on-Trent City Council v W & J Wass Ltd* (1988) 87 LGR 129 at 143. *Quaere* whether exemplary damages may be awarded in a market case where a defendant's conduct justifies such award: the point was raised by Nicholls LJ in *Wass above*, but not further discussed.

50 *Great Eastern Rly Co v Goldsmid* (1884) 9 App Cas 927; *Wilcox v Steel* [1904] 1 Ch 212; *London Corpn v Lyons Son & Co (Fruit Brokers) Ltd* [1936] Ch 78 at 140; *Scottish Co-operative Wholesale Society Ltd v Ulster Farmers' Mart Co Ltd* [1960] AC 63; *Kingston-upon-Hull City Council v Greenwood* (1984) 82 LGR 586.

51 *Wilcox v Steel* [1904] 1 Ch 212 at 218; *London Corpn v Lyons Son & Co (Fruit Brokers) Ltd* [1936] Ch 78 at 131, 132, 140. See further as to defences, *below*, pp 83 to 85.

52 *Yard v Ford* (1670) 2 Saund 172; *Morpeth Corpn v Northumberland Farmers' Auction Mart Co Ltd* [1921] 2 Ch 154 at 160, per Sargant J.

53 *Great Eastern Rly Co v Goldsmid* (1884) 9 App Cas 927; *Moseley v Chadwick* (1782) 3 Doug KB 117; *Birmingham Corpn v Foster* (1894) 70 LT 371.

54 *Dorchester Corpn v Ensor* (1869) LR 4 Exch 335; *Elwes v Payne* (1879) 12 Ch D 468; *London Corpn v Low* (1879) 49 LJQB 144; *Morpeth Corpn v Northumberland Farmers' Auction Mart Co* [1921] 2 Ch 154.

55 *Dorchester Corpn v Ensor* (1869) LR 4 Exch 335; *Marquis of Downshire v O'Brien* (1887) 19 LR Ir 380.

56 (1825) Sm & Bat 395.

goods for sale at the depot (through the instrumentality of the tenants) and to come and buy. *Held* (by HL, affirming the decision of CA) that the defendant's depot, although not technically a market, nevertheless constituted a rival market and a disturbance of the plaintiff's market: *Great Eastern Rly Co v Goldsmid*[57].

The plaintiff enjoyed a right by charter to hold markets every week on Wednesdays, Thursdays and Saturdays. The defendant held sheep and cattle auctions on alternate Saturdays in a neighbouring field belonging to the co-defendant M, either let by M for that purpose, or jointly occupied by E and M for that purpose. Evidence was given of M's active co-operation at sales held there. *Held* that M's involvement amounted to a disturbance of the plaintiff's market rights without the necessity of showing that M had actually sold: *Dorchester Corpn v Ensor*[58].

Where the defendant does not publicly invite sellers indiscriminately, but sells the goods of others under contract or by private arrangement, he is not levying a rival market but is selling outside the market; and the fact that such goods are sold by auction does not necessarily alter the situation.

ILLUSTRATION

The defendant company dealt in the same commodities as those sold in the plaintiff's franchise market, and held a number of auction sales in its own building situated outside the plaintiff's market but within the common law distance. For reasons other than lack of room, the plaintiff had previously declined to allow the defendant to sell goods by auction within the market, and had also declined to accept the defendant's offer to pay reasonable tolls in respect of goods sold outside. The defendant sold goods owned by a limited number of persons, and sale notices expressly stated that buyers only would be admitted and that goods were being offered to wholesale buyers only. The plaintiff claimed disturbance by the levying of a rival market and sought an injunction. *Held* (by CA) in refusing relief, that a trader has a right to conduct sales by auction in a market if he chooses, and that the defendant's auction sales outside the market did not, on the facts, constitute disturbance by the levying of a rival market: *London Corpn v Lyons Son & Co (Fruit Brokers) Ltd*[59].

The court in *Lyons* was satisfied that there was no rival market because there was no concourse of sellers and only a limited concourse of buyers. There can be no market, in whatever sense, without a concourse both of buyers and of sellers[60]. 'Concourse' in the market sense, describes the coming together in one place of persons for a common purpose; it does not signify a succession of persons (even if two or more happen to arrive at the same time) coming with the predetermined objective of buying from or selling to a particular individual, and then departing.

ILLUSTRATION

The respondent market owners claimed that the setting up, with the approval of the Ministry of Agriculture, of the appellant Society's own abattoir within the market area, and the introduction of a scheme under which the Ministry undertook to use the appellant's

---

57 (1884) 9 App Cas 927.

58 (1869) LR 4 Exch 335.

59 [1936] Ch 78. See also *Scottish Co-operative Wholesale Society Ltd v Ulster Farmers' Mart Co Ltd* [1960] AC 63. As to disturbance by selling outside the market, see *below*, pp 85, 86.

60 *Great Eastern Rly Co v Goldsmid* (1884) 9 App Cas 927; *Marquis of Downshire v O'Brien* (1887) 19 LR Ir 380; *Scottish Co-operative Wholesale Society Ltd v Ulster Farmers' Mart Co Ltd* [1960] AC 63; *Kingston upon Hull City Council v Greenwood* (1984) 82 LGR 586.

premises as a collecting centre to which producers could bring live pigs for sale, constituted the levying of a rival market and thus an actionable interference with the respondent's market rights. *Held* (by HL) in allowing the appeal, that there was no concourse of buyers and sellers since the buyers could only be the Ministry or the appellant Society: *Scottish Co-operative Wholesale Society Ltd v Ulster Farmers' Mart Co Ltd*[61].

Whilst the essential feature of a rival market is the provision of facilities for a concourse both of buyers and of sellers, there is no requirement that it should be levied in a public place to which both may freely resort. Apart from auction cases, there will sometimes be rival markets where, so far as numbers, mobility and variety of sellers are concerned, the concourse falls short of that which may be expected in a lawful market. This will not necessarily affect the status of the rival operation even if the operator attempts to exercise control over sellers by conducting personal interviews of applicants for units or stalls and by granting licences to successful applicants which will result in some degree of security of tenure. The space available to sellers will often be limited, and control of this nature may sometimes be justified if chaos is to be avoided.

ILLUSTRATIONS

The defendant constructed about 30 solid, semi-permanent, individual units for the sale of goods on part of the ground floor of retail premises about half a mile from the plaintiff Council's franchise market. The front of each unit was open and sales were conducted from within the unit. At night, each unit and the two entrances to the 'arcade' (as the defendant described it) within the premises were securely boarded up so that goods could be safely left there overnight and at weekends. The defendant advertised in the local trade and general press inviting traders to trade from the units. Licences were granted to about 20 occupants determinable on a week's notice. *Held*, in granting injunctive relief to the plaintiff, that the defendant was providing facilities for a concourse of buyers and sellers and that this operation constituted a rival market: *Kingston-upon-Hull City Council v Greenwood*[62].

The defendants acquired on lease part of a building, which had previously housed a well known department store, and advertised in the local press an 'antiques and collectors' fair' to be held there inviting traders to take 'tables/spaces by the day'. Because the building was within 6⅔ miles of the Council's statutory markets, Council representatives visited the premises and found that 100 'market stalls' could be accommodated and that approximately 60 had been erected from which individual traders were offering articles for sale to the public, including articles of the kind normally offered for sale in the Council's markets. The stalls were of flimsy construction, and in some cases there was no physical barrier between them. The defendants granted oral licences to the traders, at first daily, later weekly and, at the time of the trial, monthly. The defendants claimed to interview all applicants for licences. The Council claimed that the defendants were operating a rival market and obtained an injunction restraining them from so doing. *Held* (by CA) dismissing the defendants' appeal against the grant of an injunction: (1) that there was sufficient concourse of buyers and sellers at the defendants' premises to constitute a rival market; (2) that the individual trading units did not come within the definition of 'shops' for the purpose of the Shops Act 1950 so as to fall outside the field of the Council's exclusive market rights: *Manchester City Council v Walsh*[63].

But the Court of Appeal in the *Walsh* case, *above*, doubted the wisdom of attempting to lay down fixed criteria to test the existence of a market, or of a

61 [1960] AC 63.
62 (1984) 82 LGR 586.
63 (1986) 84 LGR 1. The Shops Act 1950 is now repealed.

concourse of buyers and sellers, as Nourse J had attempted to do in *Greenwood, above*, and declined to do so:

> 'Each case will have to be judged on its own facts taking into account a number of factors including, but not necessarily exclusively, the nature of the invitation to sellers and buyers, the numbers of each, the nature and size of the individual units, the nature and sources of the goods, the proximity of individual sellers one to another, and the degree of control retained and exercised by the organisers[64].'

F Sales in shops and other premises

It is not normally a disturbance for a person to sell his own goods in the ordinary course of business in his own shop or private house near the market place on market days[65]. There is, however, a substantial difference between that and the case of a person who provides premises from which others may sell their goods without taking them into the market. From a misunderstanding of an early case[66], it was once supposed that a grant of a market carried with it a right to prevent persons from selling their goods on market days in their own shops or private houses; but it is now settled that such a right is not incident to a grant of a market.

ILLUSTRATION

The plaintiff Corporation brought an action to restrain the defendants from selling eggs and dried fish on market days in their shop. The shop was situated in a street which adjoined one side of one of the plaintiff's markets, and was on the opposite side of the street from but not opposite to, the entrance from the street to the market. The defendants sold only their own goods in their shop in the ordinary course of business. *Held* (by CA) that there was no disturbance of the plaintiff's statutory right of market: *Manchester Corpn v Lyons*[67].

---

64 *Manchester City Council v Walsh* (1986) 84 LGR 1 at 12. Compare the tests suggested on p 82, *below*. Nourse J had attempted in *Kingston upon Hull City Council v Greenwood, above*, to lay down three criteria, one of which was the retention by the defendant of a sufficient degree of control in particular by granting to the sellers little or no security of occupation: this test was rejected by the CA in *Walsh, above*. See also the cases of *Northampton Borough Council v Midland Development Group of Companies Ltd* (1978) 76 LGR 750; *Leicester City Council v Oxford and Bristol Stores Ltd,* (21 December 1978, unreported), pp 81, 82, *below*, and *East Staffordshire County Council v Windridge Pearce (Burton-on-Trent) Ltd* [1993] EGCS 186. In the last case the Vice-Chancellor held that the defendant's operation constituted a rival market because the defendant's original intention to grant exclusive nine month leases to all sellers had not, in fact, been implemented so that there was insufficient security of occupation resulting in a concourse of sellers. The Vice-Chancellor's approach was followed in *In Shops Centres plc v Derby City Council* (1997) 95 LGR; [1996] NPC 150 where it was held that proposed leases for five year terms (excluded by court order from the security of protection provisions of the Landlord and Tenant Act 1954) of separate self-contained retail units would give each trader sufficient security to take the proposed operation out of the definition of a market for the purposes of market law, ie there would be no general concourse of sellers and therefore no rival market.

65 *Macclesfield Corpn v Chapman* (1843) 12 M & W 18; *Macclesfield Corpn v Pedley* (1833) 4 B & Ad 397; *Penryn Corpn v Best* (1878) 3 Ex D 292; *Manchester Corpn v Lyons* (1882) 22 Ch D 287, 311.

66 *Prior of Dunstable's Case* YB II Hen VI, ff 19, 25; see *Macclesfield Corpn v Chapman* (1843) 12 M & W 18 at 20, per Parke B.

67 (1882) 22 Ch D 287.

Nevertheless, if the shop is in or next to the market place, and the owner opens it for selling in the market, he may be liable to stallage[68]; and a right to exclude sales in shops or private houses within the limits of the franchise on market days may exist by immemorial custom or by prescription. Such a right may formerly have been acceptable on the basis that, whilst it enabled the owner of the market to take an increased profit, it also benefited the public by securing the owner's supervision over all articles for sale on market days[69]. The only cases in which the right has been established have been those concerning ancient markets in which the owner claimed the right as from time immemorial, and the evidence supported that claim. If the market is ancient, and the owner at all times appears to have prevented a sale in shops or private houses, the exercise of such control is evidence of the right[70].

It is probable that a clause in a modern grant of a market purporting to confer such a right would be void[71].

It is not possible to lay down a precise definition by which sales in a private shop may be distinguished from such a system of selling which amounts to establishing a rival market. The mere fact that the sale in a shop attracts some persons who would otherwise buy in the market is not enough to constitute a disturbance, nor is the character or name of the building in which the sale is conducted. All the circumstances of the case must be taken into consideration including the nature and method of the business done[72] and the character and management of the premises[73].

ILLUSTRATIONS

The defendants fitted out with booths one floor of a shopping centre situated 3½ miles from the plaintiff Council's market, with the intention of granting three-monthly licences to individual traders. It was also the defendants' intention to install good lighting and to carpet the whole area. *Held,* granting interlocutory relief, that the defendants' proposed activities would constitute the levying of a rival market: *Northampton Borough Council v Midland Development Group of Companies Ltd*[74].

The defendant's business in a building about 200 yards from the plaintiff Council's market was initially conducted in the manner of a market with a concourse both of sellers and of buyers. After about a fortnight, the *modus operandi* was altered and the defendant claimed that there was no longer a concourse of sellers but merely a series of sales by the defendant,

---

68 *Newington Fair Case* (1608) 2 Roll Abr 123, B I; Com Dig Market (F) 2.

69 See the argument in *Mosley v Walker* (1827) 7 B & C 40. See also Abb Plac, p 113, where the Bishop of Hereford claimed the right to prevent persons selling marketable goods in their own houses in Hereford during the fair. The townsmen, on the other hand, claimed the right to sell in their own shops, but admitted the right of the bishop to toll.

70 *Mosley v Walker* (1827) 7 B & C 40 (where Bayley J justifies the right in a somewhat different manner); *Macclesfield Corpn v Chapman* (1843) 12 M & W 18; *Macclesfield Corpn v Pedley* (1833) 4 B & Ad 397; *Devizes Corpn v Clarke* (1835) 3 Ad & El 506; *Penryn Corpn v Best* (1878) 3 Ex D 292; *Prior of Dunstable's case* YB II Hen VI ff 19, 25.

71 See *Mosley v Walker* (1827) 7 B & C 40, per Holroyd J; *Penryn Corpn v Best* (1878) 3 Ex D 292 at 295.

72 *Great Eastern Rly Co v Goldsmid* (1884) 9 App Cas 927, 947; *McHole v Davies* (1875) 1 QBD 59; *Fearon v Mitchell* (1872) LR 7 QB 690; *Dorchester Corpn v Ensor* (1869) LR 4 Exch 335.

73 *Cork Corpn v Shinkwin* (1825) Sm & Bat 395, 400; *Pope v Whalley* (1865) 34 LJMC 76; *Great Eastern Rly Co v Goldsmid* (1884) 9 App Cas 947. See also the cases next illustrated, *below*, and the cases under the Markets and Fairs Clauses Act 1847, s 13, footnote at pp 182, 183, *below*.

74 (1978) 76 LGR 750.

as sole vendor, in the manner of a department store. Licences previously granted to stall holders were terminated, and under a new agreement individual traders supplied goods to the defendant for sale at the store, the property in such goods passing to the defendant on delivery (as evidenced by invoices). In addition, although traders were to find their own sales staff, these were employed and paid by the defendant, and were required to wear the defendant's uniform. Takings were delivered to the defendant's manager each day and banked in the defendant's bank account. *Held*, refusing interlocutory relief, that there was no real evidence which cast doubt on the genuineness of the defendant's scheme and, since there was no concourse of sellers, there could be no rival market: *Leicester City Council v Oxford and Bristol Stores Ltd*[75].

In the context of the market law provisions of the 1984 Food Act it is suggested that the definition of 'shop' should be construed so as to give 'shop' its ordinary, everyday meaning, and applied by adopting the approach propounded in *Pope v Whalley*[76]. This will mean that a stall, by virtue of its physical attributes and the nature of its tenure, cannot normally be a 'shop' and even if some units in a rival operation might properly be considered to be shops, that may not preclude injunctive relief against an individual as organiser of such operation[77].

In seeking, therefore, to determine whether sales are from stalls rather than shops, and whether there is a concourse of buyers *and* sellers, it is suggested that the following questions be asked[78]:

1 Has the operator, by public advertisement, issued a general invitation to the public to sell on land or in a building owned by him or under his control?
2 Can anyone come and buy?
3 Do the sellers have little or no security of tenure or exclusive right to use occupy their stalls or any others?
4 Is there provision or space for casual traders?
5 Are most stalls owned and erected by individual sellers? If not, are they generally of insubstantial construction and/or do they lack storage space and/or are they insufficiently self-contained and secure for goods to be stored there overnight and at weekends?
6 Are the goods sold of the same type, or substantially of the same type, as in the established market?

If the answer to most of these questions is in the affirmative, then sales will probably be from stalls and not shops, there is likely to be a concourse of buyers and sellers, and

75 (21 December 1978, unreported). This case, and that in footnote 74, *above*, also, of course, have relevance in determining whether there is a concourse of sellers: see pp 78 to 80, *above*.

76 (1865) 34 LJMC 76: see *Manchester City Council v Walsh* (1986) 84 LGR 1 at 15 and *Greenwood v Whelan* [1967] 1 QB 396. See further the cases cited in footnote 3 to s 13 of the Markets and Fairs Clauses Act 1847, at p 181, *below*.

77 The point was raised, but not decided, in *Kingston-upon-Hull City Council v Greenwood* (1984) 82 LGR 586, and in *Manchester City Council v Walsh* (1986) 84 LGR 1 at 15. See also *In Shops Centres plc v Derby City Council* (1996) 95 LGR 161.

78 See *Walsh*, *above*, at p 12 and also the tests in *Windridge Pearce*, footnote 64, *above*. In *Nuneaton and Bedworth Borough Council v Russell* (17 April 1986, unreported), Millet J said in the course of his judgment:

> 'I do not regard the terms "market" on the one hand, and "shopping arcade" or "arcade of shops" on the other, as mutually exclusive terms. Even if the units, or some of them, may properly be described as shops, so that a prosecution would not lie against an individual shopkeeper, it does not, in my judgment, follow that the activities of the defendant . . . which are what are here in question . . . do not constitute the setting up of a rival market.'

the operation, if situated within the common law distance, may constitute a disturbance of the lawful market[79].

G Defences to holding a rival market

(1) Consent of the owner

The consent or licence of the owner of the lawful market or fair to the holding of a rival is a defence to an action by the owner but is not, of course, a bar to proceedings by the Crown if the market is otherwise unlawful[80].

(2) Grant from the Crown

In an action for disturbance by levying a rival market, it is not usually a defence to plead a grant from the Crown, since the Crown cannot derogate from its own earlier grant by making a grant of a new market to the injury of the old[81]. If, however, by the terms of the original grant, the market was to be held in a fixed placed defined by metes and bounds, and those limits are insufficient but the market owner has no power to enlarge them, then it is possible that a grant of a new market will be justified to such an extent as to meet the deficiency, but no more[82]. In answer to one of the further questions proposed to them by the House of Lords when considering the *Islington Market Bill*[83], Littledale J, on behalf of himself and two other judges[84], said:

> '. . . if those limits are not sufficient for the accommodation of buyers and sellers at the market, and the owner of the market has no power to enlarge the limits, that circumstance, coupled with the fact that it would be for the advantage of the public that a new market should be erected, would be sufficient ground for the Crown to take such steps as would according to law have the effect of erecting a new market, to such an extent as would remedy the inconvenience, without affecting the rights of the owners of the market; . . . the new market can only be legally granted to such an extent as to provide for what may be called the surplus accommodation of the public beyond what the old market can afford, and that the old market is not to be affected by the new market. For instance, if the public require twenty acres of accommodation, and the old market could only furnish ten, the new market could not be granted

---

79 A 'car-boot' sale is a rival market, if within the common-law distance, since there is normally an open invitation to both buyers and sellers: *Newcastle-upon-Tyne City Council v Noble* (1991) 89 LGR 618. On the other hand, a jumble sale might not fall within this description if stalls are manned by representatives of the organiser; but cf the situation in *Great Eastern Rly Co v Goldsmid, above*, where goods belonging to others were sold through the instrumentality of the stall holders. Compare, also, 'bring and buy' sales. In practice, since the proceeds of jumble and bring and buy sales are often applied for charitable purposes, the consent of the market owner (*below*), if required, is likely to be forthcoming; or, if, as no doubt is normally the case, prior consent has not been sought, the market owner is likely to turn a blind eye. See *below*, p 133.

80 Bracton, bk iv, c 46, f 235b; *Tamworth Borough Council v Fazeley Town Council* (1978) 77 LGR 238 at 266. For the nature of an action for disturbance, see *below*, p 89. As to the effect of acquiescence in barring an action by the owner, see *below*, pp 89, 90. As to proceedings by the Crown, see *below* pp 99, 100.

81 2 Inst 406; *Re Islington Market Bill* (1835), 3 Cl & Fin 513, 519, 520 *Tamworth Borough Council v Fazeley Town Council* (1978) 77 LGR 238. See also *above*, pp 15, 16. The new grant will be void, and the Crown may repeal it by *scire facias*, and recover damages for disturbance: *Weston's Case*, YB 11 Hen IV, ff 5, 6.

82 *Re Islington Market Bill* (1835) 3 Cl & Fin 513.

83 *Ibid.*

84 Parke B and Bosanquet LC.

for the whole twenty acres, but only for the additional ten acres, so as, upon the whole, the twenty should be capable of being used by the public; . . . For if a new market were granted for twenty acres, that would be to the damage of the old market, and might have the effect of totally ruining it, when there was no default in the owners of that market, but the necessity for a new market arose from the increase in population'[85].

The judges further suggested that the same principle would apply to the case of a market which, although not defined by metes and bounds, was held in a district so narrow and otherwise so occupied, that further space could not be acquired by the market owner to meet the increased needs of the public.

These opinions were, however, delivered with some diffidence, since the three judges had not had an opportunity of hearing argument on the matter, nor of conferring with the remaining six judges to whom the original questions were put[86].

(3) Statute

It is a good defence to an action for disturbance that the new market was established by an Act of Parliament[87]; but such statutes normally make provision for compensation[88] or require the consent of the owners of the markets affected[89].

(4) Lack of accommodation

A claim of insufficient accommodation for the public in the plaintiff's market is not a good defence to an action for disturbance[90], although it may provide a plea in mitigation of the damage claimed[91]. Lack of room in a market may justify an individual in selling his goods outside it[92], but cannot excuse the levying of a market without lawful authority[92]. If the defendant's acts amount to the setting up of a rival market, the question as to whether or not he intended to do so is immaterial[93].

(5) Irregularities or abuse of franchise by market owner

If the market or fair is lawfully established, it is no answer to a charge of unlawfully levying a rival market to say that the market owner has been guilty of irregularities by

---

85 Pages 520–521.

86 Pages 521–522; *Hammersmith and City Rly Co v Brand* (1869) LR 4 HL 171.

87 *Great Eastern Rly Co v Goldsmid* (1884) 9 App Cas 927 at 961–962; *Re Islington Market Bill* (1835) 3 Cl & Fin 513; *Tamworth Borough Council v Fazeley Town Council* (1979) 77 LGR 238 at 266. A grant of planning permission for a market will not, of itself, amount to the establishment of a market within the meaning of s 50 of the Food Act 1984 so enabling the owner of the land in question to claim protection under s 50(2) of the 1984 Act against an owner of a later established statutory market: *Delyn Borough Council v Solitaire (Liverpool) Ltd* (1995) 93 LGR 614 (and see *below*, p 129).

88 ie by a clause in the special Act.

89 See the Food Act 1984, s 50(3), but cf the Local Government (Miscellaneous Provisions) Act 1982, s 3 and Sch 4, *below*, pp 233 *et seq*, which, although requiring a district council to publish notice of its intention to resolve to designate a street for trading purposes, does not require it to do more than consider any representations received before so resolving.

90 *Re Islington Market Bill* (1835) 3 Cl & Fin 513; *Great Eastern Rly Co v Goldsmid* (1884) 9 App Cas 927; *Tamworth Borough Council v Fazeley Town Council* (1979) 77 LGR 238 at 266–267. As to the duty of the owner to supply sufficient accommodation for the public, see *above*, pp 31, 32.

91 *Cork Corpn v Shinkwin* (1825) Sm & Bat 395.

92 *Prince v Lewis* (1826) 5 B & C 363; *Mosley v Walker* (1827) 7 B & C 40; see *below*, p 86.

93 *Wilcox v Steel* [1904] 1 Ch 212.

demanding illegal tolls or unreasonable stallages[94], or by holding his market on days other than those authorised by charter[95]. Nor is an abuse or neglect of franchise, though it may entitle the Crown to take proceedings against the owner, any justification for setting up a rival market[96].

3 DISTURBANCE BY SELLING OUTSIDE THE MARKET

A Sale without payment of toll

If a person seeks to take, and takes, the benefit of a market without payment of toll, that is a fraud upon the market for which an action for disturbance will lie. An actionable wrong is committed against the market owner if a person takes advantage of a concourse of persons assembled in the market but sells outside it in order to evade toll[97].

ILLUSTRATION

By a private Act of Parliament, the market owner and his lessees were entitled to take tolls from any persons bringing goods or articles into the market. The defendant, a cattle dealer, brought sheep to a public house situated about 40 yards from the market limits, left them there, and went into the market to look for customers which he brought back to the public house and there sold them the sheep. He refused to pay toll to the plaintiff, as lessee of the market owner. *Held* that the defendant's actions constituted a fraud upon the market for which an action lay: *Bridgland v Shapter*[98].

B Intention to evade toll essential

Such acts, in order to be actionable, must be done designedly, and with an intention to obtain the benefit of the market without payment of toll. There is no disturbance if a person, in the ordinary course of his business, happens to sell goods on market day outside the market without any such design or intention[99].

ILLUSTRATION

The plaintiff Corporation was the owner of a statutory market. The defendant's son went, on market day, to a shop situated within the borough but outside the limits of the market, and there, on behalf of his father, sold some corn by sample to the shop owner which was delivered on the following market day. *Held* that, in the absence of any evidence that the defendant had intended to take the benefit of the market, or had deprived the market owner

---

94 *Cork Corpn v Shinkwin* (1825) Sm & Bat 395; *Lord Middleton v Power* (1886) 19 LR Ir 1; *Kingston-upon-Hull City Council v Greenwood* (1984) 82 LGR 586.

95 *Cork Corpn v Shinkwin* (1825) Sm & Bat 395.

96 *Middleton (Lord) v Power* (1886) 19 LR Ir 1.

97 *Bridgland v Shapter* (1839) 5 M & W 375; cf *Blakey v Dinsdale* (1777) 2 Cowp 661; *Great Eastern Rly Co v Goldsmid* (1884) 9 App Cas 927 at 960, per Lord Blackburn; *Horner v Freeman* [1884] WN 223; *Scottish Co-operative Wholesale Society Ltd v Ulster Farmers' Mart Co Ltd* [1960] AC 63, per Viscount Simmonds.

98 (1839) 5 M & W 375. Note that the seller and not the buyer was here liable to pay toll: see pp 55, 56, *above*.

99 *Brecon Corpn v Edwards* (1862) 1 H & C 51; *Tewkesbury Corpn v Diston* (1805) 6 East 438; *Blakey v Dinsdale* (1777) 2 Cowp 661; *Sprosley v Evans* 1 Roll Abr 103; *Scottish Co-operative Wholesale Society Ltd v Ulster Farmers' Mart Co Ltd* [1960] AC 63; and see footnote 108, *below*.

of some profit which would otherwise have been obtained, there was no disturbance of the plaintiff's market: *Brecon Corpn v Edwards*[100].

In the *Prior of Dunstable's case*[101], the allegation was that the defendant sold in his shop, adjoining the market, secretly (*occulte*); and this raised the question of fraud, upon which issue alone the case was tried. The mere selling in a shop, unless done secretly to evade toll, would not have been actionable.

C Defences to selling outside the market

In addition to the defence of no intention to evade toll (*above*), it is a good defence to show that, at the time of the sale outside the market, there was insufficient room to sell within it[102]; or that the market is normally overcrowded and the market owner did not, on that particular occasion, give notice to the defendant that there was room[103].

ILLUSTRATION

The plaintiffs were the lessees of a charter market (Covent Garden) granted to be held within certain specified limits for the sale of vegetables, fruit and flowers. The grantee of the market had, for his own profit, permitted part of the market place to be used for purposes other than those specified in the grant with the result that the remainder of the market place was ordinarily fully occupied. The defendant sold vegetables from a wagon stationed in a street immediately adjoining but outside the market place, and refused to pay toll. The plaintiffs claimed that, on the day in question, there was sufficient space for the defendant to place his wagon within the market. *Held* that as the market was ordinarily fully occupied, and the plaintiffs did not inform the defendant that, at the time of the sale, there was room within the market, an action against the defendant for selling outside could not be maintained: *Prince v Lewis*[104].

The defendant is not bound to attend the market day by day for the purpose of seeing whether or not there is room[105].

This defence may be raised when the market owner fails to provide sufficient accommodation[106] whether or not the market is limited by metes and bounds[107]; and it appears that it can also be raised when the lack of room occurs without any default on the part of the owner, provided the defendant has done nothing which amounts to the unlawful levying of a rival market[108].

---

100 (1862) 1 H & C 51.

101 YB 11 Hen VI, f 19b; 11 Hen VI, f 25. See *above*, pp 80, 81 as to sales in shops.

102 *Prince v Lewis* (1826) 5 B & C 363; *Re Islington Market Bill* (1835) 3 Cl & Fin 513; *Great Eastern Rly Co v Goldsmid* (1884) 9 App Cas 927 at 960, per Lord Blackburn; 25 Ch D 542, per Cotton LJ; and see footnote 108, *below*.

103 *Prince v Lewis* (1826) 5 B & C 363, per Bayley and Littledale JJ. See per Cotton LJ in *Great Eastern Rly Co v Goldsmid, loc cit, above*.

104 (1826) 5 B & C 363.

105 *Ibid* at 372, per Bayley J and 375, per Littledale J.

106 See *above*, p 31.

107 *Prince v Lewis* (1826) 5 B & C 363; *Re Islington Market Bill* (1835) 3 Cl & Fin 513.

108 *London Corpn v Lyons Son & Co (Fruit Brokers) Ltd* [1936] Ch 78, see p 77 *above*. The defendant's willingness to pay tolls and the refusal of the market owner to allow him to sell in the market in the manner in which he desires to sell, are matters to be taken into consideration: *ibid* at 132, 145.

4 DISTURBANCE BY SELLING BY SAMPLE IN THE MARKET

Toll is payable, as a general rule, by the buyer and not the seller[109]. In markets where the *seller* is responsible (eg by custom or prescription) for toll, it is an actionable disturbance to sell by sample in the market goods which are deliberately kept out of the market in order to evade toll[110].

ILLUSTRATION

The plaintiff Corporation was the owner of a charter market. Up until about 30 or 40 years previously, all corn and grain were sold in the market in bulk, but since that time the practice had grown up of selling in the market by sample but nevertheless with the plaintiff taking the customary toll on delivery of the bulk. The defendant sold beans by sample in the market, the bulk later being delivered in Tewkesbury, but refused to pay the toll. The plaintiff alleged that the defendant had wilfully and fraudulently not brought the beans to market so as to deprive the plaintiff of the toll to which it was entitled. *Held* that as a seller by sample in the market derives benefit from the market, an action would lie against the defendant for refusing to pay toll on the bulk to the injury of the market: *Bailiffs of Tewkesbury v Bricknell*[111].

Selling by sample in or near a market is not in itself a disturbance[112], but it will be if there is evidence that the seller intended to take the benefit of the market without payment of toll[113]. In a market in which the buyer customarily pays toll, a seller may nevertheless be liable in an action for disturbance if there is evidence that he intended to defraud the market owner. But equally, a buyer who buys by sample may be liable if, for example, he conspires with the seller to evade toll by some trick or fraud[114].

To buy by sample in a market is not, however, in itself actionable; and a distinction should, in this context, be drawn between buyers and sellers.

The seller has a choice as to whether to sell by sample or bring the bulk into the market; the buyer usually has no such choice. Moreover, the buyer does not get the benefit of the market unless the bulk is in the market: he is unable to view the bulk, nor does he have the advantage of a reduction in price which often results from the seller's reluctance to carry back his commodity in bulk unsold. All these circumstances will make it more difficult to establish a case of designedly buying by sample in order to evade toll; they rather support the view that the buyer has bought by sample because he had no opportunity to buy in bulk[115].

ILLUSTRATION

The plaintiff Corporation alleged that the defendant fraudulently bought corn by sample in its market with the intention of depriving the plaintiff of the toll to which it was entitled by

---

109 See p 56, *above*.

110 *Tewkesbury (Bailiffs etc) v Bricknell* (1809) 2 Taunt 120. See also *Brecon Corpn v Edwards* (1862) 1 H & C 51; *Moseley v Pierson* (1790) 4 Term Rep 104.

111 (1809) 2 Taunt 120.

112 *Brecon Corpn v Edwards* (1862) 1 H & C 51.

113 See footnote 110, *above*.

114 See *Tewkesbury Corpn v Diston* (1805) 6 East 438; and see also *Loughrey v Doherty* [1928] IR 103 at 117, per Kennedy CJ.

115 *Tewkesbury Corpn v Diston* (*below*), per Lord Ellenborough at 461. See also the remarks of Fitzgibbon J (dissenting judgment) in *Loughrey v Doherty* [1928] IR 103 at 120–121.

prescription. It was proved that the defendant bought by sample in the market, knowing of the claim to toll, and refused to pay toll on the subsequent delivery of corn outside the market. *Held* that no cause of action was disclosed since it did not appear that the defendant induced the seller to keep the corn out of the market if the defendant had not bought by sample: *Tewkesbury Corpn v Diston*[116].

5 DISTURBANCE BY OBSTRUCTING OR HINDERING THE MARKET

An action for disturbance will lie for hindering or stopping tollable goods from coming to the market[117], or for threatening or assaulting persons on their way to the market so that the owner loses his toll[118]; or for wrongfully collecting toll due to the owner[119], or for obstructing the owner's toll collector[120]. It will also be a disturbance to obstruct physically any part of the market place (for example, by erecting a building) so as to exclude the public from it[121]; or to obstruct the approaches to the market place[122]. It may also be an actionable disturbance to buy goods on the way to the market, although no toll is payable on such goods in the market[123].

ILLUSTRATION

The plaintiff's predecessor in title was granted a Royal patent to hold weekly markets. He built a market house in which markets were held pursuant to the patent. No tolls were leviable under the patent, and tolls were not levied; but a considerable income was derived from charges made for weighing and storing commodities brought into the market. About 15 to 25 years prior to the action, the practice had grown up amongst certain buyers, including the defendants, of intercepting farmers on their way to the market and of buying their produce before it reached the market. The produce so purchased was usually sent to the railway station or to the defendant's premises for weighing with the result that the plaintiff's market was seriously affected. *Held* (by CA) that this constituted an actionable disturbance of the plaintiff's market entitling her to an injunction, since even if market tolls

---

116 (1805) 6 East 438.

117 *Turner v Sterling* (1672) 2 Vent 25 at 26, per Wylde B citing YB 41 Ed III, f 24, pl 17, an observation of Belknap, counsel, in argument (cf 2 Ventr 28, per Vaughan J); *Ashby v White* (1703) 6 Mod Rep 45 at 49, per Powell J.

118 *Denesham's (Abbot) Case* (1355) YB 29 Edw III, f 18; *Gloucester Grammar School Case* (1410) YB 11, Hen IV f 47b, where Skrene, counsel, states in argument that such is the law; *Ashby v White* (1703) 6 Mod Rep 45 at 49, approved in *Tewkesbury Corpn v Diston* (1805) 6 East 438.

119 *Dent v Oliver* (1607) Cro Jac 122; *Barton's Case* YB 9 Hen IV, f 45; Viner, 'Toll', 1, 4, and 'Actions [Case]', (NC)4; FNB 91 GH; *Ramsey's (Abbot) Case*, Abb Plac, p 151b; *de Kenedon's Case*, *ibid*, p 233. In the Rot Parl (Temp Ed 1), the Prior of St Freswide in Oxford complains that the Chancellor and Scholars of Oxford made an affray and riot in his fair 'to the perpetual and final destruction of it': Rot Parl Vol iii, p 176b.

120 *de Chaunce v de Twenge and de Ros* (1337) YB 11 Edw III, p 38; *Dent v Oliver* (1607) Cro Jac 122.

121 *Thompson v Gibson* (1841) 7 M & W 456.

122 *Horner v Whitechapel District Board of Works* (1885) 53 LT 842.

123 *Loughrey v Doherty* [1928] IR 103, notwithstanding apparently the repeal, by 12 Geo 3, c 71 and 7 & 8 Vict, c 24, of the criminal offences of forestalling, regrating and ingrossing. See also another Irish case: *Wynne v Martin*, Batty's Reports 110.

are not chargeable by the market owner, buyers can disturb (in an actionable sense) the market by buying outside the limits: *Loughrey v Doherty*[124].

6 NATURE OF ACTION FOR DISTURBANCE

A Possessory action

The action for disturbance is a possessory action[125] and the owner is entitled to damages and an injunction[126]. The plaintiff must prove the existence of the franchise[127] and that, at the time of the disturbance, he was in possession of it; but he need not regularly deduce his title because, as against a stranger and wrongdoer, possession is sufficient[128].

The owner of a fair who has been compelled to discontinue it, owing to the absence of buyers and sellers, may nevertheless be in possession of the franchise for the purpose of an action for disturbance[129]. But if the owner of several markets has voluntarily discontinued to hold some of them, he will be unable to recover in an action for disturbance except in respect of the markets he continues to hold; and this will be so even although he may be entitled to revive the discontinued markets[130].

B Limitation of actions

It has been suggested that the undisturbed possession of a rival market for twenty years is a bar to an action for disturbance[131]. But the better opinion is that the uninterrupted user of a rival market for 20 years is merely evidence from which the court may infer that the rival market has had a lawful origin in a grant from the Crown[132], supported by a consent by the owner of the older market, without which a grant from the Crown would be invalid[133]. The Prescription Act 1832 has no application to market rights[134].

---

124 [1928] IR 103.

125 *Yard v Ford* (1670) 2 Saund 172(1); *Fitzgerald v Connors* (1871) 5 IR 5 CL 191.

126 See, for example, *Dorchester Corpn v Ensor* (1869) LR 4 Exch 335; *Elwes v Payne* (1879) 12 Ch D 468; *Great Eastern Rly Co v Goldsmid* (1884) 9 App Cas 927; *Wilcox v Steel* [1904] 1 Ch 212; *Morpeth Corpn v Northumberland Farmers' Auction Mart Co Ltd* [1921] 2 Ch 154; *Birmingham Corpn v Perry Barr Stadium Ltd* [1972] 1 All ER 725. As to the necessity for proof of damage, see pp 73 to 75 *above*.

127 As to evidence of the existence of a franchise, see 'Evidence of Market Rights' in Ch 11, *below*; and see *Wyld v Silver* [1963] Ch 243; *Birmingham Corpn v Perry Barr Stadium Ltd* [1972] 1 All ER 725; *Leicester Corpn v Maby* (1971) 70 LGR 209; *Kingston-upon-Thames Royal Borough Council v Sherman and Waterman Associates Ltd* (6 July 1976, unreported).

128 *Dent v Oliver* (1607) Cro Jac 122; *De Rutzen v Lloyd* (1836) 5 Ad & El 456.

129 *Marquis of Downshire v O'Brien* (1887) 19 LR Ir 380, 389, where the fair had been discontinued because of the defendant's activities.

130 See *Mayor of Dorchester v Ensor* (1869) LR 4 Exch 335 at 339, per Channell B. See also footnote 24, p 72 *above* and cases cited in relation to whether or not a market owner is entitled to protect his property rights when his own market is not in fact established.

131 *Holcroft v Heel* (1799) 1 Bos & P 400, as explained in the notes to *Yard v Ford* (1670) 2 Saund 172.

132 *Holcroft v Heel*, *above*, as explained by le Blanc J in *Campbell v Wilson* (1803) 3 East 294, 298.

133 See pp 15, 16, *above*.

134 See pp 17, 18, *above*.

In an action for disturbance, the period of limitation for recovery of damages is six years[135]; but it seems that no length of adverse user creates a positive bar to the action[136].

7 REMEDIES FOR DISTURBANCE OF STATUTORY MARKETS AND FAIRS

A market established under a local or public Act enjoys all the incidents and privileges of a market created by charter, unless the statute otherwise provides[137]. A monopoly created by statute differs only in name from a monopoly of the same kind created by charter, the latter being known as a franchise[138]. Thus, a statutory market will normally have the same degree of protection as a franchise market against, for example, disturbance by setting up a rival market within the common law distance; and the market owner will be entitled to the same remedies.

Protection expressly given by statute is not in substitution for, but in addition to, the common law rights[139]. It would be odd if statutory provisions designed to increase the franchise in strength or character had the effect of diminishing the protection against disturbance already afforded at common law[140]. But, nevertheless, those common law rights may be modified or excluded by the express terms of the statute, or by implication.

The statute may amount to a confirmation or re-enactment of the franchise market rights, with modifications and additions[141], or be in such terms as to extinguish the

---

135 Limitation Act 1980, s 2. The provisions of the Act relating to recovery of land have no application to franchises: see *ibid*, ss 15, 38(1). See also Ch 2, p 25 footnote 120.

136 See *Morpeth Corpn v Northumberland Farmers' Auction Mart Co* [1921] 2 Ch 154 at 163; *Loughrey v Doherty* [1928] IR 103 at 113, per Johnston J at first instance. In *Warwick Corpn v Maby (No 2)* (1971) 116 Sol Jo 137, delay in seeking relief in respect of a different day rival market, which had been held for eight months without effective protest, was held to be a bar to the grant of an *interlocutory* injunction.

137 *Birmingham Corpn v Foster* (1894) 70 LT 371; *Hailsham Cattle Market Co v Tolman* [1915] 1 Ch 360; *Birmingham Corpn v Perry Barr Stadium Ltd* [1972] 1 All ER 725; *Leicester City Council v Oxford and Bristol Stores Ltd* (21 December 1978, unreported;) *Halton Borough Council v Cawley* [1985] 1 WLR 15; *East Lindsey District Council v Hamilton*, Times, 2 April; *Manchester City Council v Walsh* (1985) 84 LGR 1; *Newcastle-upon-Tyne City Council v Noble* (1990) 89 LGR 618.

138 *Birmingham Corpn v Perry Barr Stadium Ltd* [1972] 1 All ER 725 at 728.

139 *Wakefield City Council v Box* [1982] 3 All ER 506; *Manchester City Council v Walsh* (1985) 84 LGR 1.

140 *Leicester Corpn v Maby* (1971) 70 LGR 209 at 213–214; and see also *Northampton Borough Council v Midland Development Group of Companies Ltd* (1978) 76 LGR 750 at 751; *Leicester City Council v Oxford and Bristol Stores Ltd*, (21 December 1978, unreported).

141 See the first class of cases stated by Willes J in *Wolverhampton New Waterworks Co v Hawkesford* (1859) 28 LJCP 242, 246; see also *Stevens v Chown, Stevens v Clark* [1901] 1 Ch 894; *Birmingham Corpn v Perry Barr Stadium Ltd* [1972] 1 All ER 725. The three classes of cases referred to by Willes J in the *Wolverhampton* case, *above*, are: '[first] that class where there is a liability existing at common law and which is only re-enacted by the statute with a special form of remedy; there unless the statute contains words necessarily excluding the common-law remedy, the plaintiff has his election of proceeding either under the statute or at common law. Then there is a second class, which consists of those cases in which a statute has created a liability but has given no special remedy for it; there the party may adopt an action of debt or other remedy at common law to enforce it. The third class is where the statute creates a liability not existing at common law, and gives also a particular remedy for enforcing it.'

franchise market and substitute a statutory one[142].

Local Acts regulating statutory markets often incorporate s 13 of the Markets and Fairs Clauses Act 1847, or apply s 56 of the Food Act 1984[143], or contain sections to like effect.

Section 13 of the 1847 Act and s 56 of the Food Act 1984 make it an offence punishable by fine on summary conviction for any person other than a certificated pedlar to sell or expose for sale in any place within certain limits, except in his own dwelling place or shop, articles normally sold in the market. It should, however, be noted that s 56 of the 1984 Act defines the limits within which sales are prohibited by reference to the area of the market authority (in s 13, the 'prescribed limits'[144]) *and* 'such distance from the market as the authority may by byelaw declare'[145]. The position of the owner of a statutory market in relation to actions for disturbance appears to be as follows[146]:

A There is no disturbance if a person merely sells tollable articles in his own dwelling place or shop although situated within the limits prescribed by the statute[147]. It will not, therefore, be a ground of complaint if a person sells such articles in his dwelling place or shop outside the limits so prescribed.

B If an offence is committed against the relevant section, the penalty imposed may be recovered in a court of summary jurisdiction. If the offence amounts also to an injury to a right of property, the power of a court of competent jurisdiction to protect that right by injunction is not excluded unless the statute so provides[148]. But for a mere offence against the section, it is probable that no action for damages lies[149].

Both sections appear to create a liability not existing at common law[150] and, as each prescribes the particular remedy for enforcing it, that remedy must be adopted[151].

---

142 *Manchester Corpn v Lyons* (1882) 22 Ch D 287; *Abergavenny Improvement Comrs v Straker* (1889) 42 Ch D 83 and cf *New Windsor Corpn v Taylor* [1899] AC 41.

143 As amended by the Food Safety Act 1990, Sch 2, paras 2–11.

144 ie 'prescribed for that purpose in the special Act': see s 2, p 180, *below*.

145 In addition, under s 56 of the 1984 Act, the articles must be specified in the byelaw. There is no such requirement in s 13 of the 1847 Act.

146 See *Wakefield City Council v Box* [1982] 3 All ER 506.

147 See per Romer J, *Birmingham Corpn v Foster* (1894) 70 LT 371, 372. The common law does not prohibit such sales unless by custom and no such prohibition would be included in a modern grant or statute; see pp 80, 81 *above*.

148 See *Cooper v Whittingham* (1880) 15 Ch D 501, 506; *Stevens v Chown, Stevens v Clark* [1901] 1 Ch 894 (in which ancient rights were preserved by a statute which gave an additional remedy for sale in avoidance of tolls outside the market but within the prescribed limits). In the absence of any statutory limitation of the common law rights, a local authority market owner is entitled to an injunction restraining a rival market operator notwithstanding that the rival market is outside the district of the local authority: *Halton Borough Council v Cawley* [1985] 1 WLR 15.

149 See, for example, *Halton Borough Council v Cawley* [1985] 1 WLR 15.

150 The offence created by the sections appears to differ in several respects from the common law wrong of intentionally taking the benefit of the market with intent to avoid payment of toll (see pp 85, 86, *above*).

151 See the third class of cases stated by Willes J in *Wolverhampton New Waterworks Co v Hawkesford* (1859) 28 LJCP 242, 246, footnote 141 *above*; see also *Stevens v Chown, Stevens v Clark* [1901] 1 Ch 894; *Hailsham Cattle Market Co v Tolman* [1915] 1 Ch 360, CA; *Birmingham Corpn v Perry Barr Stadium Ltd* [1972] 1 All ER 725.

C If, on the other hand, the market is disturbed by the unlawful levying of a rival market in a manner which does not constitute any offence against the relevant section, an action lies for damages, as well as for an injunction[152]. It should be noted that a person may set up a rival market without committing an offence under the sections, for the sections only prohibit selling and exposing for sale, acts which someone setting up a rival market does not necessarily commit[153]. Consequently, if the remedy by action did not exist, the market owner might be without remedy against very serious infringements of his rights.

D It is probable that, on similar grounds, an action is maintainable against persons who disturb the market by wrongful acts other than that of setting up a rival market, provided that the wrongful acts complained of amount to more than the commission of an offence under the sections. But there seems to be no authority directly on this point[154].

E The effect of, in particular, s 13 of the 1847 Act on the market owner's rights of action may be complicated by the fact that the section sometimes has to be read in conjunction with other sections of the special Act which incorporates it. This may considerably alter its effect, and acts outside the exception in s 13 in respect of sales in a dwelling place or shop (and which would therefore constitute a disturbance) may nevertheless escape prohibition because the scope of the exception has been widened by another section[155].

F If no byelaws have been made under s 56 of the 1984 Act, or its predecessor, specifying the proscribed articles or defining the distance from the market within which sales are prohibited, a local authority cannot, it seems, prosecute under this section[156]. Also, even in the case of a market *established* under a private or public Act, the common law right to protection for disturbance will be available unless the wording of the relevant statute modifies that right[157].

8 DISTURBANCE OF MARKET RIGHTS VESTED IN A PERSON OTHER THAN THE OWNER

On the basis that 'prescription and antiquity of time fortifies all titles, and supposeth the best beginning the law can give them'[158], it appears that actions for disturbance may be brought, not only by the market owner, but also by any person who has a prescriptive or

---

152 *Birmingham Corpn v Foster* (1894) 70 LT 371; and see cases cited in footnotes 138, 139 and 140 *above*.

153 See pp 77 to 80, *above*, and *Halton Borough Council v Cawley* [1985] 1 WLR 15.

154 See, however, the dictum of Morris CJ in *Newtownards Town Comrs v Wood* (1877) IR 11 CL 506 at 509.

155 See *Abergavenny Improvement Comrs v Straker* (1889) 42 Ch D 83; *Birmingham Corpn v Foster* (1894) 70 LT 371; *Hailsham Cattle Market Co v Tolman* [1915] 2 Ch 1.

156 *Halton Borough Council v Cawley* [1985] 1 WLR 15; *Manchester City Council v Walsh* (1985) 84 LGR 1 at 7.

157 *Ibid.* The court in *Walsh* declined to follow, as being against the weight of authority (see cases cited in footnotes 137–140, *above*) the reasoning of the CA, and in particular, Pickford LJ, in *Hailsham Cattle Market Co v Tolman* [1915] 1 Ch 1, that a provision in a local Act similar to s 13 of the 1847 Act and s 56 of the 1984 Act in effect constituted the only remedy available to the owner of a statutory market in the event of a disturbance of his rights.

158 Per Lord Hobart in *Slade v Drake* (1618) Hob 295.

other well established right to place a stall in the market in front of his shop, such right being appurtenant to the premises.

ILLUSTRATION

The defendant Corporation was owner of a prescriptive market held in the High Street and the plaintiff was the owner of a house in the same street. The plaintiff and previous owners and occupiers of his house, and of other neighbouring houses, had from time immemorial erected stalls on market days opposite their houses and exposed goods for sale on them, but had never paid toll to the Corporation for that privilege. The Corporation removed its market to another part of the borough to the injury of the plaintiff. *Held* that as the holding of the market in High Street would have necessarily diminished the trade on market days of the shops kept in the plaintiff's and neighbouring houses, the shopkeepers were probably originally granted in return the right and privilege of advancing their shops into the market itself by having stalls in the street commensurate with the fronts of their houses; and such right was sufficiently connected with the enjoyment of those houses to entitle the plaintiff to maintain an action for unlawful disturbance of his enjoyment of the right: *Ellis v Bridgnorth Corpn*[159].

---

159 (1863) 15 CBNS 52.

CHAPTER 7

Sales in Markets and Fairs

1 THE LAW AS TO SALE OF GOODS IN MARKET OVERT

A The rule for protection of buyers

As a general rule, where goods[1] are sold by a person who is not the owner, and who does not sell them under the authority or with the consent of the owner, the buyer acquires no better title than the seller had, unless the owner of the goods is by his conduct precluded from denying the seller's authority to sell[2]. By s 22(1) of the Sale of Goods Act 1979[3], however (substantially repeating a similar provision of the Sale of Goods Act 1893[4] which itself re-enacted the common law[5]), where goods were sold in market overt according to the usage of the market, the buyer acquired a good title to the goods provided he bought them in good faith[6] and without notice of any defect or want of title on the part of the seller.

The general rule has now been restored in that the law relating to goods sold in market overt is repealed in relation to contracts for the sale of goods made after 3 January 1995 by the provisions of the Sale of Goods (Amendment) Act 1994, s 1. There is therefore no need to refer to the earlier law.

2 STOLEN GOODS

It was formerly the law that where goods had been stolen and the offender was prosecuted to conviction, the property in the goods so stolen revested in the person who was the owner of them, notwithstanding any intermediate dealing with them, whether by sale in market overt or otherwise. In short, the title acquired by a buyer in market overt was liable to be defeated[7]. That provision however, was repealed by the Theft Act 1968[8] and it is now provided by s 31(2) of that Act that notwithstanding any enactment to the contrary, where

1 'Goods' includes all personal chattels other than things in action and money: see the Sale of Goods Act 1979, s 61(1).
2 *Ibid*, s 21(1).
3 By s 22(2) the section does not apply to Scotland. Further, the rules of market overt do not apply in Wales, see s 47, Laws in Wales Act 1542 (as amended by the Theft Act 1968, ss 33(3), 35(1), and Sch 3, Pt II) which provides that the sale of stolen goods in a market or fair conveys no title. But it would appear that a title acquired in Ireland will be recognised in Scotland, see *Todd v Armour* (1882) 9 R 901; (*quaere* the position if the title has been acquired in England, see *Winkworth v Christie, Manson and Woods Ltd* [1980] Ch 496).
4 Sale of Goods Act 1893, s 21.
5 For a clear statement of the common law, see Lord Cairns in *Cundy v Lindsay* (1878) 3 App Cas 459 at 463; see 2 Co Inst 713, and the 12 exceptions thereto, and 2 Bl Com 449–50. Lord Coke's 12 exceptions apply to *all* sales in market overt including shops in the City of London (*below*).
6 'A thing is deemed to be done in good faith within the meaning of this Act when it is done honestly, whether it is done negligently or not'; Sale of Goods Act 1979, s 61(3): see also 2 Co Inst 713 (5th, 6th and 7th exceptions); 2 Bl Com 449–450.
7 See Sale of Goods Act 1893, s 24.
8 Section 33(3), Sch 3, Pt III. But see s 63(3) and Sch 4, para 3, to the Sale of Goods Act 1979.

property has been stolen or obtained by fraud or other wrongful means, the title to that or any other property shall not be affected by reason only of the conviction of the offender. The effect of this provision is to leave consideration of the question of title and wrongful interference with goods to the civil courts. The only remaining function which a criminal court can perform is under s 28 of the Theft Act 1968[9] which empowers a court where goods have been stolen to make a restitution order in the case of a defendant convicted of an offence with reference to the theft whereby the goods may be restored to the person entitled to recover them. But where it appears to the court that the person convicted has sold the goods to a person acting in good faith the court may order that a sum not exceeding the value of the goods be paid to the purchaser out of any money of the person convicted which was taken out of his possession on apprehension. This provision is clearly designed to avoid any hardship to the *bona fide* purchaser.

Further, the buyer can acquire a good title in law if he can avail himself of the provisions of the Factors Acts[10] or any enactment enabling the apparent owner of goods to dispose of them as if he were the true owner[11] or has purchased the goods under any contract of sale pursuant to any special common law or statutory power of sale[12].

Formerly, a seller of goods in market overt who after an agreement for sale discovered that the goods were stolen but still handed them over to the buyer representing that he had good title was not guilty of obtaining the purchase price by deception, for property and title in the goods would have passed to the buyer on the agreement to sell at which point there was no dishonesty[13].

3 SALE OF HORSES IN MARKETS AND FAIRS

The former elaborate provisions[14] relating to the formalities for the sales of horses, mares, geldings, colts and fillies in markets and fairs were repealed by the Criminal Law Act 1967[15], and the sale of these animals is now governed by the normal rules.

4 SALE OF HAY AND STRAW IN MARKETS IN AND NEAR THE METROPOLIS

Markets for the sale of hay or straw held in or within 30 miles of the City of London and Westminster were subject to the provisions of the Hay & Straw Acts 1796, 1834 and 1856[16]. These were repealed by the Theft Act 1968[17].

---

9 As amended by the Criminal Law Act 1977, Sch 12.
10 See *Payne v Wilson* [1895] 1 QB 653, 661, [1895] 2 QB 537; *Pearson v Rose and Young Ltd* [1951] 1 KB 275; *Du Jardin v Beadman Bros Ltd* [1952] 2 QB 712.
11 Sale of Goods Act 1979, s 21.
12 *Ibid.*
13 *R v Wheeler* (1990) 92 Cr App Rep 279, CA.
14 Sale of Horses Act 1555 (2 & 3 Ph & M, c 71), Sale of Horses Act 1588 (32 Eliz, c 12).
15 Criminal Law Act 1967, s 10(2), Sch 3, Pt 1. This Act also repealed the saving provisions of s 22(2) of the Sale of Goods Act 1893 (see s 10(2), Sch 3, Pt III). But see s 22(3) of and Sch I, para 3 to the Sale of Goods Act 1979.
16 36 Geo III, c 88, s 2; 4 & 5 Will IV, c 21; 18 & 20 Vict, c 114.
17 Theft Act 1968, s 33(3), Sch 3, Pt II.

CHAPTER 8

Forfeiture and Extinction of Markets and Fairs

1 FORFEITURE

A General

The owner of a market or fair is liable to be deprived of his franchise by forfeiture to the Crown if he misuses or abuses it, or if he neglects to use it[1].

A franchise is granted by the Crown on the implied condition that it is duly exercised according to the grant, and if this condition is broken the grant is liable to be repealed[2].

A franchise can also be extinguished by Act of Parliament[3], but it cannot be abandoned[4]. Prescriptive markets are liable to forfeiture for misuse or abuse or neglect, as well as markets created by grant. But the Crown cannot take proceedings to forfeit statutory markets[5]. Neglect or abuse does not justify the setting up of a rival market.

B Non-user of the franchise

The non-user of a franchise which is merely to the profit or pleasure of the owner is no ground for its loss or forfeiture; but a fair or market is held not merely for the profit of the owner but also for the benefit of the public, who suffer a loss if the fair or market is not duly held; accordingly the non-user of a fair or market, or the neglect to hold it, is a good ground for the Crown taking the necessary steps to seize the franchise[6]. Further, if a market owner has not actually established his market although entitled to do so he may well find that a court is unsympathetic to his attempt to suppress a rival market which has either commenced or is about to commence[7].

---

1 'Retinet possessionem per usum . . . donec amiserit per abusem vel non usum', Bracton, lib 2, c 24, fol 56, cited 2 Co Inst 222. See also Cru Dig 4th ed, vol iii, p 268.

2 '. . . a franchise-right to a market or fair with the tolls belonging thereto, imports a holding by the owner of the right under the Crown, either upon foot of an extant charter or by prescription which assumes the former existence of such a charter, and such a right of market is in its very nature an exclusive right, and one which imports not merely a title in the grantee to enjoy the benefits conferred upon him by the grant under which he claims title, but also a correlative obligation to provide proper accommodation for the market, and for its due regulation, and the grant is held by the grantee subject to an implied liability to its being recalled by the Crown, by proceedings by *scire facias*, in the case of his failure properly to discharge its accompanying obligations', per Little V-C, *Manchester Corpn v Peverley* (1876) 22 Ch D 294n; also see per Holt CJ, *City of London v Vanacre* (1700) 12 Mod Rep 270 at 271; YB 20 Edw IV ff 5, 6. As to repeal of a grant by *scire facias* see pp 98, 139, *below*.

3 *Manchester Corpn v Lyons* (1882) 22 Ch D 287; *Manchester Corpn v Peverley* (1876) 22 Ch D 294n; *New Windsor Corpn v Taylor* [1899] AC 41 at 45, 48 and 50; and see *below*, pp 102, 103.

4 Per Lord Denning MR in *Wyld v Silver* [1963] Ch 243 at 245; and see per Chatterton V-C, *Marquis of Downshire v O'Brien* (1887) 19 LR Ir 380 at 389; but see *Gloucestershire County Council v Farrow* [1983] 2 All ER 1031; and see *below*, pp 98, 99.

5 See *New Windsor Corpn v Taylor* [1899] AC 41 at 50; and see *below*, p 104.

6 Per Sir Edward Coke, 4 March 1987, *Leicester Forest Case* (1608) Cro Jac 155.

7 *Stoke on Trent City Council v W & J Wass Ltd* (4 March 1987, unreported at first instance; (1989) 87 LGR 129, CA; *Birmingham City Council v Anvil Fairs* (1989) 87 LGR 394.

The printed volume of the 'Placita Quo Warranto' contains many instances of forfeiture for non-user[8], but the franchise was generally re-granted on payment of a fine. In one case the defendants produced a charter containing a clause that 'although they have not used any liberty, yet they may lawfully use it' and so justified a market which they had been holding, since the date of this charter, by virtue of an earlier market-charter upon which they had not acted until that date[9].

In several cases, however, the defendant pleaded successfully that he had held his fair or market as far as he could if any chose to attend it, but that it often happened that there was no access to buyers and sellers[10].

It seems that a market or fair cannot be forfeited for non-user of a part of the franchise which is not necessary to the due holding of the market or fair. If a market or fair is granted with a right to take toll, the grant of the market or fair cannot be repealed on the ground that no toll is taken[11]. Toll is not an incident of the market or fair[12], and the grant of toll benefits the lord, and not the public. The franchise of market being separate and independent from the franchise of toll, it cannot be forfeited by the failure to take toll. So if the franchise of toll were to be forfeited the market or fair would remain[13].

C Abuse of the franchise

Amongst abuses which entitle the Crown to take proceedings to forfeit the franchise of market or fair may be mentioned that of holding a market or fair outside the lawful area[14], holding a fair on additional days beyond those authorised by the grant[15], or of holding a market on a day other than the authorised day[16]. However, to hold a market on an additional day as well as on the authorised day seems to be treated not as abuse of the franchise granted but as usurpation of another and separate franchise[17].

---

8 For example, Leamington (pp 128, 129); Sandiacre (pp 162, 163); Orlandston (p 329).
9 Melcheburne (pp 6, 7).
10 Placita de Quo Warranto, Wardon (p 64); Ilkeston (p 137); Ashton-in-Weston (pp 143, 144); Hovingham (pp 218, 219); Fiskarton (p 635); Lib Rad'i de Berners (p 742); Lib Prioris de Novo Loco (p 747); Lib Joh'is de Sc'o Joh'e (p 748).
11 *Newcastle (Duke) v Worksop UDC* [1902] 2 Ch 145 at 156, 157.
12 See *above*, p 52.
13 *R v Maidenhead Corpn* (1620) Palm 76 at 78, 82. Formerly pursuant to the Statute of Westminster the First, 1275 (3 Edw I, c 31) it was possible for the franchise of market to be forfeited if outrageous toll were taken. But since the repeal of this Statute by the Theft Act 1968 (s 33(3), Sch 3, Pt I) the power of the Crown to forfeit the franchise of market for taking outrageous toll has been abolished, and the only process of forfeiture is now at common law by *scire facias*; and see pp 98, 139, *below*. But in the case of *Newcastle (Duke) v Worksop UDC* [1902] 2 Ch 145 at 158, Farwell J.considered that it was not easy to see how a subordinate franchise of toll if surrendered or forfeited could vest in the Crown whilst the franchise of fair could remain in the lord. Also see *below*, pp 101, 102, neglect to take toll does not of itself destroy the right to toll.
14 See *above*, p 34.
15 See *above*, pp 45, 46.
16 See *above*, pp 48, 49.
17 See *above*, pp 45, 46.

Abuse may be of a negative character, consisting in the neglect of something which ought of necessity to be done, or non-user of an essential part of the franchise[18].

In the case of a market not confined by metes and bounds, neglect to provide sufficient accommodation for the public may be abuse on account of which the grant may be repealed[19], but neglect to take toll is not a ground of forfeiture of the franchise of market or the franchise of toll[20].

D Effect of non-user and abuse

The non-user or neglect of the franchise, or its abuse, does not of itself destroy the right, but it entitles the Crown to obtain a repeal of the grant by *scire facias*[21]. An abuse of the franchise may entitle the Crown to take proceedings for its forfeiture, but it does not entitle third persons to usurp market or fair rights and thereby disturb the franchise[22]. Notwithstanding that he himself is in default, the owner of the franchise has a remedy against such wrong-doers[23].

If a fair becomes unfrequented and useless, and to that extent discontinued, the franchise right nevertheless remains unimpaired[24], and it cannot be abandoned[25].

But after a period of 20 years' non-user, it seems that a highway can be re-dedicated free from the reservation of market rights pursuant to the presumption of dedication contained in s 31 of the Highways Act 1980 so as to prevent the exercise of the franchise[26]. In such circumstances, any attempt on the part of the owner of the franchise to exercise his rights would amount to an unreasonable obstruction of the highway

---

18 YB 2 Hen VII, Hilary Term, f 10, per Brian CJ, who refers, as an example, to 'an office of clerk of the market'. One of the grounds of forfeiture of frequent occurrence in the printed volume of the 'Placita de Quo Warranto' is the neglect to keep judicial instruments of pillory or tumbrel for the punishment of persons breaking the assize of bread and ale, or the neglect to use those instruments and the substitution of fines in cases where corporal punishment is due, eg Wahull (p 36), Hegham (p 133), Lilleburn (pp 536, 537), see *above*, p 6. The pillory, however, was abolished by statute in 1816; see 56 Geo III, c 138; and in 1844 the statute called 'Judicium Pillorie', or 'Statute of the pillory and tumbrel and of the assize of bread and ale', 51 Hen III, st 6 (Ruff), was entirely repealed by 7 & 8 Vict, c 24, s 2.

19 See *above*, pp 31, 32.

20 See note 13, *above*, p 98 and *below*, pp 101, 102.

21 See per Bayley J, *Peter v Kendal* (1827) 6 B & C 703; *Middleton (Lord) v Power* (1886) 19 LR Ir 1. There was formerly a remedy by information in the nature of *quo warranto*, but *quo warranto* proceedings were abolished by the Administration of Justice (Miscellaneous Provisions) Act 1938, s 9(1), and replaced by statutory provisions, now re-enacted in the Supreme Court Act 1981, s 30.

22 *Middleton (Lord) v Power* (1886) 19 LR Ir 1; *Newcastle (Duke) v Worksop UDC* [1902] 2 Ch 145 at 158; and see *Re Islington Market Bill* (1835) 3 Cl & Fin 513 at 519.

23 *Middleton (Lord) v Power* (1886) 19 LR Ir 1.

24 *Downshire v O'Brien* (1887) 19 LR Ir 380 at 389.

25 '. . . I know of no way in which the inhabitants of a parish can lose a right of this kind once they have acquired it except by Act of Parliament. Mere disuse will not do. I do not see how they can waive it or abandon it. No one or more of the inhabitants can waive or abandon it on behalf of the others. Nor can all the present inhabitants waive or abandon it on behalf of future generations . . .', per Lord Denning MR, *Wyld v Silver* [1963] Ch 243 at 255; and also see per Harman LJ at 263. See also *Hall v Nottingham* (1875) 1 Ex D 1, and *Hammerton v Honey* (1876) 24 WR 603.

26 *Gloucestershire County Council v Farrow* [1985] 1 WLR 741.

contrary to s 137(1) of the Highways Act 1980, there being no lawful authority or excuse, thereby effectively extinguishing the right[27].

ILLUSTRATION

Pursuant to a market franchise granted by Royal Charter to the Abbey of Evesham before the commencement of legal memory and in the reign of King Henry I of England, the lord of the manor of Stow-on-the-Wold by succession had the right to hold a weekly market in the market square of Stow By the late nineteenth century the square in question had been dedicated as a highway in connection with the market and, consequently, a public right of way had been created subject to the market right. Apparently in about 1900 the use of the square for the purposes of market ceased, but in 1979 it was proposed that the market (which had been held on Thursdays) should be revived, and the lord of the manor leased his rights to a company in order to effect this purpose.

However, Gloucestershire County Council in its capacity as highway authority commenced proceedings seeking, *inter alia*, a declaration that as the market square was a highway by virtue of the Highways Act 1980 the company was not entitled to exercise its alleged rights to hold a market in the square, and, further, seeking an order restraining the defendant from so doing.

The highway authority contended that the market place had been continuously used and enjoyed by the public as of right and without interruption as a highway for a full period of over 20 years during which the right to hold a market had not been asserted, and, therefore, by virtue of s 31(1) of the Highways Act 1980 the public had a right of way over the square unqualified by the manorial market right, which was in effect extinguished.

Held: since s 31 of the 1980 Act, and its statutory predecessor, was enacted to avoid the need for lengthy and expensive antiquarian investigation when highway rights were called in question, s 31 was to be given a broad interpretation. Accordingly, despite the fact that the highway was originally dedicated subject to the right to use the land for a periodic market, it could subsequently be rededicated free from that reservation pursuant to the presumption of dedication contained in s 31(1) of the Act, thereby effectively extinguishing the market right: *Gloucestershire County Council v Farrow*[28].

E Waiver of forfeiture

It has been laid down that if a franchise becomes liable to forfeiture, the Crown may waive the forfeiture by any act, such as a receipt of rent, which recognises a continuance of the right to the franchise, and that the Crown cannot take advantage of any forfeiture which has been so waived[29].

ILLUSTRATION

In 1958 the defendant purchased a parcel of land in the parish of Wraysbury and obtained planning permission for the purpose of constructing five bungalows. It transpired that the

---

27 See per Goulding J in *Gloucestershire County Council v Farrow* [1984] 1 WLR 262 at 269. *Quaere* whether the section presumes an unqualified dedication and whether a highway originally dedicated subject to market rights can subsequently be dedicated free from that reservation having regard to *A-G v Horner* (1884) 14 QBD 245, (1885) 11 App Cas 66, and the presumption of long usage, and see *above*, pp 37 to 39. See also *Wyld v Silver* [1963] Ch 243 and p 38, *above*.

28 [1985] 1 WLR 741. This did not, however, prevent the right being exercised elsewhere within the market boundaries: see pp 38, 39 *above*.

29 *Middleton (Lord) v Power* (1886) 19 LR Ir 1. As to waiver of forfeiture, see notes to *Dumpor's case*, 1 Sm LC 10 ed 31.

parcel in question had comprised part of an area of open and common fields, and waste lands, enclosed by a private Act of Parliament in 1799.

The Act recited that the inhabitants of the parish were by ancient usage entitled to hold an annual fair or wake on the Friday in Whitsun week on part of the waste lands, and enacted that the Commissioners appointed to determine Inclosure Awards should appoint a parcel of waste land for the purpose of holding the fair as near as possible to the place where it was most commonly held. The inhabitants of the parish should thereafter have the same right to hold it on the same day on the appointed parcel and enjoy and exercise all the rights and privileges thereof as they had before the Act. The Act further provided that no person was to have any right, *inter alia*, to build on the land in question.

The Award was made and three adjoining parcels allocated for the purpose of holding a fair or wake thereon, and the Award was enrolled in the Court of Common Pleas.

Held: on the defendant's appeal to the Court of Appeal, that the plaintiffs were entitled:

(1) to a declaration that they had a right to hold an annual fair or wake on the land including the defendant's land;

(2) to an injunction restraining the defendant from doing acts which would interfere with the holding of the fair or wake on the ground that, *inter alia*, they were entitled to do so by virtue of a statutory right which could not be waived nor lost by disuse, or by right of franchise which could not be abandoned: *Wyld v Silver*[30].

F Effect of forfeiture

Markets and fairs, when forfeited to the Crown, are not extinguished, but continue *in esse* in the Crown's hands[31], and unless re-granted are placed under the management of the Crown Estate Commissioners[32] who are entitled to collect the tolls and other dues. Formerly the Commissioners had the power at any time, with the consent of the Treasury, to abandon or discontinue, either permanently or for a limited time, the collection of any tolls or profits of any markets or fairs belonging to the Crown which might have been considered inexpedient to collect, and also, with the consent of the Treasury, by deed, absolutely to relinquish any such tolls or profits. But rigorous Treasury control was abolished by the Crown Estate Act 1956 (now repealed by the Crown Estate Act 1961), and the Commissioners are now free to act without approval but subject to directions and an obligation to furnish accounts and estimates[33].

G Neglect to take toll

There remains the question, however, whether the right to toll can be lost by non-user. We have seen that non-user does not of itself appear to destroy the right to toll[34], and cannot create a forfeiture of the market or fair[35]. But it may be that if the public have

30 [1963] Ch 243.

31 2 Co Inst 222. In *Heddy v Wheelhouse* (1597) Cro Eliz 591, it was held by Popham, Gawdy, and Fenner that 'such liberties, which a common person hath by grant, or prescription, which the King (if such prescription had not been) could not have by his prerogative, was warren, park, fayre, market with toll, etc, if these come to the Crown, etc, they remain *in esse*, and are not extinct; for if the King should not have them by this means, they would be lost', and see *Abbot of Strata Mercella* (1591) 9 Co Rep 24a at 25b. *Contra* the position if the rights form part of royal prerogative as 'flowers of the Crown' such as wrecks, treasure trove and royal mines, and see *above*, p 24.

32 Crown Estate Act 1961, s 1. Formerly markets and fairs were placed under the management of the Commissioners of Crown Lands pursuant to the Crown Lands Acts 1829 and 1885, but these Acts were repealed by the Crown Estate Act 1961, Pt II, Sch 3.

33 Formerly the Crown Lands Act 1852, s 6. See now the Crown Estate Act 1961, ss 1, 2.

34 See per Sir Edward Coke, *Leicester Forest Case* (1608) Cro Jac 155; *Newcastle (Duke) v Worksop UDC* [1902] 2 Ch 145 at 156; and see *above*, p 98.

35 See *above*, pp 97, 98.

been using a market or fair for a great number of years without any demand of toll being made, this fact may, in the absence of any other explanation, warrant the inference that the right of toll has been at some time or other surrendered to the Crown[36], or otherwise become extinguished, or, at any rate, that it has become severed from the ownership of the market or fair. Probably a forfeiture would not be presumed if there is no evidence that there was at any time any ground of forfeiture; for a forfeiture implies a wrong done by the owner of the franchise, and, as a general rule, the presumption is against wrong[37]. But this objection does not apply to a presumption of a voluntary surrender.

An abuse of the franchise of toll by taking outrageous toll renders that franchise liable to forfeiture, but does not at common law, it seems, create a forfeiture of the market or fair[38]. Formerly it was possible pursuant to the Statute of Westminster the First, 1275, to forfeit the franchise of market or fair for taking outrageous toll[39].

Thus the effect of the surrender or forfeiture of the right to toll is that the franchise of market or fair will remain in the owner and the subordinate franchise of toll, which exists only as appurtenant to the franchise of market or fair, will be in the Crown[40].

2 SURRENDER

Prescriptive and charter markets and fairs may be lost by their surrender to the Crown[41], but they are not extinguished but continue to exist in the Crown's hands[42].

It has been said that if the owner of prescriptive franchises accepts from the Crown a grant of the same liberties, he cannot afterwards claim them by prescription, but he must rely upon the grant[43].

3 EXTINCTION BY ACT OF PARLIAMENT

A By general or special Act

All franchises are liable to be extinguished by Act of Parliament, and a market or fair created by statute can only be extinguished by statute[44]. A statute of 25 Henry VI expressly annulled all grants of markets and fairs in North Wales which had been made

---

36 Cru Dig, 4th ed, Vol iii, p 267.

37 See *Doe d Tatum v Catomore* (1851) 16 QB 745.

38 See *above*, p 55 and footnote 13, p 98.

39 *Ibid.*

40 See *above*, footnote 13, p 98, and the comments of Farwell J, in *Newcastle (Duke) v Worksop UDC* [1902] 2 Ch 145 at 158.

41 Cru Dig, 4th ed, Vol iii, p 267; and see *above*, p 24.

42 See *above*, pp 24 and 101.

43 Com Dig, 5th ed, Vol vii, p 100, title 'Prescription G'; cited by Smith LJ, in *Taylor v New Windsor Corpn* [1898] 1 QB 186, (on appeal sub nom *New Windsor Corpn v Taylor* [1899] AC 41); Cru Dig, 4th ed, Vol iii, p 428, citing Finch Bk 1, c 3, s 23, who in turn cites YB 21 Hen VI, f 5; but the decision in the Year Book supports the contrary proposition; and see also *Goodson v Duffield* (1612) Cro Jac 313. The effect of the grant is probably a matter of construction in each case. See also *Addington v Clode* (1775) 2 Wm Bl 989; *Carnarvon (Earl) v Villebois* (1844) 13 M and W 313; *Grant on Corporations*.

44 See, for example, *New Windsor Corpn v Taylor* [1899] AC 41 at 50. It is not liable to forfeiture, and see *below*, p 105.

at any time to Welshmen[45]. Express words, however, are not necessary to cause extinguishment; and a statute may abolish a franchise by implication. Where the owners of a prescriptive Saturday market obtained an Act of Parliament which empowered them to hold the markets on every weekday over an extended area, and with higher tolls, it was decided that the prescriptive rights were superseded by the Parliamentary rights, and that the statute, on its true construction, conferred the latter in substitution for, and not by way of addition to, the former[46]. The intervention of Parliament for some subordinate purpose which presupposes the continuance of the old rights does not necessarily merge or extinguish the tenure of the old rights[47]; but in each case the effect of the statute is a question of construction[48].

ILLUSTRATIONS

In 1838 the charter incorporating the Borough of Manchester was granted. The manor was coterminous with the township of Manchester, but the Borough included not only the township but also five other townships. In 1846 the Corporation purchased the manorial rights of the manor of Manchester pursuant to the powers of an Act of 1844 and this purchase included an ancient prescriptive franchise to hold a market, which appears to have been a Saturday market, and to levy tolls and stallages in connection therewith.

The lords of the manor were the Mosley family, and prior to this purchase they had established by a series of actions their monopoly of market on various weekdays for the sale of different products.

In 1846 the Manchester Markets Act was enacted, *inter alia*, to provide new market places and to regulate markets and fairs within the Borough.

On the question of whether this Act operated to extinguish the prior manorial franchises in respect of markets and fairs formerly dependent upon prescription, it was *held* that the rights granted by Parliament superseded those which the grantee previously held from the Crown alone and that the old franchise was extinguished. The effect of a change of time, a change of place, an alteration of the old charges, an imposition of new charges and an extension of the market from the township to the Borough meant that the plaintiffs could not fall back on and assert the continuance of the original franchise right: *Mayor of Manchester v Lyons*[49].

---

45 25 Hen VI, repealed by 21 Ja I, c 28, s 11.

46 *Manchester Corpn v Lyons* (1882) 22 Ch D 287. 'But if after such a grant has been made by the Crown the three estates which conjointly constitute Parliament step in, whether on the solicitation of the grantee or otherwise, and by their joint act create the same rights or larger or different rights of the same nature and character in favour of the grantee, it seems to me that of necessity these Parliamentary rights, emanating as they do from a paramount authority, must supersede those which the grantee was previously holding from the Crown alone, and that after the passing of such an Act there can be no continuing tenure by the grantee under his original title, nor a continuance of his prior accountability on foot thereof to the Crown . . . I think, therefore, that the franchise rights have been superseded by the Parliamentary rights on the grounds just now stated . . . The question then arises, can the Plaintiffs, having solicited and obtained this Act of Parliament, now fall back upon and assert the continuance of their original franchise rights? And it seems to me that the ruling of Wood V-C, in the case of *Ellis v Bridgnorth Corpn* ((1861) 4 LT 112, 2 John & H 67), is distinctly in point against their being able to do so', per Little V-C, in *Manchester Corpn v Peverley* (1876) 22 Ch D 294n. See also *New Windsor Corpn v Taylor* [1899] AC 41; *Hammerton v Honey* (1876) 24 WR 603; *Wyld v Silver* [1963] Ch 243. See also *Bishopsgate Motor Finance Ltd v Transport Brakes Ltd* [1949] 1 KB 322. See also p 21, *above*.

47 *Manchester Corpn v Peverley* (1876) 22 Ch D 294n at 296n.

48 See *above*, p 21.

49 (1882) 22 Ch D 287.

'I can hardly imagine a plainer case of a new market as distinguished from a mere alteration or enlargement of an old one. It appears to be perfectly plain that, applying the law as laid down, and in my opinion correctly laid down, by Vice-Chancellor Little[50], there is a new market which is intended to be a new market, or rather a series of new markets, and that the old franchise was intended to be extinguished.'[51]

From a time long before living memory down to 1734, the New Windsor Corporation had taken certain tolls for passage over a wooden bridge which crossed the River Thames at Windsor. In 1734 a local Act was passed which, after reciting the Corporation's right to take the customary tolls, enacted that the customary tolls should be and remain vested in it and its successors. In 1819 the Corporation obtained another local Act which repealed the former Act and empowered it to take down the old bridge and build a new one and to take tolls which varied from the old tolls in amount and subject matter. The Act was for a specific term which had expired.

Held: that the prescriptive rights to take tolls had merged in and been extinguished by the statutory right given in 1734. Further, this prescriptive right had not been nor could have been revived by the later Act, and the right to take tolls expired with the later Act: *New Windsor Corporation v Taylor*[52].

B Abolition of fairs under the Fairs Act 1871

By the Fairs Act 1871[53] (as amended) special powers are given to the Home Secretary which enable him, under certain circumstances, to make an order abolishing any fair held in England or Wales.

The Secretary of State cannot make such an order without the previous consent in writing of the owner for the time being of the fair or of the tolls or dues payable in respect thereof[54]; but he can only make the order in cases where he has received a representation that it will be for the convenience and advantage of the public that the fair be abolished, and where it appears to him that such is the fact[55]. The representation, to entitle him to act upon it, must be made either

(1) by the owner of a fair, or
(2) by the district council of the district in which the fair is held, or London borough within which it is held[56].

Before the representation is considered by the Home Secretary, notice of the representation, and of the time when he will take it into consideration, must be published once in the *London Gazette*, and in three successive weeks in some one and the same newspaper published in the county, city or borough in which such fair is held, or if there are no

50 *Manchester Corpn v Peverley* (1876) 22 Ch D 294n, '. . . what is there left subsisting of the ancient franchise capable of being held under the Crown? It is in my opinion clear that the answer to this question must be "nothing", for the rights to the holding of the markets, and to the receipt of tolls in respect of those markets were not merely incidents of the holding under the Royal franchise, but were in truth the sole constituent element of that franchise. I therefore arrive at the conclusion and I hold, that the franchise rights were superseded or extinguished on the passing of the Act of 1846, and that whatever rights do now exist in the plaintiffs in respect of markets and fairs must be asserted on the footing of their Parliamentary title' (per Little VC at 298n).

51 Per Jessel MR at 305, 306.

52 [1899] AC 41.

53 35 & 34 Vict, c 12; see *below*, p 189.

54 *Ibid*, s 3.

55 *Ibid*, s 3.

56 *Ibid*, s 3, as amended by the Local Government Act 1894, ss 21(3), 27(1)(e), 32, 35; Local Government Act 1972, ss 1(10), 179(3); and London Government Order 1965, SI 1965/654, art 3(24), Sch 1.

such newspapers, then in the newspaper of some county adjoining or near thereto[57]. As soon as the order that the fair be abolished has been made the notice of the making of the order must be similarly published, and thereupon the fair becomes abolished[58], but the order appears to have no force until such publication has been completed.

For the purpose of the Act ' "owner" means any person, or persons, or body of commissioners or body corporate entitled to hold any fair, whether in respect of ownership of any lands or tenements, or under any charter, letters patent, or Act of Parliament or otherwise howsoever'[59].

4 EXTINCTION OF STATUTORY MARKETS

As we have seen the Crown cannot take proceedings by *scire facias* to forfeit a statutory market[60]. If abuses arise in connection with statutory markets, and the remedies provided by the statutes regulating them prove to be inadequate, they may be restrained by information at the suit of the Attorney-General[61] or recourse must be had to Parliament to pass a further statute which will provide adequate remedies[62]. Recourse to Parliament will undoubtedly be necessary in the case of a public or local Act where certain powers and duties have been given to the statutory market owner to hold the market in effect for the benefit of the public.

5 SUPPRESSION OF UNLAWFUL MARKETS AND FAIRS

A person who held a market or fair or levied toll without charter or other lawful authority could formerly be proceeded against by information in the nature of *quo warranto* to compel him to show by what authority the market was held or the toll levied; but that remedy has been abolished[63].

A simple process is provided, however, to prevent the holding of unlawful fairs within the limits of the Metropolitan Police District.

By the Metropolitan Police Act 1839 (as amended)[64], if it appears to the Commissioners of Police that any fair held within the Metropolitan Police District[65] has been held

---

57 Fairs Act 1871, s 3.
58 *Ibid*, s 4.
59 *Ibid*, s 2.
60 'The root of title is an Act of Parliament, and it is sufficiently proved by the production of that Act of Parliament, instead of being evidenced whenever it is called in question by the more or less precarious proof which is necessary to support a prescription. And it differs also in its incidence; it is not liable to be disproved in various ways which are familiar to lawyers, nor is it liable to forfeiture or to be called in question by any process of *scire facias*', per Davey LJ in *New Windsor Corpn v Taylor* [1899] AC 41 at 50.
61 *A-G v Tynemouth Corpn* (1900) 17 TLR 77 at 78.
62 Fairs Act 1871 (p 189 *below*), however, gives power to extinguish a fair.
63 See *above*, footnote 21, p 99.
64 2 & 3 Vict, c 47, s 39 and *below*, p 173.
65 As from 1 April 1965 the Metropolitan Police District comprises Greater London (excluding the City, Inner Temple and Middle Temple) and adjacent small parts of Essex, Hertfordshire and Surrey, see London Government Act 1963, s 76(1)(a)–(d), and Police Act 1964, s 62(4), Sch 6. The London Government Act 1963, s 76, may be amended (as to the alteration of police areas) by orders made by the Secretary of State under the Police Act 1964, s 2, as substituted by the Police and Magistrates' Courts Act 1994, s 14.

without lawful authority, or that any fair lawfully held has been held for a longer period than is warranted[66], the Commissioners may cause the owner or occupier of the ground upon which the fair is held to appear before a magistrate and show his title to hold a fair or hold it beyond the given period as the case may be. If the owner or occupier does not attend before the magistrate, or cannot show a right and title to hold the fair or hold it for the given period, the magistrate may declare the fair to be unlawful altogether or beyond the stated period. The Commissioners on such a declaration may give notice thereof and take steps to suppress the fair so far as it is unlawfully held[67] unless the owner or occupier exercises their right to have the legality of the fair raised before the High Court[68].

Furthermore, by the Metropolitan Fairs Act 1868 (as amended)[69], if a fair is held or notice given of any fair proposed to be held, on any ground within the Metropolitan Police District[70], other than that on which a fair has been held during each of the seven years immediately preceding, the Commissioner of Police, can, under that Act, have the question of whether the fair is legal summarily raised before a magistrate and, if the fair is declared unlawful, he can take summary steps to suppress it[71].

6 LANDLORD AND TENANT ACT 1954, PART II

The application of Part II of the Landlord and Tenant Act 1954 to markets was considered by the Court of Appeal and House of Lords in *Graysim Holdings Ltd v P & O Property Holdings Ltd*[72]. The tenant had taken a lease from the landlord of a building and had agreed to operate a general market in the premises. Individual stalls were fitted with lock up roller-blinds with the stall holders paying a weekly rent and service charge. The tenant employed a manager and provided basic facilities for the traders who were not allowed access outside market hours. The landlord served a notice to terminate the tenancy, objecting to the grant of a new lease on the ground it intended to demolish or reconstruct the building. The tenant then served a counter notice stating that it did not wish to give up possession on the basis it was operating a market. It was held by the judge that the tenant did not have exclusive possession of the building and accordingly was not entitled to the protection of the Landlord and Tenant Act 1954.

The tenant appealed and the Court of Appeal overturned the judgment at first instance on the grounds that although the tenant did not physically occupy the individual stalls, it exercised sufficient management control required by that type of business for it to be considered to be in 'occupation' for the purposes of the Act. The Court of Appeal also considered the point as to whether the tenant operated a market. The landlord had contended that the operation was similar to a downmarket shopping centre on the basis that there was no concourse of sellers and buyers. Nourse LJ considered that whilst a concourse is essential to the tort of levying a rival market, it is

66 As to the permitted hours, see Metropolitan Police Act 1839, s 38, *below*, p 173.
67 *Ibid*, s 39.
68 *Ibid*, s 40; Supreme Court of Judicature (Consolidation) Act 1925, s 19(2); and see *below*, p 174.
69 31 & 32 Vict, c 106, s 2; and see p 187, *below*.
70 See *above*, footnote 65.
71 Metropolitan Fairs Act 1868, s 2. For service of the summons and description of owner, etc, see s 3, *below*, p 187. The powers under this Act are additional to the powers contained in the Metropolitan Police Act 1839, ss 39, 40, *below*, pp 173, 174.
72 [1994] 1 WLR 992, [1996] AC 329.

not so for the purpose of determining whether the business conducted by the tenant is a market.

On appeal by the landlord, the House of Lords held, allowing the appeal and in effect restoring the decision at first instance, that the tenant did not 'occupy' for the purposes of its business that part of the building taken up by the stalls, and as the stalls were no longer part of 'the holding' under the 1954 Act, the tenant was not entitled to a new tenancy of them, or to recover compensation. Without the stalls, and the rents receivable from them, the retained parts of the market were useless to the tenant.

This decision has serious implications for those market operators holding premises under a headlease. Care must be taken, in these circumstances, to ensure that stall holders hold on licence only, or, where stalls are relatively substantial or self-contained (as in *Graysim*), that security of tenure is excluded by the court prior to the sub-letting, which should be for a term expiring not less than fourteen months before the expiry of the headlease, so as to enable the market operator to regain physical occupation of the whole property prior to the expiry of the term under the headlease.

CHAPTER 9

Regulation, Administration and Control

1 BYELAWS

A Franchise markets and fairs

The lord of a market or fair had, at common law, extensive powers for regulating it, but these powers have now been surrendered or fallen into disuse[1]. The private owner of a franchise market or fair has, as such, no power except under statute to make byelaws or regulations enforceable by fine or imprisonment.

Where, however, a local authority has acquired a franchise market, it has the same powers under the Food Act 1984 to make byelaws[2] regulating that market as it has in relation to markets established by it under that Act

The council of a district or London borough may also make byelaws for the good rule and government of the whole or any part of the district or borough, and for the suppression of nuisances[3], and these powers may be utilised to some extent to control conduct at markets and fairs[4]. In addition, local authorities[5] have powers under the Public Health Act 1961[6] to make byelaws regulating pleasure fairs. These local authority powers are exercisable irrespective of the ownership of the market or fair and are exercisable also in relation to statutory markets and fairs.

B Under the Markets and Fairs Clauses Act 1847

If the empowering or special Act incorporates the Markets and Fairs Clauses Act 1847, s 42, then the persons authorised by the special Act to construct or regulate the market or fair[7] may, from time to time, make such byelaws as they think fit for all or any of the following purposes[8]:

1 for regulating the use of the market place and fair, and the buildings, stalls, pens and standings in it, and for preventing nuisances or obstructions there or in the immediate approaches to it;

---

1 Thus, he had a court of pie powder for the determination of disputes arising in the market or fair; see pp 6, 7, *above*; and he was bound to keep in the market place a pillory and tumbrel for the punishment of offenders; see p 9, *above*. How far the duties in connection with these and other matters belonged to the owner of a market or fair as such, or how far they properly belonged to other jurisdictions usually held along with that franchise, is a somewhat obscure subject and not now of practical importance. For fuller consideration, see Chapter 1.

2 That is, under the 1984 Act, s 60; see p 250 *below*.

3 Local Government Act 1972, s 235(1). As to procedure for confirmation of all local authority byelaws for which specific provision is not otherwise made, see *ibid*, s 236 and Appendix pp 301, 302 *below*.

4 But a byelaw prohibiting or restricting market rights in streets would be bad: see *Elwood v Bullock* (1844) 6 QB 383.

5 That is, a district council, a London borough, the Common Council of the City of London and, in the Inner Temple and Middle Temple, the Sub Treasurer and Under Treasurer respectively: see the Public Health Act 1961, s 2(3) and the Local Government Act 1972, s 180(1), (3).

6 Section 75: see pp 207, 208, *below*.

7 That is, the undertakers: 1847 Act, s 2. For the 1847 Act, see *below*, pp 179 *et seq*.

8 1847 Act, ss 2 and 42.

2 for fixing the days, and the hours during each day, on which the market or fair shall be held[9];
3 for inspection of slaughterhouses, for keeping them in a clean and proper state, for removing filth and refuse at least once in every twenty-four hours, for requiring that a sufficient supply of water be provided and for preventing cruelty in them;
4 for regulating carriers resorting to the market or fair and fixing the rates for carrying articles from it within the limits of the special Act;
5 for preventing the sale or exposure for sale of unwholesome provisions in the market or fair.

The byelaws must not be repugnant to the laws of that part of the United Kingdom where they are to have effect, nor to the provisions of the 1847 Act or the special Act; and they may be repealed or altered[10].

The 1847 Act makes, in addition, specific provision for the confirmation of byelaws by the Secretary of State for the Environment[11], and for their publication[12] and enforcement[13].

C Under the Food Act 1984

A local authority which maintains a market, whether or not it is a market authority within the meaning of the Food Act 1984[14], may make byelaws:
1 for regulating the use of the market place, and the buildings, stalls, pens and standings in it;
2 for preventing nuisances or obstructions in the market place, or in the immediate approaches to it;
3 for regulating porters and carriers resorting to the market, and fixing the charges to be made for carrying articles from the market within the district;
4 after consulting the fire authority for the area in which the market is situated, for preventing the spread of fires in the market[15].

A market authority may also make a byelaw specifying the distance from the market within which articles commonly sold in the market, and specified in the byelaw, may not be sold or exposed for sale by unauthorised persons on market day[16]. The market

9 But any provision of a local Act which confers power on a local authority to make byelaws appointing days on which or hours during which markets or fairs are to be or may be held must be construed as conferring on the authority a power to appoint such days or hours by resolution: Local Government (Miscellaneous Provisions) Act 1976, s 36(1).
10 1847 Act, s 42.
11 *Ibid*, ss 44–46.
12 1847 Act, ss 47–49.
13 *Ibid*, s 43. The maximum penalty which may be imposed is level 1 on the standard scale. Where the special Act incorporates the 1847 Act, penalties are recoverable on summary conviction in accordance with the Railway Clauses Consolidation Act 1845: 1847 Act, s 52; and see *below*, pp 175 *et seq*.
14 That is, a local authority which maintains a market established or acquired under s 50(1) of the 1984 Act or under the corresponding provisions of any earlier enactment: 1984 Act, s 61. 'Local authority' means a district council, a London borough council or a parish or community council: *ibid*.
15 1984 Act, s 60. For model byelaws see Appendix A, p 295 *below*, and for model regulations see Appendix B, p 303 *below*. For procedure for the confirmation of such byelaws, see the Local Government Act 1972, s 236 and the Department of the Environment's Memorandum 7D set out in Appendix A, p 301, *below*.
16 1984 Act, s 56(1); and see p 91, *above*.

authority must keep exhibited in conspicuous places near the market notices stating the effect of any such byelaw[17].

Byelaws made under this Act must be confirmed by the Secretary of State for the Environment[18].

Offences under byelaws are triable summarily[19].

D Under the Animal Health Act 1981

A wharf or other place provided by a local authority under the Animal Health Act 1981[20], s 54(1), is a market within the Market and Fairs Clauses Act 1847[21], and the 1981 Act is deemed to be the special Act.

Byelaws must be approved by, in England, the Minister of Agriculture, Fisheries and Food, and in Scotland or Wales, the Secretary of State[22]. Notice of application for approval must be given and, before application, the proposed byelaws published as required by the 1847 Act[23]. The local authority may charge for the use of the wharf or other place provided by it under the 1981 Act such sums as may be imposed by byelaws, and those sums are deemed to be tolls authorised by the special Act[24].

E Validity of byelaws

Byelaws will be valid and may regulate trade in a market provided all the following conditions are satisfied:

(1) Must not be ultra vires

A byelaw is invalid and of no effect if not made in the manner (if any) directed by statute, charter or other authority under which it is purported to be made[25]. A power to make byelaws regulating trade cannot be used to justify the prohibition of a lawful trade carried on in a lawful manner[26].

(2) Must not be repugnant to the general law

A byelaw is not repugnant to the general law merely because it creates a new offence and says that something shall be unlawful which the law does not say is unlawful. It is repugnant if it expressly, or by necessary implication, proposes to alter the general law, or deprives the defendant of a defence which he would have under the general law.

---

17 *Ibid*, s 56(2).

18 In accordance with the procedure in the Local Government Act 1972, s 236: see footnote 15, *above.*

19 Food Act 1984, s 93(1), (3)(g). Byelaws under the Food Act 1984 may provide for the imposition of fines not exceeding level 2 on the standard scale: Local Government Act 1972, s 237. Where byelaws provided for a fine on breach, it was held in *R v Barnsley Metropolitan Borough Council, ex p Hook* [1976] 1 WLR 1052 (per Lord Denning MR and Sir John Pennycuick) that the market owner could not deprive the stall holder of his common law right to trade, and thereby indirectly of his livelihood, by revoking his licence, as an alternative to taking him before the justices.

20 See p 214, *below*.

21 See pp 109 and 110, *above*, p 179, *below*, and p 113 *below*.

22 Animal Health Act 1981, ss 54(3)(b) and 86(1)(b).

23 *Ibid*, s 54(3)(b).

24 Animal Health Act 1981, s 54(4).

25 *Parry v Berry* (1717) 1 Com 269; *Parker v Bournemouth Corpn* (1902) 86 LT 449. For the proper test to be applied when determining whether the bad parts of a byelaw are severable to enable the legislative purpose to be served, see *DPP v Smith; DPP v Hutchinson* [1990] 2 AC 783, HL.

26 *Toronto (City) Municipal Corpn v Virgo* [1896] AC 88.

Again, a byelaw will be repugnant if it adds something inconsistent with the provisions of a statute creating the same offence; but if it adds something not inconsistent, that is not sufficient to make the byelaw bad as repugnant[27].

(3) Must not be unreasonable

A byelaw may be unreasonable if it is partial and unequal in its operation, or because it is manifestly unjust or discloses bad faith or involves oppressive or gratuitous interference with the rights of those subject to it. But it will not be unreasonable merely because it goes further than is prudent, necessary or convenient, or because it does not contain an exception or qualification which it might well contain. The elected representatives of a local authority understand the requirements of their locality better than judges, and if something can be a nuisance in law it is for the local authority to decide whether it ought to be controlled by byelaw[28].

As indicated in paragraph (1) above, byelaws in restraint of trade are bad unless made under an express power or supported by custom[29]. But byelaws involving partial restraint are not necessarily unreasonable. For example, a byelaw may confine sales of a particular article to special parts of the market[30]; or it may appropriate a part of the market to sales by wholesale[31] or by public auction[32]; and where part of the market is properly set aside for sales by public auction, a byelaw prohibiting sales by private auction in that part is good[33].

A byelaw may not, however, prohibit without the consent of an officer of the market authority, all dealing in a particular article in a market, or in any special part of the market, if the article is one of those for which the market was established[34]. Similarly, a byelaw is bad if it purports to prohibit sales by auction in the market, or to prohibit such sales without the consent of the market authority; for a seller is entitled to fix the conditions on which his goods should be offered for sale[35].

It has been held that a byelaw which regulates the times at which sales by auction may take place in a market is valid[36], but this decision has, in effect, been overruled[37].

It is for the person who asserts that a byelaw is unreasonable to prove that it is[38].

---

27 *Gentel v Rapps* [1902] 1 KB 160 at 166, per Channell J; *Strickland v Hayes* [1896] 1 QB 290; *Dyson v London and North Western Rly Co* (1881) 7 QBD 32.

28 *Kruse v Johnson* [1898] 2 QB 91 at 100, per Lord Russell of Killowen CJ; *White v Morley* [1899] 2 QB 34; *Elwood v Bullock* (1844) 6 QB 383; *Dodd v Venner* (1922) 20 LGR 574. A byelaw which is unreasonable in part may nevertheless be upheld as to the rest if it is divisible into separate and distinct parts: see *Strickland v Hayes* [1896] 1 QB 290; *Dyson v London and North Western Rly Co* (1881) 7 QBD 32.

29 *Parry v Berry* (1717) 1 Com 269; *Elwood v Bullock* (1844) 6 QB 383.

30 *Savage v Brook* (1863) 15 CBNS 264; *Wortley v Nottingham Local Board* (1869) 21 LT 582; *Player v Jenkins* (1666) 1 Sid 284.

31 *Strike v Collins* (1886) 55 LT 182.

32 *Scott v Glasgow Corpn* [1899] AC 470; *Nicholls v Tavistock UDC* [1923] 2 Ch 18.

33 *Scott v Glasgow Corpn* [1899] AC 470.

34 *Wortley v Nottingham Local Board* (1870) 21 LT 582. A byelaw which indirectly prevents dealing in an article is also bad: see *Sutton Harbour Improvement Co v Foster* (1920) 89 LJ KB 829; but not if it is merely restrictive and is otherwise reasonable: see *Sutton Harbour Improvement Co v Foster (No 2)* (1920) 89 LJ Ch 540.

35 *Nicholls v Tavistock UDC* [1923] 2 Ch 18.

36 *Collins v Wells Corpn* (1885) 1 TLR 328.

37 By *Scott v Glasgow Corpn* [1899] AC 470; see *Nicholls v Tavistock UDC* [1923] 2 Ch 18 at 30.

38 *Belfast Corpn v Daly* [1963] NI 78 at 85; *Associated Provincial Picture Houses Ltd v Wednesbury Corpn* [1948] 1 KB 223 at 228, per Lord Greene MR.

(4) Must be certain

A byelaw must clearly specify the action which is to be taken or avoided, and identify the person whom it affects[39]. If the words of a byelaw are ambiguous, the courts will, however, construe it so as to give effect, as far as reasonably possible, to the intention of the authority which made it[40].

2 CONTRACT

No one has the right at common law to occupy exclusively any particular part of the soil of the market place, for example by erecting a stall, without the consent of the owner of the soil, or other person entitled to actual possession or control of the land[41]. The landowner may stipulate such terms as he thinks fit when granting a licence to occupy a stall including the level of stallage (charge) and the class of goods to be sold.

ILLUSTRATION

The Council, as market owner and owner of the market building, granted the defendants a licence to use a stall in the building. The licence restricted the defendants to selling 'high class salads'. The defendants failed to comply with the restriction and sold various green vegetables and fruit not on an agreed list of items. The Council obtained an order for possession of the stall. On appeal by the defendants: *Held* dismissing the appeal, that the general law, which was not displaced by any rule of law of market franchise, was that the landowner was entitled to exact from an intending occupier of land such terms as he thought fit and, accordingly, since the defendants were in breach of the provisions of the licence, the Council was entitled to possession of the stall: *Gloucester City Council v Williams*[42].

A local authority or other public authority market owner should ensure, however, that any licence to occupy a stall is, in its terms, clear and unambiguous[43] with specific provision for determination in the event of breach of conditions. Care should be taken to ensure that a trader is not given cause to complain that he has been treated unfairly or in an arbitrary manner. Failure to give attention to proper procedures may lead to review by the court on the basis that any resulting threat to a trader's livelihood affects his common law rights, so bringing the issue within the ambit of public law[44].

---

39 *Kruse v Johnson* [1898] 2 QB 91 at 108, per Mathew J.

40 *Tuck & Sons v Priester* (1887) 19 QBD 629 at 638, per Lord Esher MR; *London and North Eastern Rly Co v Berriman* [1946] AC 278.

41 See pp 28, 57, 58 *above* and *A-G v Colchester Corpn* [1952] Ch 586.

42 (1990) 88 LGR 853.

43 See, for example, Parker LJ's *obiter* remarks (at 862) on the meaning of 'high class salads' in *Gloucester City Council v Williams, above*. Any rules and regulations made by an authority will not be deemed to be incorporated into the contract (and will therefore be unenforceable) unless a copy is given to each stall holder: *Rickard v Forest Heath District Council* (1 May 1991, unreported). For model rules and regulations, see pp 303–307 *below*.

44 As in *R v Barnsley Metropolitan Borough Council, ex p Hook* [1976] 1 WLR 1052; *R v Basildon District Council, ex p Brown* (1981) 79 LGR 655; *R v Wear Valley District Council, ex p Binks* [1985] 2 All ER 699; *Rickard v Forest Heath District Council* (1 May 1991, unreported); *R v Birmingham City Council, ex p Dredger and Paget* (1993) 91 LGR 532 and *Camden London Borough Council v Paddock* [1996] CLY 3691.

3 STATUTE

A Street trading

The Local Government (Miscellaneous Provisions) Act 1982[45] introduced an adoptive code for the control of street trading[46]. Many of the provisions were previously found in local Acts[47].

Under the 1982 Act, a district council may, by resolution, designate any street as a prohibited street, a licence street or a consent street[48]. The system of control by licensing is rather more involved than that by consent, but generally the former is intended to cover street markets and the latter itinerant or mobile traders[49].

It should be noted that although the definition of 'street trading'[50] appears wide, it is cut down quite considerably by the exemption from control of certain specified activities[51]. The activities exempted include, notably, trading by a person acting as a pedlar[52] (ie going from door to door); and anything done in a market or fair the right to hold which was acquired by virtue of a grant (including a presumed grant) or acquired or established by virtue of an enactment or order[53]. These exemptions provide defences from prosecution under para 10.

The licensing system is an attempt to maintain a balance between stall holders, who are dependent on street trading for their livelihood, and councils, who must maintain control and recover costs[54]. On the one hand, a council is not entitled to refuse, revoke

45 Section 3 and Schedule 4. See pp 233 *et seq*, *below*.

46 'Street' includes: (a) any road, footway, beach or other area to which the public have access without payment; and (b) a service area defined in s 329 of the Highways Act 1980; and also includes any part of a street: 1982 Act, s 3, Sch 4, para 1(1). 'Street trading' means the selling or exposing or offering for sale of any article (including a living thing) in a street: *ibid*; but note the exemptions in Sch 4, para 1(2).

47 For example, the County of South Glamorgan Act 1976 (C XXXV): See *Voisey v Cardiff City Council* (1981) 79 LGR 185 and *Yeates v Cardiff City Council* (1981) 79 LGR 577. Note the protection in the 1982 Act, Sch 4, para 3(8), for the rights of existing fixed traders. See also Appendix A to Home Office Circular 62/82 (DoE Circular 19/82, Welsh Office Circular 34/82).

48 1982 Act, Sch 4, para 2(1). The procedure for designation is set out in *ibid*, para 2; and it should be noted, in particular, that the consent of the highway authority is required before a street maintainable by such authority is designated as a licence street: 1982 Act, Sch 4, para 2(3) and (4).

49 But see *ibid*, para 7(8) and text, *below*.

50 See footnote 46, *above*.

51 See 1982 Act, Sch 4, para 1(2) and (3).

52 Under the Pedlars Act 1871: see p 190, *below*. For the distinction between acting as a street trader and a pedlar see *Watson v Malloy* [1988] 3 All ER 459; *R v Westminster City Council, ex p Elmasoglu* [1996] COD 357; *Shepway District Council v Vincent* [1994] COD 451; *Stevenage Borough Council v Wright* (1996) 95 LGR 404 and *Chichester District Council v Wood* (14 March 1997, unreported).

53 1982 Act, Sch 4, para 1(2)(a) and (b). See also the savings in *ibid*, para 11. But note that if the local authority market owner validly restricts the holding of the market to an area smaller than that over which the market rights subsist (see pp 30, 31, *above*), a street trader trading without authorisation in a consent street outside the designated market area will not be entitled to avail himself of the defence under Sch 4, para 1(2)(b): *Jones v Lewis* (1989) Times 14 June. In this case, the Queen's Bench Division (per Glidewell LJ) held that initially the burden of proof lay on the trader to show that the place where he was trading was a market (eg by the production of the indenture granting market rights) following which the onus fell on the local authority to prove that it had exercised the power to limit the market area.

54 Councils may charge reasonable fees for the grant or renewal of a street trading licence or consent: 1982 Act, Sch 4, para 9(1) and (2); and may (but in relation to licences only) recover reasonable charges for the collection of refuse, the cleansing of streets and other services rendered: *ibid*, para 9(6). Note, however, that since the purpose of the Act is to

or vary a licence, except on certain specified grounds[55], but on the other, it has absolute control over the number of stalls in the street, the number of traders dealing in the same goods and the minimum number of days on which a licence holder must trade[56]. Reasonable conditions may be attached to a licence[57].

Reasonable conditions may also be attached to street trading consents[58]. Control is, however, much stricter, with no rights of appeal for the trader against refusal, revocation or variation of a consent[59]. Although consents are intended primarily to control mobile trading (which may include a flower seller with a single basket or a hot-dog stall), power is given to a council to permit trading in a consent street from a stationary van, cart, barrow or other vehicle; or from a portable stall[60].

Licences and consents may be granted for any period not exceeding 12 months[61]. They cannot be granted to anyone under the age of 17 years, nor where a control order under the Local Government (Miscellaneous Provisions) Act 1976, s 7, is in force and applies[62].

The system of control is intended to be flexible, and different controls may be applied to different parts of the same street[63]. If one form of control proves to be inappropriate, another may be adopted in its place[64].

A person guilty of an offence under the provisions is liable on summary conviction to a fine[65].

In London, further powers to control street trading are conferred upon local authorities by the London Local Authorities Act 1990, Part III[66] (as amended by the London Local Authorities Act 1994, s 6 and Sch). The Act received Royal Assent on 22 February 1990 and comes into force in the area of the participating council[67] on the day appointed by each council[68], when certain specified local enactments shall cease to have effect[69]. Under the Act, it is unlawful for a person to engage in street

---

control street trading, a council is not empowered to raise revenue generally by means of fees: *R v Manchester City Council, ex p King* (1991) 89 LGR 696.

55 See 1982 Act, Sch 4, paras 3(6), 5(1) and 6.

56 *Ibid*, para 6(5).

57 1982 Act, Sch 4, para 4(4) and (5). These are 'subsidiary terms' and are additional to the 'principal terms' which *must* be specified in a licence. 'Principal terms' are: (a) the street or particular place in the street in which the licence holder is permitted to trade; (b) the days on which and the times between which he is permitted to trade; and (c) the description of the articles in which he is permitted to trade: *ibid*, para 4(1), (2) and (3).

58 1982 Act, Sch 4, para 7(4), (5) and (9); and these may be varied: *ibid*, para 7(6).

59 1982 Act, Sch 4, para 7(2), (6) and (10). See *R v Bristol City Council, ex p Pearce* (1984) 83 LGR 711, where it was held that a district council is not obliged to hear oral representations from applicants for consents or to give reasons for its decisions although the applicant has a right to know the contents of any letters of objection (other than from the council's own officers or the police) so that he may have an opportunity to comment.

60 *Ibid*, para 7(8). For conditions, see para 7(9). Obviously, it is for a council to decide whether, if a trader stays sufficiently long and often in the same place, the street ought to be re-designated as a licence street.

61 1982 Act, Sch 4, paras 4(6) and 7(10).

62 *Ibid*, paras 3(4) and 7(3).

63 For definition of 'street', see footnote 46, *above*.

64 1982 Act, Sch 4, para 2(13).

65 *Ibid*, para 10. The maximum fine is level 3 on the standard scale.

66 Sections 21 to 41. The City of London (Various Powers) Act 1987, Part III (ss 6–26) makes provision for the control of street trading and related activity in Middlesex Street.

67 That is, a borough council mentioned in Sch 1 to the 1990 Act.

68 *Ibid*, ss 3 and 22.

69 1990 Act, ss 24, 40 and Sch 2.

trading[70] in any licence street[71], so designated[72] by a borough council, without a street trading licence[73] or a temporary licence[74]. Provision is made for succession rights[75], conditions of licences[76] and grant, renewal, variation and revocation of licences[77]. There are rights of appeal to a magistrates' court by a person aggrieved[78] and thence (by street trader or borough council) to the Crown Court[79]. Borough councils may charge fees for licences to cover reasonable costs[80], and may provide receptacles or containers for use in street trading[81]. Further provisions relate to offences and penalties[82], the employment of assistants[83] and itinerant ice cream traders[84]. There are savings in respect of sales prohibited under other enactments[85] and a saving for sales in legal markets and fairs[86].

B Temporary markets

Section 37 of the Local Government (Miscellaneous Provisions) Act 1982[87] enables a district council or a London borough to adopt, by resolution, a limited power of control over temporary markets[88]. 'Temporary market' is defined[89] as a concourse of buyers and sellers of articles held otherwise than in a building or on a highway, and comprising not less than 5 stalls, stands, vehicles[90] (whether movable or not) or pitches from which articles are sold. Excluded from the definition are charter, prescriptive or statutory markets and fairs, and sales by auction of farm livestock or deadstock[91]. The section also does not apply to a market in respect of which planning permission has been obtained[92].

---

70 As defined in the 1990 Act s 21(1), and see *ibid*, s 38. As to what falls within the definition of street trading in London, see *R v Westminster City Council, ex p Elmasoglu* [1996] COD 357 and *Wandsworth London Borough Council v Rosenthal* (1996) 95 LGR 84. In the latter case it was held that the exposing of goods for sale on a pavement outside the shop for payment within the shop was street trading for the purposes of the 1990 Act s 21(1). This activity is specifically excluded from the definition of 'street trading' under the Local Government (Miscellaneous Provisions) Act 1982, applicable to areas outside London.

71 'Street' and 'licence street' are defined in the 1990 Act, s 21(1); and see *O'Gorman v Brent London Borough Council* (1993) 91 LGR 555.

72 In accordance with the 1990 Act, s 24.

73 For licence application, see *ibid*, s 25.

74 1990 Act, ss 21(1) and 31.

75 *Ibid*, s 26.

76 1990 Act, s 27.

77 *Ibid*, ss 25, 28 and 29.

78 1990 Act, s 30(1).

79 *Ibid*, s 30(4). Cf *R v Crown Court at Southwark, ex p Watts* (1989) 153 JP 666, a case under the London County Council (General Powers) Act 1947, s 64. Also see p 164, *below*.

80 1990 Act, s 32.

81 *Ibid*, s 33. Power to remove receptacles is given by the 1990 Act, s 35.

82 1990 Act, ss 34 and 38. The maximum fine is level 3 on the standard scale.

83 *Ibid*, s 36.

84 1990 Act, s 37.

85 *Ibid*, s 39.

86 1990 Act, s 41.

87 See p 232, *below*.

88 1982 Act, s 37(1). Within 14 days of the passing of the resolution, notice of it must be advertised in a local newspaper.

89 In *ibid*, s 37(6).

90 Thus, it appears, 'car boot sales' will be caught.

91 1982 Act, s 37(6).

92 *Ibid*, s 37(8). For the necessity for planning permission, see pp 127–130, *below*.

Where the provision is in force, at least one month's notice of an intention to hold[93] a temporary market must be given to the local authority by both the intending promoter and by the occupier of the land on which it is to be held[94]. There is no prescribed form of notice, but it must state the names and addresses of the promoter and the occupier of the land; the day or days on which and the times between which the market is to be held; and the site[95]. If, however, the proceeds of the market are to be applied solely or principally for charitable, social, sporting or political purposes, no notice is required[96].

Holding a temporary market (or permitting land to be used for the purposes of such) without giving the required notice is an offence punishable on summary conviction by a fine[97].

The provision is a useful addition to a local authority's common law and statutory powers to control markets. Although it does not give authorities the power to prohibit markets completely, it does give them a prior opportunity to discuss with market promoters or occupiers of land the problems normally associated with activities of this kind: for example, traffic control and litter disposal[98]. It may also provide local authorities with valuable time within which to consider whether an effort should be made under other powers to prevent the market from taking place; for example, where there is likely to be an infringement of franchise rights[99]. A local authority may also wish, in exceptional circumstances, to consider making the proposed market subject to planning control by means of a general direction under Article 4 of the Town and Country General Development Order 1988[100].

C Employment

(1) Health and safety at work

The Health and Safety at Work, etc Act 1974, s 2(1) imposes a duty on employers to ensure, so far as reasonably practicable, the health, safety and welfare of their employees at work. Section 3 of the Act requires that employers do not expose their employees to risk to their health and safety and failure to do so is an offence liable on summary conviction to a fine not exceeding £5,000 or on conviction on indictment to an unlimited fine. Action against employers is, however, more usually taken under ss 21 and 22. Section 21 empowers the local authority inspector to issue an improvement notice if he believes an offence has been committed, or is likely to be committed. The improvement notice requires remedial action to be taken. Under s 22 an inspector may issue a prohibition notice if he believes an activity involves a risk of serious personal injury. The prohibition notice requires certain actions to be taken before the activity is resumed. Non-compliance with either notice is an offence liable on summary conviction to imprisonment for a term not exceeding six months or a fine not exceeding £20,000, or both, or on conviction on indictment to imprisonment for a term not exceeding two years or an unlimited fine, or both. There is provision for appeal to the Industrial Tribunal under each procedure.

---

93 1982 Act, s 37(7) describes the circumstances in which a person is deemed to hold a temporary market.
94 *Ibid*, s 37(2).
95 1982 Act, s 37(4).
96 1982 Act, s 37(3).
97 *Ibid*, s 37(5). The maximum fine is level 4 on the standard scale.
98 See Home Office Circular 62/82, DoE Circular 19/82 and Welsh Office Circular 34/82.
99 See Chapter 6.
100 See p 130, *below*.

(2) Children

Under the Children and Young Persons Act 1933, s 20[101], generally, no child may be employed[102] in street trading[103]. Byelaws made by a local authority[104] under this section may, however, authorise children[105] who have attained the age of fourteen years to be employed by their parents in street trading to such extent as may be specified in the byelaws[106]. Byelaws may also regulate street trading by children; and such byelaws may distinguish between persons of different ages and sexes and between different localities[107].

If a person is employed[102] in contravention of this provision, or of any byelaw made under it, the employer and any person responsible for the contravention (but not the employee) will be liable on summary conviction to a fine[108]. A child who engages in street trading in contravention of this section will, nevertheless, also be liable on summary conviction to a fine, albeit on a lower scale[109].

D Weights and measures: goods generally

(1) Under the Markets and Fairs Clauses Act 1847

The weighing and measuring provisions of the Markets and Fairs Clauses Act 1847[110] apply to all markets and fairs subject to the special Act which incorporates those provisions[111]; and to all markets established under the Animal Health Act 1981[112]. The

---

101 As amended by the Children and Young Persons Act 1963, s 35(1) and by the Employment Act 1989, s 10(2), Sch 3, Pt III, para 2(a), (b).

102 A person who assists in a trade or occupation carried on for profit is deemed to be 'employed', notwithstanding that he receives no reward for his labour: Children and Young Persons Act 1933, s 30.

103 'Street trading' includes the hawking of newspapers, matches, flowers and other articles, playing, singing or performing for profit, shoe blacking and other similar occupations carried on in streets or public places: *ibid*, and cf the narrower definition in the Local Government (Miscellaneous Provisions) Act 1982, s 3, Sch 4, para 1(1), *above*, p 114. Note also that street trading licences and consents cannot be granted under the 1982 Act to anyone under the age of 17 years: *ibid*, paras 3(4)(a) and 7(3)(a). See also: *Stratford Co-operative Society Ltd v East Ham Corpn* [1915] 2 KB 70 (delivery of bread to customers' doors not street trading); *Morgan v Parr* [1921] 2 KB 379 (newsagent authorising boys to sell newspapers as his agent commits offence); *Vann v Eatough* (1935) 154 LT 109 (selling from stall in market is 'street trading'). 'Street' is defined in the Children and Young Persons Act 1933, s 107(1) as including any highway and any public bridge, road, lane, footway, square, court, alley or passage, whether a thoroughfare or not. However, nothing in *ibid*, s 20, or in byelaws made thereunder, restricts the engagement or employment of any person in the carrying on in any place of a retail trade or business on any occasion on which it is customary for retail trades or businesses to be carried on in that place: Children and Young Persons Act 1963, s 35(2).

104 That is, a local education authority or the Common Council of the City of London: *ibid*, ss 96, 97; Children Act 1948, s 60(2) and Sch 3.

105 'Child' is defined as a person who is not (for the purposes of the relevant legislation) over compulsory school age: Children and Young Persons Act 1933, s 30(1) (as amended).

106 *Ibid*, s 20(2).

107 Children and Young Persons Act 1933, s 20(2). For provisions which may be included in byelaws, see *ibid*.

108 Children and Young Persons Act 1933, s 21(1). Maximum fine now level 3 on the standard scale. For defence, see 1933 Act, s 21(1), proviso.

109 *Ibid*, s 21(3); Children and Young Persons Act 1963, s 36(6).

110 That is, ss 21, 22, 24 and 34.

111 See 1847 Act, ss 1, 2, pp 179, 180, *below*.

112 Animal Health Act 1981, s 54(2).

provisions of the 1847 Act, some of which are set out in full elsewhere[113], require the undertakers[114] to provide sufficient and proper weighing houses or places and to keep there proper weights, scales and measures[115]. Proper persons must be appointed to attend to weighing and measuring[115], and everyone offering articles[116] for sale must have them weighed or measured, if required to do so by the buyer, with a penalty in default[117].

Tolls, if any[118], are payable before the commodities are weighed or measured to the person authorised by the undertakers[119].

Similar provisions[120] apply to the weighing of carts in which goods are brought for sale within the market or fair or the prescribed limits[121].

E Weights and measures: cattle

(1) Under the Markets and Fairs (Weighing of Cattle) Acts

These provisions are dealt with in some detail because of the somewhat confusing nature of their current application.

Markets and fairs in which, for the time being, tolls[122] are authorised to be taken and actually are taken in respect of cattle[123], are subject to the provisions of the Markets and Fairs (Weighing of Cattle) Acts 1887 and 1891[124]. It should be noted, however, that these Acts, and the Markets and Fairs (Weighing of Cattle) Act 1926, *below*, are now effectively repealed so far as they relate to any local authority which is a market authority for the purposes of Part III of the Food Act 1984[125].

Under the 1887 and 1891 Acts, certain duties are imposed on the market authority[126] unless exemption is granted by an order of the Ministry of Agriculture, Fisheries and Food[127]. These duties are:

(a) to provide and maintain in or near the market or fair sufficient and proper buildings or places for weighing cattle brought for sale within the market or fair[128];

---

113 See p 179, *below*.
114 See 1847 Act, s 2.
115 1847 Act, s 21.
116 For the meaning of 'articles', see 1847 Act, s 22. 'Articles' is not specifically defined in the 1847 Act but appears to mean all things for the buying and selling of which the market is held, including horses and cattle: *Llandaff and Canton District Market Co v Lyndon* (1860) 8 CBNS 515 at 521, per Byles J.
117 1847 Act, s 22. Maximum penalty level 1 on the standard scale.
118 That is, if authorised by the special Act.
119 1847 Act, s 34.
120 That is, *ibid*, ss 24, 34.
121 For 'prescribed limits' see 1847 Act, s 13, note (4), pp 180, 181, *below*.
122 *Quaere* whether the provision applies to markets and fairs in which only payments in the nature of stallage are taken. It may be, however, that the provision covers payments for standing room for cattle: see *R v Casswell* (1872) LR 7 QB 328; *Bedford (Duke) v Overseers of St Pauls, Covent Garden* (1881) 51 LJMC 41 and cf *Heddy v Wheelhouse* (1597) Cro Eliz 558.
123 Defined in the Markets and Fairs (Weighing of Cattle) Act 1926, s 3, as including ram, ewe, wether, lamb and swine. Compare the definition in the Markets and Fairs (Weighing of Cattle) Act 1926, s 1(3), pp 120 and 204, *below*.
124 See pp 201 and 202, *below*.
125 See p 243, *below*.
126 Defined in the 1887 Act, s 2, as being any company, corporation or person by whom tolls in respect of cattle are taken.
127 Under the 1887 Act, s 9.
128 1887 Act, s 4. Where a cattle market is held on a highway dedicated subject to the right to hold a market thereon, the highway authority cannot prevent the market authority from

(b) to keep there, or nearby, weighing machines and weights for the purpose of weighing cattle[128];

(c) to appoint proper persons in charge of such machines and weights[128];

(d) to make the machines and weights available for use by the public for weighing cattle[128];

(e) generally, to provide and maintain to the satisfaction of the Ministry sufficient and suitable accommodation for weighing cattle[129].

Unless it is otherwise expressly provided in any Act, the market authority may take tolls in respect of the weighing of cattle[130]; but failure to comply with any of the above duties will make it unlawful for the market authority to demand, receive or recover tolls in respect of cattle brought to the market or fair for sale[131]. And if during the time the market authority is in default any person demands or receives toll, he will be liable on summary conviction to a fine[132].

Every person selling, offering for sale, or buying cattle in a market or fair provided with accommodation for weighing cattle, may require such cattle to be weighed; and the toll payable for weighing shall be paid by such person to the person authorised by the market authority to receive it[133]. Sections 36 to 41 of the Markets and Fairs Clauses Act 1847 (which deal with such matters as recovery of tolls by distress, disputes and exhibition of a list of tolls) apply to this toll as if the Markets and Fairs (Weighing of Cattle) Act 1887 were the special Act, and the market authority were the undertakers[134].

Upon the application of a market authority, the Ministry of Agriculture, Fisheries and Food has power to make an order exempting the market or fair from the provisions of the 1887 and 1891 Acts; but the order must limit the time, not exceeding three years, during which it is to be in force; and such order may be wholly or partly rescinded, altered or extended by subsequent order[135].

The conduct of auctioneers is governed by the 1891 Act, s 4, and by the 1926 Act[136].

An auctioneer is prohibited, unless exempted by order of the Ministry of Agriculture, Fisheries and Food[137], from selling cattle at any mart where cattle are habitually or periodically sold, unless there are provided at that mart similar facilities for weighing

---

setting up, in accordance with the Acts, a permanent weighing machine: *McIntosh v Romford Local Board* (1889) 60 LT 185.

129 Markets and Fairs (Weighing of Cattle) Act 1891, s 2 which, in effect, imposes the additional requirement of satisfying the Minister of Agriculture, Fisheries and Food.

130 That is, in addition to tolls on sale. The Acts do not apply unless tolls on sale are payable: see 1887 Act, s 2, p 201, *below*. Tolls on weighing must not exceed the amounts specified in the Schedule to the 1926 Act (which superseded the Schedule to the 1887 Act) or such other amounts as may be authorised by the Secretary of State for the Environment to be taken by the market authority: see 1887 Act, s 8. The maximum tolls specified in the Schedule to the 1926 Act were 6d (now 2½p) for every head of cattle, other than sheep or swine; and 3d (now about 1½p) for every 5 or less number of sheep or swine.

131 1887 Act, s 4; 1891 Act, s 2.

132 *Ibid.* Maximum fine now level 1 on the standard scale.

133 1887 Act, s 5. As to what constitutes an offer for sale see, for example, *Partridge v Crittendon* [1968] 2 All ER 421 and *British Car Auctions Ltd v Wright* [1972] 3 All ER 462.

134 1887 Act, s 8. 'The special Act' and 'the undertakers' are defined in the Markets and Fairs Clauses Act 1847, s 2, p 180, *below*.

135 1887 Act, s 9; 1891 Act, s 1; 1926 Act, s 2.

136 See, respectively, pp 202, 204, *below*.

137 That is, in circumstances where the Minister is of the opinion that enforcement of the requirements would be inexpedient: 1926 Act, s 2.

cattle as are required under the above provisions[138]. Failure to comply with this requirement will render the auctioneer, or his employee, liable to a fine[139] on summary conviction.

An auctioneer is also prohibited (unless exempted as above) from offering for sale in any market, fair or mart in or near which a weighing machine is provided in compliance with the requirements of the 1887 and 1891 Acts[140] any cattle, ie bulls, cows, oxen, or heifers[141], which are fit for immediate slaughter ('fat cattle') unless they have been weighed on the weighing machine and their weight is then effectively communicated to intending purchasers at the time of the offer for sale[142]. Failure to comply will render the auctioneer, on summary conviction, to a fine for each head of cattle offered for sale[143]. The Ministry may, however, declare by order that these provisions shall not apply to any market, fair or mart[144].

(2) Under the Food Act 1984

The Markets and Fairs (Weighing of Cattle) Acts 1887 and 1891[145] do not apply to a market authority within the meaning of the Food Act 1984[146]. Such authority, in whose market cattle, sheep and swine are sold, must (unless the Minister[147] declares by order that in the circumstances it is unnecessary) provide one or more weighing machines adapted for weighing those animals, and must appoint officers to attend to the weighing[148]. The market authority may, in return for weighing, demand such charges as it may from time to time determine[149].

The provisions as to notice of the weight of fat cattle to be given by auctioneers under the Markets and Fairs (Weighing of Cattle) Act 1926, s 1[150] are not excluded with respect to markets under the 1984 Act; and a weighing machine provided under s 57(2) of the 1984 Act is sufficient machine for the purpose of requiring the auctioneer to comply with the provisions of the 1926 Act, s 1[151].

F Diseases and welfare of animals

By the Animal Health Act 1981[152], the Minister of Agriculture, Fisheries and Food[153] has extensive powers of control over the holding of markets and fairs for the purpose of

---

138 1891 Act, s 4(1). Where the cattle sale yard in a market was let exclusively by the market authority to the auctioneers, the provision of weighing facilities by the authority in the market place, although outside the sale yard, was held to exempt the auctioneers from the necessity of providing weighing facilities in the sale yard: *Knott v Stride* (1913) 11 LGR 534.
139 See 1891 Act, s 4(3), p 203, *below*.
140 See pp 119, 120, *above*.
141 Compare definition in 1887 Act, s 3.
142 1926 Act, s 1(1), (3).
143 *Ibid*, s 1(2), p 204, *below*.
144 1926 Act, s 1(4).
145 *Above* pp 119, 120.
146 See 1984 Act, s 61, p 251 *below*.
147 Defined in the 1984 Act, s 132(1).
148 *Ibid*, s 57(2).
149 1984 Act, s 53(2).
150 *Above*, and p 204, *below*.
151 1984 Act, s 57(2).
152 See p 214, *below*.
153 Or, as appropriate, in Scotland or Wales, the Secretary of State: see the Animal Health Act 1981, s 86.

preventing or checking pleuro-pneumonia, foot-and-mouth disease and other diseases[154] of animals[155], and diseases of poultry[156].

The Minister may make such orders[157] as he thinks fit:

1 for prohibiting or regulating the holding of markets or fairs and sales of animals or poultry[158];
2 for prohibiting or regulating the exposure of diseased or suspected animals or poultry in markets or fairs, and the placing of them in lairs or other places adjacent to or connected with markets or fairs or where animals are commonly placed before exposure for sale[159];
3 for dealing with animals found to be affected with pleuro-pneumonia or foot-and-mouth disease whilst exposed for sale in a market or fair, or in transit[160];
4 for prescribing and regulating the cleansing and disinfection of places used for the holding of markets and fairs, or for lairage[161];
5 generally, for preventing the spread of disease[162].

The Minister may also make orders for the purpose of protecting animals and poultry from unnecessary suffering[163].

The Welfare of Animals at Markets Order 1990[164] provides for the protection and welfare of animals[165] kept in a market[166], or while being exposed for sale[167] in a market, or while awaiting removal after being exposed for sale in a market, or which are being kept temporarily in a market (without being exposed for sale) pending completion of their inland transit in Great Britain[168]. In a market it is an offence[169] to expose for sale an unfit[170]

---

154 For meaning of 'disease', see *ibid*, s 88.

155 'Animals' means cattle, sheep and goats and all other ruminating animals and swine; but the Minister may extend the definition to comprise any kind of mammal except man and any kind of four-footed beast which is not a mammal: 1981 Act, s 87(1) and (2). The definition may be further extended by order to comprise for any purpose except disease, fish, reptiles, crustaceans or other cold-blooded creatures of any species: *ibid*, s 87(3).

156 'Poultry' means birds of the following species: (a) domestic fowls, turkeys, ducks, guinea fowls and pigeons; and (b) pheasants and partridges; but the Minister may by order extend the definition to include any other species of bird or restrict the definition to exclude any of the species in para (b): 1981 Act, s 87(4).

157 Such orders as affect the holding of markets and fairs have been made partly under ss 1, 7, 8, 25, 26, 27 and 37 of the 1981 Act or partly have effect thereunder by virtue of the Interpretation Act 1978, s 17(2)(b). For a list of current orders see pp 225–231, *below*.

158 1981 Act, ss 8(1)(e), 87(4).

159 *Ibid*, ss 25(a), 87(4). For 'expose for sale' see, for example, *Crane v Lawrence* (1890) 25 QBD 152; *Keating v Horwood* (1926) 135 LT 29; *Newman v Lipman* [1951] 1 KB 333.

160 1981 Act, s 26. For 'expose for sale' see footnote 159, *above*.

161 1981 Act, s 7(1)(a).

162 *Ibid*, ss 1, 87(4).

163 1981 Act, s 37(1).

164 SI 1990/2628 (in force on 1 March 1991).

165 'Animals' means cattle, sheep, goats and all other ruminating animals, pigs, rabbits and poultry: 1990 Order, arts 2(a) and 3(1). The definition of 'poultry' in the 1981 Act, s 87(4) is extended so as to comprise quails: 1990 Order, arts 2(b) and 3(1).

166 'Market' means a market place or sale-yard or any other premises or place to which animals are brought from other places and exposed for sale and includes any lairage adjoining a market and used in connection with it and any place adjoining a market used as a parking area by visitors to the market for parking vehicles: 1990 Order, art 3(1).

167 For 'expose for sale' see footnote 159 *above*.

168 For scope of application, see 1990 Order, art 4.

169 For offences, see 1990 Order, art 20.

170 'Unfit' includes infirm, diseased, ill, injured and fatigued: 1990 Order, art 3(1). Proof of knowledge of unfitness is not required: *Davidson v Strong* (1997) Times, 20 March.

animal or an animal likely to give birth[171] or to cause or permit any injury or unnecessary suffering to an animal[172]. It is also an offence to handle or tie animals in a market in a particular way[173], to use excessive force to control animals[174] or knowingly to obstruct or wantonly or unreasonably to annoy an animal[175].

It is the duty of a market authority[176] to ensure that:

(a) in the case of certain specified animals, covered accommodation is provided for such animals[177];

(b) all passageways and sale rings in the market and pens in which animals are kept are constructed and maintained in such manner as not to cause injury or unnecessary suffering to animals, and that certain other facilities are provided for the welfare of animals[178];

(c) ramps are provided for the loading and unloading of certain specified animals in and out of vehicles[179].

It is the duty of the market operator[180] (or, in the case of (b) below, such other person for the time being in charge of an animal) to ensure that:

(a) no animal is kept in a pen, cage or hutch which is unsuitable for the size and species of that animal, and that no injury or unecessary suffering is otherwise caused through the penning and caging of animals[181];

(b) adequate lighting is available to enable animals in the market to be inspected and to be fed and watered, and that an adequate supply of suitable bedding is kept for certain specified animals[182];

(c) certain specified animals are kept in the covered accommodation to be provided by the market authority (see above)[183];

(d) where a calf[184] is sold, certain information is supplied to a purchaser, and a record of such is kept[184];

(e) suitable pens are available to enable the separation of unfit from other animals, with pens so used being clearly marked as such[185]. A market operator must render such reasonable assistance to an inspector[186] in relation to the moving and detention of an unfit animal, pending examination by a veterinary inspector, as the inspector may reasonably require and must give to the inspector such

---

171 1990 Order, art 5.
172 *Ibid*, art 6.
173 1990 Order, art 7.
174 *Ibid*, art 8.
175 1990 Order, art 9.
176 'Market authority' means the local authority or other person responsible for the upkeep of a market or for the provision of fixed penalties there: 1990 Order, art 3(1).
177 *Ibid*, art 13(1).
178 1990 Order, art 15.
179 *Ibid*, art 19.
180 'Market operator' means the person for the time being responsible for managing the reception or the sale of animals in a market: 1990 Order, art 3(1).
181 *Ibid*, art 10.
182 1990 Order, art 12.
183 *Ibid*, art 13(2).
184 1990 Order, art 14(5) and (6). In this article, 'calf' means a bovine animal under 12 weeks of age: *ibid*, art 14(8)(a).
185 1990 Order, art 16.
186 'Inspector' means a person appointed to be an inspector for the purposes of the 1981 Act by the Minister or by a local authority and, when used in relation to a person appointed by the Minister, includes a veterinary inspector: 1990 Order, art 3(1).

information as he possesses as to the ownership of such animal[187].

Additionally it is the duty of the owner (or his duly authorised agent) or the person in charge of an animal to ensure that the animal is adequately fed and watered whilst kept in the market[188], and to remove any calf from the market within four hours of the time of the last sale by auction of a calf[189].

There are restrictions on the sale of calves[190]. An inspector may mark or cause to be marked any animal for identification purposes[191].

The Welfare of Horses at Markets (and Other Places of Sale) Order 1990[192] makes similar provision for the protection and welfare of horses and foals.

Orders under the Act are made by statutory instrument[193], and severe penalties are imposed for disobedience[194].

G Inspection and seizure of fish

By the Sea Fish (Conservation) Act 1967, any officer of a market authority acting within the limits of any market which that authority has power to regulate, may at all reasonable times board any fishing boat or enter any premises used for carrying on any business in connection with the treatment, storage or sale of sea fish. He may search for and examine any sea fish in any place, whether on board a fishing boat or elsewhere, and whether in a receptacle or not, and may seize any sea fish which have been landed, sold[195] or exposed or offered for sale[196] by any person, or which any person has in his possession[197] in contravention of an order restricting fish sizes[198]. An officer will not be liable in any civil or criminal proceedings following the purported exercise of these powers if the court is satisfied that he acted in good faith and there were reasonable grounds for so acting[199].

Any officer of a market authority[200], acting within the area of the jurisdiction of that authority, may seize any salmon, trout or freshwater fish bought, sold or exposed for sale by, or in the possession of for the sale by, any person in contravention of the

187 *Ibid*, art 17.
188 1990 Order, art 11.
189 *Ibid*, art 14(7).
190 1990 Order, art 14.
191 *Ibid*, art 18.
192 SI 1990/2627 (in force on 1 March 1991).
193 1981 Act, s 91(5).
194 1981 Act, ss 72, 73, 75.
195 To constitute a sale, the property in the goods must pass: Sale of Goods Act 1979, s 2(4), (5). An agreement for sale will not, therefore, constitute a sale. See, for example, *Mischeff v Springett* [1942] 2 KB 331 and *Watson v Coupland* [1945] 1 All ER 217.
196 On what constitutes an offer for sale see, for example, *British Car Auctions Ltd v Wright* [1972] 3 All ER 462. On what constitutes exposure for sale see, for example, *Keating v Horwood* (1926) 135 LT 29 and *Newman v Lipman* [1951] 1 KB 333.
197 'Possession' probably should be construed in its popular sense: see, for example, *Towers & Co Ltd v Gray* [1961] 2 QB 351 and *Warner v Metropolitan Police Comr* [1968] 2 All ER 356.
198 Sea Fish (Conservation) Act 1967, s 16(1). Orders are made under *ibid*, s 1 (as substituted in the Fisheries Act 1981, s 19(1)) and are: the Sea-Fishing Industry (Crabs and Lobsters) Order 1981, SI 1981/551; the Immature Sea-Fish Order 1980, SI 1980/1808; the Immature Bass Order 1981, SI 1981/535, as amended by SI 1983/552; the Sea Fish (Conservation) (Revocation) Order 1983, SI 1983/255 and the Immature Scallops (Wales) Order 1983, SI 1983/1384.
199 Sea Fish (Conservation) Act 1967, s 16(3) (as inserted by the Fisheries Act 1981, s 25(5)).
200 Defined as including any corporation, local authority, body of trustees or other persons having power to maintain or regulate any market: Salmon and Freshwater Fisheries Act 1975, s 41(1).

Salmon and Freshwater Fisheries Act 1975[201].

Any officer of a market authority[200], acting within the area of the jurisdiction of that authority, may open any package consigned or sent by any common or other carrier, or brought to any place to be so consigned or sent, and suspected to contain salmon or trout[202]. If any such package is found to contain salmon or trout, and is not conspicuously marked 'salmon' or 'trout' (as the case may be) on the outside as required[203], the officer may detain the package and its contents until proof is forthcoming that the fish is not being dealt with contrary to law. He may also detain in like manner and conditions any salmon or trout not packaged in a package[204].

If any salmon or trout so detained becomes unfit for human food before proof is given that it is not being dealt with contrary to law, the officer may destroy it or cause it to be destroyed[205].

H Food safety

It is an indictable offence at common law knowingly to bring into a market food for human consumption which is not fit for that purpose[206], or to sell or expose for sale such food in the market[207].

In markets or fairs to which the Markets and Fairs Clauses Act 1847 applies[208], it is also an offence, punishable on summary conviction[209], to sell or expose for sale any unwholesome meat or provisions[210]. An inspector of provisions appointed by the undertakers[211] may seize such unwholesome meat or provisions which may be destroyed, or otherwise disposed of, on the order of a justice if found to be unfit for human consumption[212]. There are similar powers in relation to cattle or carcases of cattle deposited in a slaughter-house and found on inspection to be unfit for human consumption[213].

Under the Food Safety Act 1990, it is an offence to sell or offer or expose or advertise for sale, or possess for the purpose of such sale, any food for human consumption which

---

201 *Ibid*, ss 37, 41(1) and Sch 4, para 7. By the Salmon and Freshwater Fisheries Act 1975, s 22(1), any person who buys, sells, exposes for sale or has in his possession for sale any salmon between 31 August and the following 1 February, or any trout (other than rainbow trout) between 31 August and the following 1 March is guilty of an offence. Actual physical possession is not necessary: *M'Attee v Hogg* (1903) 5 F 67, Ct of Sess.

202 Salmon and Freshwater Fisheries Act 1975, s 24(2).

203 That is, as required by *ibid*, s 24(1).

204 Salmon and Freshwater Fisheries Act 1975, s 24(3). A person who contravenes the above provisions, or refuses to allow an officer to exercise his powers, or obstructs him, is guilty of an offence: *ibid*, s 24(6).

205 Salmon and Freshwater Fisheries Act 1975, s 24(5).

206 *R v Jarvis* (1862) 3 F & F 108; *R v Crawley* (1862) 3 F & F 109; *Shillito v Thompson* (1875) 1 QBD 12.

207 *R v Stevenson* (1862) 3 F & F 106. From the earliest times butchers and victuallers committing such an offence were punishable by statute: see Judicium Pillorie, 51 Hen III, Stat 6 (Ruff), repealed by 7 & 8 Vict, c 24, s 2.

208 See p 179, *below*.

209 Maximum penalty level 1 on the standard scale.

210 Markets and Fairs Clauses Act 1847, s 15.

211 As defined in *ibid*, s 2.

212 'Unfit for the food of man'. See Markets and Fairs Clauses Act 1847, ss 15, 20.

213 *Ibid*, s 20. Anyone obstructing or hindering an inspector is liable on summary conviction to a maximum penalty of level 1 on the standard scale. See 1847 Act, s 20.

fails to comply with food safety regulations[214]. Contravention of regulations is an offence liable on summary conviction to a fine not exceeding £5,000 or on conviction on indictment to a fine and/or imprisonment for a term not exceeding two years. If a breach of the regulations is proved and the court believes that a serious health risk has occurred or may occur, the court must issue a prohibition order under s 11 of the 1990 Act prohibiting the use of processes, treatments, equipment and/or the premises. Breach of a prohibition order is an offence liable on summary conviction to a maximum fine of £20,000 and/or imprisonment for a term not exceeding six months or on conviction on indictment to an unlimited fine and/or imprisonment for a term not exceeding two years, or both. The court may also prohibit the food business proprietor or manager from participating in the management of any food business.

Section 10 of the Food Safety Act 1990 provides that an inspector who has reasonable grounds for believing the regulations are being contravened may issue an improvement notice requiring remedial action to be taken. An appeal lies to the magistrates' court but an offence is committed if the notice is then breached. Breach of an improvement notice is an offence liable on summary conviction to a fine not exceeding £5,000 or to imprisonment for a term not exceeding six months, or both, or on conviction on indictment to an unlimited fine or to imprisonment for a term not exceeding two years, or both.

I Licences for the sale of intoxicating liquors

A holder of a justices' on-licence[215] for premises situated in the immediate neighbourhood[216] of a public market[217] may apply to justices of the peace having jurisdiction for the purpose[218] for a general order of exemption[219]. The effect of the order is to add to the permitted hours[220] in the premises such hours as may be specified[221]. The order may have general application or may apply to certain specified days only[221]; but an order must not be made unless the justices are satisfied, after hearing evidence, that it is desirable to do so for the accommodation of any considerable number of persons attending the market[222].

---

214 1990 Act, s 8. The current regulations are the Food Safety (General Food Hygiene) Regulations 1995 (SI 1995/1763) and the Food Safety (Temperature Control) Regulations 1995 (SI 1995/2200).

215 For the meaning of 'justices' on-licence' see Licensing Act 1964, s 1(2).

216 See *R v Dewisland and Haverfordwest Licensing Justices* (1961) Times, 28 January.

217 In *R v Bungay Justices, ex p Long* (1959) 123 JP 315, it was held that premises in the immediate neighbourhood of a discontinued public market, where farmers met on former market days to trade amongst themselves and with commercial travellers, did not fall within this provision.

218 The justices having power to grant, revoke or vary a general order of exemption are two justices acting for the petty sessions area in which the premises are situated sitting in open court in a petty sessional court house: Licensing Act 1964, s 75(1); Magistrates' Courts Act 1980, s 121. In London, if the premises are in the City of London, instead of the justices, the powers are exercisable by the Commissioners of Police for the City acting with the approval of the Lord Mayor and, if the premises are in the metropolitan police district, by the Commissioner of Police for the Metropolis acting with the approval of the Secretary of State: Licensing Act 1964, s 74(6).

219 *Ibid*, s 74(1).

220 That is, the permitted hours under Licensing Act 1964, s 60, as amended by the Licensing (Sunday Hours) Act 1995, s 1, Sch 1, para 3, Sch 2.

221 *Ibid*, s 74(1).

222 Licensing Act 1964, s 74(2).

The justices may revoke or vary a general order of exemption[223], and until such revocation or variation, the order remains in force notwithstanding a change in the licence-holder. Even if an order is revoked or varied, a licence-holder will not be guilty of an offence in respect of a breach of permitted hours unless it is proved that he had notice of the revocation or variation[224].

The licence holder must keep posted in some conspicuous place outside his premises a notice stating the effect of the order and, if granted for certain days only, the days on which it applies[225]. Failure to do so is an offence[226].

The holder of a general order of exemption must, on being ordered by a justice of the peace or a constable, produce it for examination within a reasonable time, and failure to do so is an offence[227].

Justices may also make a special order of exemption which has the effect of adding specified hours to the permitted hours on such special occasion or occasions as may be specified[228]. The question as to what constitutes a special occasion is one of fact to be determined by the justices[229]; but a regularly occurring market or fair will not normally be a special occasion[230].

Justices may also, on the application of the holder of a justices' on-licence, grant an occasional licence authorising the sale by him of intoxicating liquor at some place other than the premises in respect of which his on-licence was granted, such as at a fair[231].

J Town and country planning

(1) The need for planning permission

Market activities clearly may have serious implications in terms of, for example, disturbance to local residents and traffic control. But it is also clear that such activities may be subject to control as being a material change of use of land and thus development requiring planning permission under the Town and Country Planning Act 1990[232]. Two factors should be considered in relation to this basic proposition.

(a) Existing market rights. A market owner seeking to revive an ancient market, the rights in respect of which have not been exercised for many years, may find himself in conflict with the local planning authority. The question arising in these circumstances is whether the market activity is subject to control under the planning legislation.

---

223 *Ibid*, s 74(3).
224 Licensing Act 1964, s 74(3).
225 *Ibid*, s 89(1).
226 Licensing Act 1964, s 89(2). Anyone contravening this section is liable on summary conviction to a maximum fine of level 1 on the standard scale.
227 Licensing Act 1964, s 185. Maximum fine level 1 on the standard scale.
228 Licensing Act 1964, s 74(4).
229 See *Devine v Keeling* (1886) 50 JP 551.
230 *R v Inglis, ex p Cole-Hamilton* (1921) 85 JP 114; *R v Butt, ex p Brooke* (1922) 38 TLR 537.
231 For procedures, see Licensing Act 1964, s 180, as amended by the Local Government (Wales) Act 1994, s 66(6), Sch 16, para 22(5), as from a date to be appointed.
232 Section 57. For Ministerial planning decisions on the use of land for a market, see [1973] JPL 617, [1975] JPL 371 and [1976] JPL 113. See also *Tidswell v Secretary of State for the Environment and Thurrock Borough Council* [1977] JPL 104 (the appeal from the last cited Ministerial decision); *Thanet District Council v Ninedrive Ltd* (1978) 76 LGR 320; and *Scott Markets Ltd v Waltham Forest London Borough Council* (1979) 77 LGR 565. If the local authority is also a market owner, the question of disturbance to established market rights may also, of course, arise: see Chapter 6, *above*.

Section 335 of the 1990 Act declares 'for the avoidance of doubt' that the provisions of the Act and any restrictions or powers in relation to land imposed or conferred by it, apply and may be exercised notwithstanding any enactment authorising or regulating any development in force at the time of the Town and Country Planning Act 1947. 'Enactment' is defined[233] as including 'an enactment in any local or private Act of Parliament, and an order, rule, regulation, byelaw or scheme made under an Act of Parliament'. Thus if the charter or letters patent[234] conferring market rights is expressed as having been granted by the Crown 'with Parliament's assent'[235], or words to that effect, it is clear that such grant would be in the nature of an 'enactment' for the purposes of ss 335 and 336 of the 1990 Act, and so subject to planning control. It was until recently, however, less certain as to whether the grantee of market rights given by the Crown in exercise of its prerogative was subject to the controls imposed by the 1990 Act. Whilst the Crown itself is not bound by the provisions of the 1990 Act in respect of development of its own land[236], this immunity will not extend to licensees or tenants of the Crown[237], nor, it has been decided[238], to those in whom market rights are vested by virtue of a Crown grant; and this is so notwithstanding the undoubted duties towards members of the public which the law imposes on a market owner[239].

ILLUSTRATION

On 29 June 1638, Charles I, by Deed, granted to Anthony Bourchier, his heirs and assigns, the right to 'hold forever a market to be held on Tuesday in every week at the town of Moreton Henmarsh'. The market was held in the High Street until 1923 and from that date until 1956 it continued as a cattle market in Station Road. No market at all was held between 1956 and 1976 when the appellant acquired the market franchise and sought to revive a general retail market on its former site in High Street. Conceding that such revival constituted a material change of use for the purposes of section 22 of the Town and Country Planning Act 1971[240], the appellant contended that it was entitled to the Crown's exemption from planning control since in exercising rights granted under the royal prerogative it was acting on the Crown's behalf and exercising its prerogative power. Planning permission was sought, but without prejudice to the argument that no permission was required. Permission was granted subject to conditions limiting the area within which the market might be held and the local planning authority served enforcement notices requiring compliance with those conditions. The Secretary of State dismissed the appellant's appeal and on appeal to the High Court[241] Macpherson J *held*, that in exercising rights granted by the Crown the owners were not thereby exercising the Crown's prerogative power and that accordingly planning control applied. *Held* (by CA) in dismissing the appeal, that a market franchise granted by the royal prerogative gave rise to a private right for the exclusive

---

233 In the 1990 Act, s 336.
234 For the difference between charters and letters patent see p 15, *above*.
235 As was the case in *Great Eastern Rly Co v Goldsmid* (1884) 9 App Cas 927, where a charter of Edward III was expressed to have been granted by the King 'with the assent of the prelates, earls, barons and all the commons of our realm assembled in our present Parliament convoked at Westminster'. Selborne LC said of this document, at *ibid* p 934 (and again at 936), that it was '. . . strictly in the nature of a private grant, or at all events, a local and personal Act of Parliament, and ought to be construed and to receive effect according to its nature'.
236 1990 Act, s 293.
237 See *Minister of Agriculture Fisheries and Food v Jenkins* [1963] 2 QB 317.
238 In *Spook Erection Ltd v Secretary of State for the Environment* (1988) 86 LGR 736.
239 See pp 27 *et seq*, *above*.
240 Now the 1990 Act, s 55.
241 (5 June 1987, unreported).

enjoyment of the owner but that the exercise of such right was not an exercise of the prerogative itself and, since the owner was in no sense acting on the Crown's behalf, there was no exemption from planning control: *Spook Erection Ltd v Secretary of State for the Environment*[242].

Thus, the Crown's immunity from planning control will not extend to those to whom exclusive rights are given by the Crown in the exercise of its prerogative.

Whilst planning permission is required for the siting of a franchise market in a particular place where the market had not been held since before 1 July 1948[243], the refusal of permission to site a market in that place, or the imposition of restrictions on the permission unacceptable to the market owner, will not affect the market owner's absolute right to hold the market elsewhere within the market area defined by the grant[244], albeit subject again to the requirement to obtain planning permission[245] and the consent of the landowner.

The grant of planning permission will not, in itself, confer on the owner of land a market right nor a universal 'right' destroying any legal obstacles having nothing to do with the planning laws; and nor will it amount to a statutory authority giving immunity from suit.

ILLUSTRATION

The plaintiff Council established in 1991 a statutory Saturday market in the centre of Holywell under s 50 of the Food Act 1984. In July 1994 the defendants re-opened a Saturday market within three miles of the Council's new market pursuant to planning permissions granted by the Council in 1981 and 1983. In granting the Council an interlocutory injunction to prevent the defendants from continuing to operate their Saturday market within the common law distance Jacob J *held* that planning permission does no more than remove the impediment on use or development of land imposed by the planning laws and conferred no universal 'right' on the defendants: *Delyn Borough Council v Solitaire (Liverpool) Ltd*[246].

Interestingly, the judge also held that the defendants did have an arguable defence on the basis that modern public law might, in some circumstances, interfere with the exercise of a market right, for example, where lack of good faith on the part of the local authority could be demonstrated, or where a trader had established a long standing and thriving market which, especially when coupled with a grant of planning permission, gives rise to a 'legitimate' or 'reasonable' expectation that the local authority will not obstruct. The case did not proceed to a full hearing.

(b) Permitted development. Under Part 4, Class B of the Town and Country Planning (General Permitted Development) Order 1995[247], land[248] may be used for the purpose of

---

242 (1988) 86 LGR 736.

243 The date of the coming into force of the Town and Country Planning Act 1947. In the case of a market held on a particular site at that date, subsequently not held for a period but then sought to be revived on the same site, the question of whether previous existing use rights have been lost through abandonment may have to be considered.

244 Compare the position with regard to the impact on market rights of the operation of the Highways Act 1980, s 31: see *Gloucestershire County Council v Farrow* [1984] 1 WLR 262; affirmed [1985] 1 WLR 741 and pp 38, 39, *above*.

245 *Spook Erection Ltd v Secretary of State for the Environment*, per Macpherson J at first instance (5 June 1987, unreported).

246 (1995) 93 LGR 614.

247 SI 1995/413.

248 That is, open land.

the holding of markets for not more than 14 days in total (not necessarily consecutive) in any calendar year without the necessity of obtaining planning permission[249].

(2) Control under the 1990 Act

(a) By direction. Article 4 of the Town and Country Planning General Development Order 1988 enables a local planning authority to make a direction which, in effect, negatives the general permission conferred by Part 4, Class B of the General Permitted Development Order 1995[250]. A local planning authority may make such direction without the approval of the Secretary of State if it considers that the development would be prejudicial to the proper planning of its area or constitute a threat to the amenities of the area[251]. A direction so made expires at the end of six months unless approved beforehand by the Secretary of State, whose approval is also required to any second or subsequent direction relating to the same development or to development of the same class in the same area[252].

(b) By enforcement action. Where it appears to a local planning authority that a market is being conducted in breach of planning control, the authority may issue an enforcement notice under the 1990 Act, s 172, requiring the breach to be remedied. Copies of the notice must be served on the owner and on the occupier of the land in question, and on any other person having an interest in the land, which interest is, in the opinion of the local planning authority, materially affected by the notice[253].

Whether a copy of the notice ought to be served on each individual stall holder depends on the nature of the stall holder's interest. If stall holders are in occupation of pitches neither as tenants[254] nor as licencees other than on a casual or transient basis, and if it cannot be argued that they enjoy at least an equitable interest in the land, then copies of the enforcement notice need not be served on them[255].

---

249 Each day is a grant of planning permission: *South Buckinghamshire District Council v Secretary of State for the Environment* [1989] JPL 351, CA: *Strandmill v Secretary of State for the Environment and South Buckinghamshire District Council* [1988] JPL 491. An article 4 notice may, therefore, be served after any day's use. And where it is apparent from the outset that the character of the user is permanent rather than temporary, the local planning authority may take enforcement action even although the 14 day period permitted by the GDO has not expired: *Tidswell v Secretary of State for the Environment and Thurrock Borough Council* [1977] JPL 104 (following *Miller-Mead v Minister of Housing and Local Government* [1963] 2 QB 196). In *Tidswell*, a market advertised as 'open every Sunday' had been held for nine successive Sundays only, but the High Court dismissed the appeal against the Minister's decision to uphold the enforcement notice, Slynn J drawing a distinction (at 105) between a permanent user, which was not covered by the GDO, and a temporary casual user, which was.

250 *Above.*

251 GDO 1988, article 5(4). Guidance issued by the Secretary of State states that clear justification is required for withdrawal of permitted development rights including a full assessment of the area and evidence of local support for the decision.

252 *Ibid*, article 5(5), (6). For a case concerning a market where an article 4 direction was employed, see *Thanet District Council v Ninedrive Ltd* (1978) 76 LGR 320; and see *South Buckinghamshire District Council v Secretary of State for the Environment* [1989] JPL 351, CA where it was held that every time the temporary use was implemented a material change of use occurred and a grant of planning permission was necessary.

253 1990 Act, s 172(6).

254 Such relationship with the landowner or market operator will not exist if there is a genuine concourse both of buyers and sellers: see p 1, *above*.

255 *Munnich v Godstone RDC* [1966] 1 All ER 930, 934; *Stevens v Bromley London Borough Council* [1972] 1 All ER 712, 719; and see also the Ministerial planning decision in *Tidswell*, *above* [1976] JPL 113. Note, however, the advice contained in PPG 18 (Guidance on

Enforcement procedure under the 1990 Act is, however, slow and cumbersome, and singularly ill equipped to control market activities. This situation is, to a certain extent, ameliorated by the power given to local planning authorities by s 183 of the 1990 Act to serve a stop notice which has the effect of prohibiting the carrying on of the activity alleged by the enforcement notice to constitute a breach of planning control[256]. A stop notice may not, however, be utilised so as to remove the permitted development rights to hold a market on 14 days in each calendar year. It may not be necessary for a local authority, in coming to a decision to issue a stop notice in a market case, to carry out a 'cost benefit analysis' of the type implicit in paragraph 19 of Annex 3 to DoE Circular 21. But before issuing a stop notice a local authority ought to satisfy itself that there is good reason to require the immediate discontinuance of the offending market, for example, to safeguard the amenities of the area, or public safety, or to abate a nuisance, or to prevent serious damage to the environment[257].

(c) By injunction. Proceedings for an injunction under the 1990 Act, s 187B cannot remove permitted development rights and may be commenced only when an offence has occurred or is about to occur. Other remedial action (the issue of an enforcement or a stop notice) can be taken concurrently and it is not a condition of the commencement of proceedings that enforcement action be started first.

An injunction is an equitable remedy and the court has a discretion whether or not to grant it. The local authority applicant has to satisfy the court that an injunction is 'necessary or expedient' and demonstrate why other available remedies would not be effective. Evidence must be submitted showing that the market is causing damage and inconvenience justifying its cessation.

(d) Advertisements. The Town and Country Planning (Control of Advertisements) Regulations 1992[258] may be utilised to render advertisements for markets less visually offensive. Class 3B of Schedule 3 to the Regulations permits the advertising of a market on land on which the market is to take place. Only one advertisement may be displayed at any one time, and where more than one is displayed, the first is taken as the one permitted. There are restrictions on the size, appearance and positioning of the advertisement.

An advertisement must not be displayed earlier than 28 days before the sale starts and must be removed within 14 days after it ends. This allows an advertisement to be displayed for a maximum period of 20 weeks (14 weeks being the maximum duration of the sale, plus four weeks before the sale and two weeks following the sale).

Express consent is required to exceed any of the limitations imposed by the Regulations. A common breach is exceeding the maximum permitted size (1.2 sq m in area) of advertisement. Breach is an offence liable on summary conviction to a fine not exceeding £1,000.

Enforcing Planning Control Generally) concerning unauthorised development by small businesses and self-employed persons.

256 But note the effect of *Scott Markets Ltd v Waltham Forest London Borough Council* (1979) 77 LGR 565 (12 month limitation period on the service of a stop notice under the 1990 Act, s 183(3), begins to run from the commencement of the use, not from the breach of planning control). Note, also, the entitlement, in certain circumstances, to compensation for loss due to a stop notice: *ibid*, s 186.

257 *R v Elmbridge Borough Council, ex p Wendy Fair Markets Ltd* [1994] EGCS 159, [1995] JPL 928, CA.

258 SI 1992/666.

K Environmental protection

(1) Statutory nuisance

Where a local authority believes that disturbance caused by a market constitutes a statutory nuisance within the meaning of the Environmental Protection Act 1990, s 79, it may take remedial action by issuing an abatement notice.

The definition of 'statutory nuisance' in s 79 includes any premises (including land) the condition of which is prejudicial to health or a nuisance, and any noise emitted from premises which is prejudicial to health or a nuisance. 'Nuisance' must be an enduring event and have substantial effect on enjoyment of the land. 'Noise' includes vibration; 'prejudicial to health' means injurious or likely to cause injury to health.

When a local authority believes a statutory nuisance exists, or is likely to occur, it can serve an abatement notice requiring the abatement of the nuisance within a specified period of time. There is a right of appeal to the magistrates' court but on conviction the offender is liable to a fine not exceeding £20,000 in cases of land used for trade or business.

(2) Litter

Under the Environmental Protection Act 1990, s 87, the leaving of litter in a public open space is an offence, and s 90 gives local authorities power to designate any land within their area as a Litter Control Area if they believe that the presence of litter or refuse renders the land detrimental to the amenities of the locality. The 1990 Act, s 89 imposes a requirement on the occupier of land in a Litter Control Area to ensure that the land is kept clear of litter and refuse. If he fails in this, the local authority may issue a litter abatement notice, breach of which is an offence.

4 OTHER RELATED ACTIVITIES

A Restrictions on Sunday opening of 'large shops'

The Sunday Trading Act 1994, s 1(a) and Sch 1 imposes restrictions on the Sunday opening of large shops. By Schedule 1, paragraph 1 'large shop' means a shop which has a relevant floor area exceeding 280 square feet. 'Relevant floor area', in relation to a shop, means the internal floor area of so much of the shop as consists of or is comprised in a building, but excluding any part of the shop which, throughout the week ending with the Sunday in question, is used neither for the serving of customers in connection with the sale of goods nor for the display of goods. 'Shop' means any premises where there is carried on a trade or business consisting wholly or mainly of the sale of goods.

A large shop may be open on a Sunday only if the occupier gives 14 days' notice to the local authority that he proposes to open, and specifies the Sunday opening hours which must be a continuous period of six hours beginning no earlier than 10 am and ending no later than 6 pm[259]. There are exemptions[260] which are not relevant here.

The question arises as to whether a market hall containing individually occupied stalls or units will be caught by the definition of 'large shop' if the relevant floor area of the building as a whole exceeds 280 square feet, even though the relevant floor area of the individual units is less.

---

259 1994 Act, Sch 1, para 2.
260 *Ibid*, Sch 1, para 3, and Sch 2.

First, 'building' should probably be given its ordinary meaning, ie 'a structure of considerable size and intended to be permanent or at least endure for a considerable time'[261]. Secondly, 'premises' appears to mean a whole property in either one occupation or one ownership according to the context in which it is used[262].

To help answer the question raised above, it may be useful to contrast (1) a shop or unit in a modern retail centre, and (2) an area of floor in a large building licensed by the owner of the building to a retailer selling his own goods. In (1), the individual shop or unit within the centre will be of substantial construction, be completely self-contained with its own washing and lavatory accommodation for staff and customers (albeit there will be common entrances and exits to and from the centre), and the occupier will normally have security of tenure under the Landlord and Tenant Act 1954, Pt II. In (2), the areas of floor will have, at most, a rudimentary system of division designed primarily to demarcate space rather than for security reasons, and most, if not all, facilities (water, light, heat, cleaning services) will be provided by the owner of the building and paid for through the licence fee. The individual occupiers will have no security of tenure perhaps even to the extent of there being a genuine concourse of sellers. In (1) above, it seems clear that it is the floor area of the individual shop or unit in the retail centre which will be 'relevant'; in (2), the floor area of the building as a whole.

The closer the operation is to a market in law, ie a genuine concourse of sellers and buyers, the more it seems likely that it will be the floor area of the building as a whole which will be relevant for the purpose of determining whether the statutory restrictions apply. Inevitably, there will be 'grey' areas but these must await judicial consideration on the facts of each individual case[263].

B Car boot sales

There is no doubt that a car boot sale is a market in law and is subject to the same controls as an 'ordinary' market. There is currently no legislation specifically designed to control car boot sales although there has been discussion in Parliament and an attempt made to introduce a Private Member's Bill with the object of regulating those activities. Since car boot sales may be controlled and regulated under the legislation discussed above, it seems somewhat unnecessary to introduce further controls to deal with a market under another name. Furthermore, a car boot sale can constitute a rival market at common law and so is susceptible to action by a local authority under its general powers[264].

C Pedlars

'Pedlar' is defined comprehensively by statute[265] as any hawker, pedlar, petty chapman, tinker, caster of metals, mender of chairs or other person who, without any horse or other beast bearing or drawing burden, travels and trades on foot and goes from town to town or to other men's houses, carrying to sell or exposing for sale any goods, wares or merchandise immediately to be delivered, or selling or offering for sale his skill in handicraft. A pedlar is, therefore, someone who sells on the move and not from a stall[266]

---

261 *Stevens v Gourley* (1859) 7 CBNS 99 at 112, per Byles J.
262 See, eg, *Cadbury Bros Ltd v Sinclair* [1934] 2 KB 389 at 393.
263 See, in the context of determination of a rival market, *Manchester City Council v Walsh* (1986) 84 LGR 1, *above*, p 79.
264 See *Newcastle-upon-Tyne City Council v Noble* (1991) 89 LGR 618.
265 The Pedlars Act 1871, s 3 and see p 190 *below*.
266 *Watson v Malloy* [1988] 3 All ER 459.

and although, generally, no one may operate as a pedlar without a pedlar's certificate[267], a certificate is not required if goods are sold or offered for sale in a legally constituted market or fair[268]. Thus, although strictly the code regulating sales by pedlars is outside the scope of the law governing sales in markets and fairs, there is probably historical justification for including it in this work and the Pedlars Act 1871 is set out below[269].

---

267 The Pedlars Act 1871, s 4. The maximum penalty is level 1 on the standard scale: *ibid.*

268 *Ibid*, s 23, para 3. A sale in a market held without grant or statutory authority falls outside this exception: *Benjamin v Andrews* (1858) 5 CBNS 299. For other exemptions from the requirement for a certificate, see the 1871 Act, s 23, paras 1 and 2.

269 See pp 190–197 *below*. For the distinction between acting as a pedlar and a street trader, see the cases cited in footnote 52 above.

CHAPTER 10

Accounts, Rates and Taxes

1 RETURNS AND ACCOUNTS

At common law, the owner of a market or fair, as such, is under no obligation to keep accounts or publish returns of his receipts or expenditure in connection with his franchise; and at the present day, apart from the law relating to rates and taxes, no such obligation lies upon private persons who own common law markets or fairs and take tolls under charters or by prescription for their private benefit.

A wharf or other place provided by a local authority under the Animal Health Act 1981[1] for the reception and disposal of imported or other animals is deemed to be a market within the Markets and Fairs Clauses Act 1847[2]; and charges for the use of such places are deemed to be tolls[3]. All such sums received by a local authority must be carried to a separate account and applied in payment of interest and repayment of principal in respect of money borrowed by it under the 1981 Act; and any balance must be applied towards the discharge of the local authority's expenses under that Act[4].

The local authority must make such periodical returns to the appropriate Minister[5], as the Minister may require, of its expenditure and receipts in respect of the wharf or other place[6].

Annual returns of receipts and expenditure are also prescribed by the Markets and Fairs Clauses Act 1847, s 50[7], which is deemed to be incorporated with the Animal Health Act 1981[8].

2 RATES

A Stallage

Payments made for stalls or standing places (stallage) or pens (pennage) in a market, or for making holes in the ground for support (piccage), are profits of the soil and must be taken into account in estimating the rateable value of the market place[9]. A test as to whether the charge is attributable to the use of the soil (as opposed to the right to hold a market) is whether its payment confers upon the payer some right, privilege or advantage of user of the soil over and above that made available to every member of the

---

1 Section 54(1); see p 218, *below*.
2 1981 Act, s 54(3).
3 *Ibid*, s 54(4).
4 1981 Act, s 54(5).
5 That is, in relation to England, the Minister of Agriculture, Fisheries and Food, and in relation to Scotland or Wales, the Secretary of State: 1981 Act, s 86(1)(b).
6 1981 Act, s 54(6).
7 Penalty for omitting to prepare a return, level 2 on the standard scale.
8 See 1981 Act, s 54(2).
9 *Roberts v Overseers of Aylesbury* (1853) 1 E & B 423; and see *Worcester Corpn v St Clements Overseers* (1858) 22 JP Jo 319; *R v Derby Justices* (1856) 28 LTOS 89; *R v Barnard Castle Inhabitants* (1863) 27 JP 534; and as to deductions see *Brecon Markets Co v St Mary's, Brecon* (1877) 36 LT 109.

public attending the market with goods to sell[10]. Payments satisfying such test enhance the value of the occupation.

Payments need not necessarily be made in respect of each separate stall, but may be in respect of a separate portion of the market place specifically allotted for the sale of certain types of goods[11]. It is enough if payment is made for some standing room in the market, as distinct from the mere entrance into it, even although the exclusive occupation of the soil is of short duration[12], or the market owner is liable to alter the location of the portion of soil so occupied from time to time[13].

ILLUSTRATION

In Deptford Foreign Cattle Market, payments were taken on the landing of cattle there for 'wharfage, lairage, market dues and charges'. Consignees had a right to keep cattle in the market for ten days but had no right to have them kept in any particular pens but only in such pens as the clerk of the market authority might direct, and the clerk was entitled to have the cattle shifted from one pen to another. *Held* that the payments were for the use and occupation of the soil, and therefore rateable: *Mayor of London v Assessment Committee of Greenwich Union*[14].

B Tolls

Franchise tolls, whether granted by charter or payable under statute, are incorporeal hereditaments and are not incident to the occupation of the soil of the market place[15]. They are usually payable in respect of goods sold in the market place, and are quite different in their nature from the compensation paid to the owner of the soil, or to his lessee, for the use of the soil[16]. The payment of such tolls is the fruit of the incorporeal hereditament and not the profit of the soil of the market place; and payment constitutes a condition of the public right to resort to the market place and does not confer on the payer any position or privilege[17]. As such, tolls should not be taken into account in estimating the rateable value of the market place; and this is the case whether tolls are payable upon the entry of goods into the market or upon the sale of goods in the market place; and whether they are granted by charter or payable by statute[18].

It matters not that the market place is laid out in such a way that cattle may be exposed for sale only in pens; for if such pens, or other amenities such as roofing, drainage, clean flooring and lighting are common to all, then no right or advantage in the soil may be implied so as to give rise to an assessment to rates[19].

---

10 *Bedford (Duke) v Overseers of St Pauls, Covent Garden* (1881) 51 LJMC 41 at 45, per Bowen J; *Oswestry Corpn v Hudd (Valuation Officer)* [1966] 1 WLR 363 at 380, per Russell LJ.
11 *Bedford (Duke) v Overseers of St Pauls, Covent Gardent* (1881) 51 LJMC 41.
12 *R v Barnard Castle Inhabitants* (1863) 27 JP 534.
13 *London Corpn v Assessment Committee of Greenwich Union* (1883) 48 LT 437.
14 (1883) 48 LT 437.
15 *R v Casswell* (1872) LR 7 QB 328; *R v Bell* (1816) 5 M & S 221; *Horner v Stepney Assessment Committee* (1908) 24 TLR 500; *Oswestry Corpn v Hudd (Valuation Officer)* [1966] 1 WLR 363.
16 *Roberts v Overseers of Aylesbury* (1853) 1 E & B 423.
17 *Oswestry Corpn v Hudd (Valuation Officer)* [1966] 1 WLR 363 at 378, per Russell LJ.
18 *R v Casswell* (1872) LR 7 QB 328; *London Corpn v Overseers of St Sepulchre* (1871) LR 7 QB 333n; *Oswestry Corpn v Hudd (Valuation Officer)* [1966] 1 WLR 363.
19 *Oswestry Corpn v Hudd (Valuation Officer)* [1966] 1 WLR 363.

ILLUSTRATION

By a local Act of 1848 'persons occupying or using any stand, stall, shed, pen or place in the market place . . . or bringing into such market place . . . any marketable commodities . . . cattle or other livestock . . . specified in Schedule (B)' to the Act were required to pay 'such stallage, rents, and tolls as the council shall . . . appoint, not exceeding' those in Schedule (B). A second local Act of 1885 repealed and replaced Schedule (B) and after itemising the charges for every bull, cow and other types of cattle, provided for the 'several rents tolls and stallages before mentioned to be payable and paid for and in respect of the occupation or use of any pen, stall, standing place, bench, compartment, or space of ground as well by the original taker or occupier thereof for a part or portion of the day in case he shall not occupy the same the whole day as also by any subsequent taker or occupier of the same for the residue . . . of the same day'. In addition to the above payments, Oswestry Corporation received entry tolls for each head of cattle entering the market for sale as provided for by the revised Schedule in the 1885 Act. Although the evidence showed a history which included tolls referable only to a franchise of market, it showed also that the cattle market had since its earliest days involved a layout which did not permit cattle to be exposed otherwise than in the pens provided. *Held*, dismissing the Valuation Officer's appeal, that on the true construction of the local Acts the entry tolls paid for cattle were purely for bringing cattle into the market in pursuance of a general public right so to do, and were not attributable to the use of the soil of the market place. Accordingly they had the character and quality of franchise tolls and ought not to be taken into account in ascertaining the rateable value of the market place: *Oswestry Corporation v Hudd (Valuation Officer)*[20].

But charges made by the occupier of a market for admission to it are necessarily incidental to the use of the soil if they cannot be shown to be derived from a franchise, whether by charter, prescription, statute or otherwise; and such charges must be taken into consideration in estimating the value of the occupation[21]. This rule, it seems, must apply equally whether the market can be supported by franchise, or not.

The onus of showing that a charge is derived from a franchise lies upon the person who asserts that it is[22]. It is not enough that the payments are called 'tolls'[23] or 'market dues and charges'[24].

C Stall holders

Holders of stalls in markets are not generally rateable in respect of their occupation of such stalls since a degree of permanence is an essential element in rateable occupation[25].

ILLUSTRATION

In 1880, an attempt was made to rate a stall holder in Bodmin market. It appeared that his stalls were capable of being removed, and were liable to be removed from one spot to another, provided that they continued in the same position relative to other stalls. *Held* that

---

20 [1966] 1 WLR 363.
21 *Percy v Ashford Union* (1876) 34 LTNS 579.
22 *Ibid*, per Field J.
23 *Roberts v Overseers of Aylesbury* (1853) 1 E & B 423.
24 *London Corpn v Assessment Committee of Greenwich Union* (1883) 48 LT 437.
25 *Roberts v Overseers of Aylesbury* (1853) 1 E & B 423; but cf *Williams v Wednesbury and West Bromwich Churchwardens and Overseers Union Assessment Committee* (1890) Ryde Rat App (1886–1890) 327 (exclusive occupation of market on two days a week held rateable); and see also *R v Mosley* (1823) 2 B & C 226.

the stall holder had no exclusive right to occupy any definite portion of the soil, and therefore had no rateable occupation: *Spear v Guardians of Bodmin Union*[26].

Stall holders may, however, be liable to be rated if they occupy fixed places exclusively and such occupation is more than fleeting or intermittent[27].

3 INCOME TAX

Profits or gains arising out of property in the case of rights of markets and fairs and tolls, are chargeable to income tax, not under Schedule A, but under Case I of Schedule D[28]. Tax is assessed and charged on the person carrying on the concern, or on the agents or other officers who have the direction or management of the concern, or who receive its profits[29].

The general rules for estimating the amount of the profits or gains are contained in the Income and Corporation Taxes Act, 1988, ss 60 to 63. Under these rules, tax is charged on the full amount of profits or gains of the year preceding the year of assessment[30].

The owner or occupier or receiver of profits of a market, fair or tolls is answerable for the tax charged, and may retain and deduct the same out of any such profits[31].

Local authorities are exempt from all charge to income tax in respect of their income[32].

Provisions for collection and recovery of tax are contained in the Taxes Management Act 1970, Part VI.

---

26 (1880) 49 LJMC 69.

27 *Roberts v Overseers of Aylesbury* (1853) 1 E & B 423; *Williams v Wednesbury and West Bromwich Churchwardens and Overseers Union Assessment Committee* (1890) Ryde Rat App (1886–1890) 327; and see *Westminister City Council v Southern Rly Co* [1936] AC 511.

28 See the Income and Corporation Taxes Act 1988, s 15, Sch A, para 3(b); and s 55(2)(e).

29 *Ibid*, s 59(2).

30 Income and Corporation Taxes Act 1988, s 60(1).

31 *Ibid*, s 59(3).

32 Income and Corporation Taxes Act 1988, s 519(1)(a).

CHAPTER 11

Practice, Procedure and Evidence

1 SCIRE FACIAS

The appropriate process for obtaining the repeal or forfeiture of a grant, charter or letters patent for holding a market or fair is that by writ of *scire facias* on the Crown side of the Queen's Bench Division[1]. The process does not apply, however, unless the grant is of record[2]. The action of *scire facias* to repeal a grant, charter or letters patent is a proceeding taken by or on behalf of the Crown upon information that the grant is void by reason of being inadvisedly made or improperly obtained, or that it has become forfeited through misuse or abuse, or through non-fulfilment of conditions expressly or impliedly attached to the grant[3]. These grounds for instituting proceedings by *scire facias* have been already referred to in earlier pages of this work[4].

The process of *scire facias* was formerly issued from the Petty Bag Office in Chancery. Since the abolition of that office in 1889 it now issues from the Crown Office[5]. It can only issue upon a *fiat* of the Attorney-General, who has the right and duty of controlling the action, and of determining upon what and whose information, and on what terms and security as to costs, he will permit the action to be prosecuted[6]. He endorses his *fiat* upon a draft of the proposed writ, which must be submitted to

1 The writ is a prerogative original judicial writ and is not affected by the Crown Proceedings Act 1947, and must be distinguished from *scire facias* on the Revenue side of the Queen's Bench Division which was abolished by s 13, s 38(2) and Sch 1 of that Act. It must also be distinguished from the obsolete writ of *scire facias* formerly used in the process of execution. The reason why such proceedings are preserved is because proceedings on the Crown side are not included in the definition of 'civil proceedings' in s 38(2).

2 *R v Hughes* (1866) LR 1 PC 81. The grant or charter must be sealed or enrolled in a court of record. *Quaere* the position where rights are acquired by prescription.

3 *R v Eastern Archipelago Co* (1853) 1 E & B 310; affirmed sub nom *Eastern Archipelago Co v R* (1853) 2 E & B 856; *Great Eastern Rly Co v Goldsmid* (1884) 9 App Cas 927 at 965; *Peter v Kendal* (1827) 6 B & C 703 at 710; 3 Bl Comm 261; 4 Co Inst 72 at 88; *R v Aires* (1717) 10 Mod Rep 258 at 354 sub nom *R v Eyre* I Stra 43; *Butler's Case* (1680) 2 Vent 344;affd sub nom *R v Butler* (1685) 3 Lev 220; *Bassett's Case* (1568) Dyer 276b; See also Dyer, 197, 198; *R v Miles* (1797) 7 TR 367. *Foster on Scire Facias*; *Godson on Patents,* 2nd ed, p 269; 2 *Tidd's Practice*, 9th ed, pp 1093 *et seq*; Chitty, *Prerog of Crown* 330, 331; 2 Saund Rep 72a; 1 *Webster's Patent Cases*, 64n(a), 669n(f); *Grady and Scotland's Practice*, 290; 2 *Richardson's CP Practice*, 391 *et seq*. To every Crown grant, there is annexed by the common law an implied condition that it may be repealed by *scire facias* by the Crown, or by a subject grieved using the prerogative of the Crown on the *fiat* of the Attorney-General, per Sir John Jervis CJ in *Eastern Archipelago v R* (1853) 2 E & B 856 at 914. The fact that there is available the concurrent common law remedy in nuisance was no reason for refusal of *scire facias* by the Crown since the King had an undoubted right to repeal a patent whereby he or his subject suffered prejudice: *Butler's Case* (1680) 2 Vent 344; affd sub nom *R v Butler* (1685) 3 Lev 220.

4 See pp 16, 17, 99, *above*.

5 RSC, 30 January 1889; Short and Mellor, *Crown Office Practice*, 2nd ed, 399; Great Seal (Offices) Act 1874, s 5.

6 *Robertson's Civil Proceedings by and against the Crown*, 537.

him[7]. The writ issues as of right to every subject aggrieved, though not as of course (*de cursu*) to any subject asking for it[8].

The process may be issued from the Crown Office to the Sheriff of the county[9] in question and it directs the sheriff to make known[10] to the defendant that he must appear and show cause why the grant, charter or letters patent should not be cancelled. The sheriff, by a summons to the defendant, warns him to appear in answer to the writ. It is not necessary to file declarations and other pleadings but they must be delivered to the opposing party[11].

If in the event judgment is obtained in favour of the applicant, either after trial or in default, the judgment orders that the Crown grant, charter or letters patent is to be restored to Chancery and there to be cancelled and the seal cut off and the enrolment vacated[12]. But, as we have seen, markets and fairs when forfeited to the Crown are not extinguished but continue *in esse* in the Crown's hands[13].

The process of *scire facias* appears to have fallen into disuse and it is uncertain that such proceedings will in future be taken in connection with the market or fair although it is clearly still available[14].

2 QUO WARRANTO

Formerly[15] there was a remedy by an information in the nature of *quo warranto*[16] but such proceedings were abolished by the Administration of Justice (Miscellaneous Provisions) Act 1938, s 9(1), and replaced by statutory provisions, now re-enacted in the Supreme Court Act 1981, s 30. This provides that in any case where any person acts in an office in which he is not entitled to act, and an information in the nature of *quo warranto* would have lain against him, the High Court may grant an injunction restraining him from so acting and may declare the office to be vacant, provided that the

---

7 *Webster's Patent Cases*, 64n(a); *Foster on Scire Facias*, 249; *Robertson's Civil Proceedings by and against the Crown*, 487; See also RSC Ord 15, r 11. Formerly the practice was for the Attorney-General not to grant his *fiat* until he had received a warrant under the sign manual directing him to cause the writ to be issued; and the warrant had to be obtained by a petition or a memorial to the Crown and was only issued upon the Attorney-General's advice. But the modern practice seems to be for the Attorney-General to act on his own initiative; See *Richardson's CP Practice*, 391–398; *Tidd's Practice*, 9th ed, 1094; Chitty, *Prerog of Crown*, 331; 1 *Webster's Patent Cases*, 669n(f); *Foster on Scire Facias*, 247.

8 *R v Prosser* (1848) 11 Beav 306; *Eastern Archipelago v R* (1853) 2 E & B 856. It was held in the latter case (affirming the decision of the QBD) that it was *not* necessary for the Crown to make a writing under the Great Seal or sign warranties as a condition precedent to the forfeiture of the latter patent. It could repeal the grant *ex meno motu.* See also *Butler's Case*, (1680) 2 Vent 344.

9 Petty Bag Act 1849, s 29, now repealed by Courts Act 1971, s 56(4).

10 Hence the title, *scire facias*.

11 Petty Bag Act 1849, s 30. As to the procedure rules of 1848 and 1849, see S R & O Revised 1908 Vol 12, p 925.

12 For the form of judgment see *Brynner v R* (1846) 9 QB 523, Ex Ch; *R v Eastern Archipelago Co* (1853) 1 E & B 310; affirmed sub nom *Eastern Archipelago Co v R* (1853) 2 E & B 856.

13 See p 101, *above*.

14 See the remarks of Lord Goddard in *A-G (at the relation of Allen) v Colchester Corpn (or BC)* [1955] 2 QB 207 at 215, where it was suggested that the writ would still be available at the suit of the Attorney-General where the owner of a franchise of ferry failed in his duty. See also *Foster* at p 12.

15 See pp 97, 98, *above*.

16 For the former practice, see Short and Mellor, *Crown Office Practice*, 2nd ed, pp 172 *et seq.*

proceedings are brought by a person who would have been entitled to apply for such information. The proper procedure for such an application is by way of judicial review. The order is not issued as of course (*de cursu*) and the court may inquire into the conduct and motives of the applicant[17].

3 DECLARATORY RELIEF

In appropriate circumstances a person may make an application for a declaration to ascertain and determine the rights of parties or for the determination of a point of law. It is a procedural device utilising the provisions of Order 15, Rule 16 of the Rules of the Supreme Court, which provide as follows:

> 'No action or other proceeding shall be open to objection on the ground that a merely declaratory judgment or order is sought thereby, and the Court may make binding declarations of right whether or not consequential relief is or could be claimed.'

For a recent case where declaratory relief was sought and granted see *In Shops plc v Derby City Council*[18].

4 THE RIGHT TO INJUNCTIVE RELIEF

Section 37 of the Supreme Court Act 1981 (which replaced s 45 of the Supreme Court of Judicature Act 1925) provides that:

> '(1) the High Court may by order (whether interlocutory or final) grant an injunction or appoint a receiver in all cases in which it appears to the Court to be just and convenient to do so.
>
> (2) any such order may be made either unconditionally or on such terms and conditions as the court thinks just.'

Further, by Order 29, Rule 1, of the Rules of the Supreme Court[19], an application for the grant of an injunction:

> '(1) . . . may be made by any party to a cause or matter before or after the trial of the cause or matter, whether or not a claim for the injunction was included in the party's writ, originating summons, counterclaim or third party notice, as the case may be.'

and must be made by motion or summons, except where the applicant is the plaintiff and the case is one of urgency in which circumstances such an application may be made *ex parte* on affidavit[20]. However,

> '(3) the plaintiff may not make such an application before the issue of the writ or originating summons by which the cause or matter is to be begun except where the case is one of urgency, and in that case the injunction applied for may be granted on terms providing issue of the writ or summons and such other terms, if any, as the Court thinks fit.'

---

17 See *Everett v Griffiths* [1924] 1 KB 941 at 958; and Supreme Court Act 1981, s 31.
18 (1997) 95 LGR 161.
19 *The Supreme Court Practice* (1997 ed) Vol 2 para 5166.
20 O 29, r 1(2).

Thus, the court has wide and flexible powers to grant injunctions which can be exercised in any case which it is right or just to do so having regard to settled reasons or principle. However, the question whether an injunction ought to be granted is to be determined by reference to the circumstances and the state of the law at the date when the question falls to be determined, whether before or at trial, and not at the date of the issue of the writ. Further, it will only be granted in support of a legal right, and at the suit of the person whose legal right has been infringed[21].

A Interlocutory relief

In the case of a plaintiff seeking to enjoin a defendant by means of an interlocutory injunction, which is a temporary and discretionary remedy sought pending disposal of the issues at trial (and which in a case of real urgency may be sought *ex parte*) the court is invited to anticipate the results of the determination of such issues prior to trial. It is therefore reluctant to do so unless adequate safeguards are accorded to the parties.

> '. . . When an application for an interlocutory injunction to restrain a defendant from doing acts alleged to be in violation of the plaintiff's legal right is made upon contested facts, the decision whether or not to grant an interlocutory injunction has to be taken at a time when *ex hypothesi* the existence of the right or the violation of it, or both, is uncertain and will remain uncertain until final judgment is given in the action. It was to mitigate the risk of injustice to the plaintiff during the period before that uncertainty could be resolved that the practice arose of granting him relief by way of interlocutory injunction; but since the middle of the nineteenth century this has been made subject to his undertaking to pay damages to the defendant for any loss sustained by reason of the injunction if it should be held at trial that the plaintiff had not been entitled to restrain the defendant from doing what he was threatening to do[22].'

However, at the same time

> '. . . the Court is not justified in embarking upon anything resembling a trial of the action upon conflicting affidavits in order to evaluate the strength of either party's case[23].'

(1) A serious question to be tried

Although on an application for the grant of an interlocutory injunction anything resembling a trial of the action itself should be avoided, it is necessary to determine on enquiry the essential preliminary point as to whether there is a serious question to be tried entitling the plaintiff to interim relief. In this regard, it has been said that such expressions as 'a probability' or 'a *prima facie* case' or 'a strong *prima facie* case' are confusing[24]. If such an enquiry reveals that there is a serious question to be tried[25], and that the claim 'is not frivolous or vexatious', and that the material before the court does not fail to disclose that the plaintiff 'has any real prospect of succeeding in his claim for a permanent injunction at the trial'[26], then (provided it is appropriate) it is necessary to

21 29/1/2 RSC.

22 Per Lord Diplock in *American Cyanamid Co v Ethicon Ltd* [1975] AC 396 at 406.

23 *Ibid*, at 409.

24 *Ibid*, at 407.

25 That is, one for which there is some supporting material and of which the outcome is uncertain (see *Cayne v Global Natural Resources plc* [1984] 1 All ER 225).

26 *Americas Cyanamid*, footnote 22, *above*, at 408.

consider the question whether the balance of convenience is in favour of granting or refusing the interlocutory relief sought.

(2) Balance of convenience and damages

The determination of the question of balance of convenience involves the consideration of the governing principle as to whether damages would be an adequate remedy to the plaintiff if relief is refused at the interlocutory stage, but the plaintiff succeeds at trial of the action; and the converse, whether damages would be an adequate remedy for the defendant if relief is granted to the plaintiff at the interlocutory stage but the defendant succeeds at trial.

> 'It is where there is doubt as to the adequacy of the respective remedies in damages available to either party or to both, that the question of balance of convenience arises . . . Where other factors appear to be evenly balanced it is a counsel of prudence to take such measures as are calculated to preserve the *status quo*. If the defendant is enjoined temporarily from doing something that he has not done before, the only effect of the interlocutory injunction, in the event of his succeeding at the trial, is to postpone the date at which he is able to embark upon a course of action which he has not previously found it necessary to undertake; whereas to interrupt him in the conduct of an established enterprise would cause much greater inconvenience to him since he would have to start again to establish it in the event of him succeeding at the trial[27].'

Consideration of the question of the balance of convenience will not arise, however, in circumstances when the relevant matters are all before the court and are plain and uncontroversial, or when there is plainly no defence, eg where the defendant is acting in breach of a right, covenant or statute[28]. This is of particular relevance where a local authority has commenced proceedings pursuant to s 222(1) of the Local Government Act 1972 in order to enforce its market rights, eg where a 'same day' rival market is involved, or where breaches of planning law are involved (*below*).

(3) When interlocutory relief will be granted

Thus, provided the plaintiff establishes that there is a serious question to be tried, and that the defendant's conduct is unjustified, and that damages are not an adequate remedy in the event of his succeeding at the later trial, the court will normally grant an interlocutory injunction. This will be so even though the plaintiff is unable to show a reasonable prospect of obtaining a permanent injunction at trial. Further, an injunction may be granted even though the plaintiff would obtain thereby substantially all or even the whole of the remedy or relief claimed in the action.

However, it has been said that where the grant or refusal would have the practical effect of putting an end to an action, the court should approach the case on the broad principle of what it can do in its best endeavour to avoid injustice, and to balance the risk of doing an injustice to either party. In such a case the court should bear in mind that to grant the injunction sought by the plaintiff would mean giving him judgment in the case against the defendant without permitting the defendant the right of trial. Accordingly, the established guidelines requiring the court to look at the balance of convenience when deciding whether to grant or refuse an interlocutory injunction do

27 *Ibid*, at 408.

28 *Hampstead and Suburban Properties Ltd v Diomedous* [1969] 1 Ch 248; *Warder v Cooper* [1970] Ch 495; *Manchester Corpn v Connolly* [1970] Ch 420.

not apply in such a case, since, whatever the strengths of either side, the defendant should not be precluded by the grant of an interlocutory injunction from disputing the plaintiff's claim at a trial[29].

It must also be remembered that although the court has jurisdiction to grant a *mandatory* injunction upon an interlocutory application, it is only done in exceptional circumstances and will not be granted on affidavit evidence where the issues of fact are strongly contested.

(4) The cross-undertaking as to damages

The question of a local authority being obliged to give a cross-undertaking as to damages has also arisen for consideration. In the case of *Kirklees Metropolitan Borough Council v Wickes Building Supplies Ltd*[30] (a case involving breaches of the Shops Act 1950 (now repealed) and the former laws against Sunday trading), the local authority declined to give a cross-undertaking in damages on the basis that it was entitled to the same exemption as the Crown when seeking an interlocutory injunction. At first instance the judge granted an injunction without requiring the local authority to give a cross-undertaking. The Court of Appeal allowed the appeal against this order and discharged the injunction on the basis that the special privilege afforded to the Crown did not extend to local authorities. Further, it was held that the defendants should be protected by a cross-undertaking pending the decision of the European Court as to the position of Sunday trading and the interpretation of Article 30 of the Treaty of Rome

On appeal by the local authority to the House of Lords the appeal was allowed and it was held that:

(1) Section 71(1) of the 1950 Act was sufficiently broad in its terms to embrace any proceedings necessary to secure observance of the Act and accordingly a local authority could institute not only criminal proceedings but also civil proceedings for an injunction in its own name under s 222 of the 1972 Act to secure observance of the former 1950 Act when proceedings were necessary. Furthermore, the court could exercise its jurisdiction to grant an injunction to restrain a breach of the criminal law notwithstanding that the defendant had a defence, eg a Community law defence, to the alleged crime, since the existence of an alleged defence was not a matter of jurisdiction but was instead to be taken into account in the exercise of the court's discretion when deciding whether it was just and convenient to grant interlocutory relief[31].

(2) Where the Crown brought a law enforcement action, in which an injunction was sought to restrain a subject from breaking a law where the breach would be harmful to the public or a section of it, the court had a discretion not to require an undertaking in damages from the Crown and that special privilege afforded to the Crown as law enforcer not to give a cross-undertaking in damages on the grant of an interlocutory injunction also applied to other public authorities, including a local authority, when exercising a law enforcement function in the public interest. Since the appellant local authority was under a duty to enforce the law under the former 1950 Act, including bringing proceedings for an injunction, which in practice were the only proceedings by which the law could effectively be enforced, the judge was entitled to decide, in the

---

29 *Cayne v Global Natural Resources plc* [1984] 1 All ER 225.

30 [1993] AC 227, [1992] 3 All ER 717.

31 [1993] AC 227. *R v Braintree District Council, ex p Willingham* (1982) 81 LGR 70 and dicta of Lord Roskill and Lord Templeman in *Stoke-on-Trent City Council v B & Q (Retail) Ltd* [1984] 2 All ER 332 at 335–336, 341–342 applied.

exercise of his discretion, that no undertaking in damages should be required of the local authority on the grant of an interlocutory injunction[32].

(3) The mere fact that the respondent might have a Community law defence founded on Art 30 of the EEC Treaty did not compel the court to require an undertaking in damages from the local authority since if the European Court were to hold that s 47 of the 1950 Act (now repealed) was invalid as being in conflict with Art 30 of the EEC Treaty the United Kingdom government would be under an obligation, irrespective of any undertaking in damages given by the local authority, to make good any damage caused to individuals by the breach of Art 30 for which it was responsible by its failure to amend or repeal s 47. Accordingly, any undertaking by the local authority as to damages would be superfluous. Moreover the local authority would be liable on the undertaking irrespective of whether the respondent was found to have a right to damages. Even if the respondent was held to be entitled to damages the effect of requiring an undertaking from the local authority would be wrongly to impose liability in damages on the council instead of on the United Kingdom government which would properly be the party so liable. It followed that the court was not bound by Community law to require an undertaking in damages from the local authority if an interlocutory injunction was granted and the judge was right to decide the question on ordinary principles of English domestic law[33].

(4) Since it was clear that the respondent intended to continue to act in breach of s 47 of the Act (now repealed) unless restrained and that proceedings by way of injunction were the only way open to the council to enforce the provisions of the Act, the judge was fully entitled to decide, in the exercise of his discretion, that no undertaking in damages should be required of the council.

(5) The importance of interlocutory relief for the market owner

The availability and use of the procedure invoking the court's jurisdiction in order to obtain interlocutory relief have considerable practical importance for the market owner. For instance, the jurisdiction can be invoked in those cases where the market owner has sought to restrain certain activities on the part of a defendant which amount to disturbance of his market franchise. Such an application, whether by way of interlocutory relief or at the trial of the action, seeks the protection of the court in the exercise of its discretion in any case in which it is just and right to do so.

The court also has the power independently to enforce obedience to the law as enacted, notwithstanding that the relevant statute may provide a sanction for its breach. This power is of particular importance to local authorities, who prior to its repeal had increasing difficulty in enforcing the provisions of the Shops Act 1950 against organisations deliberately prepared to flout the law by trading on Sundays. But recourse to the civil courts was not confined to persistent breaches of the Shops Act 1950, and there are a number of cases in which the jurisdiction of the court has been invoked as a means of enforcing planning decisions[34], although planning considerations alone may not be sufficient.

---

32 Dictum of Lord Diplock in *F Hoffmann-La Roche & Co AG v Secretary of State for Trade and Industry* [1974] 2 All ER 1128 at 1152–1153 explained.

33 *Bougoin SA v Ministry of Agriculture, Fisheries and Food* [1985] 3 All ER 585 doubted.

34 See, for example, *A-G v Chaudry* [1971] 1 WLR 1614; *A-G v Ashborne Recreation Ground Co* [1903] 1 Ch 101; *Kent County Council v Batchelor* (1976) 75 LGR 151, *(No 2)* [1979] 1 WLR 213; *Westminster City Council v Jones* (1981) 80 LGR 241.

Thus, the courts have a reserve power which will be utilised in order to support and supplement the law as enacted where the circumstances justify judicial intervention. Such power is not restricted to cases where other means have been exhausted. Indeed it may be utilised in circumstances where other means of ensuring compliance have not been commenced provided that it can be shown the offender is not merely infringing the law but that he is deliberately and flagrantly flouting it[35].

A more recent example of this principle can be seen in *Delyn Borough Council v. Solitaire (Liverpool) Limited*[36] where Jacob J considered whether the grant of a planning permission could itself amount to the establishment of a market within the meaning of s 50 of the Food Act 1984. The plaintiff Council established in 1991 a statutory Saturday market in the centre of Holywell under s 50. In July 1994 the defendants re-opened a Saturday market within three miles of the Council's new market pursuant to planning permissions granted by the Council in 1981 and 1983. In proceedings for an injunction to prevent the defendants from continuing to operate their Saturday market within the common law distance, it was held that a grant of planning permission does not confer on the owner of land a market right or a universal 'right' destroying any legal obstacles having nothing to do with the planning laws; nor will it amount to a statutory authority giving immunity from suit. Planning permission does no more than remove the impediment on use or development of land imposed by planning laws. Jacob J also, however, held that the defendants did have an arguable defence on the basis that modern public law might, in some circumstances, interfere with the exercise of a market right; for example, where lack of good faith on the part of a local authority could be demonstrated, or where a trader had lawfully established a long-standing and thriving market which, especially when coupled with a grant of planning permission, gives rise to a 'legitimate' or 'reasonable' expectation that the authority will not obstruct it. The balance of justice and convenience, and the merits of the claim, however, favoured the granting of a temporary interlocutory injunction against the defendants pending hearing of the case.

On 3 October 1996 Solitaire withdrew their defence and agreed in an out of court settlement to pay the Council's entire legal costs. The Council's market rights were thereby preserved and its Holywell Saturday market protected.

B Disturbance of the market owner's franchise.

In those cases where relief has been sought by a market owner in order to restrain disturbance of its franchise, it is necessary to consider in what circumstances the courts will grant such relief. The vast majority of the reported cases relating to disturbance involve applications made at the interlocutory stage by way of motion in the Chancery Division in which interim relief has been sought pending the trial of the action.

In the main, these cases relate to applications brought by market owners against entrepreneurs who have sought to challenge the monopoly of market by attempting to establish rival markets, in whatever form, within the common law distance of 6⅔ miles. Such applications have usually been successful in preventing the holding of rival markets, pending trial of the action. Thereafter, in many cases, the case itself has never proceeded to a full hearing. Often (as is a common practice in the Chancery Division) the motion itself has been treated as the trial of the action. In other cases, where interim relief has either been granted or been refused, a speedy trial has been ordered. It must be

35 *Stafford Borough Council v Elkenford* [1977] 1 WLR 324 and see *Stoke-on-Trent City Council v B & Q (Retail) Ltd* [1984] 2 WLR 929.

36 (1995) 93 LGR 614.

said, however, that as almost all of the reported cases are decisions made at the interlocutory stage (some of which have been upheld on appeal), they must be treated with some circumspection. The evidence required to satisfy a court at this stage is not of the standard required at the trial of the action, in that the contentions raised by the plaintiff or the defendant on affidavit may not have been challenged in the opposing affidavits at the interlocutory stage and will not have been tested by cross-examination. Thus, although these cases will be authoritative with regard to the circumstances as to when the court will grant or refuse interlocutory relief, they may not necessarily be authoritative, for example, as to whether a particular set of activities constitutes a rival market.

There are several points of importance to which regard must be had if a market owner is to succeed in obtaining interlocutory relief prior to trial.

In order to establish whether or not there is a serious issue to be tried there are three preliminary considerations:

(1) it is necessary to establish the market authority's monopoly right pursuant to charter, prescription or statute;

(2) it is necessary to demonstrate that the defendant is disturbing that right;

(3) if it is a 'different day' market it is necessary to demonstrate actual loss (or the 'likelihood of loss'[37], as it was put in one case) on the part of the plaintiff.

If, on consideration of these factors, it can be established that there is a serious issue to be tried, then the court will go on to consider the question of the balance of convenience and damages.

C Evidence of right

Practitioners should be aware of a number of procedural hurdles which have been encountered in cases over recent years. First, the source of the deponent's belief should be clearly stated. In *Leicester City Council v Maby*[38] the plaintiff Corporation nearly came to grief on a motion for interlocutory relief. Goff J was concerned as to the failure of the deponent's solicitor to specify in his evidence the source of his belief with regard to the holding of the market which, as the solicitor stated, had been held in the market place '. . . on such days for as long as anyone can remember . . .'[39]. Clearly a relevant issue was whether the Corporation had made out a *prima facie* case that they had such a common law right. As this was a question of the right being in dispute, and not merely the question of its infringement, it should be a strong *prima facie* case. Therefore, such a statement by the solicitor was '. . . inadmissible even on a motion . . .'[40].

Further, in another paragraph in the same affidavit the same solicitor failed to explain the source of his knowledge as to the history of the market to which he had deposed, and which presumably had been obtained from the archives of the Corporation. Thus, the judge could attach little or no weight to this although had such an explanation been given it might have been admissible as having been derived from knowledge gained in his capacity as an officer of the plaintiff Corporation.

Fortunately for the plaintiff Corporation, however, the local Acts to which the attention of the judge had been drawn themselves contained recitals which in one form

---

37 Per Pennycuick V-C in *Birmingham Corpn v Perry Bar Stadium Ltd* [1972] 1 All ER 725; and see pp 74, 75 *above*.

38 (1971) 70 LGR 209.

39 *Ibid*, at 211.

40 *Ibid*, at 211–212.

or another referred to the existence of the market on the relevant day. Referring to the judgment of Harman LJ in *Wyld v Silver*[41], Goff J held that:

> '. . . those statements in the local Acts appear to me to afford the requisite strong prima facie evidence . . . It was argued that those provisions in the local Acts could not avail the Corporation because they do not recite that the Corporation have any rights in the market or what those rights were, but for the purpose of an interlocutory application I cannot accept that submission. Those statutory references are, on the authority which I have cited, strong *prima facie* evidence of the factual existence of a market at least since 1846 and, of course, one of the species of evidence to prove a common law market is to prove long user, the other being, of course, reputation. For the puposes of a motion, in my judgment, the Corporation have well discharged the *onus* upon them by producing those statutory references'[42].

Secondly, it is clearly necessary for the market authority to establish precisely in its evidence to the court the exact status of its market rights. If it is possible to provide evidence from sources other than placing sole reliance upon a statutory market established under the Food Act 1984, it is advisable to do so having regard to the case of *East Lindsey District Council v Hamilton*[43].

Thirdly, in relation to the production of public documents, such as a royal charter, the general rule is that if the charter is in the plaintiff's possession it could be proved by affidavit evidence on motion by establishing that it was in his possession and that the document exhibited to the affidavit was a correct copy or extract from the original. To make such a statement the deponent must have examined the copy against the original. If the deponent does not do this the evidence adduced is clearly insufficient, even for the purposes of interlocutory proceedings, as being secondary evidence, and an injunction will be refused[44].

D Evidence of disturbance of right

Provided that the right to the monopoly of market can be established, evidence of disturbance of that right is usually not too difficult to demonstrate, except in those cases where the defendant is able to contend successfully that the activities generated by him do not constitute a concourse of buyers and sellers.

---

41 [1963] Ch 243 at 258ff.

42 *Leicester City Council v Maby*, footnote 38, *above*, at 211.

43 (27 July 1983, unreported). (A case under the Food and Drugs Act 1955, now repealed and re-enacted as the Food Act 1984.) It was held by Whitford J, in this case at first instance that whilst statutory markets are entitled to the same degree of protection as franchise markets unless the statute otherwise provides, the only protection available to markets set up under the 1955 Act was that afforded by bringing into operation, by byelaw, the provisions of s 55. The decision was reversed on appeal (1984) Times, 2 April the Court of Appeal holding (per Oliver LJ) that the Council should be entitled to argue, when the matter came to trial, that s 49(3) of the 1955 Act (now re-enacted as s 50(3) of the Food Act 1984 as amended by the Food Safety Act 1990) extended to statutory markets the protection enjoyed by franchise markets against the establishment of a rival market within the local authority's district. The case, however, went neither to further appeal nor to trial. See also *Hailsham Cattle Market Co v Tolman* [1915] 1 Ch 360, and *Halton Borough Council v Cawley* [1985] 1 WLR 15, in which it was held that the common law right to protection was available to any market even though created under the provisions of a statute and despite the fact the rival market was outside the local authority's district.

44 *Warwick Corpn v Maby* (1971) 115 Sol Jo 965.

Such evidence of disturbance can be provided by employees or agents of the market owner deposing to the activities of the defendant. Reliance can be placed on advertisements in the local press or trade journals, and in hand bills, posters, etc, all of which may indicate by advertisement to the trade and/or to the public the time and venue of the rival market. It is also usual for evidence to be obtained from eye-witnesses who have been present when the rival market has operated, and who can depose to the size of the undertaking, the number of stalls, the identity of the stall holders, the nature of the goods sold and the number of persons present thereat.

The market owner may be assisted in his endeavours in circumstances when the defendant has made it clear that he is not willing to abandon the project, or is not willing to comply with an order of the court, or has refused to give certain undertakings as to the activities carried out by him. There have also been cases where the defendant has attempted to conceal his activites, and to mislead the market authority and the courts.

Not unnaturally such considerations have not assisted defendants seeking to contend that their activities do not offend the law. The *bona fides* of the defendants is put in issue at the interlocutory stage, and this may have a considerable effect upon the court when it considers the question of the balance of convenience.

In several cases the court has taken a somewhat circumspect view of the defendant's behaviour. In *The Mayor, Aldermen and Burgesses of the Royal Borough of Kingston-upon-Thames v Sherman and Waterman Associates Ltd*[45], as Walton J indicated in his judgment, the plaintiffs:

> '... did not obtain that full and frank statement of the defendants' intentions which one would have expected the defendants to have made if they were really doing something which they thought they had a right to do. Ultimately, Kingston had to find out by the backstairs what was actually happening, and, as a result, they only obtained an *ex parte* injunction on the very eve of the opening of the market and, indeed, it proved too late to prevent a few stalls opening'[46].

There were attempts at concealment, and also a deliberate failure on the part of the defendants to put their cards on the table after having been invited to do so by the plaintiffs at a very early stage. These factors, combined with the great difficulties which the plaintiffs faced in connection with service of the proceedings, and also the fact that 'the market was not advertised in the press in the normal manner, in which any honest market would have been expected to be advertised ...'[47] did not find favour with the court, and indicated clearly to the judge that 'the whole operation was planned as a clandestine one destined to present both the Council and the court with a *fait accompli* ...'[46].

Again, in *Bassetlaw District Council v Zaccaria*[48] there was strong evidence of concealment. The defendants initially advertised in a trade journal (the *Worksop Trader*) which included the statement 'The organisers have asked not to be named. It would appear legal action is expected to be taken by Bassetlaw Council', and apparently elsewhere in this journal the organiser gave his reasons for starting up a Sunday market

---

45 (6 July 1976, unreported).
46 *Ibid*, transcript, p 6.
47 *Ibid*, at pp 14–15.
48 [1980] CLY 300 (and transcript).

despite previous bans placed by High Court orders[49]. Further means of identifying persons concerned in the sale had been obstructed; for example, car number plates had been covered up, and there was an absence of any information as to the names and addresses of the stall holders. One name and address obtained from a trader proved to be false.

In the unreported case of *Birmingham City Council v In Shops plc*[50], the defendants were criticised by Hoffman J for deliberately attempting to create a *fait accompli* without informing the plaintiffs about what they were doing as part of their tactics in negotiation. They overplayed their hand, it was said, and only had themselves to blame for any loss of goodwill. An injunction was granted in the circumstances restraining the defendants from operating a rival market.

Shams

As has been indicated above, it sometimes proves more difficult for the market authority to provide the necessary evidence of disturbance of its franchise where there is an attempt to circumvent its rights by the creation of what purports to be, for example, a department store, or an arcade of shops, or a supermarket. Ultimately, the success or failure of the defendant's contention in this regard must rest on the standard and quality of the evidence provided. If the scheme proposed or operated by the defendant can be shown to be a sham, however, then evidence of disturbance of the monopoly of market will necessarily follow.

Cases in which it has been held by the courts that schemes or activities have constituted shams tend to have been concerned with Sunday trading and the Shops Act 1950 (now repealed), rather than with rival markets, the sham being the method adopted by the defendant to avoid the provisions of the Shops Act 1950. But it is submitted that similar considerations apply to the latter. In *Leicester City Council v Oxford and Bristol Stores Ltd*[51], however, the Vice-Chancellor held on an interlocutory application that the plaintiff Council had failed to show that the defendant's scheme, which, it was contended, was in the nature of a department store rather than a concourse of buyers and sellers, was a mere sham entitling the plaintiff Council to interlocutory relief. The fact that the *modus operandi* had been altered, after about a fortnight, from that of a concourse of sellers as well as buyers to a scheme under which it was claimed that there was merely a series of sales by the defendant company as the sole vendor, together with other possible areas of doubt and uncertainty which, not unnaturally, the plaintiff Council desired to challenge and investigate, was not enough to support the contention that there was a serious issue to be tried:

> '. . . what is needed is something which in fact is a "serious question" and shows a "real prospect of success", and not a mere possibility of one[52].'

---

49 *Ibid*, transcript, p 3. See also *Waller v Hardy* (1972) 70 LGR 331, where the defendants, who ran a furniture shop, attempted to avoid the Sunday trading provisions by ostensibly selling carrots and giving away with each carrot a free gift. One carrot sold for £250 and others for £20, the price including purchase tax. It was held by the Queen's Bench Division that an intention to buy furniture could not be changed into an intention to buy carrots merely by describing the articles sold as carrots and the furniture as free gifts.

50 [1992] NPC 71.

51 (21 December 1978, unreported), p 82 *above*.

52 *Ibid*, transcript, p 10.

E Evidence of damage

Reference has already been made to the well-established principle that in the case of a 'same day' market injury and damage is presumed to be a disturbance of the old. In the case of a 'different day' market, however, injury and actual damage must be proved.

In the case of *Birmingham Corpn v Perry Barr Stadium Ltd*[53], a 'different day' market, for the purposes of the motion (and accepted by counsel for one of the defendants) it was considered sufficient by Pennycuick V-C that the plaintiff Corporation would show a 'likelihood of damage'.

> 'It is apparent that if some other party, unauthorised by the plaintiff Corporation, established a market within the City of Birmingham, the value of the plaintiff Corporation's monopoly rights must be reduced. Obviously if it is known that traders can get away with establishing a market without recourse to the licence of the plaintiff Corporation, other traders are less likely to spend their money on obtaining a licence from the plaintiff Corporation. There is also the point as to interference with the existing markets carried on by the plaintiff Corporation itself[54].'

The decision in the Birmingham Corporation case was followed in *Leicester City Council v Maby*[55]. In this case the unfortunate solicitor for the Corporation was once again criticised by Goff J for his failure to produce evidence of actual damage (which, as the judge indicated, it should have been possible to do, in view of the fact that the rival market had been in operation for some three months). But the judge endorsed the remarks of Pennycuick MR in the *Birmingham Corporation* case and the observations of Sir George Jessel MR, at first instance, in *Elwes v Payne*[56] and granted the relief sought. In the *Kingston-upon-Thames* case[57] Walton J followed his reasoning and held, for the purposes of the motion, that evidence of the likelihood of damage was sufficient to justify the granting of interlocutory relief.

> 'I must make it perfectly clear what, so far as I can see, the nature of that damage is. It is not, I think, that people from outside Putney accustomed to go to the Kingston market will be pulled to the Putney market. That seems to me, at any rate on the evidence in front of me at the moment, to be rather unlikely. But man being a lazy animal, what is much more likely to happen is that the good people of Putney who have been accustomed to resorting to Kingston on a large number of matters and then to go on and complete their shopping in Kingston market will now, since their market is not only just around the corner in Lacy Road, not bestir themselves to go to Kingston, Or, if they go to Kingston, they will not collect their market shopping in Kingston, but will collect it on their own doorstep. That appears to me to be in the nature of the damage[58].'

Again Walton J in *Northampton Borough Council v Midland Development Group of Companies Ltd*[59] held that (following *Morpeth Corpn v Northumberland Farmers' Auction Mart Co*[60]) even if damage had to be shown in the case of a same day market, it would not be necessary to show economic damage to the holder of the market, but

53 [1972] 1 All ER 725, p 75, *above*.
54 *Ibid*, at 730.
55 (1971) 70 LGR 209, p 75 *above*.
56 [1879] 12 Ch D 468 (reversed on appeal [1879] 12 Ch D 475).
57 (6 July 1976, unreported).
58 *Ibid*, transcript, pp 13–14.
59 (1978) 76 LGR 750, p 81, *above*.
60 [1921] 2 Ch 154.

would be quite sufficient to show damage to his stall holders. In this case, unchallenged evidence had been given that the holding of the rival market would seriously impair the viability of many of the marginal stalls.

But, irrespective of whether or not damage is to be presumed in the case of a same day market, or damage must be proved in the case of a different day market, it is clearly to the market owner's advantage, and may have an important bearing on the question of balance of convenience, if the market owner is able to produce firm evidence of injury and damage, especially if that injury and damage are challenged by the defendant in his evidence.

Thus, if it can be demonstrated by the market owner that there has been a fall in trade in his market, or a decrease in turnover at any markets licensed by him, with the consquential loss of toll or stallage, or if it can be shown that there has been a loss of income to individual stall holders, especially if it can be demonstrated that the loss would affect the viability of the more marginal stalls, then such evidence can only be of assistance to the market owner's case both at the interlocutory stage and at the trial of the action. Conversely, the failure of the market owner to produce such evidence could have serious consequences for his case (as almost happened in the case of *Leicester City Council v Maby*[61]).

It is appreciated that it may be difficult to quantify such damage, especially if the rival undertaking has not in fact been commenced. The longer the rival market has been in existence, however, the easier it should be for the market owner to quantify his loss, and failure by him to do so must weaken his case, particularly at the interlocutory stage[62].

F Balance of convenience

If, after consideration of the factors, there is a serious question to be tried, then, if it is appropriate, the court will consider the question of balance of convenience and damages. A number of points can be discerned from the cases in the interpretation of the principle by the courts in market cases.

(1) A local authority market owner is certainly good for any damages which might ultimately be awarded to a defendant, ie a local authority should clearly be in a position to make good any loss sustained by a defendant who at the later trial succeeds in his opposition to the grant of the injunction. However, it must be remembered that since the case of *Kirklees Metropolitan Borough Council v Wickes Building Supplies Ltd*[63] a cross-undertaking in damages is not an essential prerequisite to the grant of an injunction, but lies within the discretion of the Court[64].

(2) If a defendant is permitted to continue his activities, pending trial of the action, such may well threaten the profits, viability and existence of the market owner's existing market, and those activities may be copied by others to the further detriment of the existing market.

(3) If a defendant has incurred substantial capital expenditure, then the balance of convenience may favour a refusal to grant an interlocutory injunction unless the defendant has incurred such expenditure after having been warned not to do so by the market owner. Such disregard for the plaintiff's apparent rights will indicate a firm and continuing intention to establish a market which may well be disadvantageous to a

61 (1971) 70 LGR 209.

62 For measure of damages, see *Stoke-on-Trent City Council v W & J Wass Ltd* (1988) 87 LGR 129, CA and pp 76, 77 *above*.

63 [1993] AC 227, [1992] 3 All ER 717, [1992] 3 WLR 170.

64 See *above*, p 144.

defendant on an interlocutory application. Any apparent flagrant invasion of the market owner's rights, especially in circumstances where the profits are high, will not commend itself to a court. However, if a defendant is genuinely willing to undertake to desist from such activities then interlocutory relief is usually not granted. But such cases are rare.

(4) If a market owner wishes to prevent activities on the part of a defendant which are apparently a disturbance of his rights he should act speedily, otherwise the *status quo* could be affected by the establishment and operation of such a rival undertaking. If the market owner does act with speed, then the *status quo* will be maintained until trial, unless other factors in the assessment of the balance of convenience are not in favour of granting the relief prayed.

(5) A further consideration relates to the ease with which the prospective loss on the part of the plaintiff or the defendant can be quantified. The loss to the plaintiff market owner is often incalculable or substantial. The defendant not only often fails to provide evidence of his ability to pay damages but also his loss usually can be easily quantified; for instance, by the loss to him of stallage at the prospective rival market. In the case of an established market owner the loss may be very difficult to calculate.

G Local authorities and their powers under s 222(1) of the Local Government Act 1972

At common law a local authority was in no different position than any other plaintiff and could only sue for interference with its private rights or for interference with a public right when it had suffered special damage peculiar to itself. Breach of statute such as the Shops Act 1950 (now repealed) could not constitute an interference with the private rights of a local authority nor cause it special damage. Accordingly, at common law a local authority could not bring civil proceedings complaining of such breaches. Such proceedings could only be instituted by the Attorney-General.

Now, however, since the enactment of s 222(1) of the Local Government Act 1972 in a proper case a local authority can utilise its powers under the section 'to restrain' anticipated breaches of the criminal law without recourse to the Attorney-General. Such powers are additional to and are not in derogation of the power of the Attorney-General *ex officio* or *ex relatione* to enforce obedience to the public law[65].

Section 222(1) provides that:

> 'Where a local authority considers it expedient for the promotion or protection of the interests of the inhabitants of their area—
>
> (a) they may prosecute or defend or appear in any legal proceedings and, in the case of civil proceedings, may institute them in their own name;
>
> (b) . . .'

In recent years there was a marked increase in organisations prepared to flout deliberately the provisions of the Shops Act 1950 (now repealed) by trading on Sundays by selling goods other than those permitted by Sch 5 thereto. The penalties provided by s 59 (as increased by the Criminal Justice Act 1982, ss 35–48) were clearly inadequate to deter such organisations, many of which found Sunday trading a highly profitable venture, particularly with regard to DIY articles.

It is in these circumstances that a number of cases have reached the civil courts in which the local authorities concerned have sought, pursuant to their powers under

---

65 See *Stoke-on-Trent City Council v B & Q (Retail) Ltd* [1984] 2 WLR 929.

s 222(1), to invoke the aid of the civil courts to ensure compliance with the criminal law, and to restrain such breaches by way of injunction. Such actions have, in the main, been successful.

The use of such a power by a local authority however, to invoke the assistance of the civil courts in the aid of the criminal law is, in the view of Lord Diplock in *Gouriet v Union of Post Office Workers*[66]:

> '... appropriate ... only in the most exceptional of cases. It is not accurate to describe it as preventative justice. It is a deterrent and punitive procedure ...'

which may be anticipatively invoked before any crime, even inchoate, has actually been committed. However, as profits from Sunday trading were considerable, and as the fines provided by the Shops Act 1950 were not likely to be a deterrent, and as law-abiding citizens were placed in a disadvantageous position in relation to those who were willing to flout the law, the civil courts appeared to be increasingly willing to grant such relief as a means of ensuring compliance with the criminal law. As a result the courts are now more sympathetic towards local authorities, and are apparently more prepared to recognise the difficulties inherent in prosecuting individual offenders for persistent breaches of eg market rights and planning legislation. All local authorities have finite resources and considerable strain can be placed upon small departments in relation to the expenditure of time, effort and money in attempting to enforce the criminal law. It is in such circumstances that the civil courts have stepped in and granted relief.

A precursor of s 222(1) of the Local Government Act 1972 was contained in s 276 of the Local Government Act 1933 (itself a replacement of an earlier enactment), which provided that, 'where a local authority deem it expedient for the promotion or protection of the interests of the inhabitants of their area, they may prosecute or defend any legal proceedings', but the local authority had no power, if it thought criminal proceedings an inadequate remedy, to bring proceedings in its own name for injunctive relief. In *Prestatyn UDC v Prestatyn Raceway Ltd*[67] it was held by Goff J[68] that, in a case where a local authority wished to take proceedings in respect of a public nuisance, it was bound to sue on the relation of the Attorney-General and not in its own name. Thus, the previous enactment did not authorise the institution by a local authority of proceedings for the suppression or prevention of a public nuisance in the absence of the Attorney-General's *fiat*.

Clearly, the additional wording contained in the new section was designed to alter this position and to reverse the decision of Goff J, and to confer limited powers on a local authority to enable it to sue in its own name and without the intervention of the Attorney-General in order to ensure compliance with public duties, in cases where, prior to the Act, it had been necessary to obtain his concurrence[69].

This was the view taken by Oliver J in *Solihull Metropolitan Borough Council v Maxfern Ltd*[70] who considered that the intention of the legislature was to vest the discretion formerly exercised by the Attorney-General in the local authority in cases

---

66 [1978] AC 435 at 498. See also the sentiments expressed by Lord Wilberforce at 481.

67 [1970] 1 WLR 33.

68 Applying the dictum of Kay LJ in *Tottenham UDC v Williamson & Sons Ltd* [1896] 2 QB 353 at 354–355. See also *Hampshire County Council v Shonleigh Nominees Ltd* [1970] 1 WLR 865.

69 *Stoke-on-Trent City Council v B & Q (Retail) Ltd* [1984] 2 WLR 929.

70 [1977] 1 WLR 127 (Sunday market, shopping 'club', a sham). See also the reported further part of the proceedings *(No 2)* (1977) 75 LGR 392.

where the local authority thought it necessary to promote or protect public rights in its area[71].

This interpretation was approved by the House of Lords in *Stoke-on-Trent City Council v B & Q (Retail) Ltd*[72].

The discretion of the Attorney-General had previously been exercised in proceedings involving, for example, the granting of injunctions to restrain breaches of planning provisions (*A-G v Bastow*[73] and *A-G v Smith*[74]), or where there had been persistent contraventions of byelaws (*A-G v Kerr & Ball*[75]), and although the *Solihull* case confirmed that a local authority could now in such circumstances sue in its own name, the constraining words '. . . for the promotion or protection of the interests of the inhabitants of their area . . .' awaited judicial consideration.

The phrase was not judicially defined by Oliver J in the *Solihull* case, since although the case concerned a market and breaches of the Shops Act (now repealed), the only argument before the court was as to whether an action for the enforcement of a public right had still to be instituted in the name of the Attorney-General notwithstanding s 222 of the 1972 Act.

The Court of Appeal's decision in *Stafford Borough Council v Elkenford Ltd*[76] also concerned a Sunday market and breaches of the Shops Act 1950 (now repealed); which the defendants had attempted to circumvent by the setting up of a proprietary club. The use of the land also contravened the then Town and Country Planning Act 1971. However, again, the scope of the constraining words of the section was not considered, the point not being taken. This case also came before Oliver J at first instance, and counsel for the defendant company submitted that, as injunctive relief is an ancillary remedy, he who seeks it must first demonstrate that the statutory remedy has been exhausted and that it is inadequate. He also submitted that an injunction should be granted only where there are persistent breaches of statute which demonstrate the inadequacy of the statutory remedy, and he cited as an example *A-G v Harris*[77], where the two defendants had been prosecuted and convicted for illegal street trading on no fewer than 142 and 95 occasions respectively.

Whilst Oliver J accepted that the court must at least consider the extent to which statutory remedies have been exhausted before exercising its discretion, he quoted with approval the dictum of Lord Denning MR in *A-G v Chaudry*[78].

> 'Whenever Parliament has enacted a law and given a particular remedy for the breach of it, such remedy being in an inferior court, nevertheless the High Court always has a reserve power to enforce the law so enacted by way of an injunction or declaration or other suitable remedy. The High Court has jurisdiction to ensure obedience to the law whenever it is just and convenient to do so[79].'

The learned judge did not consider that the court was restricted to granting injunctions only in those cases where permanent damage to the public interest is being

---

71 Approving the passage in *The Supreme Court Practice* at 15/11/5.
72 [1984] 2 WLR 929.
73 [1957] 1 QB 514.
74 [1958] 2 QB 173.
75 (1915) 79 JP 51.
76 [1977] 1 WLR 324.
77 [1961] 1 QB 74 (Sunday Market, proprietary 'club', a sham).
78 [1971] 1 WLR 1614.
79 *Ibid*, at 1624.

done, as, for instance, in *A-G v Ashborne Recreation Ground Co*[80] (threat to build in front of the building line), or where the intervention of the court is required as a matter of urgency because, for example, there is an element of public danger, as in *A-G v Chaudry*[81] (defendant restrained from using building as a hotel pending the grant of a certificate under the London Building Acts). The High Court has a wider jurisdiction where it is a case of a defendant

> '. . . who is quite deliberately organising and maintaining a system which, from first to last, is designed to break the law, relies for its existence on breach of the law, and assists and encourages others to break the law and to expose themselves to the risk of prosecution. It is a state of the conscious and deliberate provision of facilities by the use of which the individual traders in the market are invited and encouraged to participate in or assist regular and persistent contraventions of an Act of Parliament. And it is a case where the company's own evidence makes it perfectly plain that it intends to go on doing what is complained of. These considerations, as it seems to me, take the case right outside the ordinary run of cases where the court declines its assistance until exhaustion of the statutory remedies. It is perfectly plain that the fines provided by the Act are not in the slightest degree likely to deter the company from engaging in what is obviously a lucrative activity by which it obtains an advantage which is not open to those more law abiding tradesmen who consider it their duty, however unpalatable it may be, to observe the decrees of Parliament[82].'

The Court of Appeal supported the reasoning of Oliver J and dismissed the appeal against the grant to the local authority of the relief it sought by way of motion. Lord Denning was of the opinion that a local authority can, where there is a plain breach of a statutory provision which is likely to continue, apply immediately for an injunction:

> 'When there is a plain breach of the Act I do not think that the authorities concerned need wait at all for finality anywhere. They can take proceedings in the High Court before any other proceedings are even started. It is open to the court in its discretion to grant an injunction straight away, at all events when the breach of the law is plain and where there appears to be intention by the defendants to continue with the breach[83].'

However, Bridge LJ was somewhat more cautious in his approach.

> 'The reason why it is ordinarily proper to ask whether the authority seeking the injunction has first exhausted the statutory remedies is because in the ordinary case it is only because those remedies have been invoked and have proved inadequate that one can draw the inference, which is the essential foundation for the exercise of the court's discretion to grant an injunction, that the offender is, in the language of Oliver J, "deliberately and flagrantly flouting the law". In the appropriate case it may be possible, as Lord Denning MR has said, to draw that inference before there has been any resort to the statutory remedies at all. It would have to be shown that the scale of the operations was such that it could be legitimately inferred that they would continue unless and until effectively restrained by law. In some cases it may be apparent from the start that the profits the defendants are likely to make are such that nothing short

80 [1903] 1 Ch 101.
81 [1971] 1 WLR 1614.
82 [1977] 2 All ER 519 at 525.
83 [1977] 1 WLR 329.

of an injunction will be effective to restrain them. Finally, of course, in such a case it must be plain beyond doubt that there is no defence to a prosecution under the Act[84].'

The judgment of Bridge LJ was expressly approved by the House of Lords in *Stoke-on-Trent City Council v B & Q (Retail) Ltd*[85].

In another club case, *Bassetlaw District Council v Zaccaria*[86], the Court of Appeal upheld the decision of Whitford J that a 'members' club' was designed to avoid the provisions of the Shops Act and was a camouflage incapable of concealing the true nature of the transactions, which were sales between traders and persons coming to the site. The district council involved had not prosecuted under the Shops Act (now repealed) before commencing proceedings for injunctive relief, and it was considered by the legal department concerned that such prosecutions would prove ineffective in securing the cessation of breaches.

The scope of s 222(1) was considered to a limited degree in *Kent County Council v Batchelor*[87]. In this case the local authority had previously obtained an interlocutory injunction against a farmer restraining him from damaging or destroying trees on his land which had previously been made the subject of a tree preservation order. The local authority sought to have the defendant committed for breach of the terms of the injunction (a previously successful committal order having been quashed by the Court of Appeal on the ground that there was insufficient evidence). The defendant opposed this application and applied to have the interim injunction discharged on the grounds (*inter alia*) that the original proceedings should have been brought by the Attorney-General by way of a relator action and, in any event, the Attorney-General could exercise his discretion only where criminal acts were being committed and the penalties were wholly inadequate, or where urgent action was required.

Talbot J rejected the defendant's arguments and confirmed that the effect of s 222(1) was to enable a local authority to institute civil proceedings without first necessarily obtaining the concurrence of the Attorney-General. Furthermore, a local authority was not limited to obtaining an injunction in circumstances where the penalties for criminal offences were wholly inadequate. A local authority's statutory duty to protect areas of natural beauty did not stop at making tree preservation orders, but extended to enforcing those orders in order to protect areas of natural beauty, and to ensure that they are preserved. Since this concerned the interest of the inhabitants of its area, the local authority was empowered by s 222(1) to take proceedings to protect such areas.

The subsection again appears to have been considered to a limited degree by Goulding J in *Stoke-on-Trent City Council v Saxon Scaffolding Ltd*[88], where the headnote states that:

> 'The public interest . . . was much wider than nuisances by noise, excessive traffic and the like, and a local authority could bring an action against a single shop as in the present case without joinder of the Attorney-General. The offences alleged on the motion might yet be prosecuted in the Magistrates' Court; while the defendant might be in jeopardy of more serious penalities in that court than under the Shops Act 1950, there was nothing constitutionally wrong with granting the injunction sought.'

---

84 *Ibid*, at 330; and see also *Runnymede Borough Council v Ball* [1986] 1 WLR 353.
85 [1984] 2 WLR 929.
86 [1980] CLY 300 (and transcript).
87 [1979] 1 WLR 213.
88 (26 October 1979, unreported).

Similar considerations applied in *Westminster City Council v Jones*[89], a case which concerned a failure by the defendant to comply with the terms of a stop notice, and to cease using premises for the purposes of an amusement arcade. The plaintiffs sought an injunction (under s 222(1)) which was granted by Whitford J. In this case the court was not prepared to wait even one month for criminal proceedings relating to the stop notice to be heard, and considered it right that an injunction should be granted against a defendant who was determined to flout the law for as long as possible, and who was in flagrant disregard of the views of the local authority and in defiance of the notice.

Again, Whitford J in *Barking and Dagenham London Borough Council v Essexplan Ltd*[90] considered the scope of the subsection to a limited degree, in a case where the organisers of a market contended that, pending applications for registration of stall holders as Jewish traders pursuant to the provisions of s 53 of the Shops Act 1950 (now repealed), they were entitled to operate a Sunday market. The learned judge held that, as s 71(1) imposes a duty on councils to secure compliance with the provisions of the Shops Act 1950, such compliance with these provisions must be in the interests not only of those who live within the council's area but also of all inhabitants of the country.

H The Wolverhampton and Stoke-on-Trent cases

However, a new element was introduced into the debate regarding the scope of a local authority's powers pursuant to s 222(1) by the reported decision of Nourse J in the case of *Wolverhampton Borough Council v B & Q (Retail) Ltd*[91] (and followed, albeit with some apparent reluctance, by Goulding J in another reported decision against B & Q (Retail) Ltd[92]) in which the learned judge dismissed the plaintiff's motion for an interlocutory injunction, which sought to restrain deliberate and persistent breaches of the 1950 Act by the defendant company.

Within the area of Wolverhampton Borough Council B & Q (Retail) Ltd operated three DIY retail shops selling building materials and tools. On various Sundays between late spring and summer of 1982 the company carried on trading in contravention of s 47 of the 1950 Act (now repealed) at all three premises. Despite a warning letter from the Environmental Health Control Committee of the local authority in October 1982, and the company's conviction at Wolverhampton Magistrates' Court in November 1982 of 24 offences under s 47, when it was fined £50 in respect of each offence and ordered to pay £120 costs, further contraventions occurred.

The basis of the decision of the learned judge at first instance rested on a submission by defence Counsel (the same point apparently not having been taken in any previously reported case since the enactment of s 222), that as the motion was to restrain breaches of the criminal law it could only be made by the Attorney-General in relator proceedings, unless the evidence disclosed circumstances in which the plaintiff could properly consider it to be expedient, for the promotion or protection of the interests of the inhabitants of its area, that the application should be made.

It was held by Nourse J that the facts disclosed by the evidence did not establish that the case fell within s 222(1), and, accordingly, the proceedings were not properly constituted. Neither a local authority's desire to prevent the commission of crime in its area, was said to be sufficient. Although a local authority might consider it to be in the

---

89 (1981) 80 LGR 241.
90 (1983) 81 LGR 408.
91 (1983) 127 Sol Jo 68.
92 *Poole Borough Council v B & Q (Retail) Ltd* (1983) Times, 29 January.

interests of the inhabitants that its area should be respectable and as free from crime as possible, that was equally the concern of the public in general:

> '. . . it was not a special interest of the inhabitants of a particular area . . . it could not be assumed that the plaintiff's Environmental Health and Control Committee had a number of purely local considerations in mind. The evidence did not point to any particular prejudice to the inhabitants as opposed to the public in general[93].'

If s 222(1) were to be construed widely it might result in a very considerable number of cases being removed from the discretion of the Attorney-General and, as counsel submitted, this would involve the usurpation of his function, the importance of which had been emphasised in the *Gouriet* case[94] and which demonstrated that it should be exceptional for the aid of the civil court to be involved in support of the criminal law. As the learned judge stated in his judgment:

> 'The solemnity thus attaching to a decision made by the Crown's Senior Law Officer, whose office and experience in both fields give him a unique grasp of politico-legal considerations, emphasise that the power to make it was not to be regarded as having been removed from him and entrusted to a local authority unless the circumstances in which it was made fell fairly and squarely within s 222 . . .[95].'

However, the Court of Appeal allowed the appeal of Wolverhampton Borough Council against the decision of Nourse J at first instance, and also dismissed the appeal of B & Q (Retail) Ltd against the decision of Whitford J to grant an injunction to Stoke-on-Trent City Council. In a third appeal heard at the same time (*Barking and Dagenham London Borough Council v Home Charm Retail Ltd*), the defendant company's appeal against the decision of Falconer J to grant injunctive relief was allowed[96].

This decision, insofar as Stoke-on-Trent was concerned, was the subject of an unsuccessful appeal by B & Q to the House of Lords, where the decision of the Court of Appeal was affirmed[97].

The principles which can be distilled from this case, and which are still of considerable relevance, are as follows:

(1) Parliament has in some instances conferred limited powers on local authorities to institute and maintain proceedings to ensure compliance with public duties and has supplemented the power of the Attorney-General to act in the national interest with the power for a local authority to act in the interests of the public within its area.

(2) The terms of s 222(1) are sufficiently explicit to enable a local authority to bring proceedings in its own name without recourse to the Attorney-General. Such power was additional to and does not derogate from the power of the Attorney-General to enforce obedience to the public law.

(3) However, the power of a local authority to act arises only if it considers it expedient for the promotion or protection of the interests of the inhabitants of its area, and is in any event subject to the well-established principles relating to judicial review enunciated in *Associated Provincial Picture Houses Ltd v Wednesbury Corpn*[98].

---

93 (1983) 127 Sol Jo 68.
94 [1978] AC 435.
95 (1983) 127 Sol Jo 68.
96 [1983] 3 WLR 78.
97 [1984] 2 WLR 929.
98 [1948] 1 KB 223.

(4) Furthermore, as a matter of caution, something more than infringement of the criminal law (in this case s 47 of the Shops Act 1950 (now repealed)) must be shown before it is proper for the assistance of the civil process to be invoked by the local authority. It must be demonstrated that the offender is deliberately and flagrantly flouting the criminal law and that his unlawful operations will continue unless and until effectively restrained by law, and that nothing short of an injunction will be effective to restrain him[99].

(5) *Per curiam*. In carrying out the duty imposed on it by s 71(1) of the Shops Act 1950 (now repealed) a local authority had first to decide whether the conduct in question *prima facie* constitutes a contravention of the Act. If so, then it had to consider whether it is necessary to institute and carry on proceedings in respect of that *prima facie* contravention in order to secure observance of the provisions of the Act. In this connection, in similar enforcement cases the local authority is entitled to have regard in the particular case or cases in question to the financial consequences of any suggested action. If, for example, there is a serious or doubtful question of law involved which may invoke a series of appeals and thus cast a heavy financial burden on ratepayers, whatever the result but especially if the prosecution ultimately fails, the local authority after taking proper legal advice is not debarred from taking that factor among others into account before reaching its final decision whether or not it is necessary to institute and carry on proceedings[100].

Thus, the scope of a local authority's power under section 222(1) has been clarified by these decisions. But what lessons can be drawn from these judgments, and to what considerations should a local authority have regard before embarking upon injunctive relief to restrain breaches of the criminal law which it has a duty to enforce, bearing in mind that the section can be used in support of a wide range of breaches?

First, it must be remembered that this decision does not extend the general principle that a local authority is not entitled to use the civil courts to control criminal conduct and injunctive relief should not be sought as a general means of planning control.

Secondly, it is vitally important for a local authority to adopt correct procedures. In its deliberations on the merits of commencing proceedings pursuant to section 222, a local authority should consider the action taken hitherto by way of warnings to the offender, and subsequent prosecutions, if any. It should consider whether further warnings and/or prosecutions are likely to have any effect. If so, then clearly this should be the next step. On the other hand, the record of the offender in other areas or the terms in which any warning has been rejected may lead the local authority reasonably to infer that a further prosecution, or even a first prosecution, would have no deterrent effect, and would be a waste of time and money. Generally speaking, however, injunctive relief will be more readily granted if criminal sanctions have failed to deter.

Thirdly, it is important that those matters be incorporated into a written report to the appropriate committee possessing delegated powers. The committee's attention must be specifically drawn to section 222 and the limitation thereunder. The resolution should specifically state that it is considered expedient for the promotion or protection of the interests of the inhabitants of that area that proceedings for injunctive relief be instituted. If there has been some procedural failure then consideration must be given to the question of a subsequent ratification in order to regularise the position.

---

99 Dictum of Bridge LJ in *Stafford Borough Council v Elkenford Ltd* [1977] 1 WLR 324 at 330: applied in *Runnymede Borough Council v Ball* [1986] 1 WLR 353 and in *Wychavon District Council v Midland Enterprises (Special Events) Ltd* (1988) 86 LGR 83.

100 Dictum of Webster J in *R v Braintree District Council, ex p Willingham* (1983) 81 LGR 70 at 79 approved.

Fourthly, it goes without saying that these matters must be fully deposed to on affidavit by the appropriate officers of the local authority concerned.

5 RECENT DEVELOPMENTS AND THE EUROPEAN DIMENSION

There have been in recent years what could be described as a concerted set of challenges upon the rights held by the market owner, whether as an individual or as a local authority. There have been numerous attempts by rival market operators to seek to challenge the efficacy of such rights in the courts.

A Nature of the challenges

The nature of the challenges can be divide into two categories. First, there have been numerous reported and unreported cases in the courts where rival market operators have contended successfully or unsuccessfully that the market owner does not possess or is unable to seek to assert his market rights on a variety of different grounds. These include the failure of the market owner to provide sufficient evidence of title or sufficient evidence of loss and damage or the likelihood of loss and damage in an 'other day' rival market case, together with other assertions to which reference has been made above.

The second area of challenge has been based upon various Articles contained in the Treaty of Rome. This category can be sub-divided into two parts. First, those challenges which related to local authorities operating in their role as law enforcement agencies seeking to suppress breaches of the Shops Act 1950 (now repealed) by rival shop or market undertakings where the provisions of the Treaty of Rome have been raised. These have arisen particularly in relation to Article 30, which deals with the prohibition between the member states of quantitative restrictions on imports and all measures of an equivalent effect.

Following this, there has been the more recent development where rival market operators have sought to challenge the whole basis of private market law as being in breach of Article 85 (which deals with the question of restriction or distortion of competition) and Article 86 (which deals with the question of abuse of dominant position). Such challenges have also sought to pray in aid the provisions of Articles 30 and 52, the latter being directed to the position of market traders and the rights of self-employed nationals of one state to establish themselves within another member state.

B The Shops Act challenge

These developments seem to have first been recorded with arguments advanced by the defendants in the case of *Wychavon District Council v Midland Enterprises (Special Events) Ltd*[101] to the effect that the restrictions on Sunday trading imposed by the Shops Act 1950 (now repealed) were incompatible with Article 30. These arguments were rejected by the court.

Thereafter, this theme was taken up in a case brought before the Cwmbran Justices by Torfaen District Council in which the magistrates' court was required to give a decision on an information laid before it alleging that B & Q plc contravened the provisions of

---

101 (1988) 86 LGR 83.

sections 47 and 59 of the Shops Act 1950 (now repealed). The particular allegations related to retail premises owned by B & Q plc being open for serving customers on Sundays in Cwmbran for transactions other than those permitted by Schedule 5 to that Act.

In April 1988 the court referred the matter to the European Court of Justice for a preliminary ruling under Article 177 of the Treaty of Rome, raising three questions on the interpretation of Articles 30 and 36.

At about the same time convictions were imposed by Peterborough Magistrates' Court upon W H Smith Do-It-All Ltd and Payless DIY Ltd in respect of unlawful Sunday trading which were the subject of appeals to the Crown Court and eventually by way of cases stated to the Divisional Court. These were eventually dismissed after lengthy argument relating to the provisions of Article 30[102].

Eventually in November 1989[103] in the *Torfaen* case the European Court of Justice held that the national rules such as those imposed by the Shops Act 1950 (now repealed) with regard to the opening hours of retail premises constituted a legitimate part of economic and social policy consistent with the objects of public interest pursued by the EEC Treaty. They reflected certain political and economic choices insofar as their purpose was to ensure working and non-working hours were so arranged as to accord with national or regional socio-cultural characteristics. Such rules were not designed to govern patterns of trade between member states but were a matter for member states. Whether the effects of specific national rules extended what was necessary to achieve the aim in view was a question of fact to be determined by the national court. Thus, it followed that the prohibitions in Article 30 against measures having an effect equivalent to a quantitative restriction on imports did *not* apply to national rules prohibiting Sunday trading where the restrictive effects on Community trade which might result therefrom did not exceed the effects intrinsic to rules of that kind.

In paragraph 14 of its answer to the first of the three questions posed by Cwmbran Justices the European Court of Justices stated as follows:

> 'The same consideration [ie the national rules governing the hours of work, delivery and sale in the bread and confectionery industry constitute a legitimate part of economic and social policy, consistent with the objects of public interest pursued by the Treaty] must apply as regards national rules governing the opening hours of retail premises. Such rules reflect certain political and economic choices *insofar as* their purpose is to ensure that working and non-working hours are so arranged as to accord with national or regional socio-cultural characteristics, and that, in the present state of community law, is a matter for the member states. Furthermore, such rules are not designed to govern the patterns of trade between member states[104].'

In short, the European Court held that the validity of the law restricting Sunday trading in England and Wales depended on whether:

(a) It pursued an object justified under EEC law. In the *Torfaen* case it was held to be justified as the restriction on Sunday trading protected people from having to work on Sundays.

---

102 *Smith (WH) Do-It-All Ltd v Peterborough City Council, Payless DIY Ltd v Peterborough City Council* [1991] 1 QB 304, [1991] 4 All ER 193, [1991] 3 WLR 1131.

103 Caser C-145/88: *Torfaen Borough Council v B & Q plc* [1990] 2 QB 19, [1990] 1 All ER 129. The opinion of Mr Walter van Gerven, Advocate-General to the European Court, was given in June 1989; [1989] ECR 3851.

104 [1990] 2 QB 19 at 53.

(b) The test of 'proportionality' was satisfied, that is, whether the effects of the restriction on trade between member states were disproportionate to its legitimate aim. In the *Torfaen* case it was held that it was up to the national courts to determine whether on the facts the test was satisfied.

Although argument was directed towards the two further questions posed by the Cwmbran Justices, in the *Torfaen* case, the European Court of Justice said it was unnecessary to answer these questions in view of the answer to the first question[105].

The judgment in the *Torfaen* case was intended to be an authoritative interpretation of the EEC Treaty sufficient to enable the domestic courts to decide the case. Unfortunately, since the judgment there have been arguments over what the judgment in fact actually means, in particular, with regard to the issue of proportionality.

The words 'insofar as' were considered in the case of *Stoke-on-Trent City Council v B & Q plc*[106] by Hoffman J where it was held that the meaning of 'insofar as' was not 'if it is the case that' but rather 'because' and the European Court was deciding that the purpose of section 47 of the Shops Act 1950 (now repealed) satisfied this description. In any event, as Hoffman J stated, it seemed:

> '. . . plain and obvious that the purpose of section 47 was to arrange working and non-working hours in shops in England and Wales so as to accord with the "regional socio-cultural characteristics" by which people generally do not work on Sundays[107].'

However, in the *Stoke-on-Trent City Council v B & Q plc*[108] case Hoffman J had to consider a number of further points raised by counsel for B & Q particularly with regard to the second question before the European Court in the *Torfaen* case, which the Court had declined to answer on the basis that it was a question of fact to be determined by the national court. Thereafter the House of Lords, after allowing a petition by the defendants in November 1990, declined to rule upon the appeal which had been the subject of the 'leapfrogging' procedure, and referred the whole question raised in the *Stoke-on-Trent City Council v B & Q plc* case back to the European Court. The hearing of the appeals was adjourned pending receipt of the answers from the European Court of Justice.

On 8 July 1992 Mr Walter van Gerven, Advocate-General to the European Court, delivered his long-awaited opinion on the *Torfaen* case and two other cases[109].This opinion was endorsed by the European Court when it delivered its full judgment in the matter on 16 December 1992[110]. The conclusion reached supports the judgment of the European Court in the *Torfaen* case. The opinion stated that as a matter of principle it is not for the national court to determine the proportionality of a national measure under Community law on the evidence before it and in circumstances where the measure is held to be disproportionate to declare it to be incompatible with Community law and determine the consequences under national law of that declaration. The European Court of Justice in its judgment provided the unequivocal answer that Article 30 is to be interpreted as meaning that the prohibition which it lays down does not apply to

---

105 [1990] 2 QB 19 at 53.

106 *Stoke-on-Trent City Council v B & Q plc, Norwich City Council v B & Q plc* [1991] Ch 48.

107 *Ibid*, at 64.

108 [1991] Ch 48.

109 Case C-306/88: *Rochdale Borough Council v Anders* (see [1988] 3 All ER 490; and seee [1993] 1 All ER 520n). Case C-304/90: *Reading Borough Council v Payless DIY Ltd.* Case C-169/91: *Stoke-on-Trent City Council and Norwich City Council v B & Q plc.*

110 [1993] 2 WLR 730.

national legislation prohibiting retailers from opening their premises on Sundays. As a result of this ruling the House of Lords, in March 1993, dismissed the appeals in the *Stoke-on-Trent City Council v B & Q plc* case[111].

C Market rights and the Treaty of Rome

Market rights are essentially of a private nature and being incorporeal hereditaments have the same status as any other private property rights. They can be enforced or not enforced depending upon the circumstances. There should be no question of these rights giving rise to a law enforcement action as in the case of a public statute even in the case where the franchise itself may have been modified or superseded by statute. Whether the market rights in question are held by individuals or by local authorities, they still remain private rights albeit of benefit to the public. In the case of a local authority it is not, as a public body, under any public duty to enforce these rights. However, it may render itself susceptible to judicial review if it fails to adopt or follow correct procedures in seeking to invoke its rights.

Organisations seeking to challenge these private rights might attempt to draw a distinction between the rights held by a statutory market owner and the rights held by the owner of a franchise. However, case law has affirmed and re-affirmed that a market established under a local or public Act enjoys all the incidents and privileges of a market created by charter unless the statute otherwise provides. This means that the incorporeal rights associated with a charter market are ascribed to a statutory market. Thus private rights, albeit under a public Act such as the Food Act 1984, should not therefore easily be susceptible to review under the provisions of the Treaty of Rome.

No case has so far come before the English courts where *substantive* consideration has been given to Article 30, 85 or 86 in relation to market rights, although there have been a number of cases where such issues have been raised.

In one unreported case (*Birmingham City Council v In Shops plc*[112]) assertions were made with regard to the provisions of Article 86 of the Treaty of Rome on the basis that the exercise of what were called the 'monopoly rights' held by Birmingham Corporation constituted the abuse of a dominant position within a substantial part of the common market so as to affect trade between member states contrary to the Article.

A further contention was raised (but not pursued) in that case relating to Article 52 of the Treaty of Rome to the effect that the Council was infringing the prohibition on discrimination against nationalities as only UK nationals could obtain the right to operate markets in Birmingham. This was a point which had been raised in a previous case and then rejected by the Court of Appeal in *R v Crown Court at Southwark, ex p Watts*[113].

The difficulty with the proposition based upon the Article 86 point raised in the *Birmingham City Council* case[114] was that no evidence at all had been adduced to support the allegation that the City Council was abusing its dominant position (if indeed it could be construed as having one). This case went almost immediately to the Court of Appeal where Scott LJ reiterated the aspect of lack of evidence, and, as he stated, in most cases where a breach of Article 86 is successfully alleged a very great deal of evidence is required.

---

111 [1993] 2 WLR 730 at 772–774.
112 [1992] NPC 71; *on appeal* (1 June 1992, unreported).
113 2 May 1992, 156 LG Rev 343, and see p 116, (1989) 153 JP 666.
114 [1992] NPC 71; *on appeal* (1 June 1992, unreported).

The case of *Birmingham City Council v In Shops plc*[115] is also instructive not least because of the consideration of the question of the balance of convenience. It was said by Scott LJ that the raising of the Article 86 point particularly meant that the trial of the action would be likely to lie some fair distance in the future and could well result in a reference to the European Court. That would entail even greater delay in the case than the conduct of civil litigation inevitably entails. Thus, the Court of Appeal was minded not to discharge the injunction obtained by the City Council and concluded that Hoffman J was correct that the bounds of convenience favoured the grant of an interlocutory injunction pending the trial of the action.

Article 30 of the Treaty of Rome fell to be considered by Jacob J in *South Pembrokeshire District Council v Wendy Fair Markets Ltd*[116].

Here the Council, being the holder of ancient market rights, sought an interim injunction pending trial against the defendants who were threatening to hold two separate markets within the common law distance of 6⅔ miles. The defendants, *inter alia*, sought to rely upon Article 30 as a defence to the action. Article 30 provides:

> 'Quantitative restrictions on imports and all measures having an equivalent effect shall, without prejudice to the following provisions, be prohibited between member-States.'

It was argued that the *Dassonville* principle[117] applied. This was on the basis that since some goods from the EC were sold in the markets there was the possibility of a hindrance on inter-state trade either in the trading of one stall holder or in an individual product. This meant that the market right claimed would fail. Indeed on this interpretation most market rights would fail. Against this the ECJ has rejected this general approach in *Torfaen* and *Stoke-on-Trent*. Jacob J held that the Article 30 case law was unclear and that there was a triable issue. The facts needed to be fully determined before a reference were made to the ECJ, particularly as Article 85 and 86 points had also been pleaded both by way of defence and counterclaim which would have to be investigated irrespective of Article 30.

As to the interlocutory injunction, this was granted on the 'balance of convenience' since the Council was faced with a direct challenge to its alleged monopoly and damages were not an adequate remedy should the Council succeed at the trial of the action. If no injunction were granted, pending such trial, this would enable third parties to establish markets pending resolution of the case. Further, the Council's own market traders might suffer as a result of the defendants operating a competing market and there was some evidence that the Council's own market traders had suffered during the time when the defendants had operated their market. Finally, the *status quo* lay in favour of the Council.

In the case of *Keck and Mithouard*[118] there has been a further gloss on the *Dassonville* principle in relation to its treatment of Article 30 which would appear to provide further support to the continued exercise by councils of their market rights.

At the present time a substantive ruling is still awaited on the merits as to the applicability of Articles 30, 85 and 86 of the Treaty of Rome to market law and as to whether or not a Court could be persuaded to uphold the contentions that these provisions of the Treaty of Rome apply to private market rights. In the *South*

---

115 *Ibid.*
116 [1994] 1 CMLR 213.
117 *Procureur du Roi v Dassonville* (8/74) [1975] FSR 191; [1974] ECR 837.
118 Cases C-267, 268/91: [1993] ECR I-6097, 1995] CMLR 101, ECJ.

Pembrokeshire case[119] no substantive ruling was made on the interlocutory hearing as to the applicability of these Articles, the matter being stood over for trial and a possible reference to the European Court. An injunction was granted in the meantime. However, it must be said that it would be surprising if a court would even consider the question of the application of Article 30 in a non-law enforcement action when successive courts including the European Court have rejected its applicability to Sunday trading.

Perhaps the whole matter can be summed up by the words of Hoffman J in the case of *Stoke-on-Trent City Council v B & Q plc*[120] where he stated that:

> 'the member states of the Community differ widely in their histories, customs and social and cultural values. It was certainly not the object of the Community to introduce uniformity in all these matters. The purpose of the Treaty was to bring about a European Common Market but not to interfere with national laws and customs which did not constitute obstacles to the establishment of such a market . . . It is the function of the European Court of Justice in Luxembourg to interpret the Treaty and for the national court to apply it. In its interpretation of the Treaty, the European Court has tried to tread a careful line which permits both boldness in advancing the objects of the Community and sensitivity to the domestic interests and member states.'

D Deregulation

It should also be mentioned that, on 16 August 1993, the DoE published a Consultation Paper, seeking views, *inter alia*, on the proposal that there should be early legislation to remove from local authorities the common law right to object to the establishment of new markets. This government proposal emanated from the De-Regulation Panel of the DTI and the Conservative Prime Minister's Policy Review Unit generated by pressure from certain private market operators.

These proposals were eventally incorporated into three clauses in the Deregulation and Contracting Out Bill which were in effect designed to restrict a local authority's ability to suppress a rival market operation on and after the date upon which these provisions would have become law. In other words, rival markets would have been able to operate freed from the market owner's right to protection capable of being enforced by injunction and/or damages. The proposed legislation would have proscribed the right to pursue the tort of disturbance to suppress the rival market undertaking within 6⅔ miles of the market owner's established market.

On 10 May 1994 after a somewhat stormy passage in the House of Commons, the government withdrew these clauses from the Bill at the Report Stage with a view to further discussion with all interested parties as to how best to remove the adverse effects of market franchise and monopoly rights in the light of a perceived general consensus that there was a need to modernise the law. The intention was that new clauses would be produced and inserted in the Bill during the deliberations in the House of Lords.

However, on 18 October 1994 in response to a written question to the government in the House of Lords:

> 'What proposals in the Deregulation and Contracting Out Bill they are bringing forward on market franchise rights'

---

119 [1994] 1 CMLR 213, see footnote 116.
120 [1991] Ch 48.

the following written answer was provided:

> 'Following the decision to withdraw the then Clauses 22, 23 and 24 on market franchise rights from the Bill, my right honourable friend the then Minister for Industry expressed the hope that the Government would be able to come forward at a later stage with fresh proposals on the deregulation of market franchise rights which enjoyed a widespread measure of support among interested parties.
>
> The Government remain of the view that the common law on market franchise rights is antiquated. Interested parties do not dispute that the law needs revision, but say that any review would need to be more considered.
>
> In view, however, of the very short time remaining for consideration of the Deregulation and Contracting Out Bill in Parliament the Government is not intending to make changes to existing law in the context of the current Bill.'

The Bill was then enacted without any of the features being included relating to the modification of market franchise rights as had originally been envisaged. No further proposals have been made.

6 EVIDENCE OF MARKET RIGHTS

It is proposed here to treat shortly the evidence which may be available to establish market and fair rights. The right to hold a market or fair may be proved by:

(1) production of the original charter or letters patent, or properly attested copies thereof; or

(2) reference to the public Act of Parliament by which the rights are given, or, if a private Act, by production of a Queen's Printer's copy of it; or

(3) production of evidence of immemorial or long user, ie prescription or presumption of lost grant[121].

A Grants

From the close of the twelfth century to the year 1516, the king's grants of franchises were made by charter, and thenceforward by letters patent. All these grants are recorded in the Charter Rolls and Patent Rolls deposited at the Record Office. The grants recorded in the Charter Rolls may be either grants of liberties which had not been previously granted, or confirmation charters, ie charters confirming previous grants with or without the addition of further privileges. When the original grant is recited in the confirmation charter, the latter is called an inspeximus charter[122]. The origin of a fair or market may be proved by a charter of one of the above kinds, or by letters patent.

Both charters and letters patent may be proved by the production of the original under the great seal, of which the court takes judicial notice[123]. Primary evidence of charters or letters patent may also it seems, be given (without accounting for the

---

121 The question of sufficiency of evidence of the entitlement to a fair was considered by the Court of Appeal in *Wyld v Silver* [1963] Ch 243; see pp 89, 100, 101, *above*.

122 See Introduction to printed volume of the *Rotuli Chartarum*, by Sir T Duffus Hardy, 1837. Palmer's Index, No 93, in the Record Office contains a list of grants of markets and fairs from 1 John to 22 Edw IV.

123 *Lane's Case* (1586) 2 Co Rep 16b at 17b. But note the difficulties which arose in *Gloucestershire County Council v Farrow* [1983] 2 All ER 1031; affirmed [1985] 1 All ER 878 (see pp 99, 100, *above*).

original) by an exemplification or enrolment[124].

An exemplification is an exact copy sealed with the great seal[125]. An enrolment is the roll of charters and letters patent now preserved in the Public Record Office[126]; and the enrolment is itself a public document, which need not be produced in court, but may be proved by an exemplification, or by an examined copy[127], or by a copy examined and certified by the deputy keeper of the records or one of the assistant record keepers, and sealed or stamped with the seal of the Record Office[128].

B Acts of Parliament

Most local and personal Acts passed before 1851 contain a section declaring them public, and every Act passed after the year 1850 is a public Act, unless the contrary is expressly provided[129]. The courts take judicial notice of public Acts. If, however, an Act is not public, it must be proved[130]. This is most conveniently done by producing a copy purporting to be printed by the Queen's printer, or under the authority or superintendence of Her Majesty's Stationery Office[131].

C Evidence of ancient user

To establish a market or fair by prescription, or presumption of lost grant[132], or to prove customary rights therein[133], user within time of living memory will usually be proved by the evidence of living witnesses. Though not absolutely necessary[134] it is always advisable to carry the evidence further back than the date to which the memory of the oldest living witnesses can carry it. For this purpose, evidence of reputation and documentary evidence of various kinds may be used and a careful search should therefore be made in the Record Office, and in the muniment room of the supposed owner of the franchise.

D Acts of ownership

Some documents are admissible in evidence as acts of ownership. Among these are old leases and conveyances of the market or fair, or of the tolls[135], tables of tolls which have been exhibited in the market or used by collectors of toll[136], appointments of stewards,

---

124 See the Introduction to the *Rotuli Chartarum* by Sir T Duffus Hardy (1837), pp xviii and xix.

125 See the Introduction to the *Rotuli Chartarum* by Sir T Duffus Hardy (1837), p vii.

126 *Ibid*, pp i and vii; and see Public Records Act 1958.

127 That is, a copy which a witness swears he has examined with the original and found to be correct.

128 Public Records Act 1958, ss 9, 10; Evidence Act 1845, s 1; Evidence Act 1851, s 14. For the requisite evidence for the purposes of an interlocutory injunction, see pp 147–149 *above* and *Warwick Corpn v Maby* (1971) 115 Sol Jo 965.

129 Interpretation Act 1978 s 3, s 22(1), Sch 2, para 2.

130 *R v Sutton* (1816) 4 M & S 532, 542. See also *Wyld v Silver* [1963] Ch 243; *Birmingham Corpn v Perry Bar Stadium Ltd* [1972] 1 All ER 725; and *Leicester Corpn v Maby* (1971) 70 LGR 209.

131 Evidence Act 1845, s 3; Documentary Evidence Act 1882, s 2.

132 See pp 17 to 19, *above*. And see the comments of Walton J in *Kingston-upon-Thames Royal Borough Council v Sherman and Waterman Associates Ltd* (6 July 1976, unreported).

133 See pp 57, 58, *above*.

134 See pp 17 to 19, *above*.

135 *Penryn Corpn v Best* (1878) 3 Ex D 292, 296; *Bristow v Cormican* (1878) 3 App Cas 641, 653; *Malcolmson v O'Dea* (1863) 10 HL Cas 593, 672, 614; *De Rutzen (Baron) v Farr* (1835) 4 Ad & El 53; *Mosley v Walker* (1827) 7 B & C 40, 43; *Beaufort (Duke) v Smith* (1849) 4 Exch 450, 471.

136 *Brett v Beales* (1829) Mood & M 416, 419; *Lawrence v Hitch* (1868) LR 3 QB 521.

bailiffs, or other officers[137], writs, pleadings, and other proceedings in actions brought by the owner for toll or disturbance, proceedings in the court of pie powder, and proceedings relating to the market or fair in the court leet or borough court[138]. If the documents are produced from proper custody, they are presumed in the absence of evidence to the contrary to be duly executed according to their purport[139].

E Declarations against interest

Accounts made out by deceased bailiffs or stewards, wherein they debit themselves with tolls, which they profess to have collected personally, are admissible in evidence, as declarations by deceased persons against their interest, to prove that tolls were in fact paid[140]. And payments of rent for a market may be proved in the same way.

F Evidence of reputation.

The public have a right to enter and buy and sell[141], and it seems that the public interest in market rights is sufficient to let in evidence of reputation when the question is as to the existence of a market or the right to take toll[142]. If so, the mere statements of deceased persons, whether oral or written, which embody a common report, and were made before any controversy had arisen, are admissible and may be proved by a living witness[143]. Of greater value are formal written statements in the nature of reputation. Among writings of this kind are depositions[144], rates and assessments[145], recitals or descriptions in leases and conveyances[146], or in Acts of Parliament[147]. And some evidence may be found in presentments of manorial and other customary courts[148]. Extracts from Domesday Book are probably admissible as evidence of this kind. That book contains many references to markets existing at the time of its compilation[149]. Reference can also be made to the Royal Commission on Market Rights and Tolls (1888–1891).

---

137 *Penryn Corpn v Best, above; Malcolmson v O'Dea, above; Caernarvon (Earl) v Villebois* (1844) 13 M & W 313, 329.

138 *Mosley v Walker, above.*

139 *R v Farringdon Inhabitants* (1788) 2 Term Rep 466; *Wynne v Tyrwhitt* (1821) 4 B & Ald 376; *Brett v Beales* (1829) Mood & M 416.

140 *De Rutzen (Baron) v Farr* (1835) 4 Ad & El 53; *Exeter Corpn v Warren* (1844) 5 QB 773; *Doe d Webber v Thynne* (1808) 10 East 206; *Doe d Ashburnham v Michael* (1851) 17 QB 276; *Beaufort (Duke) v Smith* (1849) 4 Exch 450, 471; and see notes to *Higham v Ridgway* (1808) 10 East 109.

141 See pp 27, 28, 34, 52, 53, *above.*

142 Compare *Caernarvon (Earl) v Villebois* (1844) 13 M & W 313, 332; *Brett v Beales* (1829) Mood & M 416; *Drinkwater v Porter* (1835) 7 C & P 181; *Pim v Currell* (1840) 6 M & W 234.

143 See *Crease v Barrett* (1835) 1 Cr M & R 919, 929; *Barraclough v Johnson* (1838) 8 Ad & El 99; *Thomas v Jenkins* (1837) 6 Ad & El 525; *R v Cotton* (1813) 3 Camp 444; *R v Bliss* (1837) 7 Ad & El 550.

144 *Freeman v Phillips* (1816) 4 M & S 486.

145 See *R v Cotton* (1813) 3 Camp 444.

146 *Plaxten v Dare* (1829) 10 B & C 17; *Brett v Beales* (1829) Mood & M 416.

147 *Caernarvon (Earl) v Villebois* (1844) 13 M & W 313, 332; *R v Sutton* (1816) 4 M & S 532. See also *Wyld v Silver* [1963] Ch 243; *Birmingham Corpn v Perry Bar Stadium Ltd* [1972] 1 All ER 725; and *Leicester Corpn v Maby* (1972) 70 LGR 209.

148 See *Beaufort (Duke) v Smith* (1849) 4 Exch 450; *Roe d Beebee v Parker* (1792) 5 Term Rep 26; *Talbot v Lewis* (1834) 1 Cr M & R 495.

149 Extracts from Domesday may be proved by an examined or certified copy in accordance with the Public Records Act 1958, ss 9 and 10.

G Verdicts and judgments

Upon the same principle verdicts and judgments in previous actions in which the existence of a market or fair, or the right to take toll, was in issue are receivable in evidence in subsequent actions where the same matter is in issue, although the parties are different, provided that they have the same relative interest[150]. So the proceedings, and the judgment and finding of the jury, in *quo warranto* proceedings[151], allowances before Justices in Eyre[152], inquisitions to ascertain the extent of Crown lands[153], the returns to inquisitions post mortem[154], and extents of manors[155], may be given in evidence. The 'Placita de Quo Warranto'[156], 'Abbreviato Placitorum', and 'Rotuli Hundredorum' all contain many records relating to markets and fairs.

---

150 *Pim v Currell* (1840) 6 M & W 234; *Brisco v Lomax* (1833) 8 Ad & El 198, 214; *Caernarvon (Earl) v Villebois* (1844) 13 M & W 313, 331; *Reed v Jackson* (1801) 1 East 355; cf *Beaufort (Duke) v Smith* (1849) 4 Exch 450.

151 *Caernarvon (Earl) v Villebois* (1844) 13 M & W 313, 331; *Egremont (Earl) v Saul* (1837) 6 Ad & El 924.

152 Per Parke B in *Caernarvon (Earl) v Villebois* (1844) 13 M & W 313, 331; *Doe d William IV v Roberts* (1844) 13 M & W 520.

153 *Rowe v Brenton* (1828) 8 B & C 737, 747.

154 *Mosley v Walker* (1827) 7 B & C 40, 42, and see the *Calendarum Inquisitionum post mortem*, vol i introductory note (1806).

155 See the statute Extenta Manerii 4 Ed 1, Stat 1 (Ruff); Incert Temp (Stat Realm); repealed by SLR Act 1863.

156 The volume entitled 'Placita de Quo Warranto' was printed under the superintendance of the Record Commission in 1818. The volume contains records of most of the *quo warranto* proceedings in the reigns of Edw I, II and III. As to the nature and purpose of these proceedings, see Introduction to the volume, and *Stuart Moore on Foreshore*, pp 42–46 and 69–72.

Statutes

METROPOLITAN POLICE ACT 1839

(2 & 3 Vict, c 47)

An Act for further improving the Police in and near the Metropolis

[17th August 1839]

38. Fairs not to be carried on between 11 pm and 6 am etc

The business and amusements of all fairs(1) holden within the metropolitan police district(2) shall cease at the hour of eleven in the evening, and shall not begin earlier than the hour of six in the morning; and if any house, room, booth, standing, tent, caravan, waggon, or other place shall, during the continuance of any such fair, be open within the hours of eleven in the evening and six in the morning for any purpose of business or amusement, in the place where such fair shall be holden, [. . .](3) the person having the care or management thereof, and also every person being therein who shall not quit the same forthwith upon being bidden by such constable so to do; and the person so then having the care or management of any such house, room, booth, standing, tent, caravan, waggon, or other place, shall be liable to a penalty, not more than [level 1 on the standard scale](4) and every person convicted of having been therein, and of not having quitted the same forthwith upon being bidden by a constable so to do, shall be liable to a penalty not more than [level 1 on the standard scale](4).

(1) This section does not appear to apply to fairs which are not markets (see *above*, pp 1, 2 and 46) but which consist merely of amusements; cf *Collins v Cooper* (1893) 68 LT 450; *Walker v Murphy* [1914] 2 Ch 293; affd [1915] 1 Ch 71, CA.

(2) As from 1 April 1965 the Metropolitan Police District comprises Greater London (excluding the City, Inner Temple and Middle Temple) and adjacent small parts of Essex, Herts, and Surrey: London Government Act 1963, s 76(1)(a)–(d); Police Act 1964, s 62(4), Sch 8).

(3) Repealed by the Police and Criminal Evidence Act 1984, ss 26(1), 119(2), Sch 7, Pt I.

(4) Maximum penalties increased to £25 by the Criminal Law Act 1977, s 31(6); and by virtue of the Criminal Justice Act 1982, s 46, the reference to those amounts is converted to a reference to level 1 on the standard scale set out in s 37(2) thereof.

39. Fairs within the metropolitan police district may be inquired into, and may be declared unlawful, either altogether or beyond a stated period

If it shall appear to the commissioners of police that any fair [. . .](1) holden within the metropolitan police district has been holden without lawful authority(2), or that any fair lawfully holden within the said district has been [. . .](1) holden for a longer period than is so warranted, it shall be competent to such commissioners to direct one of the superintendents belonging to the metropolitan police force to summon the owner or occupier of the ground upon which such fair is [. . .](1) holden to appear before a magistrate at a time and place to be specified in the summons, not less than eight days after the service of the summons, to show his right and title to hold such fair, or to hold such fair beyond a given period (as the case may be); and if such owner or occupier shall not attend in pursuance of such summons, or shall not show to the magistrate who shall hear the case sufficient cause to believe that such fair has been lawfully holden for the whole period during which the same has been [. . .](1) holden, the magistrate shall declare(3) in writing such fair to be unlawful, either altogether or beyond a stated period (as the case may be); and the commissioners shall give notice of such declaration by causing copies thereof to be affixed on the parish church and on other public places in and near the ground where such fair has been [. . .](1) holden; and if, after such notices have been affixed for the space of six days, any attempt shall be made to hold such fair if it shall be declared altogether unlawful, or to hold it beyond the prescribed period if it shall be declared unlawful beyond a certain period, the commissioners of police may direct any constable to remove every booth, standing, and tent, and every carriage of whatsoever kind conveyed to or being upon the ground for the purpose of holding or continuing such fair, and [. . .](4) every person erecting, pitching, or fixing, or assisting to erect, a pitch, or fix, any such booth, standing, or tent, and every person driving, accompanying, or conveyed in every such carriage, and every person resorting to such ground with any show or instrument of gambling or amusement [shall be guilty of an offence](4); and every person convicted before a magistrate of any of the offences last aforesaid shall be liable to a penalty not more than [level 1 on the standard scale](5).

(1) The words omitted were repealed by Statute Law Revision Act 1874 (No 2) (37 & 38 Vict, c 96).

(2) As to the control of a fair held or proposed to be held within the Metropolitan Police District on ground other than that on which it has been held during the past seven years, see Metropolitan Fairs Act 1868, *below*, p 187.

As to the limitations of the hours of holding a fair in that district, see s 38 of this Act, *above*.

See also *above*, pp 29, 33, 45 as to the general restrictions on the places and days on which fairs may be held.

(3) Whether or not the magistrate has declared the fair unlawful, if the owner or occupier enters into recognizances to have the question of lawfulness decided by the High Court, the notice of declaration of unlawfulness and other measures are suspended until judgment of the High Court is given; see s 40, *below*.

(4) Words omitted repealed and words inserted by the Police and Criminal Evidence Act 1984, ss 26, 119(2), Sch 6, Pt I, para 2, Sch 7, Pt I.

(5) Words substituted by virtue of the Criminal Justice Act 1982, ss 38, 46.

40. On owner, etc, of ground entering into recognizance, the declaration of illegality shall be suspended until the right and title to the fair has been tried in the Queen's Bench

Provided nevertheless, that if the owner or occupier of the ground where on any such fair has been [. . .](1) holden shall, when summoned before the magistrate, enter into a recognizance in the final sum of two hundred pounds (which recognizance such magistrate is hereby authorized to take) with condition to appear in the Court of Queen's Bench(2) on the first day of the next term and to answer to any information which Her Majesty's attorney [. . .](3) general may exhibit against such owner or occupier touching his right and title to such fair, and to abide the judgment of the court thereon, and to pay such costs as may be awarded by the court, which costs the said court is hereby authorized to award, then, notwithstanding the magistrate may have declared such fair to be unlawful, the commissioners of police shall forbear from giving notice of such declaration, and from taking any further measures thereon, until judgment shall be given by the said court against the right and title to such fair; and the magistrate taking such recognizance shall forthwith transmit the same to one of Her Majesty's principal secretaries of state, to the end that the same may be filed in the said court, and such further directions may be given thereon as to such secretary of state may seem fit.

(1) The word omitted was repealed by Statute Law Revision Act 1874 (No 2) (37 & 38 Vict, c 96).

(2) The jurisdiction of the Court of Queen's Bench is now vested in the High Court; see Supreme Court of Judicature (Consolidation) Act 1925 (15 & 16 Geo V, c 49), s 18 (2) (*a*) (now repealed).

(3) Words omitted repealed by the Law Officers Act 1997, s 3(2), Sch.

RAILWAYS CLAUSES CONSOLIDATION ACT 1845

(8 & 9 Vict, c 20)

An Act for consolidating in One Act certain Provisions usually inserted in Acts authorizing the making of Railways

[8 May 1845]

With respect to the recovery of damages not specially provided for, and of penalties, and to the determination of any other matter referred to justices, be it enacted as follows:

Clauses 140–161 inclusive of this Act are, by s 52 of the Markets and Fairs Clauses Act 1847, incorporated with that Act, and any special Act which incorporates that section. In printing these clauses below, the word 'undertakers' has been substituted for the word 'company' pursuant to the directions in s 52 of the Act of 1847.

140. Provision for ascertainment of damages not otherwise provided for—Enforcement by distress([1])

In all cases where any damages, costs, or expenses are by this or the special Act([2]), or any Act incorporated therewith, directed to be paid, and the method of ascertaining the amount or enforcing the payment thereof is not provided for([3]), such amount, in case of dispute, shall be ascertained and determined([4]) by two justices([5]); [. . .]([6]).

([1]) Repealed in part in Northern Ireland only by the Statute Law Revision (NI) Act 1980, s 1, Sch, Pt I.

([2]) For the meaning of 'special Act', see s 2 of Markets and Fairs Clauses Act 1847, *below*.

([3]) These clauses do not, it seems, apply to the recovery of damages sustained by reason of the exercise by undertakers of the powers of constructing their undertaking; see the Markets and Fairs Clauses Act 1847, s 11.

([4]) Damages, costs and expenses to which this section applies can be recovered only in the manner provided by this section; *Blackburn Corpn v Parkinson* (1858), 1 E & E 71.

([5]) As to the justices having jurisdiction, see the Markets and Fairs Clauses Act 1847, s 3, *below* and s 55.

As to the procedure, see s 142 of this Act, *below*.

([6]) Words omitted repealed by the Statute Law (Repeals) Act 1993.

141. [. . .]([1])

([1]) Repealed (except in Northern Ireland) by the Transport Act 1962, ss 93(1), 95(1), Sch 12, Pt I.

142. Method of proceeding before justices in questions of damages, etc([1])

Where in this or the special Act([2]) any question of compensation, expenses, charges, or damages, or other matter, is referred to the determination of any one justice, or more([3]), it shall be lawful for any justice, upon the application of either party, to summon the other party to appear before one justice, or before two justices, as the case may require, at a time and place to be named in such summons; and upon the appearance of such parties, or in the absence of any of them, upon proof of due service of the summons, it shall be lawful for such one justice, or such two justices, as the case may be, to hear and determine such question, and for that purpose to examine such parties or any of them, and their witness, on oath; and the cost of every such inquiry shall be in the discretion of such justices, and they shall determine the amount thereof.

([1]) Repealed in part in Northern Ireland only by the Statute Law Revision (NI) Act 1980, s 1, Sch, Pt IV.

(2) See note (2) to s 140, *above*.
(3) See note (5) to s 140, *above*, as to the jurisdiction of justices.

143. [. . .](1)

(1) Repealed by the Transport Act 1962, ss 93(1), 95(1), Sch 12, Pt II.

144. Penalty for defacing boards used for such publication(1)

If any person pull down or injure any board put up or affixed [for the purpose of publishing any byelaw of the company or any penalty imposed by this or the special Act](2), or shall obliterate any of the letters or figures thereon, he shall forfeit for every such offence a sum not exceeding [level 1 on the standard scale](3) and shall defray the expenses attending the restoration of such board.

(1) Maximum penalty increased to £25 by the Criminal Law Act 1977, s 31(6); and by virtue of the Criminal Justice Act 1982, s 46, the reference to that amount is converted to a reference to level 1 of the standard scale set out in s 37(2) thereof.
(2) Substituted by the Transport Act 1962, ss 84(4), 93(1).
(3) Substituted by the Criminal Justice Act 1982, ss 38, 46.

145. Penalties to be summarily recovered before two justices

Every penalty or forfeiture imposed by this or the special Act, [. . .](1) the recovery of which is not otherwise provided for, may(2) be recovered by summary proceedings before two justices(3). . . .(4)

(1) Repealed by the Transport Act 1962, ss 93(1), 95(1), Sch 12, Pt II. As to forfeitures under the Markets and Fairs Clauses Act, 1847, see *ibid*, ss 50 and 59.
(2) A penalty or forfeiture to which this section applies may be recovered only in the manner provided by this section and cannot be recovered by action; *London and Brighton Rly Co v Watson* (1879) 4 CPD 118.
(3) As to the justices having jurisdiction, see the Markets and Fairs Clauses Act 1847, s 3, *below* and s 55.
(4) The words omitted were repealed by the Summary Jurisdiction Act 1884 (47 & 48 Vict, c 43), s 4 and Schedule, and Statute Law Revision Act 1892 (55 & 56 Vict, c 19). Those words related to the service of the summons, procedure before the justices and orders for payments of costs; as to which see now Magistrates' Courts Act 1980 and Costs in Criminal Cases Act 1973.

146.–153.

Ss 146, 147, 151 repealed by the Summary Jurisdiction Act 1884, s 4, Sch and the Statute Law Revision Act 1892; ss 148, 149 (as it applies to England and Wales), 152, 153, repealed by the SL(R) Act 1993; s 150 repealed by the Justices of the Peace Act 1949, s 46(2), Sch 7, Pt III.

154. Transient offenders

It shall be lawful for any officer or agent of the undertakers(1), and all persons called by him to his assistance, to seize and detain any person who shall have committed any offence against the provisions of this or the special Act(2), and whose name and residence shall be unknown to such officer or agent and convey him with all convenient despatch before some justice(3), without any warrant or other authority than this or the special Act; and such justice shall proceed with all convenient despatch to the hearing and determining of the complaint against such offender.

(1) See first note to this Act, *above*, and for the meaning of 'undertakers', see the Markets and Fairs Act 1847, s 2, *below*.

(2) As to the special Act, see note (2) to s 140, *above*. The section does not authorise the seizure or detention of a person who has committed an offence against a byelaw under ss 42 *et seq* of the Markets and Fairs Clauses Act 1847, *below*; see *Barry v Midland Rly Co* (1867) IR 1 CL 130.

(3) As to justices having jurisdiction, see s 3 of Markets and Fairs Clauses Act 1847.

155. Form of conviction

This section was repealed by the Summary Jurisdiction Act 1884 (47 & 48 Vict, c 43), s 4 and Schedule.

156. [. . .](1)

(1) Repealed by the Statute Law (Repeals) Act 1976, s 1, Sch 1, Pt XIX (including that section as incorporated in any other Act).

Appeal

157.–159. [. . .](1)

(1) Repealed by the Transport Act 1962, ss 93(1), 95(1), Sch 12, Pt II.

160. [. . .](1)

(1) Repealed by the Perjury Act 1911 (1 & 2 Geo V, c 6), s 17 and Schedule; see now *ibid*, s 1.

161. Relating to Ireland

This section was repealed by Statute Law Revision Act 1876 (39 & 40 Vict, c 20).

MARKETS AND FAIRS CLAUSES ACT 1847

(10 & 11 Vict, c 14)

An Act for consolidating in One Act certain Provisions usually contained in Acts for constructing or regulating Markets and Fairs([1]).

[23rd April 1847]

1. This Act to extend to such markets or fairs as shall be authorised by Acts hereafter to be passed which shall declare that this Act shall be incorporated therewith

This Act shall extend only to such markets or fairs as shall be authorised by any Act of Parliament hereafter to be passed which shall declare that this Act shall be incorporated therewith; and all the clauses of this Act, save so far as they shall be expressly varied or excepted by any such Act([2]), shall apply to the undertaking authorised thereby, so far as the same shall be applicable to such undertaking([3]), and shall, with the clauses of every other Act which shall be incorporated therewith([4]), form part of such Act, and be construed therewith as forming one Act

([1]) This Act, except ss 6–9 and 52–59, is incorporated, as respects England and Wales, with the Animal Health Act 1981 (see s 54(2) thereof).

([2]) As to incorporation with variations and exceptions, see *Rutherford v Straker* (1887) 42 Ch D 85n and p 20, *above*.

([3]) So, if the undertaking is merely a market, it will not be affected by provisions of this Act which relate exclusively to a fair or a slaughterhouse, unless the incorporating Act, by appropriate words, renders such provisions applicable.

So, also, as the Act assumes that a special Act will have provisions on which the clauses of this Act can operate, there may be some clauses or parts thereof which are inoperable because the special Act has made no provision to which they can apply and an obligation is not to be merely implied in such a case; cf. *Dartford RDC v Bexley Heath Rly Co* [1898] AC 210.

Where, however, the special Act contains provisions which are inconsistent with this Act, this Act will be varied or excepted so far as it is inconsistent, cf *City and South London Rly v London County Council* [1891] 2 QB 513, but the inconsistency must be clearly established; see *R v London Corpn* (1867) LR 2 QB 292; *Metropolitan District Rly Co v Sharpe* (1880) 5 App Cas 425 at 431. See also *Sparrow v Oxford, etc Rly Co* (1852) 21 LT Ch 731; *Great Western Rly v Swindon, etc Rly Co* (1884) 22 Ch 731; *Great Western Rly v Swindon, etc. Rly* (1884) 22 Ch D 677; affd (1884) 9 App Cas 787; *Re Cherry's Settled Estates* (1862) 31 LJ Ch 351; *Re Mill's Estates* (1886) 34 Ch D 24.

This Act may also be expressly varied or excepted by the special Act; see s 5.

([4]) As to the incorporation of other Acts, see note to the heading of s 2, *below*.

Interpretation

And with respect to the construction of this Act, and any Act incorporated therewith, be it enacted as follows:—

The headings to the various portions of this Act are to be referred to for determining the sense of any doubtful expression in a section occurring under a particular heading; see *Hammersmith Rly Co v Brand* (1869) LR 4 HL 171.

This Act assumes that it will be incorporated in a special Act; see note ([2]) to s 1, *above* and s 5, *below*; such Acts are usually local Acts but this Act is also incorporated in part by the Animal Health Act 1981, s 54, *below* pp 218, 219 which incorporates the whole of this Act except ss 6–9 and 54–59.

The only Act which, by this Act, is incorporated therewith is the Railways Clauses Consolidation Act, 1845, ss 140–161; see s 52 of this Act.

2. 'The special Act'—'Prescribed'—'The lands'—'The undertaking'—'The undertakers'

The expression 'the special Act' used in this Act shall be construed to mean any Act which shall be hereafter passed authorising the construction or regulation of a market or fair, and with which this Act shall be incorporated; and the word 'prescribed' used in this Act in reference to any matter herein stated shall be construed to refer to such matter as the same shall be prescribed or provided for in the special Act, and the sentence in which such word occurs shall be construed as if instead of the word 'prescribed' the expression 'prescribed for that purpose in the special Act' had been used; and the expression 'the lands' shall mean the lands which shall by the special Act be authorised to be taken or used for the purposes thereof([1]); and the expression 'the undertaking' shall mean the market or fair, and the works connected therewith, by the special Act authorised to be constructed or regulated([2]); and the expression 'the undertakers' shall mean the persons authorised by the special Act to construct or regulate the market or fair.

([1]) Under s 3 of this Act, 'lands' includes messuages, lands, tenements and hereditaments, or heritages, of any tenure.

([2]) Under s 3 of this Act, 'the market or fair' means the market or fair, and the works connected therewith, by the special Act authorised to be constructed or regulated.

* * * * * *

Citing the Act

And with respect to citing this Act, or any part thereof be it enacted as follows:—

4. Short title

In citing this Act in other Acts of Parliament, and in legal instruments, it shall be sufficient to use the expression 'The Markets and Fairs Clauses Act 1847.'

* * * * * *

Holding of market, etc

12. Before the market or fair shall be opened, notice to be given by undertakers

Before the market or fair shall be opened for public use the undertakers shall give not less than ten days' notice of the time when the same will be opened, and such notice shall be given by the publication thereof in some newspaper circulating within the limits of the special Act, and by printed handbills posted on some conspicuous place within those limits.

13. Sales elsewhere than in market, or in shops, etc, prohibited

After([1]) the market place is opened for public use([2]) every person other than a licensed hawker([3]) who shall sell or expose for sale in any place wthin the prescribed limits([4]), except([5]) in his own dwelling place or shop([6]), any articles([7]) in respect of which tolls([8]) are by the special Act authorised to be taken in the market, shall for every such offence be liable to a penalty([9]) not exceeding [level 1 on the standard scale]([10]).

([1]) The effect of this section on the undertakers' right of action for disturbance of their market is discussed *above*, pp 90 to 92.

([2]) This section (unlike ss 12 and 14–16) applies only to a market, and not to a fair. It seems that it would not apply to a fair regulated by a special Act merely because such Act incorporated this Act.

This section comes into force as soon as the market-place has been opened for public use.

The operation of the section is not confined to the days on which or the hours during which the market is held; *Hailsham Cattle Market Co v Tolman* [1915] 1 Ch 360; affirmed [1915] 2 Ch 1, CA; but a local Act may, by a grant of exemption for certain sales on market days, virtually exclude this section and make it inapplicable to non-market days for all sales; *ibid.*

([3]) A licensed hawker was a hawker licensed under the Hawkers Act 1888 (repealed by the Local Government Act 1966, ss 35(1), 43(2), Sch 3, Pt I, Sch 6, Pt I and not replaced). It also however includes a pedlar trading as such who holds a certificate for the district under the Pedlars Acts 1871 (34 & 35 Vict c 96) and 1881 (44 & 45 Vict c 45); see s 6 of the Act of 1871.

For the purposes of the Pedlars Acts, a 'pedlar' means 'any hawker, pedlar, petty chapman, tinker, caster of metals, mender of chairs, or other person who without any horse or other beast bearing or drawing burden, travels and trades on foot and goes from town to town or to other men's houses, carrying to sell or exposing for sale any goods, wares, or merchandise, or procuring orders for goods, wares, or merchandise immediately to be delivered, or selling or offering for sale his skill in handicraft' (Act of 1871, s 3). The Acts prohibit any person from acting as a pedlar without the prescribed certificate, which lasts for one year from the date of its issue, but provides that it shall not be necessary for a certificate to be obtained by certain persons, including commercial travellers and sellers of vegetables, fish, fruit, or victuals; Act of 1871, ss 4, 5, 23; Act of 1881, s 2. The Act of 1871, s 6, provides that a certificate under that Act shall, for the purposes of the Markets and Fairs Clauses Act 1847, and any Act incorporating the same, have the same effect as a hawker's licence, and that the term 'licensed hawker' in the Markets and Fairs Clauses Act shall be construed to include a pedlar holding such a certificate. A person, however, who holds only a pedlar's certificate is exempted from the provisions of the above s 13 only while trading as a pedlar; and formerly he was not exempted therefrom if he traded as a hawker with a horse and cart without a hawker's licence; *Woolwich Local Board of Health v Gardiner* [1895] 2 QB 497; nor is a person without a pedlar's certificate exempted therefrom by reason that the Act of 1871, s 23, renders it unnecessary in certain circumstances for him to take out a pedlar's certificate: *Openshaw v Oakeley* (1889) 60 LT 929. See, however, note ([5]) *below*, as to sales in the market.

Where a special Act prohibited persons from selling tollable articles in the streets without a licence from the undertakers, and made no exception in favour of licensed hawkers or certificated pedlars, it was held that such hawkers and pedlars were subject to the prohibition: *Openshaw v Oakeley* (1889) 60 LT 929; but such prohibition does not prevent them from selling non-tollable articles: *Loftos v Gleave* (1890) 55 JP 149; *Loftos v Kiggins* (1890) 55 JP 151.

([4]) 'The prescribed limits' mean 'the limits prescribed for that purpose in the special Act'; see s 2, *above*. If the special Act provides that such Act shall for all purposes be in force within a specified district, the boundaries of that district are the prescribed limits: *Caswell v Cook* (1862) 11 CBNS 637; and see *Kilminster v Fitton* (1886) 53 LT 959; *Collier v North* (1876) 35 LT 345. In the case of a market under the Animal Health Act 1981, s 54(3), the limits of the land acquired or appropriated for the purposes of the market are the prescribed limits.

There have been several decisions upon the question as to what constitutes a sale within the prescribed limits. The effect of these decisions, with regard to contracts for the sale and delivery of tollable articles, seems to be as follows:

(*a*) The section does not affect a delivery within the limits under a contract made outside the limits, provided that the goods were outside the limits at the time when the contract was made, and were appropriated to the contract before they were brought within the limits: *Bourne v Lowndes* (1858) 22 JP 354; *Stretch v White* (1861) 25 JP 485; and see *Pletts v Campbell* [1895] 2 QB 229; *Pletts v Beattie* [1896] 1 QB 519; and this is so although the property in the goods has not passed and is at the risk of the buyer until delivery since the word 'sell' is to be understood in its popular sense and not in its strict legal sense: *Lambert v Rowe* [1914] 1 KB 38. There must, however, be a binding contract and where in pursuance of a regular course of dealing goods are brought to a customer within the limits and there sold to him without a prior binding contract, the sale will be within the section;

see *Jenkins v Thomas* (1910) 104 LT 74. According to the Irish cases of *Newtownards Town Comrs v Woods* (1877) IR 11 CL 506; *Gracey v Banbridge Urban District Council* [1905] 2 IR 209 the section does not affect a delivery within the limits, under a contract of sale by sample within the limits, if the bulk of the goods was outside the limits at the time when the contract was made; but these cases seem to be at variance with the cases next mentioned.

(*b*) The section applies to cases in which the goods are delivered within the limits without having been appropriated to the contract before being brought within the limits; and it seems to be immaterial in these cases whether the contract was made within the limits or outside them: *Exeter Corpn v Heaman* (1877) 37 LT 534; *Torquay Market Co v Burridge* (1883) 48 JP 71; see *Pletts v Campbell, Pletts v Beattie, above. A fortiori*, the section applies where the contract was made within the limits and the goods appropriated to the contract were within the limits at the time when the contract was made: *Mayor of Londonderry v M'Elhinney* (1875) 9 Ir Rep CL 61. It applies notwithstanding that the seller previously bought the goods in the market: *Black v Sackett* (1869) 10 B & S 639.

Where, under a local Act toll is payable on 'the cart in which goods are exposed for sale' there is no exposure for sale by a baker of bread which he brings to a customer's house merely for the purpose of delivery; see *White v Yeovil Corpn* (1892) 61 LJMC 213, or by a mineral water man who takes his loaded cart to the houses of customers and after taking an order in the house, delivers from the cart the goods ordered; see *Newton-in-Makerfield Urban Council v Lyon* (1900) 69 LJKB 230; and in such a case where the toll is only on the cart containing the goods and not on the sale of the goods, there can be no conviction under s 13 of the Act of 1847 for selling the goods; see *Jenkins v Thomas* (1910) 104 LT 74. See also *Luke v Charles* (1861) 25 JP 148.

([5]) The only place expressly excepted is the seller's own dwelling-place or shop, but the section can scarcely be construed as prohibiting sales in the market-place while the market is in progress. A pedlar's certificate is not required by persons selling or exposing for sale goods, wares or merchandise in any public mart, market or fair legally established: Pedlars Act 1871, s 23(3).

([6]) It is a question of fact whether a place is a man's own dwelling-place or shop; but in determining that question regard must be had to the object of the section, which is, on the one hand, that the market should be protected from the establishment, within the district, of a rival market, but, on the other hand, that the established traders of the district who carry on their business in their own dwelling-places or shops should not be interfered with; *Llandaff and Canton District Market Co v Lyndon* (1860) 8 CBNS 515, 524; *Pope v Whalley* (1865) 6 B & S 303; *Ashworth v Heyworth* (1869) LR 4 QB 316; *Fearon v Mitchell* (1872) LR 7 QB 690; *McHole v Davies* (1875) 1 QBD 59.

'Dwelling-place' has been said by Earle CJ to be a wider expression than 'dwelling-house' which occurs in some local Acts, and to be capable of including a yard attached to a dwelling-house; *Llandaff and Canton District Market Co v Lyndon, above*; and per Cockburn CJ in *McHole v Davis, above*; but in *Fearon v Mitchell, above*, Cockburn CJ thought that no distinction was to be drawn between the two expressions: and in that case, and in *McHole v Davies, above*, it was held that a large yard adjoining a man's dwelling-house and used by him for extensive sales of cattle and sheep, was neither his dwelling-place nor his shop.

In considering whether a place is a shop, 'it is necessary to have regard to the nature, character, and extent of the trade' which is carried on therein; per Mellor J, *Fearon v Mitchell* (1872) LR 7 QB 690. In *Fearon v Mitchell* it was held that a large hall, used for sales of cattle by public auction, was not a shop, but a rival market. An auction-room may be a shop, and if a place is a shop 'the mode of selling therein cannot deprive it of the ordinary privilege attached to a shop'; per Byles J, *Wiltshire v Willett* (1861) 11 CBNS 240. So a place may be a shop although goods are sold wholesale and partly on commission: *Haynes v Ford* [1911] 2 Ch 237, 248, CA; or are sold by auction: *Hailsham Cattle Market Co v Tolman* [1915] 1 Ch 360 at 367; on appeal [1915] 2 Ch 1, CA; but *prima facie* auctioneers' premises are not shops: per Blackburn J and Cockburn CJ in *Fearon v Mitchell, above*.

A distinction is drawn not only between 'shop' and 'rival market', but also between 'shop' and 'stall'. 'Shop' imports something more than a mere place for sale; it imports a place for storing also, so far as the nature of the commodities admit of storing; per Mellor J in *Pope v Whalley* (1865) 6 B & S 303; *Haynes v Ford* [1911] 2 Ch 237, 248, CA; and it means a man's 'real permanent private shop', as distinguished from a mere temporary stall; per Blackburn J in *Pope v Whalley, above*. In determining whether a particular structure is a shop or stall, it is proper to consider whether the building is of a substantial character, or a mere alteration of what was formerly a stall; whether it admits of the entrance of buyers; whether it protects the goods from the weather, and admits of their being left therein at night with reasonable safety; and also what is the nature and duration of the tenant's holding of it; but no one of these considerations is conclusive of itself; *ibid* per Blackburn J. Thus it was held in *Ashworth v Heyworth* (1869) LR 4 QB 316, that a wooden shed which was affixed to a house and stood upon premises held therewith, and which had for many years been used for exposing goods for sale, was a shop; and in *Hooper v Kenshole* (1877) 2 QBD 127, that a covered and enclosed skittle-alley was not the shop of a hawker who hired it for two days to sell his goods therein; see also *Perkins v Arber* (1873) 37 JP 406. In *Pike v Jones* (1922) 128 LT 373, it was held that a stall with a mere canvas roof from which all goods were removed each day was not a shop.

A ship moored to a wharf in a canal is not a shop: *Wiltshire v Baker* (1861) 11 CBNS 237.

In *Spurling v Bantoft* [1891] 2 QB 384, a cattle market was established in a borough by the corporation, acting as a sanitary authority. Prior to the establishment of such market, they had granted to a cattle salesman a lease of a yard, with a covenant for quiet enjoyment. It was held that the lease and covenant did not exempt the tenant from the operation of this section.

(7) 'Article' is the word usually employed to cover all marketable commodities, and a horse may be an article within the meaning of the section: *Llandaff and Canton District Market Co v Lyndon* (1860) 8 CBNS 515. In local Acts other expressions are often used; see for example, *Shepherd v Folland* (1884) 49 JP 165, where it was held that 'potatoes' are 'provisions' within a prohibition of corn, grain, meat, fish, poultry or other 'provisions'; *Morgan v Kingdom* (1875) 39 JP 471, where it was held that 'bottled gingerade' is not within meat, fish, vegetable, fruit, butter, cheese or other marketable commodities; *Loftos v Gleave* (1890) 55 JP 149 ('hat-guards' not within 'flesh, cheese, butter or other things whatsoever'); *Johnson v Atkinson* (1909) 73 JP 510 ('coal' not within 'hay, straw, grass, vetches or other article, commodity or thing'); *Whittle (Hy) Ltd v Stalybridge Corpn* (1967) 65 LGR 344 ('bread and confectionery' 'not within 'meat, fish, poultry, vegetables, fruit').

(8) 'Toll' here means a market toll payable in respect of articles sold or exposed for sale in the market, and does not include a toll in the nature of stallage or rent payable for the occupation of a stall in the market-place: *Caswell v Cook* (1862) 11 CBNS 637; and where tolls are leviable under the local Act on the cart in which the goods are loaded and not on the sale of goods, a sale is not within the section: *Jenkins v Thomas* (1910) 104 LT 74.

(9) For the recovery of penalties, see s 52. The offence cannot be condoned by payment of toll, nor toll claimed in lieu of penalty: *Carter v Parkhouse* (1870) 22 LTNS 788; *Quilligan v Limerick* (1883) 14 LR Ir 265.

(10) Maximum penalty increased to £25 by the Criminal Law Act 1977, s 31(6); and by virtue of the Criminal Justice Act 1982, s 46, the reference to that amount is converted to a reference to level 1 of the standard scale set out in s 37(2). The effect of this section may be considerably altered by the provisions of the special Act, with which it must be read; see *Rutherford v Straker* (1887) 42 Ch D 85n; *Hailsham Cattle Market Co v Tolman* [1915] 1 Ch 360; affirmed [1915] 2 Ch 1, CA; see further *above*, pp 20, 90 to 92.

14. Market days

After the market place or place for fairs is opened for public use(1) the undertakers(2) shall hold markets and fairs therein(3) on the prescribed days(4) (if any), and on such other days as the undertakers shall appoint from time to time by any byelaw to be made in pursuance of this(5) or the special Act(6).

([1]) See s 12, *above*.
([2]) For the meaning of undertakers, see s 2, *above*.
([3]) The section provides no remedy for non-compliance with its provisions, which seem to be imperative; and if they are imperative, then (subject to the provisions of the special Act) mandamus is the proper legal remedy.
([4]) Ie, prescribed for that purpose in the special Act; see s 2, *above*.
([5]) As to the making of byelaws under this Act, see ss 42, 43, *below*. As to the general statutory restriction on the holding of markets on Good Friday and certain feast days, see *above*, pp 46, 47. See also the Sunday Trading Act 1994 p 255, *below*.
([6]) For the meaning of special Act, see s 2, *above*.

* * * * * *

Tolls

And with respect to the stallages, rents, and tolls to be taken by the undertakers, be it enacted as follows:—

Sections 31–41 are incorporated with respect to markets under the Animal Health Act 1981, s 54(2), see *below*, p 218, but the tolls require the approval of the Minister of Agriculture, Fisheries and Food

Sections 36–41 apply to tolls in respect of the weighing of cattle levied by a market authority under the Markets and Fairs (Weighing of Cattle) Act 1887, s 8.

* * * * * *

36. Stallages, tolls, etc, may be varied from time to time

The undertakers([1]) may from time to time change the stallages, rents, and tolls([2]) to be taken in respect of the market or fair, or for the slaughterhouses([3]), or for weighing and measuring([4]), provided that the stallages, rents, and tolls in no case exceed the amounts authorised by the special Act([5]).

Sections 36–41 are applied by the Markets and Fairs (Weighing of Cattle) Act 1887, s 8, and see the note to the heading to ss 31–41, *above*.
([1]) 'Undertakers' are defined in s 2, *above*.
([2]) Tolls taken in respect of a market provided under the Animal Health Act 1981 must be approved by the Minister of Agriculture, Fisheries and Food; see *ibid*, s 54(3), (4), *below*, p 218.
([3]) As to slaughterhouses, see ss 17–20.
([4]) As to weighing and measuring, see ss 21, 22, 24, and as to payment of tolls therefor, see ss 33, 34.
([5]) For the meaning of the special Act, see s 2, *above*.

* * * * * *

Byelaws

And with respect to the byelaws to be made by the undertakers, be it enacted as follows:—

Clauses 42–49 are incorporated by the Animal Health Act 1981, s 54(2) with respect to markets provided under that Act; see *below*, p 218. The byelaws must be approved by the Minister of Agriculture, Fisheries and Food and his approval is sufficient without any other approval or allowance, notice of application for approval being given and the proposed byelaws being published before the application in accordance with the Markets and Fairs Clauses Act 1847; see s 54(3) of the Act of 1981, *below*, p 218.

A local authority which maintains a market, whether or not a market authority under the Food Act 1984, may make byelaws under s 60 of that Act, see *below*, p 250.

Expressions used in any byelaws made since 1889 have, unless the contrary intention appears, the same respective meanings as in the Act conferring the power to make them; Interpretation Act 1889 (52 & 53 Vict c 63), s 31.

Model byelaws, applicable to markets under the Food Act 1984, are printed in Appendix A, *below*, p 295; and these may be adapted for use in other statutory markets.

42. Byelaws may be made for all or any of the purposes herein named

The undertakers([1]) may from time to time make such byelaws as they think fit for all or any of the following purposes([2]) (that is to say):—

For regulating the use of the market place and fair([3]), and the buildings, stalls, pens and standings therein, and for preventing nuisances or obstructions therein, or in the immediate approaches thereto;

For fixing the days, and the hours during each day, on which the market or fair shall be held([4]);

For inspection of the slaughterhouses, and for keeping the same in a cleanly and proper state, and for removing filth and refuse at least once in every twenty-four hours, and for requiring that they be provided with a sufficient supply of water, and preventing the exercise of cruelty therein([5]);

For regulating the carriers resorting to the market or fair, and fixing the rates for carrying articles carried therefrom within the limits of the special Act([6]);

[. . .]([7])

For preventing the sale or exposure for sale of unwholesome provisions in the market or fair([8]).

And the undertakers may from time to time, as they shall think fit, repeal or alter any such byelaws([9]); provided always, that such byelaws shall not be repugnant to the laws of that part of the United Kingdom where the same are to have effect([10]), or to the provisions of this or the special Act, or of any Act incorporated therewith([11]); and such byelaws shall be reduced to writing under the common seal of the undertakers, if they be a body corporate, or the hands and seals of two of the undertakers, if they be not a body corporate, and, if affecting other persons than the officers and servants of the undertakers, shall be printed and published as herein provided([12]).

([1]) 'Undertakers' are defined in s 2, *above*.

([2]) The contents of byelaws are controlled by this section and s 43. As to the procedure for making byelaws, see ss 44–47; as to their effect, see s 48, and as to evidence of the byelaws, see s 49.

Byelaws are invalid if they are not made in accordance with ss 43–47, and the special Act; pp 109, 110 or are repugnant to the general law or the provisions of this or the special Act, pp 111, 112 and text to notes (10), (11), *below*, or are unreasonable; see *above*, p 112.

The repeal and alteration of the byelaws are provided for in this section.

([3]) For the meaning of 'market place and fair', see note ([2]) to s 2, *above*. See also note ([2]) *above*, and as to byelaws regulating a market or fair and held to be invalid or unreasonable, see *above*, pp 111 to 113.

([4]) See note ([2]) *above*. As to market days, see s 14 *above* and as to the restriction of the days on which markets and fairs may be lawfully held, see *above*, pp 45 to 47.

([5]) See note ([2]) *above*. As to the provision of slaughterhouses, see ss 17–20.

(6) See note (2) *above*. The expression 'within the limits of the special Act' is not defined in the Act and its meaning must be sought in the special Act. A definition of this phrase should, therefore, be inserted in the special Act.

(7) Repealed by the Weights and Measures Act 1963, ss 63(1), 65, Sch 9, Pt II. See note (2) *above*. As to the provision of weighing machines and measures and their use, see ss 21–30.

(8) See note (2) *above*. As to the prohibition on the sale of unwholesome provisions, see s 15.

(9) Presumably subject to the same restrictions and by the same procedure as the byelaws are made; as to which, see note (2) *above*.

(10) See also *Dyson v London and North Western Rly Co* (1881) 7 QBD 32; *Parry v Berry* (1717) 1 Com 269; and see *above*, pp 111 to 113.

(11) See *Elwood v Bullock* (1844) 6 QB 383; and see *above*, p 111. For the meaning of the 'special Act', see s 2, and as to Acts incorporated therewith, see note to heading to s 2, *above*.

(12) For the provisions as to printing and publishing. see ss 47, 49. Byelaws relating solely to officers and servants of the undertakers seem to be impliedly included in the purposes of the section but do not require printing or publishing under the Act; see note (1) to s 43.

43. Byelaws may be enforced by penalties

The undertakers, by the byelaws so to be made by them(1), may impose such reasonable penalties as they shall think fit, not exceeding five pounds(2) for each breach of such byelaws(3); [. . .](4).

The words omitted relate to Scotland.

(1) See s 42, as to the purposes for which byelaws may be made. The purposes also include, it seems, byelaws which relate solely to the officers and servants of the undertakers since it is specially provided by s 44 that such byelaws do not require confirmation and, by s 42, that they do not require to be published.

Compare the model byelaws, *below*, p 295, issued for use by local authorities who maintain a market.

(2) Maximum penalty increased to £25 by the Criminal Law Act 1977, s 31(6) (standard scale level 1, see note (10) to s 13, *above*).

(3) The undertakers are given some discretion (which they ought to exercise) with respect to the amount of the penalty to be imposed by a byelaw for a breach. But if the penalty imposed for a breach exceeds the standard scale the byelaw is void; and since the penalty is required to be reasonable it seems that a byelaw which imposes an unreasonable penalty is void, although the penalty does not exceed the standard scale. Subject to these observations it seems to be sufficient, in making a set of byelaws, to provide by one of them that 'every person who is guilty of any breach of any of these byelaws shall be liable for each such breach to a penalty not exceeding the standard scale'. See further *above*, pp 111 to 113, as to the validity of byelaws.

(4) Repealed by the Statute Law (Repeals) Act 1993, s 1(1), Sch 1.

* * * * * *

METROPOLITAN FAIRS ACT 1868

(31 & 32 Vict, c 106)

An Act for the Prevention of the holding of unlawful Fairs within the Limits of the Metropolitan Police District.

[31st July 1868]

1. Short title

This Act may be cited for all purposes as 'The Metropolitan Fairs Act 1868'.

2. Restriction of right to hold fair, where fair not held for seven years([1])

Where any fair([2]) is holden or notice is given of any fair proposed to be holden on any ground within the Metropolitan Police District([3]) other than that on which a fair has been holden during each of the seven years immediately preceding, it shall be competent for the Commissioner of Police to direct one of the superintendents of the Metropolitan Police Force to summon the owner or occupier of the ground upon which such fair is holden to appear before a magistrate forthwith, or at a time to be specified in the summons, to show his right and title to hold such fair; and if such owner or occupier do not attend in pursuance of such summons, or does not show to the magistrate who hears the case sufficient cause to believe that such fair is lawfully holden, the magistrate shall declare in writing such fair to be unlawful, and the Commissioner shall give notice of such declaration by causing copies thereof to be affixed on and near the ground where such fair is holden or proposed to be holden; and after such notice has been affixed for the space of six hours the Commissioner of Police may direct any constable to remove every booth, standing, and tent, and every carriage of whatsoever kind, conveyed to or being upon the ground for the purpose of holding or continuing such fair, and to take into custody every person erecting, pitching, or fixing, or assisting to erect, pitch, or fix, any such booth, standing or tent; and every person hiring, accompanying, or conveyed in every such carriage, and every person resorting to such ground with any show or instrument of gambling or amusement, and every person convicted before a magistrate of any of the offences aforesaid, shall be liable to a penalty of not more than [level 1 on the standard scale]([1]).

([1]) Maximum penalty increased to £25 by the Criminal Law Act 1977, s 31(6); and by virtue of the Criminal Justice Act 1982, s 46 the reference to that amount is converted to a reference to level 1 of the standard scale set out in s 37(2) thereof.

([2]) The legality of any fair and the place of holding may, it seems, be questioned under the section. It may also be questioned under the Metropolitan Police Act 1839, ss 39, 40, *above*, pp 173, 174. See also s 4 of this Act, *below*.

([3]) As to what is included in the Metropolitan Police District, see note ([2]) to s 38 of the Metropolitan Police Act 1839 *above*, p 173.

3. Service of summons, and description of owner, etc, therein

A summons under this Act may be served on the owner or occupier of any ground personally, or by leaving the same at his usual or last known place of abode([1]), or, if the name of such owner or occupier or his place of abode is not known to the police, by putting up such summons in a conspicuous place on the ground where the fair is holden or proposed to be holden, and it shall not be necessary to name the owner or occupier in the summons but may be described as the owner or occupier of the ground.

([1]) 'Place of abode' means place of residence; see *R v Lilley, ex p Taylor* (1910) 104 LT 77.

4. Powers of Act accumulative

All powers conferred by this Act shall be deemed to be in addition to and not in derogation of any other powers conferred by any other Act of Parliament, and any such other powers may be exercised as if this Act had not passed.

See the Metropolitan Police Act 1839, ss 39, 40, *above*, pp 173, 174.

5. Construction

This Act, so far as is consistent with the tenor thereof, shall be construed as one with the Acts relating to the Metropolitan Police.

See in particular, the Metropolitan Police Act 1839, ss 39, 40, *above*, pp 173, 174.

FAIRS ACT 1871

(34 & 35 Vict, c 12)

An Act to further amend the Law relating to Fairs in England and Wales.

[25th May 1871]

1. Short title

This Act may be cited as 'The Fairs Act 1871'.

2. Interpretation

In this Act the term 'owner' means any person or persons or body of commissioners, or body corporate, entitled to hold any fair, whether in respect of the ownership of any lands or tenements, or under any charter, letters patent, or Act of Parliament, or otherwise howsoever.

As to the right to hold fairs under the titles referred to in the section, see *above*, pp 15 *et seq*.

3. Order for abolition of fair

In case it shall appear to the Secretary of State for the Home Department, upon representation duly made to him by the magistrates of any petty sessional district([1]) within which any fair is held, or by the owner of any fair in England or Wales, that it would be for the convenience and advantage of the public that any such fair should be abolished, it shall be lawful for the said Secretary of State for the Home Department, with the previous consent in writing of the owner([2]) for the time being of such fair, or of the tolls or dues payable in respect thereof, to order that such fair shall be abolished accordingly: Provided always, that notice of such representation, and of the time when it shall please the Secretary of State for the Home Department to take the same into consideration, shall be published once in the *London Gazette*, and in three successive weeks in some one and the same newspaper published in the county, city, or borough in which such fair is held, or if there be no newspaper published therein, then in the newspaper of some county adjoining or near thereto, before such representation is so considered.

([1]) The power of the magistrates has been transferred to the council of the district or London borough in which the fair is held by the Local Government Act 1894, ss 21(3), 27(1)(e) and the Local Government Act 1972, ss 1(1B), 179(3).

([2]) 'Owner' is defined in s 2, *above*.

4. Publication of order

When and so soon as any such order as aforesaid shall have been made by the Secretary of State for the Home Department, notice of the same shall be published in the *London Gazette* and in some one newspaper of the county, city or borough in which such fair is usually held, or if there be no newspaper published therein, then in the newspaper of some county adjoining or near thereto, and thereupon such fair shall be abolished.

PEDLARS ACT 1871

(34 & 35 Vict, c 96)
An Act for granting Certificates to Pedlars
[21st August 1871]

Preliminary

1. Short title

This Act may be cited as 'The Pedlars Act 1871'.

2. [Repealed by the SLR (No 2) Act 1893.]

3. Interpretation— 'Court of summary jurisdiction'

In this Act, if not inconsistent with the context, the following terms have the meanings hereinafter respectively assigned to them; that is to say,—

The term 'pedlar' means any hawker(1), pedlar, petty chapman, tinker, caster of metals, mender of chairs, or other person who, without any horse or other beast bearing or drawing burden, travels and trades on foot(2) and goes from town to town(3) or to other men's houses, carrying to sell or exposing for sale(4) any goods, wares, or merchandise, or procuring orders for goods, wares, or merchandise immediately to be delivered, or selling or offering for sale his skill in handicraft:

[* * * * * *]

[. . .](5).

The words omitted were repealed by the Statute Law Revision (No 2) Act 1893, and the Police Act 1964, s 64(3) and Sch 10, Pt I.

(1) Hawkers were formerly required to be licensed under the Hawkers Act 1888 (repealed by the Local Government Act 1966, ss 33, 35(1), 43(2)(a), Sch 3, Pt I, Sch 6, Pt I). For the purposes of the Markets and Fairs Clauses Act 1847 (*above*) the term 'licensed hawker' is construed to include a pedlar holding a certificate under that Act: see s 6.

(2) To fall within the definition a person must both travel *and* trade on foot: see *Watson v Malloy* [1988] 3 All ER 459 at 463, 86 LGR 766 at 773. In this case it was suggested that the distinction between a 'pedlar' and one who sets up a stall in different towns each week is that the former trades as he travels and the latter travels to trade: *ibid* at 463 per Hutchinson J. Compare *Sample v Hulme* [1956] 3 All ER 447n, where it was held that persons who travelled to a street in a van and then went from house to house on foot were travelling and trading within the meaning of this section. See also the cases cited in note 52, p 114, *above* for the distinction between acting as a street trader and a pedlar. A person who cannot bring his activities within its definition will probably be subject to the restrictions against street trading contained in Sch 4 to the Local Government (Miscellaneous Provisions) Act 1982, *below*.

(3) See *A-G v Woolhouse* (1827) 12 Price 65 and *Manson v Hope* (1862) 2 B & S 498.

(4) This has been held to include bartering or exchanging goods for other goods: *Druce v Gabb* (1858) 30 LTOS 98. A person soliciting orders for goods which are not in his possession at the time but which are subsequently delivered is not 'carrying to sell' or 'exposing for sale' under this section and therefore does not require a certificate: *R v M'Knight* (1830) 10 B & C 734. See also s 23, *below*.

(5) Repealed by the Statute Law (Repeals) Act 1993.

Certificates to be obtained by Pedlars

4. No one to act as a pedlar without certificate

No person shall act as a pedlar without such certificate as in this Act mentioned, or in any district where he is not authorized by his certificate so to act.

Any person who—

(1) acts as a pedlar(1) without having obtained a certificate(2) under this Act authorizing him so to act;

(2) [repealed by the Pedlars Act 1881, s 2];

shall be liable for the first offence to a penalty not exceeding [level 1 on the standard scale](3) and for any subsequent offence to a penalty not exceeding [level 1 on the standard scale]3.

(1) For meaning, see s 3, *above*.

(2) See ss 5 and 17, *below*, and the Pedlars Act 1881, *below*. By the Local Government (Miscellaneous Provisions) Act 1982, Sch 4, para 1(2)(a), *below* and the London Local Authorities Act 1990, Pt III, trading by a person acting as a pedlar under the authority of a pedlar's certificate granted under this section is not street trading for the purposes of the 1982 Act.

(3) The maximum penalties were increased to £25 each by the Criminal Law Act 1977, s 31(6), and by the Criminal Justice Act 1982, s 46 a reference to the level on the standard scale is substituted for the amount of the penalty.

5. Grant of certificate

The following regulations shall be made with respect to the grant of pedlar(1) certificates:

(1) Subject as in this Act mentioned, a pedlar's certificate shall be granted(2) to any person by the chief officer of police(3) [for the police area](3) in which the person applying for a certificate has, during one month previous to such application, resided(4) on such officer being satisfied that the applicant is above seventeen years of age, is a person of good character, and in good faith intends to carry on the trade of a pedlar(5):

(2) An application for a pedlar's certificate shall be in the form specified in Schedule 2 to this Act, or as near thereto as circumstances admit:

(3) There shall be paid for a pedlar's certificate previously to the delivery thereof to the applicant a fee of [£12.25](6):

(4) A pedlar's certificate shall be in the form specified in Schedule 2 to this Act, or as near thereto as circumstances admit:

(5) A pedlar's certificate shall remain in force for one year from the date of the issue thereof, and no longer:

(6) On the delivery up of the old certificate, or on sufficient evidence being produced to the satisfaction of the chief officer of police that the old certificate has been lost, that officer may, either at the expiration of the current year, or during the currency of any year grant a new certificate in the same manner as upon a first application for a pedlar's certificate. In Great Britain one of Her Majesty's Principal Secretaries of State, and in Ireland(7) the Lord Lieutenant(8) . . . may from time to time provide for the expiration of all pedlars' certificates at the same period of each year, and in doing so shall provide for the apportionment of the fees payable in respect of any such certificate.

The words omitted were repealed by the SLR (No 2) Act 1893.

(1) For meaning, see s 3, *above*.

([2]) For provisions relating to an appeal against refusal of a certificate, see s 15, *below*; for the power of a magistrates' court to deprive a pedlar of a certificate see s 16, *below*, and for exemption from the need to obtain a certificate, see s 23, *below*.
([3]) Substituted by the Police Act 1996, s 103, Sch 7, para 2.
([4]) 'Reside' implies a degree of permanence (and temporary absence can be discounted provided there is an intention to return): see, for example, *R v St Leonard's Shoreditch, Inhabitants* (1865) LR 1 QB 21; *Levene v IRC* [1928] AC 217; *Brokelmann v Barr* [1971] 2 QB 602.
([5]) It is not necessary for a person to obtain all or even most of his livelihood from peddling: he need show only that he derives some part of his living from regularly trading as a pedlar: *Murphy v Duke* [1985] QB 905.
([6]) The fee was substituted by the Pedlars' Certificates (Variation of Fee) Order 1985, SI 1985 No 2027.
([7]) Now applicable only to Northern Ireland.
([8]) Now the Secretary of State for Northern Ireland.

6. Effect of certificate

* * * * * *

For the purpose of the Markets and Fairs Clauses Act 1847([1]), and any Act incorporating the same, a certificate under this Act([2]) shall have the same effect, within the district for which it is granted, as a hawker's license, and the term 'licensed hawker' in the first-mentioned Act shall be construed to include a pedlar([3]) holding such a certificate.

The words omitted were repealed by the Pedlars Act 1881, s 2 and Schedule.
([1]) *Above.*
([2]) For grant of certificate, see s 5, *above*.
([3]) For meaning, see s 3, *above*.

7. [Repealed by the Pedlars Act 1881, s 2 and Schedule.]

8. Register of certificates to be kept in each district

There shall be kept in each [police area]([1]) a register of the certificates . . . granted . . . in [the area]([1]) under this Act, in such form and with such particulars as may from time to time be directed in Great Britain by one of Her Majesty's Principal Secretaries of State, and in Ireland([2]) by the Lord Lieutenant([3]).

The entries in such register, and any copy of any such entries, certified by the chief officer of police to be a true copy, shall be evidence of the facts stated therein.

The words omitted were repealed by the Pedlars Act 1881, s 2 and Schedule.
([1]) Substituted by the Police Act 1996, s 103, Sch 7, para 3.
([2]) Now applicable only to Northern Ireland.
([3]) Now the Secretary of State for Northern Ireland.

9. Forms of application to be kept at chief police office

Forms of applications for certificates([1]) shall be kept at every police office in every [police area]([2]), and shall be given gratis to any person applying for the same; and all applications for certificates shall be delivered to the police office of the division or subdivision of the [police area]([2]) within which the applicant resides([3]), and certificates, when duly signed by the chief officer of police, shall be issued at such office.

([1]) For grant of certificate, see s 5, *above*.

([2]) Substituted by the Police Act 1996, s 103, Sch 7, para 4.
([3]) See note ([4]) to s 5, *above*.

10. Certificate not to be assigned

A person to whom a pedlar's certificate is granted([1]) under this Act shall not lend, transfer, or assign the same to any other person, and any person who lends, transfers, or assigns such certificate to any other person shall for each offence be liable to a penalty not exceeding [level 1 on the standard scale]([2]).

([1]) For grant of certificate, see s 5, *above*.
([2]) For penalty, see note ([3]) to s 4, *above*.

11. Certificate not to be borrowed

No person shall borrow or make use of a pedlar's certificate([1]) granted to any other person, and any person who borrows or makes use of such certificate shall for each offence be liable to a penalty not exceeding [level 1 on the standard scale]([2]).

([1]) For grant of certificate, see s 5, *above*.
([2]) For penalty, see note ([3]) to s 4, *above*.

12. Penalty for forging certificate

Any person who commits any of the following offences; (that is to say),

1. Makes false representations with a view to obtaining a pedlar's certificate([1]) under this Act:

* * * * * *

shall [be liable to imprisonment for a term not exceeding six months or to a fine not exceeding level 2 on the standard scale, or to both such imprisonment and fine]([2]).

The words omitted were repealed by the Pedlars Act 1881, s 2 and Schedule, and by the Forgery and Counterfeiting Act 1981, s 30, Sch 1, Part I.
([1]) For grant of certificate, see s 5, *above*.
([2]) The maximum penalty was increased to £50 by the Criminal Law Act 1977, s 31(6), and, by the Criminal Justice Act 1982, s 46, a reference to the level on the standard scale is substituted for the amount of the penalty.

13. [. . .]([1])

([1]) Repealed as to England and Wales by the Statute Law (Repeals) Act 1989, s 1, Sch 1, Pt I.

14. Convictions to be indorsed on certificate

If any pedlar([1]) is convicted of any offence under this Act, the court, before which he is convicted shall indorse or cause to be indorsed on his certificate([2]) a record of such conviction.

The indorsements made under this Act on a pedlar's certificate shall be evidence of the facts stated therein.

([1]) For meaning, see s 3, *above*.
([2]) For grant of certificate, see s 5, *above*.

15. Appeal against refusal of certificate by chief officer of police

If the chief officer of police[1] refuses to grant . . . a certificate[2], the applicant may appeal to a court of summary jurisdiction having jurisdiction in the place where such grant . . . was refused, in accordance with the following provisions:

1. The applicant shall, within one week after the refusal, give to the chief officer of police notice in writing of the appeal:
2. The appeal shall be heard at the sitting of the court which happens next after the expiration of the said week, but the court may, on the application of either party, adjourn the case:
3. The court shall hear and determine the matter of the appeal, and make such order thereon, with or without costs to either party, as to the court seems just:
4. An appeal under this Act to a court of summary jurisdiction in England[3] and Ireland[4] shall be deemed to be a matter on which that court has authority by law to make an order in pursuance of the Summary Jurisdiction Acts[5], and in Scotland the court may adjudicate on matters arising under this section, in accordance with the enactments relating to the exercise of their ordinary jurisdiction:
5. Any certificate . . . granted . . . in pursuance of an order of the court, shall have the same effect as if it had been originally granted . . . by the chief officer of police.

The words omitted were repealed by the Pedlars Act 1881, s 2 and Schedule.

(1) See note (3) to s 5, *above*.

(2) For grant of certificate, see s 5, *above*.

(3) For meaning, see Interpretation Act 1978, ss 5, 22(1), Sch 1, Sch 2, para 5(a).

(4) Now applicable only to Northern Ireland.

(5) See now the Magistrates' Courts Act 1980.

16. Deprivation of pedlars of certificates by court

Any court before which any pedlar[1] is convicted of any offence[2], whether under this or any other Act, or otherwise, may, if he or they think fit, deprive such pedlar of his certificate; and any such court shall deprive such pedlar of his certificate if he is convicted of begging.

Any court of summary jurisdiction may summon a pedlar holding a certificate under this Act to appear before them, and if he fail to appear, or on appearance to satisfy the court that he is in good faith carrying on the business of a pedlar, shall deprive him of his certificate.

(1) For meaning, see s 3, *above*.

(2) A record of conviction must be endorsed on the certificate: see s 14, *above*.

Duties of Pedlars

17. Pedlar to show certificate to certain persons on demand

Any pedlar[1] shall at all times, on demand, produce and show his certificate[2] to any of the following persons; (that is to say,)

1. Any justice of the peace; or
2. Any constable or officer of police; or
3. Any person to whom such pedlar offers his goods for sale; or
4. Any person in whose private grounds or premises such pedlar is found:

And any pedlar who refuses, on demand, to show his certificate to, and allow it to be read and a copy thereof to be taken by, any of the persons hereby authorised to demand it, shall for each offence be liable to a penalty not exceeding [level 1 on the standard scale](3).

(1) For meaning, see s 3, *above*.
(2) For grant of certificate, see s 5, *above*.
(3) For penalty, see note (3) to s 4, *above*.

[Sections **18** and **19** were repealed by the Police and Criminal Evidence Act 1984, ss 7(1)(d), 26(1), 119(2), Sch 7, Pts I, VI.]

Legal Proceedings

20. Summary proceedings for offences, etc
In England and Ireland all offences and penalties under this Act may be prosecuted and recovered in manner directed by the Summary Jurisdiction Acts before a court of summary jurisdiction.

* * * * * *(1)

(1) Words omitted repealed by the Northern Ireland Act 1962, s 30(2)(d), Sch 4, Pt IV and the Statute Law (Repeals) Act 1993. Summary Jurisdiction Acts: see now Magistrates' Courts Act 1980.

21. Application of fees
All fees received under this Act in England(1) and Ireland(2) shall be applied in manner in which penalties recoverable under this Act are applicable.

* * * * * *

The paragraph omitted applies to Scotland only.
(1) See note (3) to s 15, *above*.
(2) Now applicable only to Northern Ireland.

Miscellaneous

22. Deputy of chief officer of police
Any act or thing by this Act authorised to be done by the chief officer of police(1) may be done by any police officer under his command authorised by him in that behalf, and the term 'chief officer of police' in this Act includes, in relation to any such act or thing, the police officer so authorised.

(1) See note (3) to s 5, *above*.

23. Certificate not required by commercial travellers, sellers of fish, or sellers in fairs
Nothing in this Act shall render it necessary for a certificate(1) to be obtained by the following persons as such; (that is to say,)

1. Commercial travellers or other persons selling or seeking orders for goods, wares, or merchandise to or from persons who are dealers therein and who buy to sell again, or selling or seeking orders for books as agents authorised in writing by the publishers of such books.

2. Sellers of vegetables, fish, fruit, or victuals.
3. Persons selling or exposing to sale goods, wares, or merchandise in any public mart, market, or fair legally established(2).

(1) For grant of certificate, see s 5, *above*.

(2) This will not apply to a market held without a grant or statutory authority: *Benjamin v Andrews* (1858) 5 CBNS 299.

24. Reservation of powers of local authority

Nothing in this Act shall take away or diminish any of the powers vested in any local authority or any general or local Act in force in the district of such local authority.

25. [Repealed by the SLR Act 1883.]

SCHEDULES

(*Sch 1 repealed by the Police Act 1964, s 64(3), Sch 10, Part I.*)

SCHEDULE TWO

Section 5

Form A

Form of Application for Pedlar's Certificate

1. I, *AB*, [*Christian and surname of applicant in full*] have during the last calendar month resided at
in the parish of   in the county of

2. I am by trade and occupation a [*here state trade and occupation of applicant, eg, that he is a hawker, pedlar, etc*]

3. I am   years of age.

4. I apply for a certificate under the Pedlars Act, 1871, authorising me to act as pedlar within the   [police area].

Dated this   day of

(Signed)   *AB*

[*Here insert Christian and surname of applicant.*]

Form B

Form of Pedlar's Certificate

In pursuance of the Pedlars Act 1871, I certify that *AB* [*name of applicant*] of
in the county of
aged years, is hereby authorised to act as a pedlar within the [police area] for a year from the date of this certificate. [*To be altered, if necessary, to correspond to any order of the Secretary of State or Lord Lieutenant of Ireland as to time of expiration of licenses.*]

Certified this day of AD

(signed)

[*Here insert name and description of the officer signing the certificate*]

The certificate will expire on the day of , AD

(*Form C repealed by the SLR Act 1883.*)

Words in square brackets substituted by the Police Act 1996, s 103, Sch 7, para 7.

FAIRS ACT 1873

(36 & 37 Vict, c 37)

An Act to amend the Law relating to Fairs in England and Wales.

[7th July 1873]

1. Short title

This Act may be cited as 'The Fairs Act 1873'.

2. Extent

This Act shall not extend to Scotland or Ireland.

3. Definition of terms

In this Act the term 'owner' means any person or persons, or body of commissioners or body corporate, entitled to hold any fair, whether in respect of the ownership of any lands or tenements, or under any charter, letters patent, or otherwise howsoever.

As to the right to hold fairs under the title referred to in the section, see *above*, pp 13 *et seq*.

6. Power of Secretary of State to alter days of holding fairs

In case it shall appear to . . . a Secretary of State, upon representation duly made to him by the justices([1]) acting in and for the petty sessional division within which any fair is held, or by the owner([2]) of any fair in England and Wales, that it would be for the convenience and advantage of the public that any such fair shall be held in each year on some day or days other than that or those on which such fair is used to be held or on the day or days on which such fair is used to be held and any preceding or subsequent day or days, or on or during a less number of days than those on which such fair is used to be held, it shall be lawful for a Secretary of State to order that such fair shall be held on such other day or days, or on the same day or days and any preceding or subsequent day or days, or on or during any less number of days as he shall think fit([3]): Provided always, that notice of such representation and of the time when it shall please a Secretary of State to take the same into consideration shall if such representation shall have been made by justices be given to the owner of such fair, and shall if such representation shall have been made by the owner of such fair be given to the clerk to the justices acting in and for the petty sessional division within which such fair is held, and shall also be published once in the *London Gazette*, and in three successive weeks in some one and the same newspaper published in the county, city, or borough in which such fair is held, or if there be no newspaper published therein, then in the newspaper of some county adjoining or near thereto, before such representation is so considered.

The words omitted were repealed by Statute Law Revision (No 2) Act 1893 (56 & 57 Vict, c 54).

([1]) See the Fairs Act 1871, s 3, note ([1]), *above*.
Notice of such representation must be given to the owner; see this section, *above*.

([2]) 'Owner' is defined in s 3, *above*.

([3]) As to the days on which fairs may be lawfully held, see, *above*, pp 45–47.

7. Order of Secretary of State to be published in certain newspapers.—All rights, etc, of owner to remain good

When and as soon as any such order as aforesaid shall have been made by a Secretary of State, notice of the making of the same shall be published in the *London Gazette* and in some one newspaper of the county, city, or borough in which such fair is usually held, or if there be no newspaper published therein, then in the newspaper of some county adjoining or near thereto, and thereupon such fair shall only be held on the day or days mentioned in such order; and it shall be lawful for the owner of such fair to take all such toll or tolls, and to do all such act or acts, and to enjoy all and the same rights, powers and privileges in respect thereof, and enforce the same by all and the like remedies, as if the same were held on the day or days upon which it was used to be held previous to the making of such order.

PEDLARS ACT 1881

(44 & 45 Vict, c 45)

An Act to amend the Pedlars Act 1871, as regards the district within which a certificate authorises a person to act as Pedlar

[22nd August 1881]

1. Short title

This Act may be cited as the Pedlars Act 1881.

This Act and the Pedlars Act 1871, may be cited together as the Pedlars Acts 1871 and 1881.

2. Alteration of 34 & 35 Vict c 96, as to indorsement of a pedlar's certificate

A pedlar's certificate granted under the Pedlars Act 1871, shall during the time for which it continues in force authorise the person to whom it is granted to act as a pedlar within any part of the United Kingdom . . .

The words omitted were repealed by the SLR Act 1894.

[Schedule repealed by the SLR Act 1894.]

This Act applies to Northern Ireland.

MARKETS AND FAIRS (WEIGHING OF CATTLE) ACT 1887

(50 & 51 Vict, c 27)

An Act to amend the Law with respect to weighing cattle in Markets and Fairs([1]).

[8th August 1887]

1. Short title

This Act may be cited as the Markets and Fairs (Weighing of Cattle) Act 1887([2]).

([1]) Sections 4, 5, 8, 9 repealed, so far as respects any London borough council which is a market authority for the purposes of Pt III of the Food and Drugs Act 1955, by the London Government Act 1963, s 93(1), Sch 18, Pt II.

([2]) This Act and the Markets and Fairs (Weighing of Cattle) Acts 1891 and 1926, *below*, pp 202–206, may be cited as the Markets and Fairs (Weighing of Cattle) Acts 1887 to 1926; see s 4(2) of the Act of 1926, *below*, p 205; and this Act and the Act of 1891 are to be construed as one; see s 6 of the Act of 1891, *below*, p 203.

2. Application of Act

This Act, save as is hereinafter provided([1]), shall apply to all markets and fairs in which tolls([2]) are for the time being authorised to be taken and actually are taken in respect of cattle([3]) by any company, corporation, or person; and every such company, corporation, or person is in this Act called the market authority.

([1]) See the power of the Minister to grant exemption from the Act given by s 9. Also, ss 4–9 of and the Schedule to this Act and the amending ss 1 and 2 of the Markets and Fairs (Weighing of Cattle) Act 1891, *below*, and ss 2 (in part) and 3 of and the Schedule to the Act of 1926, below, were repealed by the Food and Drugs Act 1938 (1 & 2 Geo V, c 56), ss 101, 103, Sch IV, so far as respects any local authority outside London which is a market authority for the purposes of that Act now replaced by the Food Act 1984. For market authorities within the latter Act, see *ibid*, s 61, *below*, p 251, and for their duty to provide weighing machines for weighing cattle and their duties and liabilities as to weighing under that Act, see *ibid*, s 57(2), *below*, pp 249, 250 and notes thereto. See also note ([2]) *below* and text thereto as to further restrictions on the application of this Act; see also p 121 *above*.

([2]) For the meaning of tolls, see *above*, p 51. The Act may therefore apply to markets to which the Markets and Fairs Clauses Act 1847 applies if tolls are payable: see *ibid*, ss 1, 31 *et seq*. See also *ibid*, ss 21 *et seq*.

([3]) 'Cattle' is defined in s 3, *below*.

3. Interpretation

In this Act the word 'cattle' includes ram, ewe, wether, lamb, and swine.

* * * * * *

MARKETS AND FAIRS (WEIGHING OF CATTLE) ACT 1891

(54 & 55 Vict, c 70)

An Act to amend the Markets and Fairs (Weighing of Cattle) Act 1887.

[5th August 1891]

1. Transfer of powers under 50 & 51 Vict, c 27, s 9

The powers under section nine of the principal Act([1]) of the Local Government Board as to England and Wales . . . shall be transferred to and vest in the Board of Agriculture([2]), . . .

The words omitted were repealed by the Statute Law Revision Act 1908 (8 Edw VII, c 49), or relate to Scotland and Ireland.

([1]) The principal Act, by virtue of thc repealed preamble to this Act, is the Markets and Fairs (Weighing of Cattle) Act 1887; for *ibid*, s 9, see *above*, p 201. Section 9 of that Act and s 1 of this Act were repealed as to markets of local authorities outside London under the Food and Drugs Acts; see note ([1]) to s 2 of the Act of 1887, *above*, p 201.

([2]) The powers of the Board of Agriculture were transferred to the Minister of Agriculture and Fisheries by the Ministry of Agriculture and Fisheries Act 1919 (9 & 10 Geo V, c 91), s 1. Now the Ministry of Agriculture, Fisheries and Food by virtue of the Transfer of Functions (Ministry of Food) Order 1955, SI 1955 No 554.

2. Amendment of 50 & 51 Vict, c 27, s 4, as to accommodation for weighing cattle([1])

(1) The market authority([2]) of every market and fair to which the principal Act([3]) for the time being applies([3]) shall, unless exempted by order of the Board of Agriculture([4]) from the requirements of this section, provide and maintain to the satisfaction of the Board sufficient and suitable accommodation for weighing cattle.

(2) Default in complying with the requirements of this section shall be deemed default in complying with the requirements of section four of the principal Act.

([1]) Ss 1, 2 repealed, so far as respects any London borough council which is a market authority for the purposes of Pt III of the Food and Drugs Act 1955, by the London Government Act 1963, s 93(1), Sch 18, Pt II.

([2]) 'Market authority' is defined in s 2 of the Markets and Fairs (Weighing of Cattle) Act 1887, *above*, which applies by virtue of s 6 of this Act, *below*.

([3]) The principal Act, by virtue of the repealed preamble to this Act, is the Markets and Fairs (Weighing of Cattle) Act 1887. That Act applies to any market or fair for cattle in which tolls are lawfully taken unless the market or fair is exempted by the Minister. Section 4 of that Act and s 2 of this Act were, however, repealed as to markets of local authorities outside London under the Food and Drugs Act 1955 (repealed), and special provision was made as to market authorities under that Act; see s 2 of the Act of 1887, *above*, p 201 and note ([1]) thereto.

([4]) Now the Minister of Agriculture, Fisheries and Food: see s 1 and notes thereto, *above*.

3. [Repealed by the Statute Law (Repeals) Act 1975.]

4. Application of Act to auction marts

(1) An auctioneer shall not, unless exempted by order of the Board of Agriculture([1]) from the requirements of this section, sell cattle([2]) at any mart where cattle are habitually or periodically sold, unless there are provided at that mart similar facilities for weighing cattle as are required by the principal Act([3]) and this Act([3]) in the case of cattle sold at a market or fair to which the principal Act applies([4]).

(2) [. . .]([5])

(3) If any such auctioneer makes default in complying with the requirements of this section, the auctioneer, or, if he is in the employment of any person, the person by whom he is employed, shall for each offence be liable on summary conviction to a fine not exceeding [level 2 on the standard scale], or in the case of a continuing offence to a fine not exceeding ten pounds for every day during which the offence continues([6]).

[(4) Postponement of operation to January 1892; repealed by Statute Law Revision Act 1908 (8 Edw VII, c 49).]

([1]) Now the Minister of Agriculture, Fisheries and Food; see s 1, *above*, and notes thereto. The Minister may exercise his power to exempt an auctioneer where the circumstances are, in his opinion, such as to render the enforcement of requirements under the section inexpedient; see Markets and Fairs (Weighing of Cattle) Act 1926, s 2, *below*.

([2]) 'Cattle' are defined in s 3 of the Act of 1887, *above*, which applies by virtue of s 6 of this Act, *below*.

([3]) The principal Act, by virtue of the repealed preamble to this Act, is the Markets and Fairs (Weighing of Cattle) Act 1887.

For the facilities for weighing under that Act, see *ibid*, s 4, under this Act, see *ibid*, s 2, *above*. It is sufficient if there are weighing facilities in the market-place although not actually in the auctioneer's sale yard: see *Knott v Stride* (1913) 11 LGR 534.

In the case of certain fat cattle the auctioneer must also disclose the weight; see s 1 of the Markets and Fairs (Weighing of Cattle) Act 1926, *below*.

([4]) The principal Act, that is the Act of 1887, applies to all markets and fairs at which tolls are lawfully taken unless the market or fair is exempted by the Minister; see *ibid*, s 2 and sub-s (1) thereto, *above*. This section (s 4) is not repealed as to markets of local authorities under the Food Act 1984.

([5]) Repealed, except as respects Northern Ireland, by the Statute Law (Repeals) Act 1975, s 1, Sch, Pt II.

([6]) Maximum fine increased to £50 by the Criminal Law Act 1977, s 31(6); and by virtue of the Criminal Justice Act 1982, s 46, the reference to that amount is converted to a reference to level 2 on the standard scale set out in s 37(2) thereof.

5. Application to Ireland

6. Construction and short title

This Act shall be construed as one with the principal Act, and may be cited as the Markets and Fairs (Weighing of Cattle) Act 1891, and the principal Act and this Act may be cited together as the Markets and Fairs (Weighing of Cattle) Acts 1887 and 1891.

The principal Act, by virtue of the repealed preamble to this Act, is the Markets and Fairs (Weighing of Cattle) Act 1887, *above*, p 201.

SCHEDULE

[Superseded by the Markets and Fairs (Weighing of Cattle) Returns Order 1905 (SR & O 1905 No 70) made under s 3(2), and repealed by Statute Law Revision Act 1908 (8 Edw VII, c 49).]

MARKETS AND FAIRS (WEIGHING OF CATTLE) ACT 1926

(16 & 17 Geo V, c 21)

An Act to amend the Markets and Fairs (Weighing of Cattle) Acts 1887 and 1891.

[15th July 1926]

1. Disclosure of weight of fat cattle on sale by auction

(1) Subject to the provisions of this Act(1) an auctioneer shall not offer for sale in any market, fair, or mart, in or near which a weighing machine is provided for the purpose of complying with the provisions of the principal Acts(2), any cattle(3) which are fit for immediate slaughter unless they have been weighed on the weighing machine and their weight as so ascertained is disclosed to intending purchasers at the time of the offer for sale either by announcement made by the auctioneer or in some other manner calculated to bring it to their notice.

(2) Any auctioneer who offers for sale any cattle in contravention of this section shall be liable on summary conviction to a fine not exceeding [level 1 on the standard scale] for each head of cattle so offered for sale(4).

(3) In this section the expression 'cattle' means bulls, cows, oxen and heifers(5).

(4) The Minister(6) may by order declare that the foregoing provisions of this Act shall not apply as respects any market, fair or mart.

(1) 'Cattle' has a limited meaning; see sub-s (3), *above*, and a market fair or mart may be exempt; see sub-s (4), *above*. See also note (2), *below*.

(2) The principal Acts are the Markets and Fairs (Weighing of Cattle) Acts 1887, *above*, and 1891, *above*; see s 4, *below*.

Weighing machines must be provided under s 4 of the Act of 1887, or s 4 of the Act of 1891, *above*, but a weighing machine provided will not be provided for the purpose of complying with those Acts if an exemption has been granted under s 9 of the Act of 1887, or s 4 of the Act of 1891, *above*, as extended by s 2 of this Act, *below*.

Where also weighing machines for weighing cattle, sheep or swine are provided as required by s 57(2) of the Food Act 1984, they are deemed to have been provided 'for the purpose of complying with the provisions of the principal Acts' referred to in this section. A weighing machine although provided, will not be so provided, however, where the Minister has exempted the market authority under s 57(2) of the Act of 1984.

(3) 'Cattle' are defined in sub-s (3), *above*.

(4) Maximum fine increased to £25 by the Criminal Law Act 1977, s 31(6); and by virtue of the Criminal Justice Act 1982, s 46, the reference to that amount is converted to a reference to level 1 of the standard scale set out in s 37(2) thereof.

(5) This section does not therefore apply to all the cattle as defined in s 3 of the Act of 1887, *above*.

(6) The Minister is the Minister of Agriculture, Fisheries and Food, see s 4, *below*.

2. Extension of powers of Minister to grant exemption from provisions of principal Acts(1)

The power of the Minister under [section 9 of the Act of 1887](2) to exempt any market or fair from the requirements of that Act as to the provision and maintenance of facilities for weighing cattle, and the power of the Minister under section four of the Act of 1891(3) to exempt an auctioneer from the requirements of that section in respect of the sale of cattle at a mart, may be exercised respectively with respect to any market or fair and with respect to any auctioneer where the circumstances are in the opinion of the Minister such as to render the enforcement of those requirements inexpedient.

(1) The words omitted from the beginning of this section were repealed by the Statute Law (Repeals) Act 1975, s 1(2). For the words 'the said section' are substituted the words 'section 9 of the Act of 1887' by SL(R)A 1975, s 1(2). This part of this section (as amended) relating to the power of the Minister under s 9 of the 1887 Act and the whole of s 3 and the Schedule are repealed, so far as respects any London borough council which is a market authority for the purposes of Pt III of the Food and Drugs Act 1955 (repealed), by the London Government Act 1963, s 93(1), Sch 18, Pt II.

(2) This section extends the power of exemption under s 9 of the Act of 1887 but that section is repealed as to markets of local authorities outside London under the Food and Drugs Act 1955 (repealed) and a special provision was made as to market authorities under that Act; see note (1) to s 2 of the Act of 1887, *above*, p. 201. Accordingly this section also is so repealed from the beginning of the section to the words 'weighing cattle, and' as is the word 'respectively'; see note (1) to s 2 of the Act of 1887, *above*.

(3) For s 4 of the Act of 1891, see *above*, p 202.

3. Tolls for weighing cattle(1)

The Act of 1887 shall have effect as if for the Schedule to that Act (which prescribes tolls which may be demanded in respect of the weighing of cattle) there were substituted the Schedule to this Act.

(1) Now of limited effect; see note to s 2, *above*.

See the Schedule, *below*.

The Schedule to the Act of 1887 is repealed as to markets of local authorities outside London under the Food and Drugs Acts and so also are this section and the Schedule, *below*; see note (1) to s 2 of the Act of 1887, *above*, p 201.

4. Interpretation, short title, commencement, citation and extent

(1) In this Act, unless the context otherwise requires, the following expressions have the meanings hereby assigned to them respectively, that is to say:—

'The Minister' means as respects England and Wales, the Minister of Agriculture, Fisheries and Food(1), . . .

'The Act of 1887' means the Markets and Fairs (Weighing of Cattle) Act 1887.

'The Act of 1891' means the Markets and Fairs (Weighing of Cattle) Act 1891.

'The principal Acts' means the Markets and Fairs (Weighing of Cattle) Acts 1887 and 1891.

(2) This Act may be cited as the Markets and Fairs (Weighing of Cattle) Act 1926, and shall come into operation on the first day of January, nineteen hundred and twenty-seven; and this Act and the principal Acts may be cited together as the Markets and Fairs (Weighing of Cattle) Acts 1887 to 1926.

(3) This Act shall not apply to Northern Ireland.

(1) For the words 'the Minister of Agriculture and Fisheries' were substituted the words 'the Minister of Agriculture, Fisheries and Food' by the Transfer of Functions (Ministry of Food) Order 1955, SI 1955/554.

The words omitted relate to Scotland. For the Acts of 1887 and 1891, see *above*, pp 201, 202.

Schedule(1)

	Not exceeding
For every head of cattle other than sheep or swine	[2p]
For every five or less number of sheep or swine	[1p](2)

([1]) See note ([1]) to s 2, *above*. See note to s 3, *above*.

([2]) The sums of 2½p and 1½p were substituted by the Decimal Currency Act 1969, s 10(1) and were rounded down as a consequence of the abolition of the halfpenny by Royal proclamation of 3 December 1984.

PUBLIC HEALTH ACT 1961

(9 & 10 Eliz 2, c 64)

An Act to amend the provisions of the Public Health Act 1936 . . . to make such amendments of the law relating to public health and the functions of county councils and other local authorities as are commonly made in local Acts . . .

[3rd August 1961]

* * * * * *

PART VI
MISCELLANEOUS

* * * * * *

75. Byelaws as to pleasure fairs and roller skating rinks

(1) A local authority may make byelaws—

(a) for regulating the hours during which pleasure fairs and roller skating rinks may be open to the public;

(b) for securing safe and adequate means of ingress to, and egress from, any pleasure fair or roller skating rink;

(c) for the prevention and suppression of nuisances, and the preservation of sanitary conditions, cleanliness, order and public safety, at any pleasure fair or roller skating rink;

[(d) without prejudice to the generality of the preceding paragraph, for preventing outbreaks of fire which might endanger—

(i) stands stalls or other structures used or intended for use in connection with any pleasure fair, or

(ii) caravans used or intended for use as sleeping accommodation in connection with any pleasure fair,

and for reducing the risk of, and the spread of fire from, such outbreaks]

and it shall be the duty of the local authority to enforce byelaws made by them under this section.

(2) In this section—

(a) 'pleasure fair' means any place—

(i) which is for the time being used wholly or mainly for providing, whether or not in combination with any other entertainment, any entertainment to which this section applies and

(ii) for admission to which, or for the use of the contrivances in which, a charge is made;

(b) 'roller skating rink' means any place which is for the time being used wholly or mainly for roller skating and for admission to which a charge is made.

(3) Subject to the provisions of the next following subsection, the entertainments to which this section applies are the following—

(a) circuses;

(b) exhibitions of human beings or of performing animals;

(c) merry-go-rounds, roundabouts, swings, switchback railways;

(d) coconut shies, hoop-las, shooting galleries, bowling alleys;

(e) dodgems and other mechanical riding or driving contrivances;

(f) automatic or other machines intended for entertainment or amusement;

(g) anything similar to any of the foregoing.

(4) [*Application to fair held by statute, charter etc; repealed with savings by Local Government (Miscellaneous Provisions) Act 1976, ss 22 and 81(2), Sch 2.*]

(5) Different byelaws may be made under this section for pleasure fairs and roller skating rinks and for different kinds of pleasure fairs.

(6) Section two hundred and eighty-seven of the Public Health Act 1936 (which relates to powers of entry), shall have effect as if this section were contained in that Act.

(7) Section thirty-eight of the Public Health Acts Amendment Act 1890 (under which byelaws may be made for the prevention of danger from roundabouts, swings and shooting galleries), shall cease to have effect, but any byelaws under that section in force at the commencement of this Act shall continue in force and may be revoked at any time as if they had been made under this section.

(8) The Secretary of State shall be the confirming authority as respects byelaws under this section, and the Secretary of State shall not confirm any byelaw under this section unless he is satisfied that all bodies which appear to him to be representative of the interests of those who carry on pleasure fairs and entertainments to which this section applies have been consulted on the matters dealt with by the byelaw [and, in the case of a byelaw made in pursuance of sub-section l(d) of this section, that the fire authority within the meaning of the Fire Services Act 1847 for the area to which the byelaw applies have been consulted.]

The words in square brackets were inserted by the Local Government (Miscellaneous Provisions) Act 1976, s 22(1)(3). In sub-s (2)(a), the meaning of 'notified pleasure fair' is applied by the Local Government (Miscellaneous Provisions) Act 1982, ss 1 and 19(12), Sch 1, para 22.

LOCAL GOVERNMENT (MISCELLANEOUS PROVISIONS) ACT 1976

(1976, c 57)

An Act to make amendments for England and Wales of provisions of the law which relates to local authorities or highways and is commonly amended by local Acts; to alter certain supplemental provisions of the enactments relating to public health; to provide for certain powers of local authorities to execute works to be exercisable outside their areas; to provide for certain future local enactments and orders to have effect subject to certain other enactments; to amend section 126 of the Housing Act 1974; and for purposes connected with the matters aforesaid

[15th November 1976]

PART I
GENERAL

Miscellaneous

36. Power of local authorities to appoint times and charges for markets

(1) Any provision of a local Act which confers power on a local authority to make byelaws appointing days on which or the hours during which markets or fairs are to be or may be held shall be construed as conferring on the authority a power to appoint such days or hours by resolution.

(2) A local authority which maintains a market in pursuance of a local Act([1]) may, notwithstanding anything in any enactment relating to the market, make in connection with the market such charges as the authority determines from time to time.

([1]) See the City of London (Spitalfields Market) Act 1990 (c ix), s 7(1) which applies s 36 to that Act.

* * * * * *

Supplemental

44. Interpretation etc of Part I

(1) In this Part of this Act, except where the contrary intention appears—

* * * * * *

'the Common Council' means the Common Council of the City of London;

* * * * * *

'local Act' includes a provisional order confirmed by an Act;

['local authority' means a county council [. . .]([1]) a district council, a London borough council, the Common Council and the Council of the Isles of Scilly and

* * * * * *

(b) in sections 1, 16, 19, 30, 36, 39 and 41 of this Act, a parish council and a community council;]([2])

* * * * * *

([1]) Repealed by the Local Government Act 1985, s 102, Sch 17.
([2]) Substituted by the Local Government Act 1985, s 84, Sch 14, para 53(b).

Part III
Supplemental

83. Short title, commencement and extent

(1) This Act may be cited as the Local Government (Miscellaneous Provisions) Act 1976.

(2) [*Commencement*].

(3) This Act does not extend to Scotland and Northern Ireland.

HIGHWAYS ACT 1980

(1980, c 66)

An Act to consolidate the Highways Acts 1959 to 1971 and related enactments, with amendments to give effect to recommendations of the Law Commission

[13th November 1980]

* * * * * *

PART IX
LAWFUL AND UNLAWFUL INTERFERENCE WITH HIGHWAYS AND STREETS

* * * * * *

Obstruction of highways and streets

137. Penalty for wilful obstruction

(1) If a person, without lawful authority or excuse, in any way wilfully obstructs the free passage along a highway he is guilty of an offence and liable to a fine not exceeding [level 3 on the standard scale](1).

(2) [. . .](2)

(1) By the Criminal Justice Act 1982, s 46, a reference to the level on the standard scale is substituted for the amount of the fine.

(2) Repealed by the Police and Criminal Evidence Act 1984, s 119, Sch 7.

* * * * * *

148. Penalty for depositing things or pitching booths etc on highway

If, without lawful authority or excuse—

(a) a person deposits on a made-up carriageway any dung, compost or other material for dressing land, or any rubbish, or

(b) a person deposits on any highway that consists of or comprises a made-up carriageway any dung, compost or other material for dressing land, or any rubbish, within 15 feet from the centre of that carriageway, or

(c) a person deposits any thing whatsoever on a highway to the interruption of any user of the highway, or

(d) a hawker or other itinerant trader pitches a booth, stall or stand, or encamps, on a highway,

he is guilty of an offence and liable to a fine not exceeding [level 3 on the standard scale].

Fine: see note (1) to s 137.

149. Removal of things so deposited on highway as to be a nuisance etc

(1) If any thing is so deposited(1) on a highway as to constitute a nuisance, the highway authority for the highway may by notice require the person who deposited it there to remove it forthwith and if he fails to comply with the notice the authority may make a complaint to a magistrates' court for a removal and disposal order under this section.

(2) If the highway authority for any highway have reasonable grounds for considering—

(a) that any thing unlawfully deposited on the highway constitutes a danger (including a danger caused by obstructing the view) to users of the highway, and

(b) that the thing in question ought to be removed without the delay involved in giving notice or obtaining a removal and disposal order from a magistrates' court under this section,

the authority may remove the thing forthwith.

(3) The highway authority by whom a thing is removed in pursuance of subsection (3) above may either—

(a) recover from the person by whom it was deposited on the highway, or from any person claiming to be entitled to it, any expenses reasonably incurred by the authority in removing it, or

(b) make a complaint to a magistrates' court for a disposal order under this section.

(4) A magistrates' court may, on a complaint made under this section, make an order authorising the complainant authority—

(a) either to remove the thing in question and dispose of it or, as the case may be, to dispose of the thing in question, and

(b) after payment out of any proceeds arising from the disposal of the expenses incurred in the removal and disposal, to apply the balance, if any, of the proceeds to the maintenance of highways maintainable at the public expense by them.

(5) If the thing in question is not of sufficient value to defray the expenses of removing it, the complainant authority may recover from the person who deposited it on the highway the expenses, or the balance of the expenses, reasonably incurred by them in removing it.

(6) A magistrates' court composed of a single justice may hear a complaint under this section.

For the meaning of 'deposited' see *Scott v Westminster City Council* (1995) 93 LGR 370.

* * * * * *

PART XIV
MISCELLANEOUS AND SUPPLEMENTARY PROVISIONS

* * * * * *

Prosecutions, appeals, etc

310. Summary proceedings for offences

All offences under this Act or under byelaws made under it are, except as provided by sections 292(4) and 297(3) above, punishable on summary conviction.

* * * * * *

Interpretation

328. Meaning of 'highway'

(1) In this Act, except where the context otherwise requires, 'highway' means the whole or a part of a highway other than a ferry or waterway.

(2) Where a highway passes over a bridge or through a tunnel, that bridge or tunnel is to be taken for the purposes of this Act to be a part of the highway.

(3) In this Act, 'highway maintainable at the public expense' and any other expression defined by reference to a highway is to be construed in accordance with the foregoing provisions of this section.

ANIMAL HEALTH ACT 1981

(1981, c 22)

An Act to consolidate the Diseases of Animals Act 1935, the Diseases of Animals Act 1950, the Ponies Act 1969, the Rabies Act 1974, the Diseases of Animals Act 1975, and certain related enactments

[11th June 1981]

PART I
GENERAL

General powers of Ministers to make orders and to authorise regulations

1. General powers of Ministers to make orders

The Ministers([1]) may make such orders([2]) as they think fit([3])—

(a) generally for the better execution of this Act, or for the purpose of in any manner preventing the spreading of disease; and

(b) in particular for the several purposes set out in this Act, and for prescribing and regulating the payment and recovery of expenses in respect of animals([4]).

([1]) For definition of 'The Ministers', see s 86(1)(c), *below*.

([2]) For list of orders which may affect markets and fairs see pp 225–231, *below*.

([3]) The Courts may, nevertheless, exercise their inherent jurisdiction in appropriate cases to determine whether such powers have been exceeded.

([4]) For definition of 'animals', see s 87(1)–(3), *below*.

2. Local authority regulations

The Ministers([1]) may make such orders([2]) as they think fit([3]) for authorising a local authority([4]) to make regulations([5]) for any of the purposes—

(a) of this Act, or

(b) of an order of the Minister([6])

subject to such conditions, if any, as the Ministers for the purpose of securing uniformity and the due execution of this Act, think fit to prescribe.

([1]) For definition of 'The Ministers', see s 86(1)(c), *below*.

([2]) For orders which, by virtue of the Interpretation Act 1978, s 17(2)(b), have effect as if made under this section, see pp 225 *et seq*.

([3]) See note ([3]) to s 1, *above*.

([4]) For definition of 'local authority', see s 50, *below*.

([5]) See ss 51 and 58, *below*. As to procedure, see the Animals (Miscellaneous Provisions) Order of 1927 SR & O 1927 No 290, arts 5(2) and 8 (as amended by SI 1976 No 919).

([6]) For definition of 'order of the Minister', see s 89(1), *below*.

* * * * * *

Cleansing and movement

7. Cleansing and disinfection

(1) The Ministers may make such orders([1]) as they think fit([2])—

(a) for prescribing and regulating the cleansing and disinfection([3]) of places used for the holding of markets, fairs, exhibitions, or sales of animals, or for lairage of animals, and yards, sheds, stables, and other places used for animals;

([1]) For orders under this section, see pp 227, 228, *below*.
([2]) See note ([3]) to s 1 *above*.
([3]) An owner is bound to give facilities for disinfection but in the absence of knowledge is not liable for his foreman's disobedience of an order: *Searle v Reynolds* (1866) 7 B & S 704.

8. Movement generally

(1) The Ministers([1]) may make such orders([2]) as they think fit([3])—

* * * * * *

(f) for prohibiting or regulating the holding of markets, fairs, exhibitions and sales of animals([4]).

([1]) For definition of 'The Ministers', see s 86(1)(c), *below*.
([2]) For orders under this section, see pp 229, 230, *below*.
([3]) See note ([3]) to s 1 *above*.
([4]) For definition of 'animals', see s 87(1)–(3), *below*.

* * * * * *

PART II
DISEASE

* * * * * *

Infection

* * * * * *

25. Movement of diseased or suspected animals

The Ministers([1]) may make such orders([2]) as they think fit([3]) for all or any of the following purposes—

(a) for prohibiting or regulating the exposure of diseased or suspected animals([4]) in markets or fairs or sale-yards, or other public or private places, where animals are commonly exposed for sale([5]), and their placing in lairs or other places adjacent to or connected with markets or fairs, or where animals are commonly placed before exposure for sale;

* * * * * *

([1]) For definition of 'The Ministers', see s 86(1)(c), *below*.
([2]) For list of orders under this section, see pp 230, 231, *below*.
([3]) See note ([3]) to s 1, *above*.
([4]) For definition of 'animals', see s 87(1)–(3), *below*.
([5]) On 'exposure for sale' see, for example, *Crane v Lawrence* (1890) 25 QBD 152; *Ollett v Jordan* [1918] 2 KB 41; *Newman v Lipman* [1951] 1 KB 333.

26. Pleuro-pneumonia or foot-and-mouth disease found in transit

(1) The Minister([1]) shall by orders([2]) make such provision as he thinks necessary or expedient([3]) respecting the case of animals([4]) found to be affected with pleuro-pneumonia or foot-and-mouth disease—

(a) while exposed for sale or exhibited in a market, fair, sale-yard, place of exhibition, or other place; or
(b) while placed in a lair or other place before exposure for sale; or
(c) while in transit or in course of being moved by land, water or air; or
(d) while being in a slaughter-house or place where animals are slaughtered or are kept with a view to slaughter; or
(e) while being on common or unenclosed land; or
(f) generally, while being in a place not in the possession or occupation or under the control of the owner of the animals.

(2) The Minister shall by orders under this section make such provision as he thinks fit for the consequences under this Act of animals being so found in the circumstances mentioned above—
(a) as well with regard to the animals as with regard to the places where they are when so found, and other places; and
(b) with regard to animals being or having been in the same shed or stable, herd or flock as, or in contact with, animals so found.

(3) The Minister may, by orders under this section relating to particular places, make such provision as he thinks fit for the consequences mentioned above.

(4) Every order under this section shall have full effect notwithstanding—
(a) any provision of this Act requiring the declaration of a place infected with pleuro-pneumonia or foot-and-mouth disease, or relating to any consequence of such a declaration, or to any matter connected with such a declaration; and
(b) any other provision whatsoever of this Act

(1) For definition of 'The Minister', see s 86(1)(a), *below*.
(2) For orders which, by virtue of the Interpretation Act 1978, s 17(2)(b), have effect as if made under this section, see pp 225–231, *below*.
(3) See note (3) to s 1, *above*.
(4) For definition of 'animals', see s 87(1)–(3), *below*.

* * * * * *

PART III
WELFARE AND EXPORT

Care

37. Prevention of suffering

(1) The Ministers[1] may make such orders[2] as they think fit[3] for the purpose of protecting animals from unnecessary suffering—

* * * * * *

(a) while exposed for sale[4]; or
(b) while awaiting removal after being exposed for sale.

(1) For definition of 'The Ministers', see s 86(1)(c), *below*.
(2) For list of orders under this section, see p 231, *below*.
(3) See note (3) to s 1, *above*.
(4) On 'exposure for sale', see note (5) to s 25, *above*.

* * * * * *

PART IV
LOCAL AUTHORITIES

50. Local authorities for purposes of this Act

(1) In this Act 'local authority' has the meaning given by subsections (2) and (3) below but subject to subsection (4) below, [and to section 13(3) above](1).

(2) In the application of this Act to England and Wales 'local authority' means(2)—

(a) as respects a London borough, the borough council,

[(b) as respects a non-metropolitan county, the county council(3),

[(bb) as respects a county borough, the county borough council](4)

(c) as respects a metropolitan district, the district council](3)

and the Common Council of the City of London shall be the local authority—

(i) for the City of London, and

(ii) in and for the whole of Greater London for the purpose of the provisions of this Act relating to imported animals.

(3) (*Applies to Scotland*)

(4) Where the district(5) or part of a district of a local authority is or comprises, or is comprised in—

(a) a port or part of a port, or

(b) an aerodrome or part of an aerodrome,

the appropriate Minister(6) may, if he thinks fit, in relation to either paragraph (a) or paragraph (b) above by order(7) make any body, other than the local authority under subsection (2) or subsection (3) above, the local authority for the purposes of the provisions of this Act relating to imported animals.

(5) A local authority shall execute and enforce(8) this Act and every order of the Minister so far as they are to be executed and enforced by local authorities(9).

(1) Inserted by the Environmental Protection Act 1990, s 151(2).

(2) See, however, sub-s (4) *above* as to the local authority where the district or part of a district of a local authority includes a port or part of a port; or an aerodrome or part of an aerodrome.

(3) The original sub-s (2)(b) substituted by sub-s (2)(b), (c), by the Local Government Act 1985, s 16, Sch 8, para 18.

(4) Added by the Local Government (Wales) Act 1994, s 66(6), Sch 16, para 61.

(5) That is, the area for which the local authority exercises power under this Act: *ibid*, s 89(1).

(6) For definition of 'the appropriate Minister', see s 86(1)(b), *below*.

(7) Orders made under this section, or which by virtue of the Interpretation Act 1978, s 17(2)(b) have effect as if made under this section, are local in nature.

(8) As to default powers of the Minister, see s 59, *below*.

(9) The powers of a local authority are limited to its district: see s 51, *below*. As to default powers of the Minister, see s 59, *below*.

51. Local authorities and their districts

(1) The provisions of this Act conferring powers on, or otherwise relating to, a local authority(1), or their inspectors(2) or officers shall, unless otherwise expressed, be read as having reference to the district(3) of the local authority.

(2) The powers so conferred shall, unless it is otherwise expressed, be exercisable and shall operate within and in relation to that district only.

([1]) For definition of 'local authority', see s 50, *above* and for powers of a local authority see ss 52–59, *below*.
([2]) For definition of 'inspector', see s 89(1), *below*.
([3]) The district of a local authority means the area for which the local authority exercises powers under this Act: see s 89(1), *below*. For definition of 'local authority', see s 50, *above*.

52. Inspectors and other officers

(1) Every local authority([1]) shall appoint as many inspectors([2]) and other officers as the local authority think necessary for the execution and enforcement of this Act.

(2) Every local authority shall assign to those inspectors and officers such duties, and salaries or allowances, and may delegate to any of them such authorities and discretion, as to the local authority seem fit, and may at any time revoke any appointment so made.

([1]) For definition of 'local authority', see s 50, *above*.
([2]) For definition of 'inspector', see s 89(1), *below*. It is usual to appoint the chief officers of police as inspectors for their districts. As to the duties of the inspectors to make returns, see s 81, *below*.

53. Borrowing powers

(1) A local authority([1]) may borrow for the purposes of this Act.

(2) (*Applies to Scotland.*)

([1]) For definition of 'local authority', see s 50, *above*.

54. Provision of wharves etc

(1) A local authority([1]) may provide, erect and fit up wharves, stations, lairs, sheds and other places for the landing, reception, keeping, sale, slaughter or disposal of imported([2]) or other animals, carcases, fodder, litter([2]), dung and other things.

(2) There shall be incorporated with this Act the Markets and Fairs Clauses Act 1847, except sections 6 to 9, and 52 to 59([3]).

(3) A wharf or other place provided by a local authority under this section shall be a market within that Act([4]), and this Act shall be the special Act([5]), and

- (a) the prescribed limits shall be the limits of lands acquired or appropriated for the purposes of this section([6]),
- (b) byelaws shall be approved by the appropriate Minister([7]), which approval shall be sufficient without any other approval or allowance where—
  - (i) notice of application for approval has been given, and
  - (ii) the proposed byelaws have been published before application,

as required by that Act of 1847([8]).

(4) A local authority may charge for the use of a wharf or other place provided by them under this section such sums as may be imposed by byelaws, and those sums shall be deemed tolls authorised by the special Act([9]).

(5) All sums so received by a local authority in England and Wales—

- (a) shall be carried to a separate account([10]); and
- (b) shall be applied in payment of interest and repayment of principal in respect of money borrowed by them under this Act([11]), and
- (c) subject to paragraph (b), shall be applied towards the discharge of their expenses under this Act

(6) The local authority shall make such periodical returns to the appropriate Minister as he may require of their expenditure and receipts in respect of the wharf or other place([12]).

(1) For definition of 'local authority', see s 50, *above*.
(2) For definition of 'animals', see s 87(1), *below*, and for definitions of 'imported', 'carcase', 'fodder' and 'litter' see s 89(1), *below*. By virtue of s 87(4), this section also applies to poultry.
(3) For the Markets and Fairs Clauses Act 1847 (part) see pp 179 *et seq*, *above*. The excluded sections 6–9 relate to the acquisition of land, and ss 51-60 relate to the recovery of damages and penalties. The acquisition of land under this Act is otherwise provided for by s 55, *below*, and enforcement, offences and proceedings by Part V, *below*.
(4) As to a market within the 1847 Act see *ibid*, s 3 and pp 19, 20, *above*.
(5) As to the special Act under the 1847 Act see *ibid*, s 2, p 180, *above* and pp 19, 20, *above*.
(6) As to the prescribed limits under the 1847 Act, see note (3) to *ibid*, s 12. As to the power to acquire land, see s 55, *below*.
(7) For definition of 'the appropriate Minister', see s 86(1)(b), *below*.
(8) As to the making of byelaws under the 1847 Act see *ibid*, ss 42 and 43, *above*, pp 109-110 *above*; and as to the necessity for confirmation, notice of application and publication, see *ibid*, ss 44–47 and p 110, *above*. As to validity of byelaws, see notes to *ibid*, s 42, *above* and pp 111–113 and 185, 186, *above*. Byelaws may prescribe charges: see sub-s (4), *above*.
(9) For provisions as to tolls in the special Act see the 1847 Act, ss 31–41 and pp 61, 62, 184, *above*.
(10) As to accounts under the 1847 Act, see *ibid*, s 50.
(11) As to the power of a local authority to borrow, see s 53, *above*.
(12) See also s 81, *below*.

55. Power to acquire land

(1) A local authority(1) may—

(a) purchase land by agreement, or
(b) if so authorised by the Minister or the appropriate Minister(2), purchase land compulsorily(3), or
(c) by agreement take land on lease or at a rent,

for the following purposes—

(i) for wharves or other places; or
(ii) for use for burial of carcases(4), in cases where there is not any ground suitable in that behalf in the possession or occupation of the owner of the animal, or any common or unenclosed land suitable and approved by the Minister or the appropriate Minister in that behalf; or
(iii) for any other purpose of this Act.

(2) The powers conferred by this section may be exercised by a local authority in England and Wales with respect to land within or without their district [and the Acquisition of Land Act 1981 shall apply to a compulsory purchase under this section by such a local authority](5).

(3) [. . .](6).

(1) For definition of 'local authority', see s 50, *above*.
(2) For definitions of 'the Minister' and 'the appropriate Minister', see s 86(1)(b), (c), *below*.
(3) For procedure for compulsory purchase of land, see the Compulsory Purchase Act 1965 and the Acquisition of Land Act 1981.
(4) For definition of 'carcase', see s 89(1), *below*.
(5) The words in square brackets were inserted by the Acquisition of Land Act 1981, s 34(1), Sch 4, para 32.
(6) Repealed in part by the Acquisition of Land Act 1987, s 34(3), Sch 6; the remainder applies to Scotland.

* * * * * *

58. Regulations

(1) A regulation([1]) of a local authority([2]) may be proved—

(a) by the production of a newspaper purporting to contain the regulation as an advertisement, or

(b) by the production of a copy of the regulation purporting to be certified by the clerk of the local authority as a true copy.

(2) A regulation so proved shall be taken to have been duly made, unless and until the contrary is proved.

(3) A regulation of a local authority authorised by this Act or by an order of the Minister([3]) shall alone be deemed for the purposes of this Act a regulation of a local authority.

([1]) By s 2, *above* the Ministers may authorise a local authority to make regulations. As to procedure, see the Animals (Miscellaneous Provisions) Order of 1927 SR & O 1927 No 290, art 8 (as amended by SI 1976 No 919).

([2]) For definition of 'local authority', see s 50, *above*.

([3]) For definition of 'the Minister', see s 86(1)(a), *below*.

59. Default

(1) Where a local authority([1]) fail to execute or enforce any of the provisions of this Act, or of an order of the Minister, the appropriate Minister([2]) may by order([3]) empower a person named in that order—

(a) to execute and enforce those provisions; or

(b) to procure their execution and enforcement.

(2) The expenses incurred under any such order or in respect of any such default by or on behalf of the appropriate Minister shall be the expenses of the local authority, and

(a) the treasurer or other proper officer of the local authority shall pay the amount of such expenses to the appropriate Minister on demand; and

(b) in default of payment a person appointed by the appropriate Minister to sue in that behalf may recover the amount of such expenses from the local authority.

(3) For the purposes of this section an order of the Minister shall be conclusive in respect of any default, amount of expenses, or other matters stated or appearing in it.

(4) The provisions of this section are without prejudice to the right or power of the appropriate Minister, or any other authority or any person, to take any other proceedings for requiring a local authority to execute or enforce any of the provisions of this Act or of an order of the Minister.

([1]) For definition of 'local authority', see s 50, *above*.

([2]) For definition of 'the Minister' and 'the appropriate Minister', see s 86(1)(b), (c), *below*.

([3]) As to the making and publication etc of orders by the Minister, see s 91, *below*.

* * * * * *

Part V
Enforcement, Offences and Proceedings

* * * * * *

Proceedings

77. Money recoverable summarily

Any money by this Act or an order of the Minister[1] made recoverable summarily may be so recovered as a civil debt, and in England and Wales this shall be in accordance with the Magistrates' Courts Act 1980[2].

(1) For definition of 'order of the Minister', see s 89(1), *below*.
(2) Magistrates' Courts Act 1980, s 58.

* * * * * *

Part VI
Supplemental

Reports and Information

81. Reports to Minister

Every local authority[1] and their inspectors[2] and officers shall give to the appropriate Minister[3] such notices, reports, returns[4] and information as he requires.

(1) For definition of 'local authority', see s 50, *above*.
(2) For definition of 'inspector', see s 89(1), *below*.
(3) For definition of 'the appropriate Minister', see s 86(1)(b), *below*.
(4) As to returns required of expenditure and receipts in respect of a wharf or other place by a local authority, see s 54(6), *above*.

* * * * * *

Interpretation, functions, and orders etc

86. Ministers and their functions

(1) In this Act—

(a) 'the Minister' means, in relation to the whole of Great Britain, the Minister of Agriculture, Fisheries and Food, and 'Ministry' shall be construed accordingly,
(b) 'the appropriate Minister' means, in relation to England, the Minister of Agriculture, Fisheries and Food, and in relation to Scotland or to Wales, the Secretary of State,
(c) 'the Ministers' means, in relation to the whole of Great Britain, the Minister of Agriculture, Fisheries and Food, the Secretary of State for Scotland and the Secretary of State for Wales, acting jointly,

but in the case of any function under the following provisions of this Act—

(i) section 21, so far as it is applicable in relation to brucellosis, tuberculosis, dourine or infestation with maggot of the warble fly,
(ii) any other provision so far as it is applicable in relation to brucellosis, brucellosis melitensis, tuberculosis or infestation of cattle with the maggot of the warble fly,

that function, notwithstanding that it is expressed to be exercisable by the Minister or the Ministers, shall be exercisable only by the appropriate Minister.

(2) The powers and duties conferred and imposed by this Act on the Minister shall be executed and discharged by the Minister in manner provided by the Ministry of Agriculture and Fisheries Acts 1889 to 1919, and this Act.

87. Meaning of 'animals' and 'poultry'

(1) In this Act, unless the context otherwise requires, 'animals' means—

(a) cattle, sheep and goats, and

(b) all other ruminating animals and swine,

subject to subsections (2) and (3) below.

(2) The Ministers may by order for all or any of the purposes of this Act extend([1]) the definition of 'animals' in subsection (1) above so that it shall for those or any of those purposes comprise—

(a) any kind of mammal except man; and

(b) any kind of four-footed beast which is not a mammal.

(3) The Ministers may by order for all or any of the purposes of this Act (except so far as it relates to disease) extend the definition of 'animals' in subsection (1) so that it shall for those or any of those purposes comprise—

(a) fish, reptiles, crustaceans, or

(b) other cold-blooded creatures of any species,

not being creatures in respect of which an order can be made under subsection (2) above.

(4) In this Act, subject to subsection (5) below and unless the context otherwise requires, 'poultry' means birds of the following species—

(a) domestic fowls, turkeys, geese, ducks, guinea-fowls and pigeons, and

(b) pheasants and partridges,

and subject to the provisions mentioned below, this Act has effect in relation to poultry as it has effect in relation to animals.

The provisions of this Act referred to above are sections [32(4), 63(9) and 75(5)]([2]).

(5) The Ministers may by order for all or any of the purposes of this Act, in so far as it applies to poultry—

(a) extend([3]) the definition of 'poultry' in subsection (4) above so that it shall for those or any of those purposes comprise any other species of bird; or

(b) restrict that definition so that it shall for those or any of those purposes exclude any of the species of bird mentioned in paragraph (b) of subsection (4).

([1]) So extended by the Spongiform Encephalopathy (Miscellaneous Amendments) Order 1994, SI 1994 No 2627, art 3.

([2]) Substituted by the Animal Health and Welfare Act 1984, s 2(2).

([3]) Extended to birds of all species by the Spongiform Encephalopathy (Miscellaneous Amendments) Order 1994, SI 1994 No 2627, art 3.

* * * * * *

89. Other interpretation provisions

(1) In this Act, unless the context otherwise requires—

* * * * * *

'carcase' means the carcase of an animal[1] and includes part of a carcase, and the meat, bones, hide, skin, hooves, offal or other part of an animal, separately or otherwise, or any portion thereof;

'cattle' means bulls, cows, steers[2], heifers and calves;

* * * * * *

'diseased' means affected with disease;

'district', when used with reference to a local authority, means thc area for which the local authority exercises powers under this Act[3];

* * * * * *

'fodder' means hay or other substance commonly used for food for animals;

'horse' includes ass and mule;

'imported' means brought to Great Britain from a country out of Great Britain;

'inspector' means a person appointed to be an inspector for the purposes of this Act by the Minister or by a local authority[4], and, when used in relation to an officer of the Ministry, includes a veterinary inspector;

'justice' means justice of the peace;

'litter' means straw or other substance commonly used for bedding or otherwise for or about animals;

'local authority' has the meaning given by section 50 above;

'order of the Minister' means an order under this Act of the Minister[5], the appropriate Minister, or the Ministers[6], as the case may be;

* * * * * *

(2) In the computation of time for the purposes of this Act, a period reckoned by days from the happening of an event or the doing of an act or thing shall be deemed to be exclusive of the day on which the event happened or the act or thing is done.

[1] For definition of 'animal', see s 87, *above*.
[2] 'Steers' were called 'oxen' under the Diseases of Animals Act 1950.
[3] For the area for which the local authority exercises power, see s 51, *above*.
[4] Inspectors are appointed under s 52, *above*.
[5] See s 91, *below*.
[6] For definition of 'the Minister', 'the appropriate Minister' and 'the Ministers', see s 86(1)(a), (b) and (c), *above*.

* * * * * *

91. Orders etc

(1) The Minister, the appropriate Minister or the Ministers[1], as the case may be, shall publish in the London Gazette and the Edinburgh Gazette a notice of any order of the Minister stating—

(a) that the order has been made; and
(b) where copies of the order may be obtained.

(2) Every local authority[2] shall at their own expense, publish every order of the Minister, and every licence or other instrument sent to them by the Minister, the appropriate Minister, or the Ministers—

(a) in such a manner as he or they shall direct[3]; and
(b) subject to and in the absence of any direction, by advertisement in a newspaper

circulating in the district(4) of the local authority.

(3) The validity or effect of an order of the Minister(5), or licence or other instrument issued by the Minister, the appropriate Minister or the Ministers shall not be affected by want of or defect or irregularity in its publication.

(4) Subsections (1) to (3) above do not apply to an order made under section 32 above.

(5) A power conferred by this Act to make an order of the Minister, other than by—

(a) section 14(2),

(b) section 59(1),

shall be exercisable by statutory instrument.

(6) An order of the Minister made under either of the provisions referred to in paragraphs (a) and (b) of subsection (5) above may be altered or revoked by a subsequent order made in the like manner and subject to the like conditions, but section 14(b) of the Interpretation Act 1978 shall not apply to an order made by the Ministers under section 34(7) above providing that section 34(6) shall cease to have effect.

(1) For definition of 'the Minister', 'the appropriate Minister' and 'the Ministers', see s 86(1)(a), (b) and (c), *above*.
(2) For definition of 'local authority' see s 50, *above*.
(3) For procedure, see the Animals (Miscellaneous Provisions) Order of 1927, SR & O 1927 No 290.
(4) For definition of 'district', see s 89(1), *above*.
(5) For definition of 'order of the Minister', see s 89(1), *above*.

* * * * * *

97. Short title, extent, and commencement

(1) This Act may be cited as the Animal Health Act 1981.

(2) Sections 93 and 95(6) above apply to Northern Ireland, and Schedule 6 to this Act, so far as it repeals provisions of the Diseases of Animals Act 1950 which applied to Northern Ireland, but apart from those provisions this Act does not extend to Northern Ireland.

(3) This Act shall come into force on the expiry of the period of one month beginning on the date of its passing.

Diseases of Animals Act 1950: *Corresponding Provisions in Animal Health Act 1981*

Diseases of Animals Act 1950		Animal Health Act 1981	
Section	1(1)(a)	*Section*	1(a)
	1(1)(b), 2(h)		1(b)
	2		2
	20(i)		25(a)
	20(vii)		8(1)(e)
	20(viii)		7(1)(a)
	20(x)		37(1)
	21		26
	57		86(2)
	59		50
	61(1)–(6)		54
	62		55

Diseases of Animals Act 1950	Animal Health Act 1981
63	59
64(1)	52
65	81
66	58
67	51
70	53
80	77
84(1)	87(1)–(3)
84(2)	87(4), (5)
84(4)	86(1)
84(4), (5)	89(1), (2)
85	91
91	97

Statutory Instruments

The following orders, which may affect the holding of markets and fairs, have been made partly under ss 1, 7, 8, 25, 26 and 37 of the Animal Health Act 1981 or partly have effect thereunder by virtue of the Interpretation Act 1978, s 17(2)(b).

Section 1: General powers of Ministers to make orders

Foot-and-Mouth Disease (Packing Materials) Order of 1925, SR & O 1925/1178, as amended by SR & O 1926/42.

Markets, Sales and Lairs Order of 1925, SR & O 1925/1349, as amended by SR & O 1926/546, SR & O 1927/982, SI 1995/11, SI 1996/3265.

Transit of Animals Order of 1927, SR & O 1927/289, as amended by SR & O 1927/399, SR & O 1939/501, SI 1927/971, SI 1975/1024, SI 1977/944, SI 1992/1361, SI 1992/3304, SI 1997/1480.

Animals (Miscellaneous Provisions) Order of 1927, SR & O 1927/290, as amended by SR & O 1938/197, SI 1953/37, SI 1953/38, SI 1959/1335, SI 1974/1185, SI 1976/919, SI 1992/1361.

Pleuro-Pneumonia Order of 1928, SR & O 1928/205, as amended by SR & O 1938/195, SI 1972/971, SI 1977/944.

Cattle Plague Order of 1928, SR & O 1928/206, as amended by SR & O 1938/194, SI 1972/971, SI 1977/944.

Animals (Miscellaneous Provisions) Order of 1938, SR & O 1938/197.

Isles of Scilly (Importation of Animals Regulations) Order 1949, SI 1949/2012.

Horses (Sea Transport) Order 1952, SI 1952/1291, as amended by SI 1958/1272, SI 1972/971, SI 1992/3304, SI 1997/1480.

Psittacosis or Ornithosis Order 1953, SI 1953/38.

Swine Fever (Infected Areas Restrictions) Order 1956, SI 1956/1750, as amended by SI 1958/1284, SI 1972/971, SI 1977/944.

Movement of Animals (Records) Order 1960, SI 1960/105, as amended by SI 1961/1493, SI 1972/971, SI 1977/944, SI 1989/879, SI 1989/2053, SI 1990/1868, SI 1995/11, SI 1995/12, SI 1996/28.

Swine Fever Order 1963, SI 1963/286, as amended by SI 1972/971, SI 1976/919, SI 1990/2487, SI 1991/1030, SI 1995/11, SI 1995/2922.

Hares (Control of Importation) Order 1965, SI 1965/2040, as amended by SI 1972/971, SI 1990/2371.

Export of Horses (Veterinary Examination) Order 1966, SI 1966/507, as amended by SI 1972/971, SI 1973/1178, SI 1995/2922.

Export of Horses (Excepted Cases) Order 1969, SI 1969/1742, as amended by SI 1972/971.

Export of Horses (Protection) Order 1969, SI 1969/1784, as amended by SI 1972/971.

Foot-and-Mouth Disease (Infected Areas) (Vaccination) Order 1972, SI 1972/1509.

Swine Vesicular Disease Order 1972, SI 1972/1980, as amended by SI 1973/101, SI 1977/944, SI 1993/3119.

Export Quarantine Stations (Regulation) Order 1973, SI 1973/824.

Diseases of Animals (Waste Food) Order 1973, SI 1973/1936, as amended by SI 1987/232, SI 1992/453, SI 1996/826.

Rabies (Importation of Dogs, Cats and Other Mammals) Order 1974, SI 1974/2211, as amended by SI 1977/361, SI 1984/1182, SI 1986/2062, SI 1990/2371, SI 1993/1813, SI 1994/1405, SI 1994/1716, SI 1995/2922.

Rabies (Control) Order 1974, SI 1974/2212, as amended by SI 1995/2922.

Movement and Sale of Pigs Order 1975, SI 1975/203, as amended by SI 1975/346, SI 1977/944, SI 1987/233, revoked by SI 1995/11 subject to savings.

Transit of Animals (Road and Rail) Order 1975, SI 1975/1024, as amended by SI 1979/1013, SI 1988/815, SI 1992/3304, SI 1994/3249, SI 1995/11, SI 1997/1480.

Importation of Animals Order 1977, SI 1977/944, as amended by SI 1990/2371, SI 1992/1361, SI 1992/3159, SI 1995/2922, SI 1996/1760.

Diseases of Animals (Approved Disinfectants) Order 1978, SI 1978/32, as amended by SI 1992/238, SI 1992/2290, SI 1993/1194, SI 1993/3086, SI 1994/2965, SI 1994/3141, SI 1997/2347.

Importation of Birds, Poultry and Hatching Eggs Order 1979, SI 1979/1702, as amended by SI 1990/2371.

Importation of Hay and Straw Order 1979, SI 1979/1703, as amended by SI 1990/2371.

Importation of Embryos, Ova and Semen Order 1980, SI 1980/12, as amended by SI 1984/1326, SI 1990/2371, SI 1994/2920.

Importation of Animal Products and Poultry Products Order 1980, SI 1980/14, as amended by SI 1980/1934, SI 1981/1238, SI 1982/948, SI 1990/2371, SI 1993/1331, SI 1994/2920, SI 1994/3142, SI 1994/3144.

African Swine Fever Order 1980, SI 1980/145, as amended by SI 1993/3119.

Importation of Animal Pathogens Order 1980, SI 1980/1212, as amended by SI 1993/3250.

Importation of Processed Animal Protein Order 1981, SI 1981/677, as amended by SI 1982/459, SI 1990/2371.

Export of Animals (Protection) Order 1981, SI 1981/1051, as amended by SI 1994/3249, SI 1997/1480.

Warble Fly (England and Wales) Order 1982, SI 1982/234, as amended by SI 1985/328, SI 1987/1601, SI 1989/244, SI 1994/3142.

Aujeszky's Disease Order 1983, SI 1983/344, as amended by SI 1994/3141, SI 1995/11, SI 1995/2922.

Foot-and-Mouth Disease Order 1983, SI 1983/1950, as amended by SI 1993/3119, SI 1995/2922.

Tuberculosis (England and Wales) Order 1984, SI 1984/1943, as amended by SI 1990/1869, SI 1995/2922.

Warble Fly (England and Wales) (Infected Areas) Order 1985, SI 1985/1542, as amended by SI 1994/3142.

Diseases of Animals (Ascertainment of Disease) Order 1985, SI 1985/1765, as amended by SI 1992/3159, SI 1994/2627.
Warble Fly (Ascertainment of Infestation) (England and Wales) Order 1985, SI 1985/1766.
Importation of Salmonid Viscera Order 1986, SI 1986/2265.
Infectious Diseases of Horses Order 1987, SI 1987/790, as amended by SI 1992/3159, SI 1995/2922.
Zoonoses Order 1988, SI 1988/2264, as amended by SI 1988/2299, SI 1997/2964.
Zoonoses Order 1989, SI 1989/285.
Processed Animal Protein Order 1989, SI 1989/661.
Tuberculosis (Deer) Order 1989, SI 1989/878, as amended by SI 1993/2010, SI 1995/2922.
Tuberculosis (Deer) Notice of Intended Slaughter and Compensation Order 1989, SI 1989/1316.
Poultry (Seizure of Hatching Eggs) Order 1990, SI 1990/232.
Movement of Animals (Restriction) Order 1990, SI 1990/760, as amended by SI 1991/1155, SI 1991/1251.
Welfare of Horses at Markets (and Other Places of Sale) Order 1990, SI 1990/2627.
Welfare of Animals at Markets Order 1990, SI 1990/2628, as amended by SI 1993/3085, SI 1995/12.
Anthrax Order 1991, SI 1991/2814, as amended by SI 1995/2922, SI 1996/1855.
Specified Diseases (Notification and Slaughter) Order 1992, SI 1992/3159, as amended by SI 1996/2628.
Shellfish and Specified Fish (Third Country Imports) Order 1992, SI 1992/3301.
Animal By-Products Order 1992, SI 1992/3303, as amended by SI 1996/827, SI 1997/2894.
Poultry Breeding Flocks and Hatcheries Order 1993, SI 1993/1898.
Specified Animal Pathogens Order 1993, SI 1993/3250, as amended by SI 1994/3142, SI 1994/3144.
Diseases of Poultry Order 1994, SI 1994/3141, as amended by SI 1995/2922, SI 1997/150.
Pigs (Records, Identification and Movement) Order 1995, SI 1995/11, as amended by SI 1995/2922.
Equine Viral Arteritis Order 1995, SI 1995/1755, as amended by SI 1995/2922.
Animals (Post-Import Control) Order 1995, SI 1995/2439.
Sheep and Goats (Records, Identification and Movement) Order 1996, SI 1996/28.
Cattle Passports Order 1996, SI 1996/1686.
Specified Diseases (Notification) Order 1996, SI 1996/2628.
Bovine Spongiform Encephalopathy (No 2) Order 1996, SI 1996/3183, as amended by SI 1997/2387.
Enzootic Bovine Leukosis Order 1997, SI 1997/757.
Brucellosis Order 1997, SI 1997/758.
Sheep Scab Order 1997, SI 1997/968.
Welfare of Animals (Transport) Order 1997, SI 1997/1480.
Horse Passports Order 1997, SI 1997/2789.
Specified Risk Material Order 1997, SI 1997/2964.

Section 7: Cleansing and disinfection

Markets, Sales and Lairs Order of 1925, SR & O 1925/1349, as amended by SR & O 1926/546, SR & O 1927/982, SI 1995/11, SI 1996/3265.

Transit of Animals Order of 1927, SR & O 1927, as amended by SR & O 1927/399, SR & O 1939/501, SI 1972/971, SI 1975/1024, SI 1977/944, SI 1992/1361, SI 1992/3304, SI 1997/1480.

Animals (Miscellaneous Provisions) Order of 1927, SR & O 1927/290, as amended by SR & O 1938/197, SI 1953/37, SI 1953/38, SI 1959/1335, SI 1974/1185, SI 1976/919, SI 1992/1361.

Pleuro-Pneumonia Order of 1928, SR & O 1928/205, as amended by SR & O 1938/195, SI 1972/971, SI 1977/944.

Cattle Plague Order of 1928, SR & O 1928/206, as amended by SR & O 1938/194, SI 1972/971, SI 1977/944.

Horses (Sea Transport) Order 1952, SI 1952/1291, as amended by SI 1958/1272, SI 1972/971, SI 1992/3304, SI 1997/1480.

Psittacosis or Ornithosis Order 1953, SI 1953/38.

Swine Fever Order 1963, SI 1963/286, as amended by SI 1972/971, SI 1976/919, SI 1990/2487, SI 1991/1030, SI 1995/11, SI 1995/2922.

Export of Horses (Protection) Order 1969, SI 1969/1784, as amended by SI 1972/971.

Transit of Animals (Road and Rail) Order 1975, SI 1975/1024, as amended by SI 1979/1013, SI 1988/815, SI 1992/3304, SI 1994/3249, SI 1995/11, SI 1997/1480.

Importation of Animals Order 1977, SI 19777/944, as amended by SI 1990/2371, SI 1992/1361, SI 1992/3159, SI 1995/2922, SI 1996/1760.

Diseases of Animals (Approved Disinfectants) Order 1978, SI 1978/32, as amended by SI 1992/238, SI 1992/2290, SI 1993/1194, SI 1993/3086, SI 1994/2965, SI 1994/3141, SI 1996/697, SI 1997/2347.

Importation of Birds, Poultry and Hatching Eggs Order 1979, SI 1979/1702, as amended by SI 1990/2371.

Export of Animals (protection) Order 1981, SI 1981/1051, as amended by SI 1994/3249, SI 1997/1480.

Aujeszky's Disease Order 1983, SI 1983/344, as amended by SI 1994/3141, SI 1995/11, SI 1995/2922.

Foot-and-Mouth Disease Order 1983, SI 1983/1950, as amended by SI 1993/3119, SI 1995/2922.

Tuberculosis (England and Wales) Order 1984, SI 1984/1943, as amended by SI 1990/1869, SI 1995/2922.

Infectious Diseases of Horses Order 1987, SI 1987/790, as amended by SI 1992/3159, SI 1995/2922.

Zoonoses Order 1988, SI 1988/2264, as amended by SI 1988/2299 (revoked), SI 1997/1480.

Zoonoses Order 1989, SI 1989/285.

Tuberculosis (Deer) Order 1989, SI 1989/878, as amended by SI 1993/2010, SI 1995/2922.

Anthrax Order 1991, SI 1991/2814, as amended by SI 1995/2922, SI 1996/1855.

Specified Animal Pathogens Order 1993, SI 1993/3250, as amended by SI 1994/3142, SI 1994/3144.

Diseases of Poultry Order 1994, SI 1994/3141, as amended by SI 1995/2922, SI 1997/150.

Pigs (Records, Identification and Movement) Order 1995, SI 1995/11, as amended by SI 1995/2922.

Bovine Animals (Records, Identification and Movement) Order 1995, SI 1995/12, as amended by SI 1995/2922, SI 1996/1686, SI 1997/1901.

Animals (Post-Import Control) Order 1995, SI 1995/2439.
Bovine Spongiform Encephalopathy (No 2) Order 1996, SI 1996/3183, as amended by SI 1997/2387.
Enzootic Bovine Leukosis Order 1997, SI 1997/757.
Brucellosis Order 1997, SI 1997/758.
Sheep Scab Order 1997, SI 1997/968.
Welfare of Animals (Transport) Order 1997, SI 1997/1480.

Section 8: Movement generally

Markets, Sales and Lairs Order of 1925, SR & O 1925/1349, as amended by SR & O 1926/546, SR & O 1927/982, SI 1995/11, SI 1996/3265.
Pleuro-Pneumonia Order of 1928, SR & O 1928/205, as amended by SR & O 1938/195, SI 1972/971, SI 1977/944.
Cattle Plague Order of 1928, SR & O 1928/206, as amended by SR & O 1938/194, SI 1972/971, SI 1977/944.
Horses (Sea Transport) Order 1952, SI 1952/1291, as amended by SI 1958/1272, SI 1972/971, SI 1992/3304, SI 1997/1480.
Swine Fever (Infected Areas Restrictions) Order 1956, SI 1956/1750, as amended by SI 1958/1284, SI 1972/971, SI 1977/944.
Swine Fever Order 1963, SI 1963/286, as amended by SI 1972/971, SI 1976/919, SI 1990/2487, SI 1991/1030, SI 1995/11, SI 1995/2922.
Diseases of Animals (Waste Food) Order 1973, SI 1973/1936, as amended by SI 1987/232, SI 1992/453, SI 1996/826.
Movement and Sale of Pigs Order 1975, SI 1975/203, as amended by SI 1975/346, SI 1977/944, SI 1987/233, SI 1995/11.
Transit of Animals (Road and Rail) Order 1975, SI 1975/1024, as amended by SI 1979/1013, SI 1988/815, SI 1992/3304, SI 1994/3249, SI 1995/11, SI 1997/1480.
Export of Animals (Protection) Order 1981, SI 1981/1051, as modified by SI 1994/3249, SI 1997/1480.
Warble Fly (England and Wales) Order 1982, SI 1982/234, as amended by SI 1985/328, SI 1987/1601, SI 1989/244, SI 1994/3142.
Aujeszky's Disease Order 1983, SI 1983/344, as amended by SI 1994/3141, SI 1995/11, SI 1995/2922.
Foot-and-Mouth Disease Order 1983, SI 1983/1950, as amended by SI 1993/3119, SI 1995/2922.
Tuberculosis (England and Wales) Order 1984, SI 1984/1943, as amended by SI 1990/1869, SI 1995/2922.
Warble Fly (England and Wales) (Infected Areas) Order 1985, SI 1985/1542, as amended by SI 1994/3142.
Diseases of Animals (Ascertainment of Disease) Order 1985, SI 1985/1765, as amended by SI 1992/3159, SI 1994/2627.
Warble Fly (Ascertainment of Infestation) (England and Wales) Order 1985, SI 1985/1766.
Infectious Diseases of Horses Order 1987, SI 1987/790, as amended by SI 1992/3159, SI 1995/2922.
Zoonoses Order 1988, SI 1988/2264, as amended by SI 1988/2299, SI 1997/2964.
Zoonoses Order 1989, SI 1989/285.
Tuberculosis (Deer) Order 1989, SI 1989/878, as amended by SI 1993/2010, SI 1995/2922.

Tuberculosis (Deer) Notice of Intended Slaughter and Compensation Order 1989, SI 1989/1316.
Movement of Animals (Restriction) Order 1990, SI 1990/760, as amended by SI 1991/1155, SI 1991/1251.
Welfare of Horses at Markets (and Other Places of Sale) Order 1990, SI 1990/2627.
Welfare of Animals at Market Order 1990, SI 1990/2628, as amended by SI 1993/3085, SI 1995/12.
Anthrax Order 1991, SI 1991/2814, as amended by SI 1995/2922, SI 1996/1855.
Animal By-Products Order 1992, SI 1992/3303, as amended by SI 1996/827, SI 1997/2894.
Specified Animal Pathogens Order 1993, SI 1993/3250, as amended by SI 1994/3142, SI 1994/3144.
Diseases of Poultry Order 1994, SI 1994/3141, as amended by SI 1995/2922, SI 1997/150.
Pigs (Records, Identification and Movement) Order 1995, SI 1995/11, as amended by SI 1995/2922.
Bovine Animals (Records, Identification and Movement) Order 1995, SI 1995/12, as amended by SI 1995/2922, SI 1996/1686, SI 1997/1901.
Equine Viral Arteritis Order 1995, SI 1995/1755, as amended by SI 1995/2922.
Sheep and Goats (Records, Identification and Movement) Order 1996, SI 1996/28.
Cattle Passports Order 1996, SI 1996/1686.
Specified Diseases (Notification) Order 1996, SI 1996/2628.
Bovine Spongiform Encephalopathy (No 2) Order 1996. SI 1996/3183, as amended by SI 1997/2387.
Sheep Scab Order 1997, SI 1997/968.
Welfare of Animals (Transport) Order 1997, SI 1997/1480.
Horse Passports Order 1997, SI 1997/2789.

Section 25: Movement of diseased or suspected animals
Pleuro-Pneumonia Order of 1928, SR & O 1928/205, as amended by SR & O 1938/195, SI 1972/971, SI 1977/944.
Cattle Plague Order of 1928, SR & O 1928/206, as amended by SR & O 1938/194, SI 1972/971, SI 1977/94.
Swine Fever Order 1963, SI 1963/286, as amended by SI 1972/971, SI 1976/919, SI 1990/2487, SI 1991/1030, SI 1995/11, SI 1995/2922.
Transit of Animals (Road and Rail) Order 1975, SI 1975/1024, as amended by SI 1979/1013, SI 1988/815, SI 1992/3304, SI 1994/3249, SI 1995/11, SI 1997/1480.
Warble Fly (England and Wales) Order 1982, SI 1982/234, as amended by SI 1985/328, SI 1987/1601, SI 1989/244, SI 1994/3142.
Aujeszky's Disease Order 1983, SI 1983/344, as amended by SI 1994/3141, SI 1995/11, SI 1995/2922, SI 1997/150.
Foot-and-Mouth Disease Order 1983, SI 1983/1950, as amended by SI 1993/3119, SI 1995/2922.
Tuberculosis (England and Wales Order 1984, SI 1984/1943, as amended by SI 1990/1869, SI 1995/2922.
Warble Fly (England and Wales) (Infected Areas) Order 1985, SI 1985/1542, as amended by SI 1994/3142.
Tuberculosis (Deer) Order 1989, SI 1989/878, as amended by SI 1993/2010, SI 1995/2922.

Anthrax Order 1991, SI 1991/2814, as amended by SI 1995/2922, SI 1996/1855.

Diseases of Poultry Order 1994, SI 1994/3141, as amended by SI 1995/2922.

Pigs (Records, Identification and Movement) Order 1995, SI 1995/11, as amended by SI 1995/2922.

Bovine Animals (Records, Identification and Movement) Order 1995, SI 1995/12, as amended by SI 1995/2922, SI 1996/1686, SI 1997/1901.

Sheep Scab Order 1997, SI 1997/968.

Section 26: Pleuro-pneumonia or foot-and-mouth disease found in transit

Pleuro-Pneumonia Order of 1928, SR & O 1928/205, as amended by SR & O 1938/195, SI 1972/971, SI 1977/944.

Foot-and-Mouth Disease Order 1983, SI 1983/1950, as amended by SI 1993/3119, SI 1995/2922.

Section 37: Prevention of suffering

Transit of Animals Order of 1927, SR & O 1927/289, as amended by SR & O 1927/399, SR & O 1939/501, SI 1972/971, SI 1975/1024, SI 1977/944, SI 1992/1361, SI 1992/3304, SI 1997/1480.

Horses (Sea Transport) Order 1952, SI 1952/1291, as amended by SI 1958/1272, SI 1972/971, SI 1992/3304, SI 1997/1480.

Export of Horses (Protection) Order 1969, SI 1969/1784, as amended by SI 1972/971.

Transit of Animals (Road and Rail) Order 1975, SI 1975/1024, as amended by SI 1979/1013, SI 1988/815, SI 1992/3304, SI 1994/3249, SI 1995/11, SI 1997/1480.

Importation of Animals Order 1977, SI 1977/944, as amended by SI 1990/2371, SI 1992/1361, SI 1992/3159, SI 1995/2922, SI 1996/1760.

Export of Animals (Protection) Order 1981, SI 1981/1051, as amended by SI 1994/3249, SI 1997/1480.

Homes (Landing from Northern Ireland and Republic of Ireland) (Revocation) Order 1989, SI 1989/23.

Welfare of Horses at Markets (and Other Places of Sale) Order 1990, SI 1990/2627.

Welfare of Animals at Markets Order 1990, SI 1990/2628, as amended by SI 1993/3085, SI 1995/12.

Welfare of Animals (Transport) Order 1997, SI 1997/1480.

LOCAL GOVERNMENT (MISCELLANEOUS PROVISIONS) ACT 1982

(1882, c 30)

An Act to make amendments for England and Wales of provisions of that part of the law relating to local authorities or highways which is commonly amended by local Acts, . . .

[13th July 1982]

Part III

Street trading

Power of district council to adopt Schedule 4

3. A district council may resolve that Schedule 4 to this Act shall apply to their district and, if a council so resolve, that Schedule shall come into force in their district on such day as may be specified in the resolution.

* * * * * *

Part XII

Miscellaneous

Temporary markets

37.—(1) The council of a district or a London borough may resolve that the following provisions of this section shall apply to their district or borough; and if a council so resolve and within 14 days of the passing of the resolution give notice of the resolution by advertising in a local newspaper circulating in their area, those provisions shall come into force in their district or borough on the day specified in the resolution.

(2) Subject to subsection (3) below, any person intending to hold a temporary market in a district or London borough, where the provisions of this section have come into force, and any occupier of land in such a district or borough who intends to permit the land to be used as the site of a temporary market or for purposes of that market, shall give the council of the district or the borough not less than one month before the date on which it is proposed to hold the market notice of his intention to hold it or to permit the land to be so used, as the case may be.

(3) No notice is required under subsection (2) above if the proceeds of the temporary market are to be applied solely or principally for charitable, social, sporting or political purposes.

(4) Any notice given under subsection (2) above shall state—

(a) the full name and address of the person intending to hold the market;

(b) the day or days on which it is proposed that the market shall be held and its proposed opening and closing times;

(c) the site on which it is proposed that it shall be held;

(d) the full name and address of the occupier of that site, if he is not the person intending to hold the market.

(5) A person who without giving the notice required by subsection (2) above holds a temporary market or permits land occupied by him to be used as the site of a temporary market shall be guilty of an offence and liable on summary conviction to a fine not exceeding [level 4 on the standard scale]([1]).

(6) In this section 'temporary market' means a concourse of buyers and sellers of articles held otherwise than in a building or on a highway, and comprising not less than

five stalls, stands, vehicles (whether movable or not) or pitches from which articles are sold, but does not include—

(a) a market or fair the right to hold which was acquired by virtue of a grant (including a presumed grant) or acquired or established by virtue of an enactment or order; or

(b) a sale by auction of farm livestock or deadstock.

(7) A person holds a temporary market for the purposes of this section if—

(a) he is entitled to payment for any space or pitch hired or let on the site of the market to persons wishing to trade in the market; or

(b) he is entitled, as a person promoting the market, or as the agent, licensee or assignee of a person promoting the market, to payment for goods sold or services rendered to persons attending the market.

(8) This section does not apply to a market held on any land in accordance with planning permission granted on an application made under [Part III of the Town and Country Planning Act 1990](2).

(1) By virtue of the Criminal Justice Act 1982, s 46 a reference to the level on the standard scale is substituted for the amount of the fine.

(2) Substituted by the Planning (Consequential Provisions) Act 1990, s 4, Sch 2, para 56(2).

* * * * * *

Section 3

SCHEDULE 4

STREET TRADING

Interpretation

1.—(1) In this Schedule—

'consent street' means a street in which street trading is prohibited without the consent of the district council;

'licence street' means a street in which street trading is prohibited without a licence granted by the district council;

'principal terms', in relation to a street trading licence, has the meaning assigned to it by paragraph 4(3) below;

'prohibited street' means a street in which street trading is prohibited;

'street' includes—

(a) any road, footway, beach or other area to which the public have access without payment; and

(b) a service area as defined in section 329 of the Highways Act 1980,

and also includes any part of a street;

'street trading' means, subject to sub-paragraph (2) below, the selling or exposing or offering for sale of any article (including a living thing) in a street; and

'subsidiary terms', in relation to a street trading licence, has the meaning assigned to it by paragraph 4(4) below.

(2) The following are not street trading for the purposes of this Schedule—

(a) trading by a person acting as a pedlar under the authority of a pedlar's certificate granted under the Pedlars Act 1871;

(b) anything done in a market or fair the right to hold which was acquired by virtue of a grant (including a presumed grant) or acquired or established by virtue of an enactment or order;

(c) trading in a trunk road picnic area provided by the Secretary of State under section 112 of the Highways Act 1980;
(d) trading as a news vendor;
(e) trading which—
(i) is carried on at premises used as a petrol filling station; or
(ii) is carried on at premises used as a shop or in a street adjoining premises so used and as part of the business of the shop;
(f) selling things, or offering or exposing them for sale, as a roundsman;
(g) the use for trading under Part VIIA of the Highways Act 1980 of an object or structure placed on, in or over a highway;
(h) the operation of facilities for recreation or refreshment under Part VIIA of the Highways Act 1980;
(i) the doing of anything authorised by regulations made under section 5 of the Police, Factories, etc (Miscellaneous Provisions) Act 1916.
[(j) the doing of anything authorised by any permit or order under Part III of the Charities Act 1992]([1]).

(3) The reference to trading as a news vendor in sub-paragraph (2)(d) above is a reference to trading where—
(a) the only articles sold or exposed or offered for sale are newspapers or periodicals; and
(b) they are sold or exposed or offered for sale without a stall or receptacle for them or with a stall or receptacle for them which does not—
(i) exceed one metre in length or width or two metres in height;
(ii) occupy a ground area exceeding 0.25 square metres; or
(iii) stand on the carriageway of a street.

([1]) Prospectively substituted by the Charities Act 1992, s 78(1), Sch 6 para 9, as from a day to be appointed.

Designation of streets

2.—(1) A district council may by resolution designate any street in their district as—
(a) a prohibited street;
(b) a licence street; or
(c) a consent street.

(2) If a district council pass such a resolution as is mentioned in sub-paragraph (1) above, the designation of the street shall take effect on the day specified in that behalf in the resolution (which must not be before the expiration of the period of one month beginning with the day on which the resolution is passed).

(3) A council shall not pass such a resolution unless—
(a) they have published notice of their intention to pass such a resolution in a local newspaper circulating in their area;
(b) they have served a copy of the notice—
(i) on the chief officer of police for the area in which the street to be designated by the resolution is situated; and
(ii) on any highway authority responsible for that street; and
(c) where sub-paragraph (4) below applies, they have obtained the necessary consent.

(4) This sub-paragraph applies—

(a) where the resolution relates to a street which is owned or maintainable by a relevant corporation; and

(b) where the resolution designated as a licence street any street maintainable by a highway authority;

and in sub-paragraph (3) above 'necessary consent' means—

(i) in the case mentioned in paragraph (a) above, the consent of the relevant corporation; and

(ii) in the case mentioned in paragraph (b) above, the consent of the highway authority.

(5) The following are relevant corporations for the purposes of this paragraph—

(a) the British Railways Board;

(b) the Commission for the New Towns;

(c) a development corporation for a new town;

(d) an urban development corporation established under the Local Government, Planning and Land Act 1980; and

(e) the Development Board for Rural Wales.

(6) The notice referred to in sub-paragraph (3) above—

(a) shall contain a draft of the resolution; and

(b) shall state that representations relating to it may be made in writing to the council within such period, not less than 28 days after publication of the notice, as may be specified in the notice.

(7) As soon as practicable after the expiry of the period specified under sub-paragraph (6) above, the council shall consider any representations relating to the proposed resolution which they have received before the expiry of that period.

(8) After the council have considered those representations, they may, if they think fit, pass such a resolution relating to the street as is mentioned in sub-paragraph (1) above.

(9) The council shall publish notice that they have passed such a resolution in two consecutive weeks in a local newspaper circulating in their area.

(10) The first publication shall not be later than 28 days before the day specified in the resolution for the coming into force of the designation.

(11) Where a street is designated as a licence street, the council may resolve—

(a) in the resolution which so designates the street; or

(b) subject to sub-paragraph (12) below, by a separate resolution at any time,

that a street trading licence is not to be granted to any person who proposes to trade in the street for a number of days in every week less than a number specified in the resolution.

(12) Sub-paragraphs (3)(a) and (6) to (10) above shall apply in relation to a resolution under sub-paragraph (1)(b) above as they apply in relation to a resolution under sub-paragraph (1) above).

(13) Any resolution passed under this paragraph may be varied or rescinded by a subsequent resolution so passed.

Street trading licences

3.—(1) An application for a street trading licence or the renewal of such a licence shall be made in writing to the district council.

(2) The applicant shall state—

(a) his full name and address;

(b) the street in which, days on which and times between which he desires to trade;
(c) the description of articles in which he desires to trade and the description of any stall or container which he desires to use in connection with his trade in those articles; and
(d) such other particulars as the council may reasonably require.

(3) If the council so require, the applicant shall submit two photographs of himself with his application.

(4) A street trading licence shall not be granted—
(a) to a person under the age of 17 years; or
(b) for any trading in a highway in relation to which a control order under section 7 of the Local Government (Miscellaneous Provisions) Act 1976 (road-side sales) is in force, other than trading to which the control order does not apply.

(5) Subject to sub-paragraph (4) above, it shall be the duty of the council to grant an application for a street trading licence or the renewal of such a licence unless they consider that the application ought to be refused on one or more of the grounds specified in sub-paragraph (6) below.

(6) Subject to sub-paragraph (8) below, the council may refuse an application on any of the following grounds—
(a) that there is not enough space in the street for the applicant to engage in the trading in which he desires to engage without causing undue interference or inconvenience to persons using the street;
(b) that there are already enough traders trading in the street from shops or otherwise in the goods in which the applicant desires to trade;
(c) that the applicant desires to trade on fewer days than the minimum number specified in the resolution under paragraph 2(11) above;
(d) that the applicant is unsuitable to hold the licence by reason of having been convicted of an offence or for any other reason;
(e) that the applicant has at any time been granted a street trading licence by the council and has persistently refused or neglected to pay fees due to them for it or charges due to them under paragraph 9(6) below for services rendered by them to him in his capacity as licence-holder;
(f) that the applicant has at any time been granted a street trading consent by the council and has persistently refused or neglected to pay fees due to them for it;
(g) that the applicant has without reasonable excuse failed to avail himself to a reasonable extent of a previous street trading licence.

(7) If the council consider that grounds for refusal exist under sub-paragraph (6)(a), (b) or (g) above, they may grant the applicant a licence which permits him—
(a) to trade on fewer days or during a shorter period in each day than specified in the application; or
(b) to trade only in one or more of the descriptions of goods specified in the application.

(8) If—
(a) a person is licensed or otherwise authorised to trade in a street under the provisions of any local Act; and
(b) the street becomes a licence street; and
(c) he was trading from a fixed position in the street immediately before it became a licence street; and
(d) he applied for a street trading licence to trade in the street, his application shall

not be refused on any of the grounds mentioned in sub-paragraph (6)(a) to (c) above.

4.—(1) A street trading licence shall specify—

(a) the street in which, days on which and times between which the licence-holder is permitted to trade; and

(b) the description of articles in which he is permitted to trade.

(2) If the district council determine that a licence-holder is to confine his trading to a particular place in the street, his street trading licence shall specify that place.

(3) Matters that fall to be specified in a street trading licence by virtue of sub-paragraph (1) or (2) above are referred to in this Schedule as the 'principal terms' of the licence.

(4) When granting or renewing a street trading licence, the council may attach such further conditions (in this Schedule referred to as the 'subsidiary terms' of the licence) as appear to them to be reasonable.

(5) Without prejudice to the generality of sub-paragraph (4) above, the subsidiary terms of a licence may include conditions—

(a) specifying the size and type of any stall or container which the licence-holder may use for trading,

(b) requiring that any stall or container so used shall carry the name of the licence-holder or the number of his licence or both; and

(c) prohibiting the leaving of any refuse by the licence-holder or restricting the amount of refuse which he may leave or the place in which he may leave it.

(6) A street trading licence shall, unless previously revoked or surrendered, remain valid for a period of 12 months from the date on which it is granted or, if a shorter period is specified in the licence, for that period.

(7) If a district council resolve that the whole or part of a licence street shall be designated a prohibited street, then, on the designation taking effect, any street trading licence issued for trading in that street shall cease to be valid so far as it relates to the prohibited street.

5.—(1) A district council may at any time revoke a street trading licence if they consider—

(a) that, owing to circumstances which have arisen since the grant or renewal of the licence, there is not enough space in the street for the licence-holder to engage in the trading permitted by the licence without causing undue interference or inconvenience to persons using the street;

(b) that the licence holder is unsuitable to hold the licence by reason of having been convicted of an offence or for any other reason;

(c) that, since the grant or renewal of the licence, the licence-holder has persistently refused or neglected to pay fees due to the council for it or charges due to them under paragraph 9(6) below for services rendered by them to him in his capacity as licence-holder; or

(d) that, since the grant or renewal of the licence, the licence-holder has without reasonable excuse failed to avail himself of the licence to a reasonable extent.

(2) If the council consider that they have ground for revoking a licence by virtue of sub-paragraph (1)(a) to (d) above, they may, instead of revoking it, vary its principal terms—

(a) by reducing the number of days or the period in any one day during which the licence-holder is permitted to trade; or

(b) by restricting the descriptions of goods in which he is permitted to trade.

(3) A licence-holder may at any time surrender his licence to the council and it shall then cease to be valid.

6.—(1) When a district council receive an application for the grant or renewal of a street trading licence, they shall within a reasonable time—

(a) grant a licence in the terms applied for; or

(b) serve notice on the applicant under sub-paragraph (2) below.

(2) If the council propose—

(a) to refuse an application for the grant or renewal of a licence; or

(b) to grant a licence on principal terms different from those specified in the application; or

(c) to grant a licence confining the applicant's trading to a particular place in a street; or

(d) to vary the principal terms of a licence; or

(e) to revoke a licence;

they shall first serve a notice on the applicant or, as the case may be, the licence-holder—

(i) specifying the ground or grounds on which their decision would be based; and

(ii) stating that within 7 days of receiving the notice he may in writing require them to give him an opportunity to make representations to them concerning it.

(3) Where a notice has been served under sub-paragraph (2) above, the council shall not determine the matter until either—

(a) the person on whom it was served has made representations to them concerning their decision; or

(b) the period during which he could have required them to give him an opportunity to make representations has elapsed without his requiring them to give him such an opportunity; or

(c) the conditions specified in sub-paragraph (4) below are satisfied.

(4) The conditions mentioned in sub-paragraph (3)(c) above are—

(a) that the person on whom the notice under sub-paragraph (2) above was served has required the council to give him an opportunity to make representations to them concerning it, as provided by sub-paragraph (2)(ii) above;

(b) that the council have allowed him a reasonable period for making his representations; and

(c) that he has failed to make them within that period.

(5) A person aggrieved—

(a) by the refusal of a council to grant or renew a licence, where—

(i) they specified in their notice under subparagraph (2) above one of the grounds mentioned in paragraph 3(6)(d) to (g) above as the only ground on which their decision would be based; or

(ii) they specified more than one ground in that notice but all the specified grounds were grounds mentioned in those paragraphs; or

(b) by a decision of a council to grant him a licence with principal terms different from those of a licence which he previously held, where they specified in their notice under sub-paragraph (2) above the ground mentioned in paragraph

3(6)(g) above as they only ground on which their decision would be based; or

(c) by a decision of a council—

(i) to vary the principal terms of a licence; or

(ii) to revoke a licence,

in a case where they specified in their notice under sub-paragraph (2) above one of the grounds mentioned in paragraph 5(1)(b) to (d) above as the only ground on which their decision would be based or they specified more than one ground in that notice but all the specified grounds were grounds mentioned in these paragraphs,

may, at any time before the expiration of the period of 21 days beginning with the date union which he is notified of the refusal or decision, appeal to the magistrates' court acting for the petty sessions area in which the street is situated.

(6) An appeal against the decisions of a magistrates' court under this paragraph may be brought to the Crown Court.

(7) On an appeal to the magistrates' court or the Crown Court under this paragraph the court may make such order as it thinks fit.

(8) Subject to sub-paragraphs (9) to (11) below, it shall be the duty of the council to give effect to an order of the magistrates' court or the Crown Court.

(9) The council need not give effect to the order of the magistrates' court until the time for bringing an appeal under sub-paragraph (6) above has expired and, if such an appeal is duly brought, until the determination or abandonment of the appeal.

(10) If a licence-holder applies for renewal of his licence before the date of its expiry, it shall remain valid—

(a) until the grant by the council of a new licence with the same principal terms; or

(b) if—

(i) the council refuse renewal of the licence or decide to grant a licence with principal terms different from those of the existing licence, and

(ii) he has a right of appeal under this paragraph, until the time for bringing an appeal has expired or, where an appeal is duly brought, until the determination or abandonment of the appeal; or

(c) if he has no right of appeal under this paragraph, until the council either grant him a new licence with principal terms different from those of the existing licence or notify him of their decision to refuse his application.

(11) Where—

(a) a council decide—

(i) to vary the principal terms of a licence; or

(ii) to revoke a licence; and

(b) a right of appeal is available to the licence-holder under this paragraph, the variation or revocation shall not take effect until the time for bringing an appeal has expired or, where an appeal is duly brought, until the determination or abandonment of the appeal.

Street trading consents

7.—(1) An application for a street trading consent or the renewal of such a consent shall be made in writing to the district council.

(2) Subject to sub-paragraph (3) below, the council may grant a consent if they think fit.

(3) A street trading consent shall not be granted—

(a) to a person under the age of 17 years; or
(b) for any trading in a highway to which a control order under section 7 of the Local Government (Miscellaneous Provisions) Act 1976 is in force, other than trading to which the control order does not apply.

(4) When granting or renewing a street trading consent the council may attach such conditions to it as they consider reasonably necessary.

(5) Without prejudice to the generality of sub-paragraph (4) above, the conditions that may be attached to a street trading consent by virtue of that sub-paragraph include conditions to prevent—
(a) obstruction of the street or danger to persons using it; or
(b) nuisance or annoyance (whether to persons using the street or otherwise).

(6) The council may at any time vary the condition of a street trading consent.

(7) Subject to sub-paragraph (8) below, the holder of a street trading consent shall not trade in a consent street from a van or other vehicle or from a stall, barrow or cart.

(8) The council may include in a street consent permission for its holder to trade in a consent street—
(a) from a stationary van, cart, barrow or other vehicle; or
(b) from a portable stall.

(9) If they include such a permission, they must make the consent subject to conditions—
(a) as to where the holder of the street trading consent may trade by virtue of the permission; and
(b) as to the time between which or periods for which he may so trade.

(10) A street trading consent may be granted for any period not exceeding 12 months but may be revoked at any time.

(11) The holder of a street trading consent may at any time surrender his consent to the council and it shall then cease to be valid.

General

8. The holder of a street trading licence or a street trading consent may employ any other person to assist in his trading without a further licence or consent being required.

9.—(1) A district council may charge such fees as they consider reasonable for the grant or renewal of a street trading licence or a street trading consent.

(2) A council may determine different fees for different types of licence or consent and, in particular, but without prejudice to the generality of this sub-paragraph, may determine fees differing according—
(a) to the duration of the licence or consent;
(b) to the street in which it authorises trading; and
(c) to the descriptions of articles in which the holder is authorised to trade.

(3) A council may require that applications for the grant or renewal of licences or consents shall be accompanied by so much of the fee as the council may require, by way of a deposit to be repaid by the council to the applicant if the application is refused.

(4) A council may determine that fees may be paid by instalments.

(5) Where a consent is surrendered or revoked, the council shall remit or refund, as they consider appropriate, the whole or a part of any fee paid for the grant or renewal of the consent.

(6) A council may recover from a licence-holder such reasonable charges as they may determine for the collection of refuse, the cleansing of streets and other services rendered by them to him in his capacity as licence-holder.

(7) Where a licence—

(a) is surrendered or revoked; or

(b) ceases to be valid by virtue of paragraph 4(7) above,

the council may remit or refund, as they consider appropriate, the whole or a part—

(i) of any fee paid for the grant or renewal of the licence; or

(ii) of any charges recoverable under sub-paragraph (6) above.

(8) The council may determine—

(a) that charges under sub-paragraph (6) above shall be included in a fee payable under sub-paragraph (1) above; or

(b) that they shall be separately recoverable.

(9) Before determining charges to be made under sub-paragraph (6) above or varying the amount of such charges the council—

(a) shall give notice of the proposed charges to licence-holders; and

(b) shall publish notice of the proposed charges in a local newspaper circulating in the area.

(10) A notice under sub-paragraph (9) above shall specify a reasonable period within which representations concerning the proposed charges may be made to the council.

(11) It shall be the duty of a council to consider any such representations which are made to them within the period specified in the notice.

Offences

10.—(1) A person who—

(a) engages in street trading in a prohibited street; or

(b) engages in street trading in a licence street or a consent street without being authorised to do so under this Schedule; or

(c) contravenes any of the principal terms of a street trading licence; or

(d) being authorised by a street trading consent to trade in a consent street, trades in that street—

(i) from a stationary van, cart, barrow or other vehicle; or

(ii) from a portable stall,

without first having been granted permission to do so under paragraph 7(8) above; or

(e) contravenes a condition imposed under paragraph 7(9) above, shall be guilty of an offence.

(2) It shall be a defence for a person charged with an offence under sub-paragraph (1) above to prove that he took all reasonable precautions and exercised all due diligence to avoid commission of the offence.

(3) Any person who, in connection with an application for a street trading licence or for a street trading consent, makes a false statement which he knows to be false in any material respect, or which he does not believe to be true, shall be guilty of an offence.

(4) A person guilty of an offence under this paragraph shall be liable on summary conviction to a fine not exceeding [level 3 on the standard scale](1).

(1) Substituted by the Criminal Justice Act 1982, s 46.

Savings

11. Nothing in this Schedule shall affect—

(a) section 13 of the Markets and Fairs Clauses Act 1847 (prohibition of sales elsewhere than in market or in shops etc) as applied by any other Act;

(b) section [56 of the Food Act 1984](1) (prohibition of certain sales during market hours).

(1) Substituted by the Food Act 1984, s 134, Sch 10, para 34.

FOOD ACT 1984

(Eliz II, 1984, c 30)

An Act to consolidate the provisions of the Food and Drugs Acts 1955 to 1982, the Sugar Act 1956, the Food and Drugs (Milk) Act 1970, section 7(3) and (4) of the European Communities Act 1972, section 198 of the Local Government Act 1972 and Part IX of the Local Government (Miscellaneous Provisions) Act 1982, and connected provisions.

[26th June 1984]

* * * * * *

MARKETS
PART III

50. Establishment or acquisition

(1) [A local authority](1) may(2)—

(a) establish a market(3) within [their area](1);

(b) acquire by agreement (but not otherwise), either by purchase or on lease, the whole or any part of an existing market undertaking(4) within [their area](1), and any rights enjoyed by any person(5) within [their area](1) in respect of a market and of tolls,

and, in either case, may provide(6)—

(i) a market place(7) with convenient approaches to it;

(ii) a market house and other buildings convenient for the holding of a market.

(2) A market shall not be established in pursuance of this section so as to interfere with any rights, powers or privileges(8) enjoyed(9) within [the authority's area](1) in respect of a market by any person, without that person's consent.

(3) [For the purposes of subsection (2), a local authority shall not be regarded as enjoying any rights, powers or privileges within another local authority's area by reason only of the fact that they maintain within their own area a market which has been established under paragraph (a) of subsection (1) or under the corresponding provision of any earlier enactment](10).

Sub-s (1) replaces in substantially the same terms s 49(1) of the Food and Drugs Act 1955, as partly repealed by the Local Government Act 1972, s 199(3); sub-ss (2) and (3) replace in substantially the same terms the repealed s 49(3) of the 1955 Act

(1) Words in brackets substituted by the Food Safety Act 1990, s 52, Sch 2, para 2.

(2) A local authority has no power to covenant or agree that it will not exercise the powers, or any of the powers, entrusted to it by this section, and such a covenant or agreement would be void: *Spurling v Bantoft* [1891] 2 QB 384, and cf *Ayr Harbour Trustees v Oswald* (1883) 8 App Cas 623.

(3) The powers conferred by this section are in terms limited to 'markets', and no power is conferred on a local authority by this section to establish or acquire a 'fair'. As to what constitutes a 'fair' see Introduction pp 1, 2, *above*; as to rights in relation to 'fairs', see the Markets and Fairs Clauses Act 1847, *above*, the Fairs Act 1871, *above* and the Fairs Act 1873, *above*. A market may not be established without the consent of persons with existing market rights in the district: see sub-s (2), *above*, and it may be possible to purchase those rights under sub-s (1)(b), *above*. The market will be a statutory market but it will have, it seems, all the incidents of a franchise market except insofar as they are expressly or impliedly taken away by this or any other Act: see p 21, *above*, and see note (4), *below*, note (3) to s 51, *below*, and note (1) to s 53, *below*.

(4) An existing market undertaking may be either a franchise market or a statutory market: see pp 13 *et seq*, *above*. It should be remembered that the market franchise is separate and distinct

from the franchise to levy tolls: see pp 51, 52, 55, 98, 99, *above*. The power to acquire is by agreement and not otherwise and the power to purchase land compulsorily given by s 110 does not extend the power: see *below*. Where a local authority acquires a franchise market and exercises only the powers under the franchise, the market will remain a franchise market. Where, however, it wishes to go beyond those powers, eg by altering the market days or by increasing the tolls, it may do so but in that event the franchise rights would to that extent become merged in the statutory rights, and the market will become a statutory market and will continue to enjoy the other common law or franchise rights only so far as they are not expressly or impliedly taken away by this Act or by any other Act: see *Ellis v Bridgnorth Corpn* (1861) 4 LT 112; *Manchester Corpn v Lyons* (1882) 22 Ch D 287: *Birmingham Corpn v Foster* (1894) 70 LT 371; *New Windsor Corpn v Taylor* [1899] AC 41; *Stevens v Chown* [1901] 1 Ch 894; *Leicester Corpn v Maby* (1972) 70 LGR 209; *Leicester City Council v Oxford and Bristol Stores Ltd* (21 December 1978, unreported); *Halton Borough Council v Cawley* [1985] 1 WLR 15; *Manchester City Council v Walsh* (1986) 84 LGR 1. See also pp 21, 90, 91, *above*.

Where also a local authority acquires an existing statutory market, it seems that it may continue to conduct the market under the statutes establishing it. If, however, it wishes to go beyond the powers under those statutes and exercise rights under this Act, then the powers under those statutes so far as they are inconsistent with this Act will cease, and so also any common law rights hitherto subject to those statutes will become subject also to this Act. As to how far common law rights apply to a statutory market, see pp 21, 90 and 91, *above* and note ([8]), *below*.

Where a market site is taken on lease by a local authority, the establishment of a market will not affect the freehold reversion: see *R v Basildon District Council, ex p Brown* (1981) 79 LGR 655 at 666–667 per Templeman LJ.

The exercise of the byelaw making powers conferred by s 60, *below* on local authorities who maintain franchise or statutory markets would not have the effect of converting the franchise market into a statutory market, or adversely affect an existing statutory market. See also notes to ss 51, 53, *below*.

As to the power of the owner to sell, see s 51, *below*.

([5]) 'Person' includes a body corporate: Interpretation Act 1978, s 5.

([6]) As to the power to acquire land compulsorily for a market place, etc, see s 110, *below*.

([7]) The local authority is not restricted to the provision of only one market place: *Richards v Scarborough Public Market Co* (1853) 23 LJ Ch 110. Where a market place is not confined by the charter governing the market to a particular site (ie is not 'limited by metes and bounds') the owner of the franchise may hold the market anywhere within the district to which the franchise relates, and may remove the site from time to time: see pp 33 *et seq*, *above*. The owner is however under an obligation to provide adequate accommodation for all persons wishing to buy and sell in the market, and if he does not do so he cannot complain if sales are held outside the market-place: see pp 31 and 85, *above*. In the case of a market established under sub-s (1)(a), *above*, there is, it appears, no restriction to a particular site, but the above consequences of failure to supply sufficient accommodation would seem to apply: see pp 21, 90, 91, *above*.

([8]) That is, a right, power or privilege acquired adversely to the general public and peculiar to the individual: *Fearon v Mitchell* (1872) LR 7 QB 690; *Woolwich Corpn v Gibson* (1905) 69 JP 361; and in the nature of a franchise: *Spurling v Bantoft* [1891] 2 QB 384, but not excluding rights, etc, under a wholly statutory market, it seems, except so far as excepted by sub-s (3), *above*. See also *Delyn Borough Council v Solitaire (Liverpool) Ltd* (1995) 93 LGR 614, and p 129, *above*.

([9]) With regard to the word 'enjoyed', it is not clear whether rights, powers and privileges in respect of the market can be said to be enjoyed, as that word is here used, unless there is some actual exercise from time to time of the rights, etc. Assuming however, that the rights, etc are exercised, it is not clear, again, what test needs to be applied to establish whether or not the rights, etc are 'enjoyed within' a particular area. There seem to be three possible views: (i) that the rights, etc are enjoyed only in the actual market place or area in which the market is held;

(ii) that they are enjoyed in every part of the manor or other area within which the market might lawfully be held; (iii) that the rights etc are enjoyed over the whole area within which the owner of the rights, etc can at common law prevent the levying of a rival market. If either of the first or second of these views is correct, a local authority would have power to establish a new market without the consent of the owner of a franchise or statutory market (but see *below*), although the establishment of such a new market, if it were established without statutory authority, would be an actionable disturbance of such neighbouring market — for instance, cases in which an old market is held outside but within 6⅔ miles (see pp 70, 71, *above*) of the market established in the area of the local authority. On the other hand, if (as seems likely) the third of these views is correct, a local authority has power to establish a market in its area only with the consent of the owner of the old market rights etc if the authority wishes to establish and hold it within 6⅔ miles of the area of the franchise; but if it can establish the market within its area and beyond that distance, it can do so without the consent of the owner of the old market rights, etc.

A local authority which has established a market under this Act, or under Acts preceding and replaced by this Act, is not protected: see sub-s (3), *above*. Any franchise markets purchased under these Acts would, however, be protected even if they later became statutory markets controlled by this Act since they would not have been established under this Act.

See also *Halton Borough Council v Cawley* [1985] 1 WLR 15.

([10]) The provisions in this sub-s relate only to markets established under this Act or the corresponding provisions in preceding Acts; and markets acquired under the above powers as existing markets are not excluded from the privilege.

51. Power to sell to local authority

(1) The owner of a market undertaking, or of any rights in respect of a market and of tolls, whether established under, or enjoyed by virtue of, statutory powers or not([1]), may sell or lease to a local authority([2]) the whole or any part of his market undertaking or rights, but subject to all attached liabilities([3]).

(2) A sale by a [. . .]([4]) company under this section must be authorised—

(a) if the company is a company within the meaning of the Companies Act [1985]([5]), by a special resolution of the members passed in the manner provided in [Part XI]([5]) of that Act([4]).

(b) if the company is not such a company, by a resolution passed by three-fourths in number and value of the members present, either personally or by proxy, at a meeting specially convened for the purpose with notice of the business to be transacted.

This section replaces in substantially the same terms s 50 of the Food and Drugs Act 1955.

([1]) The power therefore applies to owners of a franchise market or of a franchise of tolls or of a statutory market. The object of this section is, it seems, to give a power of sale or lease to owners who are under a disability and otherwise have no such power. As there is no power to acquire the undertaking compulsorily, the provisions of this section would not appear to relieve the owner, where he has a power of sale or lease subject to formalities or procedure, from compliance with such, even if the owner is a company. In the case of a company, the provisions of sub-s (2) should also be observed.

For transfer and devolution of market rights generally, see pp 22 *et seq*, above.

([2]) As to the corresponding power of a local authority to acquire by purchase, or on lease, see s 50(1)(b), *above*. For 'local authority', see s 61, *below*.

([3]) Where a local authority purchases a statutory or franchise market, it seems that it may, if it thinks fit, regulate the market relying entirely on the statute establishing the market or the franchise rights. A local authority may, however, whenever it thinks fit, elect to apply the provisions of this Act provided that, by so doing, any charges created upon the market or tolls, and outstanding at the date of the purchase, are left unimpaired. See also note (4) to s 50, *above* as to the general effect of applying the provisions of this Act

(4) Word omitted repealed by the Food Safety Act 1990, ss 52, 59(4), Sch 2, para 3, Sch 5.

(5) Words substituted by the Companies Consolidation (Consequential Provisions) Act 1985, s 30, Sch 2.

52. Market days and hours

A market authority(1) may appoint the days on which, and the hours during which, markets are to be held(2).

This section replaces in substantially the same terms s 51 of the Food and Drugs Act 1955, as partly repealed by the Local Government Act 1972, ss 199(4), 272(1) and Sch 30.

(1) For 'market authority', see s 61, *below*. Under the common law, a franchise market cannot be held on any day other than a day authorised by the franchise charter: see p 45, *above*; and if a local authority which has acquried a franchise market under s 50, *above* alters the market days under the powers in this section, the franchise rights would to that extent become merged in the statutory rights and the market will thereby become a statutory market subject to this Act and will continue to enjoy the other common law or franchise rights only so far as they are not expressly or impliedly taken away by this or any other Act: see note (4) to s 50, *above*. Where also a local authority has acquired an existing statutory market and alters the market days under this section, the market days will be controlled thereafter by this section only: see note (4) to s 50, *above*.

(2) By the Local Government (Miscellaneous) Provisions Act 1976, s 36(1), any provision of a local Act which confers power on a local authority to make byelaws appointing days on which or hours during which markets or fairs are held, includes a power to appoint such days or hours by resolution.

53. Charges

(1) A market authority(1) may demand in respect of the market(2), such charges . . .(3) as they may from time to time determine(4).

[(2) A market authority who provide —

(a) a weighing machine(5) for weighing cattle, sheep or swine; or

(b) a cold air store or refrigerator for the storage and preservation of meat and other articles of food,

may demand in respect of the weighing of such animals, or as the case may be, the use of the store or refrigerator such charges as they may from time to time determine(4), (9)].

(3) The authority—

(a) shall keep exhibited in conspicuous places in the market place, and in any market house, tables stating in large and legibly printed characters the several charges payable under this Part; and

(b) shall keep so much of the tables as relates to charges payable(6) in respect of the weighing of vehicles, or, as the case may be, in respect of the weighing of animals, conspicuously exhibited at every weighing machine provided by them in connection with the market for the purpose.

(4) A person who demands or accepts a charge greater than that for the time being authorised shall be liable to a fine not exceeding level 2 on the standard scale(7).

(5) Nothing in this section applies in relation to rents charged by a market authority in respect of the letting of accommodation within their market for any period longer than one week(8).

Sub-ss (1) and (2) replace in substantially the same terms s 52(1) and (2) of the Food and Drugs Act 1955, as partly repealed by the Local Government Act 1972, ss 199(4), 272(1) and Sch 30.

Sub-ss (3)–(5) replace in substantially the same terms s 52(3)–(5) of the 1955 Act as amended, in the case of sub-s (4), by the Criminal Justice Act 1982, ss 37(1), (2), 39(2), 46(1) and Sch 3.

(1) For 'market authority', see s 61, *below*. If a local authority acquires an existing market in which there is a right to take tolls, and increases the tolls, it seems that thereafter the tolls will be controlled by this section.

(2) At common law, apart from contract, toll is payable by the buyer and not the seller: see p 56, *above*. But by s 54, *below*, charges (which includes stallage or tolls: see s 61, *below*) must be paid from time to time on demand and in the case of animals are payable as soon as they are brought into the market. Under this section, it appears that toll may be made payable by the seller.

As to the right to demand preferential tolls, see note (4), *below*; and as to the penalty for demanding excessive charges, see subsection (4), *above*; and as to the recovery thereof see s 55, *below*.

(3) 'Charges' includes stallage or tolls: s 61, *below*. As to the meaning of stallage and tolls, and the distinction between them, see pp 51 *et seq*, *above*. Further tolls in respect of animals not removed within one hour of the close of the market may be levied: see s 54(3), *below*.

(4) Although the discretion to increase charges is wide, care must nevertheless be taken to ensure that such discretion is not exercised unreasonably: see *Roberts v Hopwood* [1925] AC 578 at 613; *A-G v Colchester Corpn* [1952] Ch 586; *Ricketts v Havering London Borough Council* (1981) 79 LGR 146; and pp 53–55, 59–65, *above*. There is no rule of law against preferential market tolls or stallage and the market owner may remit the whole or any part of the toll or stallage in favour of whomever he pleases: see *A-G v Colchester Corpn* [1952] Ch 586 at 597, 598 and 601; and pp 59 to 62, *above*. Under the Local Government (Miscellaneous Provisions) Act 1976, s 36(2), a local authority which maintains a market under any local Act may, notwithstanding anything in that Act, make such charges in connection with the market as it may determine from time to time.

(5) There is a duty to provide weighing machines for weighing cattle, sheep or swine: see s 57(2), *below*.

(6) The actual sums for the time being payable must be stated in the tables and not merely the maximum sums which the undertakers have power to charge: *Gregson v Potter* (1879) 4 Ex D 142.

As to articles, animals, etc not appearing in express terms in the tables, but which may be constructively therein, cf note (7) to s 13 of the Markets and Fairs Clauses Act 1847, p 183, *above*.

(7) The fine is recoverable on summary conviction: see s 93(1), (2)(a) and (3)(f), *below*. As to offences by corporations, see s 94, *below*.

(8) Where the right to occupy a space in a market and the stallages for such right are not specifically regulated, stallages are the subject of a free bargain made between the trader and the owner of the soil, and the owner may make whatever charge he pleases: see pp 59, 60, *above*. As to when bargains are not free, see pp 59, 60, *above*.

(9) Subsection substituted by the Food Safety Act 1990, s 52, Sch 2, para 4.

54. Time for payment of charges

(1) Charges[1] payable in respect of the market shall be paid from time to time on demand[2] to an authorised market officer[3].

[(2) Charges payable in respect of the weighing of cattle, sheep or swine[4] shall be paid in advance to an authorised market officer by the person bringing the animals to be weighed[5].]

(3) Charges[6] payable in respect of animals brought to the market for sale shall be payable, and may be demanded[6] by an authorised market officer[3]—

(a) as soon as the animals in respect of which they are payable are brought into the market place[6], and

(b) before they are put into any pen, or tied up in the market place,

but further charges shall be payable and may be demanded in respect of any of the animals which are not removed within one hour after the close of the market.

This section replaces in substantially the same terms s 53(1)–(3) of the Food and Drugs Act 1955.

(1) 'Charges' includes stallage or tolls: see s 61, *below*. As to the meaning of stallage and tolls, and the distinction between them, see pp 51 *et seq*, *above*.

(2) For the penalty for demanding or accepting excessive charges, see s 53(4), *above*.

(3) 'Authorised market officer' means an officer of a market authority specially authorised by it to collect charges in the market: see s 61, *below*.

(4) As to such charges, see s 53(2), *above*, and notes (5) and (6) thereto: see also note (6), *below*.

(5) Subsection (2) substituted by the Food Safety Act 1990, s 52, Sch 2, para 5.

(6) As to the charges payable, see s 53(2), *above*, and notes 4 and 5 thereto. Since charges are payable on demand under sub-s (3), *above*, as soon as the animals are brought into the market, the common law rule that tolls are payable by the buyer and not the seller (see p 56, *above*) is inapplicable.

55. Recovery of charges

If a person(1) liable to pay any charge(2) authorised under this Part does not pay it when lawfully demanded(3), the market authority(4) may, by any authorised market officer(5), levy it by distress—

(a) of all or any of the animals, poultry or other articles in respect of which the charge is payable(6), or

(b) of any other animals, poultry or articles in the market belonging to, or in the charge of, the person liable,

and any such charge may also be recovered either summarily as a civil debt(7) or in any court of competent jurisdiction.

This section replaces, in substantially the same terms, s 54 of the Food and Drugs Act 1955.

(1) 'Person' includes a body corporate: see the Interpretation Act 1978, s 5, Sch 1.

(2) See s 53, *above*, and notes thereto.

(3) For the time when the demand may be made, see s 54, *above*.

(4) For 'market authority', see s 61, *below*

(5) For 'authorised market officer', see s 61, *below*.

(6) The animals, poultry or other articles will be those appearing in the table of charges under s 53, *above*, or constructively appearing therein; cf the cases cited in note (7) to s 13 of the Markets and Fairs Clauses Act 1847, *above*.

(7) For recovery summarily as a civil debt, see s 58(1) of the Magistrates' Courts Act 1980. The complaint must be laid within six months from the date on which the matter of the complaint arose: see *ibid*, s 127(1).

56. Prohibited sales in market hours

(1) A person(1) (other than a pedlar holding a certificate under the Pedlars Act 1871(2)) who on a market day(3) and during market hours(3) sells or exposes for sale(4) any articles—

(a) which are specified in a byelaw(5) made by the market authority(6), and

(b) which are commonly sold in the market,

and such sale or exposure for sale—

(i) is in any place(7) within the authority's [area](8), and

(ii) is within such distance from the market as the authority may by byelaw declare(9),

is liable to a fine(10) not exceeding level 2 on the standard scale.

This subsection does not apply to a sale or exposure for sale([11]) in a person's own dwelling place([12]) or shop([13]), or in, or at the door of, any premises to a person resident in those premises.

(2) The market authority shall keep exhibited in conspicuous positions in the vicinity of the market notices stating the effect of any byelaw made under this section.

Sub-s (1) replaces, in substantially the same terms, s 55(1) of the Food and Drugs Act 1955, as amended by the Criminal Law Act 1977, s 31(6), Sch 6, and the Criminal Justice Act 1982, ss 37(1), (2), 46(1).

([1]) 'Person' includes a body corporate: see the Interpretation Act 1978, s 5, Sch 1.

([2]) Section 4 Pedlars Act 1871: see p 191, *above*. 'Pedlar' is defined in s 3, *ibid.* See also note ([3]) to s 13 of the Markets and Fairs Clauses Act 1847, *above.* A person who does not wholly, or predominantly, obtain his livelihood as a pedlar may nevertheless be regarded as carrying on the trade of a pedlar for the purpose of qualifying for a certificate under the Pedlars Act 1871: *Murphy v Duke* [1985] QB 905. For the distinction between acting as a street trader and a pedlar see *Watson v Malloy* [1988] 3 All ER 459; *R v Westminster City Council, ex p Elmasoglu* [1996] COD 357; *Shepway District Council v Vincent* [1994] COD 451; *Stevenage Borough Council v Wright* (1996) 95 LGR 404 and *Chichester District Council v Wood* CO/2738/96 14 March 1997.

([3]) See s 52, *above.*

([4]) Cf the cases in note ([4]) to s 13 of the Markets and Fairs Clauses Act 1847, *above*; and see also notes ([195]) and ([196]) on p 124, *above.*

([5]) For power to make byelaws, see s 60, *below*. For procedure, see note ([3]), *ibid.* 'Articles' has its ordinary meaning and not the special meaning given in s 132(1), *below.*

([6]) For 'market authority' see s 61, *below.*

([7]) In *Hooper v Kenshole* (1877) 2 QBD 127, it was held that a skittle alley used for the sale of goods was a 'place' within the corresponding provisions of a local Act.

([8]) Word substituted by the Food Safety Act 1990, s 52, Sch 2, para 6.

([9]) See note 5, *above*. If no byelaws have been made under this section a local authority cannot, it seems, prosecute under this section: see *Halton Borough Council v Cawley* [1985] 1 WLR 15 and *Manchester City Council v Walsh* (1985) 84 LGR 1, and p 92, *above.*

([10]) That is, on summary conviction: see s 93(1), (2)(a), (3)(g), *below.* As to offences by corporations, see s 94, *below*. The offence cannot be condoned by payment of toll, nor toll claimed in lieu of penalty: *Carter v Parkhouse* (1870) 22 LT 788; *Quilligan v Limerick Market Trustees* (1883) 14 LR Ir 265.

([11]) See note ([4]), *above.*

([12]) As to what is a 'dwelling place', cf the cases cited in note ([6]) to s 13 of the Markets and Fairs Clauses Act 1847, *above.*

([13]) Under s 13 of the Markets and Fairs Clauses Act 1847, *above*, it has been held that a shop must be some structure of a more or less permanent nature with a place for storing and not a mere place of sale: see note ([6]) to that section, *above*. See also *Manchester City Council v Walsh* (1985) 84 LGR 1, and pp 80–83, *above.*

57. Weighing machines and scales

(1) [Repealed by the Food Safety Act 1990, ss 52, 59(4), Sch 2, para 7, Sch 5.]

(2) A market authority([1]) in whose market cattle, sheep or swine are sold shall, unless there is in force an order of the Minister declaring that the circumstances are such as to render compliance with this subsection unnecessary—

(a) provide to that Minister's satisfaction one or more weighing machines([2]) adapted for weighing such animals; and

(b) appoint officers to attend to the weighing of such animals.

A weighing machine provided under this subsection shall for the purposes of section 1 of the Markets and Fairs (Weighing of Cattle) Act 1926([3]), be deemed to have been provided for the purpose of complying with the provisions of the principal Act referred to in that Act of 1926.

This section replaces, in substantially the same terms, s 61(1) and (2) of the Food and Drugs Act 1955, as partly repealed by the Weights and Measures Act 1963, s 63(1), Sch 9, Pt 1.

(1) For 'market authority', see s 61, *below.*

(2) The seller cannot be required to weigh animals except in the case of bulls, cows, oxen and heifers fit for immediate slaughter to be sold by auction: see note (3), *below.*

(3) Section 1 of the Markets and Fairs (Weighing of Cattle) Act 1926, *above* requires an auctioneer, unless exempted by the Minister, to have weighed, and to disclose the weight to intending purchasers of bulls, cows, oxen, heifers fit for immediate slaughter at an auction in a market in which a weighing machine is provided for the purposes of complying with the principal Act, that is, the Markets and Fairs (Weighing of Cattle) Act 1887, *above*. Furthermore, an auctioneer may not, unless exempted by the Minister, sell cattle at any mart where cattle are habitually or periodically sold and tolls are actually taken therein unless facilities for weighing cattle are provided similar to those under the Markets and Fairs (Weighing of Cattle) Acts 1887 and 1891: see s 4 of the Act of 1891, *above*; and pp 119, 120, *above.*

[57A. Provision of cold stores

(1) A market authority may provide a cold air store or refrigerator for the storage and preservation of meat and other articles of food.

(2) Any proposal by a market authority to provide under this section a cold air store or refrigerator within the area of another local authority requires the consent of that other authority, which shall not be unreasonably withheld.

(3) Any question whether or not such a consent is unreasonably withheld shall be referred to and determined by the Ministers.

(4) Subsections (1) to (5) of section 250 of the Local Government Act 1972 (which relate to local inquiries) shall apply for the purposes of this section as if any reference in those subsections to that Act included a reference to this section(1).]

(1) Section 57A inserted by the Food Safety Act 1990, s 52, Sch 2, para 8.

58. [Repealed by the Food Safety Act 1990, ss 52, 59(4), Sch 2, para 9, Sch 5.]

59. Information for market officer

The person in charge of any vehicle in which, and any other person by whom, animals(1) poultry or other articles are brought for sale in the market shall give to any authorised market officer(2) such information—

(a) as to their number and kind, or

(b) in the case of articles on which charges are made by reference to weight, as to their weight,

as that officer may require.

This section replaces, in substantially the same terms, s 58 of the Food and Drugs Act 1955.

(1) 'Animal' does not include bird or fish, see s 132(1), *below*.

(2) For 'authorised market officer', see s 61, *below*.

60. Market byelaws

A local authority(1) who maintain a market, whether or not they are a market authority within the meaning of this Act(2), may make byelaws(3)—

(a) for regulating the use of the market place, and the buildings, stalls, pens and standings in that market place;

(b) for preventing nuisances or obstructions in the market place, or in the immediate approaches to it;
(c) for regulating porters and carriers resorting to the market, and fixing the charges to be made for carrying articles from the market within the district.
[(d) after consulting the fire authority for the area in which the market is situated, for preventing the spread of fires in the market(4).]

This section replaces, in substantially the same terms, s 61 of the Food and Drugs Act 1955.
(1) For 'local authority' see s 61, *below*.
(2) See s 61, *below*. In other words, a local authority which has, apart from this Act or the preceding Acts it replaced, acquired a franchise or statutory market, or established a market under a local Act or any other Act, may make byelaws under this provision.
(3) The procedure for confirmation of byelaws is set out in the Local Government Act 1972, s 236: see Appendix A, p 301, *below*. For power to make byelaws under this and other Acts, see pp 109 *et seq*, *above*. For model byelaws, see Appendix A, pp 295 *et seq*, *below*.
(4) Paragraph inserted by the Food Safety Act 1990, s 52, Sch 2, para 10.

61. Interpretation of Part III and exclusion of City of London

In this Part, unless the context otherwise requires—
'authorised market officer' means an officer of a market authority specially authorised by them to collect charges in their market,
'charges' includes stallage or tolls(1),
['fire authority' means an authority exercising the functions of a fire authority under the Fire Services Act 1947,
'food' has the same meaning as in the Food Safety Act 1990,
'local authority' means a district council, a London borough council(2) or a parish [council but in relation to Wales, means a county council, county borough council](3) or community council,
'market authority' means a local authority who maintain a market which has been established or acquired under section 50(1) or under the corresponding provisions of any earlier enactment(4).]

This section contains provisions formerly in ss 49(2), 52(1), 53(4), 135(7) and 137(3) of the Food and Drugs Act 1955 as affected, in the case of s 49(2), by the London Government Order 1966, SI 1966 No 1305, art 2(11); and as substituted in the case of s 137(3) by the London Government Act 1963, s 54(4), Sch 13, Pt II, para 4.
(1) For the meaning of stallage and tolls, and the distinction between them, see pp 51 *et seq*, *above*.
(2) For definition of London borough council, see the London Government Act 1963, s 1, Sch 1, and the Local Government Act 1972, s 8, Sch 2.
(3) Added by the Local Government (Wales) Act 1994, s 22(3), Sch 9, para 14.
(4) Definition substituted and words omitted repealed by the Food Safety Act 1990, ss 52, 59(4), Sch 2, para 11, Sch 5.

Part IV
Sale of Foods by Hawkers

[Repealed by the Food Safety Act 1990, s 59(4), Sch 5.]

PART VI
ADMINISTRATION, ENFORCEMENT AND LEGAL PROCEEDINGS

[Repealed by the Food Safety Act 1990, s 59(4), Sch 5.]

Legal proceedings

93. Summary offences
(1) Any offence to which this section applies is triable summarily.
(2) The offences to which this section applies are—
(a) an offence under any provision of this Act specified in subsection (3);
(b)–(d) [Repealed by the Food Safety Act 1990, s 59(4), Sch.]
(3) The provisions of this Act mentioned in paragraph (a) of subsection (2) are—
(a)–(e) [Repealed by the Food Safety Act 1990, s 59(4), Sch 5.]
(f) section 53(4);
(g) section 56(1);
(h)–(i) [Repealed by the Food Safety Act 1990, s 59(4), Sch 5.]
(4) [Repealed by SI 1991 No 762, art 51(4), Sch 4.]

Sub-s (1)–(3) replace s 106A of the Food and Drugs Act 1955 as inserted by the Food and Drugs (Amendment) Act 1982, s 2.

94. Offences by corporations
[Section repealed (subsection (1) repealed except as regards offences under Part III of the Act) by the Food Safety Act 1990, s 59(4), Sch 5.]

95. Prosecutions
(1) No prosecution for an offence under this Act or regulations made under this Act which is triable either summarily(1) or on indictment shall be begun(2) after the expiry of—
(a) three years(3) from the commission of the offence, or
(b) one year(3) from its discovery by the prosecutor,
whichever is the earlier.
(2)–(8) [Repealed by the Food Safety Act 1990, s 59(4), Sch 5.]

Sub-s (1) replaces s 108(1) of the Food and Drugs Act 1955 as substituted by s 3(1) of the Food and Drugs (Amendment) Act 1982.
(1) See s 93, *above.*
(2) That is, when the information is laid: see *Beardsley v Giddings* [1904] 1 KB 847; *Brooks v Bagshaw* [1904] 2 KB 798; *R v Manchester Stipendiary Magistrate, ex p Hill* [1982] 3 WLR 331.
(3) In computing the relevant time limit, the day on which the offence was committed or discovered, as the case may be, is not to be counted: see for example, *Radcliffe v Bartholomew* [1892] 1 QB 161.

* * * * * *

PART VII
GENERAL AND SUPPLEMENTAL

Acquisition of land, and order to permit works

110. Compulsory purchase of land

A local authority([1]) may be authorised by the responsible Minister to purchase land compulsorily for the purposes of this Act, except for the purposes of paragraph (b) of section 50(1)([2]), and in relation to the compulsory purchase of land under this section—

(a) The Acquisition of Land Act 1981 applies; and

(b) 'land' includes any interest in land and any easement or right in, to or over land.

In this section 'the responsible Minister', in relation to the purposes of section 70, means the Minister([3]), and in relation to the other purposes of this Act means the Secretary of State.

This section replaces in substantially the same terms s 130 of the Food and Drugs Act 1955 as partly repealed, in the case of sub-s (1), by the Slaughterhouses Act 1974, s 47, Schs 5, 6 and as amended and partly repealed in the case of sub-s (3) by the Acquisition of Land Act 1981, s 34(1), Sch 4, para 1, Sch 6, Pt I.

([1]) For 'local authority' see s 132(1), *below*.

([2]) The power under s 50(1)(b), *above*, is a power to purchase by agreement (but not otherwise) a market undertaking and any rights enjoyed by any person in respect of a market and of tolls: see *ibid* and note ([5]) thereto.

([3]) For 'the Minister', see s 132(1), *below*.

* * * * * *

121. Byelaws

(1) The confirming authority in respect of byelaws([1]) made under this Act is the Secretary of State.

Sub-s (1) replaces s 125(1) of the Food and Drugs Act 1955 as partly repealed by the Slaughterhouses Act 1974, s 47, Sch 6.

([1]) Confirmation of byelaws is required under s 236 of the Local Government Act 1972. For power to make market byelaws under this Act, see s 60, *above*, and notes thereto.

* * * * * *

Interpretation and operation

131. Interpretation: 'food'

[Repealed by the Food Safety Act 1990, s 59(4), Sch 5.]

* * * * * *

132. Interpretation: further provision

(1) In this Act, unless the context otherwise requires, [. . .]([1])—

'animal' does not include bird or fish;

* * * * * *(1)

'the Minister' means the Minister of Agriculture, Fisheries and Food and the Secretary of State, acting jointly, except in paragraph (a) of section 5(1), section 37 so far as it relates to the Minister's power to appoint veterinary inspectors, sections 68(5), 83, 101(4), 114 and paragraph (b) of section 115(1) where it means the Minister of Agriculture, Fisheries and Food;

* * * * * *(1)

(2) All powers and duties conferred or imposed by this Act shall be deemed to be in addition to, and not in derogation of, any other powers and duties conferred or imposed by Act of Parliament, law or custom, and, subject to any repeal effected by, or other express provision of, this Act, all such other powers and duties may be exercised and shall be performed in the same manner as if this Act had not been passed.

(1) Definitions repealed by the Food Safety Act 1990, s 59(4), Sch 5.

* * * * * *

134. Transitional and saving provisions, amendments and repeals
[Repealed by the Food Safety Act 1990, s 59(4), Sch 5.]

* * * * * *

136. Citation, extent and commencement
(1) This Act may be cited as the Food Act 1984.
(2) The following provisions of this Act apply to Scotland—
(a) section 68 and 69, and paragraph 6 of Schedule 9,
(b)–(c) [Repealed by the Food Safety Act 1990, s 59(4), Sch 5.]
but apart from those provisions this Act does not apply to Scotland.
(3) [Repealed by the Food Safety Act 1990, s 59(4), Sch 5.]
(4) This Act comes into force at the end of the period of three months beginning with the day on which it is passed.

SUNDAY TRADING ACT 1994

(Eliz II, 1994, c 20)

An Act to reform the law of England and Wales relating to Sunday trading; to make provision as to the rights of shop workers under the law of England and Wales in relation to Sunday working; and for connected purposes.

[5th July 1994]

1. Reform of law relating to Sunday trading

(1) Schedules 1 and 2 to this Act shall come into force on such day as the Secretary of State may by order made by statutory instrument appoint (in this section referred to as 'the appointed day').

(2) Sections 47 to 66 of, and Schedules 5, 6 and 7 to, the Shops Act 1950 shall cease to have effect on the appointed day.

2. Loading and unloading at large shops on Sunday morning

(1) A local authority may by resolution designate their area as a loading control area for the purposes of this section with effect from a date specified in the resolution, which must be a date at least one month after the date on which the resolution is passed.

(2) A local authority may by resolution revoke any designation made by them under subsection (1) above.

(3) It shall be the duty of a local authority, before making or revoking any designation under subsection (1) above, to consult persons appearing to the local authority to be likely to be affected by the proposed designation or revocation (whether as the occupiers of shops or as local residents) or persons appearing to the local authority to represent such persons.

(4) Where a local authority make or revoke a designation under this section, they shall publish notice of the designation or revocation in such manner as they consider appropriate.

(5) Schedule 3 to this Act (which imposes restrictions on loading and unloading on Sunday before 9 am at large shops in loading control areas) shall have effect.

3. Construction of certain leases and agreements

(1) Where any lease or agreement (however worded) entered into before the commencement of this section has the effect of requiring the occupier of a shop to keep the shop open for the serving of retail customers—

- (a) during normal business hours, or
- (b) during hours to be determined otherwise than by or with the consent of the occupier,

that lease or agreement shall not be regarded as requiring, or as enabling any person to require, the occupier to open the shop on Sunday for the serving of retail customers.

(2) Subsection (1) above shall not affect any lease or agreement—

- (a) to the extent that it relates specifically to Sunday and would (apart from this section) have the effect of requiring Sunday trading of a kind which before the commencement of this section would have been lawful by virtue of any provision of Part IV of the Shops Act 1950, or
- (b) to the extent that it is varied by agreement after the commencement of this section.

(3) In this section 'retail customer' and 'shop' have the same meaning as in Schedule 1 to this Act.

4. Rights of shop workers as respects Sunday working

Schedule 4 to this Act shall have effect.

5. Exclusion of Part I of Shops Act 1950

[Repealed by the Deregulation and Contracting Out Act 1994, s 8, Sch 17.]

6. Consequential repeal or amendment of local Acts

(1) The Secretary of State may by order made by statutory instrument—

(a) repeal any provision of a local Act passed before or in the same Session as this Act if it appears to him that the provision is inconsistent with or has become unnecessary in consequence of any provision of this Act, and

(b) amend any provision of such a local Act if it appears to him that the provision requires amendment in consequence of any provision of this Act or any repeal made by virtue of paragraph (a) above.

(2) It shall be the duty of the Secretary of State, before he makes an order under subsection (1) above repealing or amending any provision of a local Act, to consult each local authority which he considers would be affected by the repeal or amendment of that provision.

(3) A statutory instrument containing an order under subsection (1) above shall be subject to annulment in pursuance of a resolution of either House of Parliament.

7. Expenses

There shall be paid out of money provided by Parliament any increase attributable to this Act in the sums payable out of such money under any other Act.

8. Meaning of 'local authority'

(1) In this Act 'local authority' means any unitary authority or any district council so far as they are not a unitary authority.

(2) In subsection (1) above 'unitary authority' means—

(a) the council of any county so far as they are the council for an area for which there are no district councils,

(b) the council of any district comprised in an area for which there is no county council,

(c) a county borough council,

(d) a London borough council,

(e) the Common Council of the City of London, or

(f) the Council of the Isles of Scilly.

(3) Until 1st April 1996, the definition of 'unitary authority' in subsection (2) above shall have effect with the omission of paragraph (c).

9. Short title, repeals, commencement and extent

(1) This Act may be cited as the Sunday Trading Act 1994.

(2) The enactments mentioned in Schedule 5 to this Act are hereby repealed to the extent specified in the third column of that Schedule.

(3) The following provisions of this Act

sections 2 to 5,

subsection (2) of this section, and

Schedules 3, 4 and 5,

shall not come into force until the appointed day (as defined in section 1 above).

(4) This Act extends to England and Wales only.

Section 1(1)

SCHEDULE 1

RESTRICTIONS ON SUNDAY OPENING OF LARGE SHOPS

Interpretation

1. In this Schedule—

'intoxicating liquor' has the same meaning as in the Licensing Act 1964,

'large shop' means a shop which has a relevant floor area exceeding 280 square metres,

'medicinal product' and 'registered pharmacy' have the same meaning as in the Medicines Act 1968,

'relevant floor area', in relation to a shop, means the internal floor area of so much of the shop as consists of or is comprised in a building, but excluding any part of the shop which, throughout the week ending with the Sunday in question, is used neither for the serving of customers in connection with the sale of goods nor for the display of goods,

'retail customer' means a person who purchases goods retail,

'retail sale' means any sale other than a sale for use or resale in the course of a trade or business, and references to retail purchase shall be construed accordingly,

'sale of goods' does not include—

(a) the sale of meals, refreshments or intoxicating liquor for consumption on the premises on which they are sold, or

(b) the sale of meals or refreshments prepared to order for immediate consumption off those premises,

'shop' means any premises where there is carried on a trade or business consisting wholly or mainly of the sale of goods, and

'stand', in relation to an exhibition, means any platform, structure, space or other area provided for exhibition purposes.

Large shops not to open on Sunday except in accordance with notice to local authority

2.—(1) Subject to sub-paragraphs (2) and (3) below, a large shop shall not be open on Sunday for the serving of retail customers.

(2) Sub-paragraph (1) above does not apply in relation to—

(a) any of the shops mentioned in paragraph 3(1) below, or

(b) any shop in respect of which a notice under paragraph 8(1) of Schedule 2 to this Act (shops occupied by persons observing the Jewish Sabbath) has effect.

(3) Where a notice under paragraph 4 below has effect in relation to a shop, sub-paragraph (1) above does not apply in relation to the shop during the permitted Sunday opening hours specified in the notice, but this sub-paragraph has effect subject to sub-paragraph (4) below.

(4) The exemption conferred by sub-paragraph (3) above does not apply where the Sunday is Easter Day or Christmas Day.

Exemptions

3.—(1) The shops referred to in paragraph 2(2)(a) above are—

(a) any shop which is at a farm and where the trade or business carried on consists wholly or mainly of the sale of produce from that farm,

(b) any shop where the trade or business carried on consists wholly or mainly of the sale of intoxicating liquor,

(c) any shop where the trade or business carried on consists wholly or mainly of the sale of any one or more of the following—

(i) motor supplies and accessories, and

(ii) cycle supplies and accessories,

(d) any shop which—

(i) is a registered pharmacy, and

(ii) is not open for the retail sale of any goods other than medicinal products and medical and surgical appliances,

(e) any shop at a designated airport which is situated in a part of the airport to which sub-paragraph (3) below applies,

(f) any shop in a railway station,

(g) any shop at a service area within the meaning of the Highways Act 1980,

(h) any petrol filling station,

(j) any shop which is not open for the retail sale of any goods other than food, stores or other necessaries required by any person for a vessel or aircraft on its arrival at, or immediately before its departure from, a port, harbour or airport, and

(k) any stand used for the retail sale of goods during the course of an exhibition.

(2) In determining whether a shop falls within sub-paragraph (1)(a), (b) or (c) above, regard shall be had to the nature of the trade or business carried on there on weekdays as well as to the nature of the trade or business carried on there on Sunday.

(3) This sub-paragraph applies to every part of a designated airport, except any part which is not ordinarily used by persons travelling by air to or from the airport.

(4) In this paragraph 'designated airport' means an airport designated for the purposes of this paragraph by an order made by the Secretary of State, as being an airport at which there appears to him to be a substantial amount of international passenger traffic.

(5) The power to make an order under sub-paragraph (4) above shall be exercisable by statutory instrument.

(6) Any order made under section 1(2) of the Shops (Airports) Act 1962 and in force at the commencement of this Schedule shall, so far as it relates to England and Wales, have effect as if made also under sub-paragraph (4) above, and may be amended or revoked as it has effect for the purposes of this paragraph by an order under sub-paragraph (4) above.

Notice of proposed Sunday opening

4.—(1) A person who is, or proposes to become, the occupier of a large shop may give notice to the local authority for the area in which the shop is situated—

(a) stating that he proposes to open the shop on Sunday for the serving of retail customers, and
(b) specifying a continuous period of six hours, beginning no earlier than 10 am and ending no later than 6 pm, as the permitted Sunday opening hours in relation to the shop.

(2) The occupier of a shop in respect of which notice has been given under sub-paragraph (1) above may, by a subsequent notice—

(a) specify permitted Sunday opening hours that could be specified under sub-paragraph (1)(b) above but are different from those specified in the earlier notice, or
(b) cancel the earlier notice.

(3) A notice under this paragraph shall not take effect until the end of the period of 14 days beginning with the day on which it is given, unless the local authority agree that it is to take effect at the end of a shorter period.

(4) A notice under this paragraph shall cease to have effect when superseded by a subsequent notice or cancelled as mentioned in sub-paragraph (2)(b) above.

Register of shops

5.—(1) Every local authority shall keep a register of shops in respect of which a notice under paragraph 4 above has effect.

(2) In relation to every such shop, the register shall contain particulars of—

(a) the name (if any) and address of the shop, and
(b) the permitted Sunday opening hours specified in the notice under paragraph 4 above.

(3) Any register kept under this paragraph—

(a) shall be open to inspection by members of the public at all reasonable times, and
(b) may be kept by means of a computer.

Duty to display notice

6. At any time when—

(a) a large shop is open on Sunday for the serving of retail customers, and
(b) the prohibition in sub-paragraph (1) of paragraph 2 above is excluded only by sub-paragraph (3) of that paragraph,

a notice specifying the permitted Sunday opening hours specified in the notice under paragraph 4 above shall be displayed in a conspicuous position inside and outside the shop.

Offences

7.—(1) If paragraph 2(1) above is contravened in relation to a shop, the occupier of the shop shall be liable on summary conviction to a fine not exceeding £50,000.

(2) If paragraph 6 above is contravened in relation to a shop, the occupier of the shop shall be liable on summary conviction to a fine not exceeding level 2 on the standard scale.

8. Where a person is charged with having contravened paragraph 2(1) above, in relation to a large shop which was permitted to be open for the serving of retail customers on the Sunday in question during the permitted Sunday opening hours specified in a notice under paragraph 4 above, by reason of his having served a retail customer after the end of those hours, it shall be a defence to prove that the customer was in the shop before that time and left not later than half an hour after that time.

Transitional provision

9. Any notice given for the purposes of paragraph 4(1) above after the passing of this Act but before the commencement of this Schedule shall, notwithstanding paragraph 4(3) above, take effect on that commencement.

Section 1(1)

SCHEDULE 2
SUPPLEMENTARY PROVISIONS

PART I
GENERAL ENFORCEMENT PROVISIONS

Duty to enforce Act

1. It shall be the duty of every local authority to enforce within their area the provisions of Schedules 1 and 3 to this Act and Part II of this Schedule.

Inspectors

2. For the purposes of their duties under paragraph 1 above it shall be the duty of every local authority to appoint inspectors.

Powers of entry

3. An inspector appointed by a local authority under paragraph 2 above shall, on producing if so required some duly authenticated document showing his authority, have a right at all reasonable hours—

(a) to enter any premises within the area of the local authority, with or without a constable, for the purpose of ascertaining whether there is or has been on the premises any contravention of the provisions of Schedules 1 and 3 to this Act,

(b) to require the production of, inspect and take copies of any records (in whatever form they are held) relating to any business carried on on the premises which appear to him to be relevant for the purpose mentioned in paragraph (a) above,

(c) where those records are kept by means of a computer, to require the records to be produced in a form in which they may be taken away, and

(d) to take such measurements and photographs as he considers necessary for the purpose mentioned in paragraph (a) above.

Obstruction of inspectors

4. Any person who intentionally obstructs an inspector appointed under paragraph 2 above acting in the execution of his duty shall be liable on summary conviction to a fine not exceeding level 3 on the standard scale.

Offences due to fault of other person

5. Where the commission by any person of an offence under this Act is due to the act or default of some other person, that other person shall be guilty of the offence, and a person may be charged with and convicted of the offence by virtue of this paragraph whether or not proceedings are taken against the first-mentioned person.

Offences by bodies corporate

6.—(1) Where an offence under this Act committed by a body corporate is proved to have been committed with the consent or connivance of, or to be attributable to any neglect on the part of, any director, manager, secretary or other similar officer of the body corporate, or any person who was purporting to act in any such capacity, he as well as the body corporate shall be guilty of the offence and shall be liable to be proceeded against and punished accordingly.

(2) Where the affairs of a body corporate are managed by its members, sub-paragraph (1) above shall apply in relation to the acts and defaults of a member in connection with his functions of management as if he were a director of the body corporate.

Defence of due diligence

7.—(1) In any proceedings for an offence under this Act it shall, subject to sub-paragraph (2) below, be a defence for the person charged to prove that he took all reasonable precautions and exercised all due diligence to avoid the commission of the offence by himself or by a person under his control.

(2) If in any case the defence provided by sub-paragraph (1) above involves the allegation that the commission of the offence was due to the act or default of another person, the person charged shall not, without leave of the court, be entitled to rely on that defence unless, at least seven clear days before the hearing, he has served on the prosecutor a notice in writing giving such information identifying or assisting in the identification of that other person as was then in his possession.

Part II
Shops Occupied by Persons Observing the Jewish Sabbath

Shops occupied by persons of the Jewish religion

8.—(1) A person of the Jewish religion who is the occupier of a large shop may give to the local authority for the area in which the shop is situated a notice signed by him stating—

- (a) that he is a person of the Jewish religion, and
- (b) that he intends to keep the shop closed for the serving of customers on the Jewish Sabbath.

(2) For the purposes of this paragraph, a shop occupied by a partnership or company shall be taken to be occupied by a person of the Jewish religion if, and only if, the majority of the partners or of the directors, as the case may be, are persons of that religion.

(3) A notice under sub-paragraph (1) above shall be accompanied by a certificate signed by an authorised person that the person giving the notice is a person of the Jewish religion.

(4) Where the occupier of the shop is a partnership or company—

(a) any notice under sub-paragraph (1) above shall be given by the majority of the partners or directors and, if not given by all of them, shall specify the names of the other partners or directors, and

(b) a certificate under sub-paragraph (3) above is required in relation to each of the persons by whom such a notice is given.

(5) Every local authority shall keep a register containing particulars of the name (if any) and address of every shop in respect of which a notice under sub-paragraph (1) above has effect.

(6) Any register kept under this paragraph—

(a) shall be open to inspection by members of the public at all reasonable times, and

(b) may be kept by means of a computer.

(7) If there is any change—

(a) in the occupation of a shop in respect of which a notice under sub-paragraph (1) above has effect, or

(b) in any partnership or among the directors of any company by which such a shop is occupied,

the notice shall be taken to be cancelled at the end of the period of 14 days beginning with the day on which the change occurred, unless during that period, or within such further time as may be allowed by the local authority, a fresh notice is given under sub-paragraph (1) above in respect of the shop.

(8) Where a fresh notice is given under sub-paragraph (1) above by reason of a change of the kind mentioned in sub-paragraph (7) above, the local authority may dispense with the certificate required by sub-paragraph (3) above in the case of any person in respect of whom such a certificate has been provided in connection with a former notice in respect of that shop or any other shop in the area of the local authority.

(9) A notice given under sub-paragraph (1) above in respect of any shop shall be cancelled on application in that behalf being made to the local authority by the occupier of the shop.

(10) A person who, in a notice or certificate given for the purposes of this paragraph, makes a statement which is false in a material respect and which he knows to be false or does not believe to be true shall be liable on summary conviction to a fine not exceeding level 5 on the standard scale.

(11) Where a person is convicted of an offence under sub-paragraph (10) above, the local authority may cancel any notice under sub-paragraph (1) above to which the offence relates.

(12) In this paragraph

'authorised person', in relation to a notice under sub-paragraph (1) above, means—

(a) the Minister of the synagogue of which the person giving the notice is a member,

(b) the secretary of that synagogue, or

(c) any other person nominated for the purposes of this paragraph by the President of the London Committee of Deputies of the British Jews (otherwise known as the Board of Deputies of British Jews),

'large shop' and 'shop' have the same meaning as in Schedule 1 to this Act, and
'secretary of a synagogue' has the same meaning as in Part IV of the Marriage Act 1949.

Members of other religious bodies observing the Jewish Sabbath

9. Paragraph 8 above shall apply to persons who are members of any religious body regularly observing the Jewish Sabbath as it applies to persons of the Jewish religion, and accordingly—

(a) references to persons of the Jewish religion shall be construed as including any person who is a member of such a body, and

(b) in the application of that paragraph to such persons 'authorised person' means a Minister of the religious body concerned.

Transitional provisions

10.—(1) Any shop which is registered under section 53 of the Shops Act 1950 at the commencement of this Schedule and is at that time a large shop within the meaning of Schedule 1 to this Act shall be taken to be a shop in respect of which a notice has been given under sub-paragraph (1) of paragraph 8 above by the person who was then registered as the occupier of the shop; and the provisions of that paragraph in relation to the cancellation of such a notice shall have effect accordingly.

(2) In paragraph 8(8) above, the reference to a certificate provided in connection with a former notice includes a reference to a statutory declaration provided under subsection (2) of section 53 of the Shops Act 1950 in connection with the registration of a shop under that section before the commencement of this Schedule.

Section 2

SCHEDULE 3

LOADING AND UNLOADING AT LARGE SHOPS ON SUNDAY MORNING

Shops to which Schedule applies

1. This Schedule applies to any shop—

(a) which is a large shop, within the meaning of Schedule 1 to this Act, in respect of which a notice under paragraph 4 of that Schedule has effect, and

(b) which is situated in an area designated as a loading control area under section 2 of this Act.

Consent required for early Sunday loading and unloading

2. The occupier of a shop to which this Schedule applies shall not load or unload, or permit any other person to load or unload, goods from a vehicle at the shop before 9 am on Sunday in connection with the trade or business carried on in the shop, unless the loading or unloading is carried on—

(a) with the consent of the local authority for the area in which the shop is situated granted under this Schedule, and

(b) in accordance with any conditions subject to which that consent is granted.

3.— (1) A consent under this Schedule may be granted subject to such conditions as the local authority consider appropriate.

(2) The local authority may at any time vary the conditions subject to which a consent is granted, and shall give notice of the variation to the person to whom the consent was granted.

Application for consent

4. An application for a consent under this Schedule shall be made in writing and shall contain such information as the local authority may reasonably require.

5. An applicant for a consent under this Schedule shall pay such reasonable fee in respect of his application as the local authority may determine.

6.—(1) Where an application is duly made to the local authority for a consent under this Schedule, the authority shall grant the consent unless they are satisfied that the loading or unloading of goods from vehicles before 9 am on Sunday at the shop to which the application relates, in connection with the trade or business carried on at the shop, has caused, or would be likely to cause, undue annoyance to local residents.

(2) The authority shall determine the application and notify the applicant in writing of their decision within the period of 21 days beginning with the day on which the application is received by the authority.

(3) In a case where a consent is granted, the notification under sub-paragraph (2) above shall specify the conditions, if any, subject to which the consent is granted.

Revocation of consent

7. Where—

(a) the occupier of a shop in respect of which a consent under this Schedule is in force is convicted of an offence under paragraph 9 below by reason of his failure to comply with the conditions subject to which the consent was granted, or

(b) the local authority are satisfied that the loading or unloading authorised by virtue of a consent under this Schedule has caused undue annoyance to local residents,

the local authority may revoke the consent.

Publication of consent

8. Where a local authority grant a consent under this Schedule, the authority may cause a notice giving details of that consent to be published in a local newspaper circulating in their area.

Offence

9. A person who contravenes paragraph 2 above shall be liable on summary conviction to a fine not exceeding level 3 on the standard scale.

Section 4

SCHEDULE 4

[Repealed by the Employment Rights Act 1996, Sch 3, Pt I and superseded by Pt IV of that Act (ss 36–43).]

RIGHTS OF SHOP WORKERS AS RESPECTS SUNDAY WORKING

Section 9(2)

SCHEDULE 5
REPEALS

Chapter	Short title	Extent of repeal
1933 c 12	The Children and Young Persons Act 1933.	Section 20(3).
1950 c 28	The Shops Act 1950.	Sections 47 to 66. In section 71(7)(b), the words 'or Part IV'. Schedules 5, 6 and 7.
1962 c 35	The Shops (Airports) Act 1962.	In section 1(1) the words from 'and of' to 'Sunday trading)'.
1963 c 33	The London Government Act 1963.	Section 51(3).
1963 c 37	The Children and Young Persons Act 1963.	Section 35(3).
1965 c 35	The Shops (Early Closing Days) Act 1965.	In section 4(2), the words from 'and, notwithstanding' to the end.
1969 c 48	The Post Office Act 1969.	In Schedule 4, in paragraph 51, the words from 'and Schedule 5' to 'on Sunday)'.
1986 c 31	The Airports Act 1986.	Section 70. In Schedule 5, paragraph 15.
1989 c 38	The Employment Act 1989.	In Schedule 3, in Part III, paragraph 2(c).

LONDON LOCAL AUTHORITIES ACT 1994

(Eliz II, 1994, c xii)

An Act to confer further powers upon local authorities in London; and for other purposes.

[21st July 1994]

1. Short title and commencement

This Act may be cited as the London Local Authorities Act 1994 and except section 5 (Night cafe licensing) of this Act shall come into operation at the end of the period of two months beginning with the date on which it is passed.

2. Interpretation

In this Act, except as otherwise expressly provided or unless the context otherwise requires—

'the Act of 1990' means the London Local Authorities Act 1990;

'authorised officer' means an officer of a borough council authorised by the council in writing to act in relation to the relevant provision of this Act;

'borough council' means London borough council but does not include the Common Council of the City of London; and 'borough' shall be construed accordingly.

3. Appointed day

(1) In this Act 'the appointed day' means such day as may be fixed in relation to a borough by resolution of the borough council, subject to and in accordance with the provisions of this section.

(2) Different days may be fixed under this section for the purpose of the application of different provisions of this Act to a borough.

(3) The borough council shall cause to be published in a local newspaper circulating in the borough notice—

(a) of the passing of any such resolution and of the day fixed thereby; and

(b) of the general effect of the provisions of this Act coming into operation as from that day;

and the day so fixed shall not be earlier than the expiration of three months from the publication of the said notice.

(4) Either a photostatic or other reproduction certified by the officer appointed for that purpose by the borough council to be a true reproduction of a page or part of a page of any such newspaper bearing the date of its publication and containing any such notice shall be evidence of the publication of the notice, and of the date of publication.

* * * * * *

6. Street trading

(1) Section 21(2)(j) (Interpretation of Part III) of the Act of 1990 is hereby amended by the insertion after 'offer for sale', of the words 'of articles'.

(2) Section 24(1) (Designation of licence streets) of the Act of 1990 is hereby amended by the substitution for the proviso of—

'Provided that a borough council shall—

(a) before passing a designating resolution, consult with the Commissioner of Police of the Metropolis on their proposal; and

(b) before rescinding or varying a designating resolution, consult with the licence holders trading in the street in question, or a body or bodies representative of them, on their proposal.'.

(3) Section 27(6) (Conditions of street trading licences) of the Act of 1990 is hereby amended by the addition, at the end of the subsection, of 'and shall notify the licence holders or a body or bodies representative of them of the making of such regulations.'.

(4) In section 30(1) (Part III appeals) of the Act of 1990, the following paragraph shall be inserted after the words 'Any person aggrieved'—

'(aa) by the refusal of a borough council to renew a licence because they are not satisfied as mentioned in subsection (4)(b) of section 25 (Application for street trading licences) of this Act;'.

(5) In section 30(1)(d) (Part III appeals) of the Act of 1990, the words, 'where that decision is based on any of the grounds mentioned in subsection (1)(d) to (h) of the said section 28' shall cease to have effect.

(6) Section 30(2)(a) (Part III appeals) of the Act of 1990 is hereby amended by the addition after 'paragraph' of '(aa),'.

(7) Section 30 (Part III appeals) of the Act of 1990 is hereby amended by the addition, after subsection (11) of the following subsection—

'(12) An appeal under subsection (11) above may be brought—

(a) in the case of an appeal under paragraph (a) or (b) of that subsection, at any time before the expiration of the period of three months beginning with the date on which notice of the passing of the resolution is published for the second time in accordance with subsection (10) of section 24 (Designation of licence streets) of this Act;

(b) in the case of an appeal under paragraph (c) of that subsection, at any time before the expiration of the period of three months beginning with the date upon which the licence holders or a body or bodies representative of them were notified of the making of the regulations;

(c) in the case of an appeal under paragraph (d) of that subsection—

(i) if it relates to the amount of a fee payable under subsection (1) of section 32 (Fees and charges) of this Act, at any time before the expiration of the period of three months beginning with the date on which the fee payable is notified to the licence holders or a body or bodies representative of them;

(ii) if it relates to the amount of a charge under subsection (2) of section 32 (Fees and charges) of this Act, at any time before the expiration of the period of three months beginning with the date on which notice of the determination of the charge has been given to the licence holders or a body or bodies representative of them.'.

(8) Section 32 (Fees and charges) of the Act of 1990 is hereby amended—

(a) (i) by the deletion in subsection (5), of 'grant or' and 'as aforesaid'; and

(ii) by the addition in that subsection after 'any' of the word 'such';

(b) by the substitution, in subsection (7) for 'or varying the amount of such charges' of the words '(whether originally or by way of variation of charges previously determined)';

(c) by the addition after subsection (7) of the following subsection—

'(7A) A notice under subsection (7)(a) above shall be accompanied by a statement showing how the proposed charges have been computed; and any body representative of licence holders may request the borough council to supply such further information or explanation with regard to the proposed charges as the body may reasonably require in order to ascertain whether the proposed charges are reasonable and have been computed in accordance with the provisions of this section.';

(d) by the addition in subsection (9)—

(i) after the first 'to' of '(a)'; and

(ii) at the end, of the words 'and (b) comply with any request made under subsection (7A) above;

and where any such request is made the period so specified, if still current, shall be treated as extended by the number of days in the period beginning with the day on which the request is made and ending with that on which it is complied with.';

(e) by the substitution for subsection (10) of—

'(10) When a borough council have determined fees under subsection (1) above or charges under subsection (2) above (whether originally or by way of variation of fees or charges previously determined) they shall give notice of the fees or charges so determined and of the date on which those fees or charges are to be brought into effect, in the manner prescribed in subsection (7) above.'.

(9) Section 34 (Offences) of the Act of 1990 is hereby amended by the addition, at the beginning of paragraph (1) of the words 'without reasonable excuse'.

(10) Section 37 (Ice cream trading) of the Act of 1990 is hereby amended by the addition, in subsection (2) after 'prohibited street' of the words 'and in the case of any London borough except the City of Westminster and the Royal Borough of Kensington and Chelsea may so designate it for such days or for such parts of days as are specified in the resolution,'.

(11) Section 38 (Unlicensed street trading) of the Act of 1990 is hereby amended—

(a) by the substitution for subsection (1) of—

'(1) A person who—

(a) is not the holder of a street trading licence or a temporary licence and who engages in street trading in a borough; or

(b) is the holder of a temporary licence and who engages in street trading in a borough on a day or in a place not specified in that temporary licence;

shall be guilty of an offence and shall be liable on summary conviction to a fine not exceeding level 3 on the standard scale.';

(b) by the addition, in subsection (4) after 'of that offence' of the words 'or may be the subject of forfeiture under subsection (5) below';

(c) by the addition, after subsection (4) of the following subsection—

'(4A)(a) The following provisions of this subsection shall have effect where any article or thing (including any receptacle) is seized under subsection (4) above and references in those provisions to proceedings are to proceedings in respect of the alleged offence in relation to which the article or thing is seized.

(b) Subject to paragraph (e) below, at the conclusion of the proceedings the article or thing shall be returned to the person from whom it was seized unless the court orders it to be forfeited under subsection (5) below.

(c) Subject to paragraph (d) below, where a receptacle seized under subsection (4) above is a motor vehicle used for ice cream trading, the borough council or the Commissioner of Police of the Metropolis (as the case may be) shall, within three days of the receipt of an application in writing by the owner or registered keeper of the vehicle, permit him to remove it.

(d) Paragraph (c) above shall not apply where—
(i) the owner or registered keeper of the vehicle has been convicted of an offence under this Part of this Act; or
(ii) the owner or registered keeper of the vehicle is being prosecuted for a previous alleged offence under this Part of this Act; or
(iii) the vehicle has been used in the commission of such an offence or previous alleged offence;
if the offence or previous alleged offence was committed or is alleged to have been committed no more than three years before the seizure and (in the case of an alleged offence) the proceedings are continuing.
(e) If no proceedings are instituted before the expiration of a period of 28 days beginning with the date of seizure, or any proceedings instituted within that period are discontinued, at the expiration of that period or, as the case may be, on the discontinuance of the proceedings, the article or thing shall be returned to the person from whom it was seized unless it has not proved possible, after diligent enquiry, to identify that person and ascertain his address.
(f) Where the article or thing is not returned because it has not proved possible to identify the person from whom it was seized and ascertain his address the borough council (whether the article or thing was seized by a constable or by an authorised officer) may apply to a magistrates' court for an order as to the manner in which it should be dealt with.';

(d) by the addition, in subsection (6) at the end, of—
'and in considering whether to make such an order a court shall have regard—
(i) to the value of the property; and
(ii) to the likely financial and other effects on the offender of the making of the order (taken together with any other order that the court contemplates making).';

(e) by the substitution, in subsection (7) for 'the article or thing' of the word 'anything';

(f) by the addition, after subsection (7) of the following subsection—
'(8) (a) This subsection shall have effect where—
(i) an article, thing or receptacle is seized under subsection (4) above; and
(ii) (A) not less than six months have passed since the date of the seizure and no information has been laid against any person for an offence under this section in respect of the acts or circumstances which occasioned the seizure; or
(B) proceedings for such an offence have been brought and either the person charged has been acquitted (whether or not on appeal) and the time for appealing against or challenging the acquittal (where applicable) has expired without an appeal or challenge being brought, or the proceedings (including any appeal) have been withdrawn by, or have failed for want of prosecution by, the person by whom the original proceedings were brought.
(b) When this subsection has effect a person who has or at the time of seizure had a legal interest in the article, thing or receptacle seized may recover compensation from the borough council or (where it is seizedby a constable) the Commissioner of Police of the Metropolis by civil

action in the County Court in respect of any loss suffered by him as a result of the seizure.

(c) The court may not make an order for compensation under paragraph (b) above unless it is satisfied that seizure was not lawful under subsection (4) above.'.

(12) Part III of the Act of 1990, as amended by this Act, is set out in the Schedule to this Act.

* * * * * *

Section 6

SCHEDULE

LONDON LOCAL AUTHORITIES ACT 1990 PART III AS HAVING EFFECT IN ACCORDANCE WITH SECTION 6 (STREET TRADING) OF THIS ACT

PART III

STREET TRADING

21. Interpretation of Part III

(1) In this Part of this Act—

'grant', unless the context otherwise requires, includes renew and renewal, and cognate words shall be construed accordingly;

'ice cream trading' means the selling, exposing or offering for sale of goods consisting wholly or mainly of ice cream, frozen confectionery or other similar commodities from a vehicle;

'itinerant ice cream trading' means ice cream trading from a vehicle which goes from place to place remaining in any one location in the course of trading for short periods only;

'licence street' means a street designated under section 24 (Designation of licence streets) of this Act;

'receptacle' includes a vehicle or stall and any basket, bag, box, vessel, stand, easel, board, tray or thing which is used (whether or not constructed or adapted for such use) as a container for or for the display of any article or thing or equipment used in the provision of any service;

'street' includes—

(a) any road or footway;

(b) any other area, not being within permanently enclosed premises, within 7 metres of any road or footway, to which the public have access without payment;

(c) any part of such road, footway or area;

(d) any part of any housing development provided or maintained by a local authority under Part II of the Housing Act 1985;

'street trading' means subject to subsection (2) below the selling or exposing or the offering for sale of any article (including a living thing) or the supplying or offering to supply any service in a street for gain or reward;

'street trading licence' means a licence granted under this Part of this Act and valid for the period specified therein being not less than six months and not more than three years;

'temporary licence' means a licence granted under this Part of this Act valid for a single day or for such period as may be specified in the licence not exceeding six months.

(2) The following are not street trading for the purposes of this Part of this Act—

(a) trading by a person acting as a pedlar under the authority of a Pedlar's Certificate granted under the Pedlars Act 1871;

(b) anything done in a market or fair the right to hold which was acquired by virtue of a grant (including a presumed grant) or acquired or established by virtue of any enactment or order;

(c) trading in a trunk road picnic area provided by the Secretary of State under section 112 of the Highways Act 1980;

(d) trading as a news-vendor provided that the only articles sold or exposed or offered for sale are newspapers or periodicals and they are sold or exposed or offered for sale without a receptacle for them or, if with a receptacle for them such receptacle does not—

(i) exceed 1 metre in length or width or 2 metres in height; or

(ii) occupy a ground area exceeding 0.25 square metre; or

(iii) stand on the carriageway of a street; or

(iv) cause undue interference or inconvenience to persons using the street;

(e) selling articles or things to occupiers of premises adjoining any street, or offering or exposing them for sale from a vehicle which is used only for the regular delivery of milk or other perishable goods to those persons;

(f) the use for trading under Part VIIA of the Highways Act 1980 of any object or structure placed on, in or over a highway;

(g) the operation of facilities for recreation or refreshment under Part VIIA of the Highways Act 1980;

(h) the doing of anything authorised by regulations made under section 5 of the Police, Factories, &c (Miscellaneous Provisions) Act 1916;

(i) trading in a highway in relation to which a control order under section 7 of the Local Government (Miscellaneous Provisions) Act 1976 is in force, other than trading to which the control order does not apply; and

(j) the sale, exposure or offer for sale of articles or offer or provision of services on any land comprised in a street (not being part of a highway) within the meaning of subsection (1) above by the owner or occupier of the land or by a bona fide employee of the owner or occupier of the land.

22. Application of Part III

This Part of this Act applies to the borough of a participating council as from the appointed day.

23. Licensing of street traders

(1) Subject to the provisions of this Part of this Act it shall be unlawful for any person to engage in street trading (whether or not in or from a stationary position) in any licence street within a borough unless that person is authorised to do so by a street trading licence or a temporary licence.

(2) For the purposes of this Part of this Act a person shall be deemed to engage in street trading whether or not he regularly carries on the business of street trading.

24. Designation of licence streets

(1) If a borough council consider that street trading should be licensed in their area they may from time to time pass any of the following resolutions—

(a) a resolution (in this Part of this Act referred to as a 'designating resolution') designating any street within the borough as a ' licence street';

(b) a resolution specifying in relation to any such street or any part of a street any class or classes of articles, things or services which they will, or other than which they will not, prescribe in any street trading licence granted by them in respect of that street;

and may from time to time by subsequent resolution rescind or vary any such resolution:

* * * * * *

Provided that a borough council shall—

(a) before passing a designating resolution, consult with the Commissioner of Police of the Metropolis on their proposal; and

(b) before rescinding or varying a designating resolution, consult with the licence holders trading in the street in question, or a body or bodies representative of them, on their proposal.

(2) At the appointed day for the purposes of this Part of this Act in a borough, the streets prescribed by any licences granted by the council of the borough in pursuance of powers contained in any of the enactments referred to in column (2) of Schedule 2 to this Act and then in force shall be deemed to have been designated as licence streets under a designating resolution.

(3) If a borough council pass a designating resolution the designation of the street shall take effect on the day specified in the resolution (which must not be before the expiration of the period of one month beginning with the day on which the resolution is passed).

(4) A borough council shall not pass a resolution or rescind or vary a resolution under this section unless—

(a) they have published notice of their intention to do so in a local newspaper circulating in their area;

(b) they have served a copy of the notice on the highway authority for that street (unless they are that highway authority); and

(c) where subsection (5) below applies, they have obtained the necessary consent.

(5) This subsection applies—

(a) where the resolution relates to a street which is owned or maintainable by a relevant corporation; and

(b) where the resolution designates as a licence street any street maintained by a highway authority;

and in subsection (4) above 'necessary consent' means—

(i) in the case mentioned in paragraph (a) above, the consent of the relevant corporation; and

(ii) in the case mentioned in paragraph (b) above, the consent of the highway authority.

(6) The following are relevant corporations for the purposes of this section—

(a) British Railways Board;

(b) London Regional Transport; and

(c) an urban development corporation established under the Local Government, Planning and Land Act 1980.

(7) The notice referred to in subsection (4) above shall

(a) contain a draft of the resolution to which it relates; and

(b) state that representations relating to it may be made in writing to the borough council within such period, not less than 28 days after the publication of the notice, as may be specified in the notice.

(8) As soon as practicable after the expiry of the period specified under subsection (7) above, the borough council shall consider any representations relating to the proposed resolution which they have received before the expiry of that period.

(9) After the borough council have considered those representations, they may if they think fit, pass such a resolution relating to the street as is mentioned in subsection (1) above.

(10) The borough council shall publish notice of the gassing of such a resolution in a local newspaper circulating in their area on two consecutive weeks.

(11) The first publication shall not be later than 28 days before the day specified in the resolution for the coming into force of the designation.

25. Application for street trading licences

(1) An application for a street trading licence or renewal of such a licence shall be made in writing to the borough council, and in the case of an application for the renewal of a licence shall be made not later than two months or earlier than three months before the date on which that licence unless revoked or surrendered will cease to be valid:

Provided that nothing in this section shall prevent a borough council from renewing a licence, other than a temporary licence notwithstanding that application has been made for such renewal at a later date than aforesaid if they consider it reasonable in the circumstances so to do.

(2) In the application, the applicant shall state—

(a) in the case of an application by an individual, his full name and address and date of birth;

(b) in the case of an application for a licence to carry on ice cream trading—

(i) by a company incorporated under the Companies Acts, the name of the company and its registered office;

(ii) by a partnership, the names of its members and the address of its principal office;

(c) the licence street in which, the days on which and the times between which he desires to trade;

(d) the description of articles, things or services in which he desires to trade; and

(e) such other particulars, relevant to street trading, as the borough council may reasonably require;

and may in the case of an individual specify the name and address of a relative of his who is associated with, or dependent upon, the business of street trading in respect of which the application is made and to whom he desires the licence to be granted in any of the events specified in subsection (1)(a) of section 26 (Succession) of this Act.

(3) No later than the date on which he submits his application, the applicant shall hand to an authorised officer two identical full-face photographs of himself, taken within the preceding 12 months, signed by the applicant on the reverse except where the application is made by a company incorporated under the Companies Acts, or by a partnership, for a licence to carry on ice cream trading.

(4) A street trading licence—

(a) shall not be granted—

(i) to a person under the age of 17 years; or

(ii) except where the application is made by a company incorporated under the Companies Acts, or by a partnership, for a licence to carry on ice cream trading to a person, on a corresponding day, days or time, who holds a street trading licence in any other licence street granted under this Part of this Act but nothing in this paragraph shall prevent the renewal of such a licence; or

(iii) except where the application is made by a company incorporated under the Companies Acts, or by a partnership, for a licence to carry on ice cream trading to a body corporate or to an unincorporated association; or

(iv) in respect of an application for a licence which is not a temporary licence to trade in a street which is not a licence street; or

(v) where the street to which the application relates is a street in respect of which the borough council have by resolution passed under subsection (1)(b) of section 24 (Designation of licence streets) of this Act specified a class of articles or things, or services which they will not prescribe in any street trading licence and the grant of the licence would be contrary to any of the terms of that resolution;

(b) shall not be granted unless the borough council are satisfied that there is enough space in the street for the applicant to engage in the trading in which he desires to engage without causing undue interference or inconvenience to persons or vehicular traffic using the street.

(5) Subject to subsection (4) above, the borough council shall grant an application for a street trading licence unless they consider that the application ought to be refused on one or more of the grounds specified in subsection (6) below.

(6) Subject to subsection (8) below the council may refuse an application on any of the following grounds—

(a) that there are enough traders trading in the street or in any street adjoining the street in respect of which the application is made in the goods in which the applicant desires to trade;

(b) that the applicant is on account of misconduct or for any other sufficient reason unsuitable to hold the licence;

(c) that the applicant is an individual who has without reasonable excuse failed personally to avail himself fully of a previous street trading licence;

(d) that the applicant has at any time been granted a street trading licence by the borough council which was revoked or could have been revoked on the grounds that he had refused or neglected to pay fees or other charges due to them in respect of the licence;

(e) that the applicant has failed to provide or to identify suitable or adequate premises for the storage of any receptacles or perishable goods in which he proposes to trade when street trading is not taking place;

(f) that—

(i) the application is for the grant (but not the renewal) of a street trading licence; and

(ii) the only available position is in that part of the street which is contiguous with the frontage of a shop; and

(iii) the articles, things or services mentioned in the application are sold or provided at the shop;

(g) that—

(i) the application is for the grant (but not the renewal) of a street trading licence; and

(ii) the only available position in the street is within the curtilage of a shop; and

(iii) the applicant is not the owner or occupier of the premises comprising the shop.

(7) If the borough council consider that grounds for refusal exist under subsection (6)(a) or (c) above they may grant the applicant a licence which permits him—

(a) to trade on fewer days or during a shorter period in each day than is specified in the application; or

(b) to trade only in one or more of the descriptions of goods specified in the application.

(8) Subject to subsection (4) above if—

(a) a person is at the appointed day licensed to trade in a street under the provisions of any local enactment; and

(b) the street becomes a licence street under this Part of this Act; and

(c) he was trading from a fixed position in the street immediately before it became a licence street; and

(d) within two months from the appointed day he applies for a street trading licence to trade in the street;

his application shall not be refused.

(9) Subject to subsections (4), (6) and (8) above a borough council when considering applications for licences to trade in licence streets under this Part of this Act shall give preference to applications from persons who immediately before the appointed day were under the provisions of any local enactment authorised to trade in a street in the borough which is not a licence street.

(10) A borough council when considering applications for licences to carry on ice cream trading in a licence street shall treat all applicants, whether companies, partnerships or individuals, on an equal footing and in particular—

(a) shall not treat individuals less favourably than companies or partnerships; and

(b) as between applicants who are companies or partnerships, shall not treat any particular company or partnership more favourably than others.

(11) A licence holder may at any time surrender his licence to the borough council and it shall then cease to be valid.

26. Succession

(1) (a) When the holder of a licence who is an individual has specified the name and address of a relative to whom he desires the licence to be granted—

(i) dies; or

(ii) retires having reached the normal age for retirement; or

(iii) notifies the borough council that owing to ill-health he is unable to continue to engage in the street trading permitted by the licence, and submits evidence to satisfy the borough council as to his ill-health;

the borough council shall not (except as provided in paragraph (b) of this subsection) grant a licence in respect of the position or place in a street at which the former licensee was entitled to engage in street trading under the authority of his licence until the expiration of 28 days from the date of the death of the licensee or his retirement or receiving the notification, as the case may be;

(b) If during the said period of 28 days the person specified by the holder of the licence, when making application for the licence, as the relative to whom he desired the licence to be granted in any of the events mentioned in paragraph (a) above makes application for the grant of a licence in respect of the position or place available in the street the borough council shall, save as provided by paragraphs (b) to (e) of subsection (6) of section 25 (Application for street trading licences) of this Act grant a licence to that person.

(2) For the purposes of this section a person shall be treated as being related to another if the latter is the wife, husband, father, mother, grandfather, grandmother, stepfather, stepmother, son, daughter, grandson, granddaughter, stepson, stepdaughter, brother, sister, half-brother or half-sister of the former and shall be deemed to be so related notwithstanding that he is so related only through an illegitimacy or in consequence of an adoption.

27. Conditions of street trading licences

(1) A licence granted under section 25 (Application for street trading licences) of this Act, shall—

(a) unless it is revoked or surrendered, be valid for a period of three years from the date on which it is granted, or for such shorter period as the borough council may determine;

(b) specify the conditions; and

(c) in the case of an individual incorporate one of the photographs of the licence holder submitted under subsection (3) of the said section 25;

and on any occasion of the renewal of a licence, or at 1st January in any year during the currency thereof, (whether on application by the licence holder or otherwise) or at any time on application by the licence holder, the borough council may vary the conditions.

(2) Where a licence is granted to a company incorporated under the Companies Acts or to a partnership to carry on ice cream trading, any individual carrying on ice cream trading in accordance with that licence shall at all times while he is so trading carry with him a recent photograph of him authenticated by the company or on behalf of the partnership, as the case may be, which holds the licence.

(3) The borough council may make regulations prescribing standard conditions which they may attach to the licence on the occasion of its grant or renewal.

(4) Before making regulations under subsection (3) above, the borough council shall—

(a) publish notice of their intention to do so in a local newspaper circulating in their area, and such notice shall—

(i) contain a draft of the resolution to which it relates; and

(ii) state that representations relating to it may be made in writing to the borough council within such period, not less than 28 days after the publication of the notice, as may be specified in the notice; and

(b) consult the licence holders or a body or bodies representative of them.

(5) As soon as practicable after the expiry of the period specified under subsection (4) above, the borough council shall consider any representations relating to the proposed regulations which they have received before the expiry of that period.

(6) After the borough council have considered those representations they may if they think fit make regulations as mentioned in subsection (3) above and shall notify the licence holders or a body or bodies representative of them of the making of such regulations.

(7) Without prejudice to the generality of subsection (3) above the standard conditions shall include such conditions as may be reasonable—

(a) identifying the street or streets in which and the position or place in any such street at which the licence holder may sell or expose or offer for sale articles or things, or offer or provide services under the authority of the licence;
(b) identifying the class or classes of articles, things or services which the licence holder may so sell or expose or offer for sale or provide;
(c) identifying the day or days on which and the time during which the licence holder may sell or expose or offer for sale articles, things or services as aforesaid;
(d) identifying the nature and type of any receptacle which may be used by the licence holder or in connection with any sale or exposure or offer for sale or provision of services and the number of any such receptacles which may be so used;
(e) requiring that any receptacle so used shall carry the name of the licence holder and the number of his licence;
(f) regulating the storage of receptacles or perishable goods;
(g) regulating the deposit and removal of refuse and the containers to be used for the deposit of such refuse and their location pending its removal;
(h) requiring that the licence holder shall commence trading or exercising his rights under the licence by a certain time on any day or forfeit his right to trade or exercise his rights under the licence on that day from the fixed position to which his licence refers.

(8) Without prejudice to the standard conditions, the borough council may in addition attach to a licence such further conditions as appear to them to be reasonable in any individual case.

(9) When granting a licence a borough council shall give to the licence holder a copy of the licence which, in the case of an individual, shall bear his photograph.

28. Revocation or variation of licences under Part III

(1) Subject to the provisions of this Part of this Act a borough council may at any time revoke a street trading licence if they are satisfied that—

(a) owing to circumstances which have arisen since the grant or renewal of the licence, there is not enough space in the street in which the licence holder trades for him to engage in the trading permitted by the licence without causing undue interference or inconvenience to persons or vehicular traffic using the street; or
(b) the licence holder is trading in a class of articles, things or services which the borough council have resolved under subsection (1)(b) of section 24 (Designation of licence streets) of this Act not to prescribe in licences granted for the licence street in which the licence holder trades; or
(c) the licence holder is an individual who has without reasonable excuse personally failed fully to avail himself of his licence; or
(d) the licence holder is on account of misconduct or for any other sufficient reason unsuitable to hold the licence; or
(e) that since the grant or renewal of the licence, the licence holder has for a period of four weeks or more failed to pay fees or charges due to the borough council in connection with the street trading licence or has failed to pay any charges due from him for accommodation provided in pursuance of subsection (2) of section 33 (Receptacles and containers) of this Act; or
(f) that since the grant or renewal of the licence, the licence holder has failed to make provision for the suitable and adequate storage of the receptacles used by

him for trading or for any perishable goods in which he trades when trading is not taking place; or

(g) that since the grant or renewal of the licence, the licence holder has persistently failed to remove to a place of storage the receptacles used by him for trading; or

(h) that the licence holder has persistently failed to comply with any condition of his licence.

(2) If a borough council consider that a licence could be revoked on any of the grounds mentioned in paragraphs (a) to (c) of subsection (1) above they may instead of revoking it, vary its conditions by attaching further conditions—

(a) reducing the number of days in any week or the period in any one day during which the licence holder is permitted to trade; or

(b) specifying a different licence street or position or place in any such street at which the licence holder may sell or expose or offer for sale articles or things or offer or provide services; or

(c) restricting the description of articles, things or services in which the licence holder is permitted to trade.

29. Further provisions relating to grant, renewal or revocation of street trading licences

(1) A borough council shall not—

(a) refuse to grant or renew a licence on any of the grounds mentioned in subsection (6) of section 25 (Application for street trading licences) of this Act; or

(b) revoke or vary a licence under section 28 (Revocation or variation of licences under Part III) of this Act; or

(c) vary a licence under subsection (1) of section 27 (Conditions of street trading licences) of this Act;

unless they shall have given to the applicant or licence holder not less than 21 days' previous notice in writing that objection has been or will be taken to such grant or renewal or that such revocation or variation is proposed, specifying the ground or grounds on which their decision would be based and giving him an opportunity to appear before the committee, sub-committee or officer determining the matter.

(2) A borough council shall not proceed to determine any of the matters referred to in subsection (1) above until after the expiry of the period specified in the notice given under that subsection; and in determining any of the matters referred to, they shall consider any representations made by an applicant or licence holder in respect of that matter.

(3) A borough council shall not refuse to grant or renew and shall not revoke a licence on the ground only that the applicant or licensee, being an individual, does not reside in the borough.

(4) If the borough council refuse to grant or renew a licence or decide to revoke or vary a licence—

(a) they shall notify the applicant or licence holder in writing of their decision and of the ground or grounds for such refusal, revocation or variation; and

(b) they shall notify the applicant or licence holder of his rights of appeal (if any) specified in the next following section.

30. Part III appeals

(1) Any person aggrieved—

(aa) by the refusal of a borough council to renew a licence because they are not satisfied as mentioned in subsection (4)(b) of section 25 (Application for street trading licences) of this Act;

(a) by the refusal of a borough council to grant or renew a licence on any of the grounds mentioned in subsection (6)(a) to (e) of section 25 (Application for street trading licences); or

(b) by a decision of a borough council under subsection (7) of the said section 25 to grant him a licence either on terms mentioned in that subsection different from those on the licence which he previously held or different from those for which he applied; or

(c) by any further condition attached by a borough council under subsection (8) of section 27 (Conditions of street trading licences) of this Act in addition to the standard conditions; or

(d) by a decision of the borough council either

(i) to vary the conditions of a licence under subsection (2) of section 28 (Revocation or variation of licences under Part III) of this Act; or

(ii) to revoke a licence under subsection (1) of the said section 28;

* * * * * *; or

(e) by a resolution of a borough council under section 37 (Ice cream trading) of this Act;

may appeal to a magistrates' court acting for the area in which the licence street is situated.

(2) An appeal under subsection (1) above may be brought—

(a) in the case of an appeal under paragraph (aa), (a), (b), (c) or (d) of that subsection, at any time before the expiration of the period of 21 days beginning with the date upon which notification in writing is given of the refusal or decision;

(b) in the case of an appeal under paragraph (e) of that subsection, at any time before the expiration of the period of 21 days beginning with the date of the second publication of the notice required by subsection (10) of section 24 (Designation of licence streets) as applied by the said section 37.

(3) A person desiring to appeal against such refusal or decision as is mentioned in subsection (1) above shall give a written notice to the magistrates' court and to the borough council specifying the refusal or decision against which he wishes to appeal and the grounds upon which such appeal is made.

(4) An appeal by either party against the decision of the magistrates' court under this section may be brought to the Crown Court.

(5) On an appeal to the magistrates' court or to the Crown Court under this section, the court may make such order as it thinks fit.

(6) Subject to subsections (7) to (9) below, it shall be the duty of the borough council to give effect to the order of the magistrates' court or the Crown Court.

(7) A borough council need not give effect to the order of the magistrates' court until the time for bringing an appeal under subsection (4) above has expired and, if such an appeal is duly brought, until the determination or abandonment of the appeal.

(8) Where a licence holder applies for renewal of his licence, his existing licence shall remain valid—

(a) until the grant by the borough council of a new licence with the same conditions; or

(b) if the borough council refuse renewal of the licence or decide to grant a licence with conditions different from those of the existing licence and he has a right of appeal under this section, until the time for bringing an appeal has expired or where an appeal is duly brought, until the determination or abandonment of the appeal; or

(c) if he has no right of appeal under this section until the borough council either grant him a new licence with conditions different from those of the existing licence or notify him of their decision to refuse his application.

(9) Where—

(a) a borough council decide—

(i) to vary the conditions of a licence under subsection (2) of the said section 28; or

(ii) to revoke a licence under subsection (1) of the said section 28; and

(b) a right of appeal is available to the licence holder under this section;

the variation or revocation shall not take effect until the time for bringing an appeal has expired or where an appeal is duly brought, until the determination or abandonment of the appeal.

(10) For the avoidance of doubt, it is hereby declared that an application under section 31 of the Supreme Court Act 1981 (application for judicial review) or under the Rules of the Supreme Court 1965 in respect of any matter which is or could be the subject of an appeal to the magistrates' court or to the Crown Court under this section shall not be treated as an appeal for the purposes of subsection (8) or (9) above.

(11) Any person aggrieved—

(a) by a resolution rescinding or varying a designating resolution,

(b) by a resolution under subsection (1)(b) of section 24 (Designation of licence streets) of this Act;

(c) by a standard condition prescribed by regulations under subsection (3) of section 27 (Conditions of street trading licences) of this Act; or

(d) by the amount of a fee or charge under section 32 (Fees and charges) of this Act;

may appeal to the Secretary of State whose decision shall be final.

(12) An appeal under subsection (11) above may be brought—

(a) in the case of an appeal under paragraph (a) or (b) of that subsection, at any time before the expiration of the period of three months beginning with the date on which notice of the passing of the resolution is published for the second time in accordance with subsection (10) of section 24 (Designation of licence streets) of this Act;

(b) in the case of an appeal under paragraph (c) of that subsection, at any time before the expiration of the period of three months beginning with the date upon which the licence holders or a body or bodies representative of them were notified of the making of the regulations;

(c) in the case of an appeal under paragraph (d) of that subsection—

(i) if it relates to the amount of a fee payable under subsection (1) of section 32 (Fees and charges) of this Act, at any time before the expiration of the period of three months beginning with the date on which the fee payable is notified to the licence holders or a body or bodies representative of them;

(ii) if it relates to the amount of a charge under subsection (2) of section 32 (Fees and charges) of this Act, at any time before the expiration of the period of three months beginning with the date on which notice of the determination of the charge has been given to the licence holders or a body or bodies representative of them.

31. Temporary licences

(1) A borough council may if they think fit on the receipt from any person of an application for that purpose and accompanied by the appropriate fee grant to that person a temporary licence.

(2) A temporary licence shall be valid only for the day or period specified in the licence and—

(a) shall be in the like form as a street trading licence with such modifications therein as the circumstances require; and

(b) shall prescribe such conditions as the borough council deem appropriate.

(3) Where the holder of a street trading licence is not for the time being exercising his rights under the licence, a temporary licence authorising street trading in the position or place prescribed by the street trading licence may be granted to any other person but shall be subject to the condition that it shall cease to be valid if during the currency thereof the holder of the licence desires to resume the exercise of his rights and gives the appropriate notice, and for the purposes of this subsection 'the appropriate notice' means—

(a) in the case of a holder of a licence who has not exercised his rights under the licence for a period of at least 14 days, 7 days' notice;

(b) in any other case, 24 hours' notice.

(4) In this section 'appropriate fee' means such fee as the borough council may have determined under section 32 (Fees and charges) of this Act.

32. Fees and charges

(1) A borough council may charge such fees for the grant or renewal of a street trading licence under this Part of this Act, the grant of a temporary licence or for the variation at the request of the licence holder of the conditions of a street trading licence as they may determine and as may be sufficient in the aggregate to cover in whole or in part the reasonable administrative or other costs in connection with their functions under this Part of this Act, not otherwise recovered.

(2) A borough council may recover from licence holders such charges as may be sufficient in the aggregate taking one year with another to cover the reasonable costs, not otherwise recovered, of—

(a) the collection, removal and disposal of refuse or other services rendered by them to such holders; and

(b) the cleansing of streets in which street trading takes place in so far as that cleansing is attributable to such trading; and

(c) any reasonable administrative or other costs incurred in connection with the administration of this Part of this Act; and

(d) the cost of enforcing the provisions of this Part of this Act.

(3) A borough council may determine—

(a) that charges under subsection (2) above shall be included in a fee payable under subsection (1) above; or

(b) that they shall be separately recoverable.

(4) A borough council may—

(a) require that every application for a licence under this Part of this Act be accompanied by the whole or part of the fee determined under subsection (1) above; and

(b) determine that the fee may be paid by instalments.

(5) Where a borough council refuse to * * renew a licence they shall repay to the person who made the application therefor the amount of any such fee paid by him * * .

(6) A borough council may determine the fees to be charged on the grant of a temporary licence under section 31 (Temporary licences) of this Act, and in doing so they shall have regard to the matters specified in subsection (2) above and such fees shall be included in the computation for the purposes of determining the fees and charges under subsections (1) and (2) above.

(7) Before determining charges to be made under subsection (2) above * * (whether originally or by way of variation of charges previously determined) a borough council—

(a) shall give notice of the proposed charges to licence holders or to a body or bodies representative of them; and

(b) shall publish notice of the proposed charges in a newspaper circulating in the area in which the licence street or streets in respect of which the charges will be applied is situated.

(7A) A notice under subsection (7)(a) above shall be accompanied by a statement showing how the proposed charges have been computed; and any body representative of licence holders may request the borough council to supply such further information or explanation with regard to the proposed charges as the body may reasonably require in order to ascertain whether the proposed charges are reasonable and have been computed in accordance with the provisions of this section.

(8) A notice under subsection (7)(a) above shall specify a reasonable period being not less than 28 days from the date of publication of the newspaper referred to in subsection (7)(b) above within which written representations concerning the proposed charges may be made to the borough council.

(9) It shall be the duty of a borough council to—

(a) consider any such representations which are made to them within the period specified in the notice; and

(b) comply with any request made under subsection (7A) above;

and where any such request is made the period so specified, if still current, shall be treated as extended by the number of days in the period beginning with the day on which the request is made and ending with that on which it is complied with.

* * * * * *

(10) When a borough council have determined fees under subsection (1) above or charges under subsection (2) above (whether originally or by way of variation of fees or charges previously determined) they shall give notice of the fees or charges so determined and of the date on which those fees or charges are to be brought into effect, in the manner prescribed in subsection (7) above.

(11) Where a licence is revoked under subsection (1)(a) or (b) of section 28 (Revocation or variation of licences under Part III) of this Act, the borough council shall refund the appropriate part of any fee paid for the grant or renewal of the licence.

(12) Where a licence is revoked otherwise than under subsection (1)(a) or (b) of section 28 (Revocation or variation of licences under Part III) or is surrendered, the borough council may remit or refund, as they consider appropriate, the whole or a part—

(a) of any fee paid for the grant or renewal of the licence; or

(b) of any charges recoverable under subsection (2) above.

33. Receptacles and containers

(1) A borough council may sell or let on hire or otherwise provide to any person holding a street trading licence or a temporary licence under this Part of this Act receptacles for use by him in street trading.

(2) A borough council may provide and maintain accommodation for the storage of receptacles and containers for the deposit of refuse arising in the course of street trading and for that purpose may—

(a) adapt any premises or erect any buildings on any land belonging to them but not already appropriated for such purpose; and

(b) make such charges as they think fit for the use of such accommodation.

34. Offences

Any person who—

(1) without reasonable excuse contravenes any of the conditions of a street trading licence or a temporary licence; or

(2) in connection with an application for a street trading licence or a temporary licence makes a statement which he knows to be false in a material particular; or

(3) resists or intentionally obstructs any authorised officer of a borough council in the execution of his duties under this Part of this Act; or

(4) fails on demand without reasonable excuse in the case of an individual licence holder to produce his licence duly signed by him and bearing his photograph, and, in the case of an individual carrying on ice cream trading under a licence granted to a company incorporated under the Companies Acts or to a partnership, to produce the photograph required by subsection (2) of section 27 (Conditions of street trading licences) of this Act to an authorised officer of the borough council or to a constable;

shall be guilty of an offence and shall be liable on summary conviction to a fine not exceeding level 3 on the standard scale.

35. Power to remove receptacles

(1) Where any receptacle used by a licence holder is not removed to a place of storage on the cessation of trading on any day it shall be lawful for the borough council to cause it to be removed to a place of storage and to recover from the licence holder the costs incurred by them in removing and storing the receptacle.

(2) Such charges as the borough council may fix as the cost of removing and storing a receptacle in pursuance of subsection (1) above, shall be payable by the licence holder before the return of the receptacle to him.

(3) The provisions of subsection (1) above are without prejudice to the power of the borough council to prosecute the licence holder for any breach of the conditions of his licence arising from the failure to remove the receptacle.

36. Employment of assistants

Subject to the provisions of this section a person holding a street trading licence may employ any other person to assist him in the conduct of street trading authorised by the licence but if any person employed by a licence holder during the temporary absence of the licence holder fails to comply with the conditions of the street trading licence held by his employer such failure shall be deemed to be a failure by the licence holder.

37. Ice cream trading

(1) Nothing in this Part of this Act shall apply to itinerant ice cream trading in any street unless—

(a) that street is a licence street; or

(b) the street has been designated as a prohibited street under the following provisions of this section.

(2) If at any time it is necessary to prohibit itinerant ice cream trading in any street in the area of a borough council which is not a licence street in the interests of preventing obstruction to traffic, or undue interference or inconvenience to persons using that street, the borough council may by resolution designate the street as a prohibited street and in the case of any London borough except the City of Westminster and the Royal Borough of Kensington and Chelsea may so designate it for such days or for such parts of days as are specified in the resolution, and may from time to time by subsequent resolution rescind or vary any such resolution.

(3) Before passing a resolution under this section, a borough council shall consult the Commissioner of Police of the Metropolis and such bodies as appear to them to be representative of persons carrying on ice cream trading in the area of the borough council.

(4) Subsections (3) to (11) of section 24 (Designation of licence streets) of this Act shall apply to a resolution under this section as they apply to a resolution under that section.

38. Unlicensed street trading

(1) A person who—

(a) is not the holder of a street trading licence or a temporary licence and who engages in street trading in a borough; or

(b) is the holder of a temporary licence and who engages in street trading in a borough on a day or in a place not specified in that temporary licence;

shall be guilty of an offence and shall be liable on summary conviction to a fine not exceeding level 3 on the standard scale.

* * * * * *

(2) In any proceedings for an offence under this section or for an offence of aiding, abetting, counselling or procuring the commission of an offence under this section where it is shown that—

(a) any article or thing was displayed (whether or not in or on any receptacle) in any street; or

(b) any receptacle or equipment used in the provision of any service was available in any street in such circumstances that a service was being offered;

the article or thing shall be presumed to have been exposed or offered for sale and the receptacle or equipment shall be presumed to have been available for the provision of a service at such time and in such position as it was displayed or available by the person having care or control or appearing to have care and control thereof unless in either case, it is shown to the satisfaction of the court that the article or thing or receptacle or equipment was brought into that street for some purpose other than for the purpose of selling it or exposing or offering it for sale or using it in the course of the provision of the service in a street.

(3) Where an offence under this section committed by a body corporate is proved to have been committed with the consent or connivance of, or to be attributable to any

neglect on the part of, any director, manager, secretary or other similar officer of the body corporate, or any person who was purporting to act in any such capacity, he, as well as the body corporate, shall be guilty of the offence and liable to the same maximum penalty as the body corporate.

(4) If an authorised officer or a constable has reasonable grounds for suspecting that a person has committed an offence under this section he may seize any article or thing being offered or exposed for sale or receptacle being used by that person which may be required to be used in evidence in any proceedings in respect of that offence or may be the subject of forfeiture under subsection (5) below provided that no article or thing which is of a perishable nature shall be seized under the provisions of this subsection.

(4A) (a) The following provisions of this subsection shall have effect where any article or thing (including any receptacle) is seized under subsection (4) above and references in those provisions to proceedings are to proceedings in respect of the alleged offence in relation to which the article or thing is seized.

(b) Subject to paragraph (e) below, at the conclusion of the proceedings the article or thing shall be returned to the person from whom it was seized unless the court orders it to be forfeited under subsection (5) below.

(c) Subject to paragraph (d) below, where a receptacle seized under subsection (4) above is a motor vehicle used for ice cream trading, the borough council or the Commissioner of Police of the Metropolis (as the case may be) shall, within three days of the receipt of an application in writing by the owner or registered keeper of the vehicle, permit him to remove it.

(d) Paragraph (c) above shall not apply where—

(i) the owner or registered keeper of the vehicle has been convicted of an offence under this Part of this Act; or

(ii) the owner or registered keeper of the vehicle is being prosecuted for a previous alleged offence under this Part of this Act; or

(iii) the vehicle has been used in the commission of such an offence or previous alleged offence;

if the offence or previous alleged offence was committed or is alleged to have been committed no more than three years before the seizure and (in the case of an alleged offence) the proceedings are continuing.

(e) If no proceedings are instituted before the expiration of a period of 28 days beginning with the date of seizure, or any proceedings instituted within that period are discontinued, at the expiration of that period or, as the case may be, on the discontinuance of the proceedings, the article or thing shall be returned to the person from whom it was seized unless it has not proved possible, after diligent enquiry, to identify that person and ascertain his address.

(f) Where the article or thing is not returned because it has not proved possible to identify the person from whom it was seized and ascertain his address the borough council (whether the article or thing was seized by a constable or by an authorised officer) may apply to a magistrates' court for an order as to the manner in which it should be dealt with.

(5) Subject to subsection (6) below the court by or before which a person is convicted of an offence under this section or for an offence of aiding, abetting, counselling or procuring the commission of an offence under this section may order anything produced to the court, and shown to the satisfaction of the court to relate to the offence, to be forfeited and dealt with in such manner as the court may order.

(6) The court shall not order anything to be forfeited under subsection (5) above where a person claiming to be the owner of or otherwise interested in it applies to be heard by the court, unless an opportunity has been given to him to show cause why the order should not be made and in considering whether to make such an order a court shall have regard—

(i) to the value of the property; and

(ii) to the likely financial and other effects on the offender of the making of the order (taken together with any other order that the court contemplates making).

(7) An authorised officer shall produce his authority if required to do so by the person having care or control of * * anything seized in pursuance of the powers in subsection (4) above.

(8) (a) This subsection shall have effect where—

(i) an article, thing or receptacle is seized under subsection (4) above; and

(ii) (A) not less than six months have passed since the date of the seizure and no information has been laid against any person for an offence under this section in respect of the acts or circumstances which occasioned the seizure; or

(B) proceedings for such an offence have been brought and either the person charged has been acquitted (whether or not on appeal) and the time for appealing against or challenging the acquittal (where applicable) has expired without an appeal or challenge being brought, or the proceedings (including any appeal) have been withdrawn by, or have failed for want of prosecution by, the person by whom the original proceedings were brought.

(b) When this subsection has effect a person who has or at the time of seizure had a legal interest in the article, thing or receptacle seized may recover compensation from the borough council or (where it is seized by a constable) the Commissioner of Police of the Metropolis by civil action in the County Court in respect of any loss suffered by him as a result of the seizure.

(c) The court may not make an order for compensation under paragraph (b) above unless it is satisfied that seizure was not lawful under subsection (4) above.

39. Savings

(1) Nothing in this Part of this Act shall affect—

(a) section 13 of the Markets and Fairs Clauses Act 1847 (prohibition of sales elsewhere than in a market or in shops etc) as applied by any other Acts;

(b) section 56 of the Food Act 1984 (prohibition of certain sales during market hours);

(c) the sale or exposure or offer for sale by London Regional Transport or (as the case may be) a designated company (within the meaning of the Transport (London) Act 1969) of refreshments at any shelter or other accommodation provided by either of them under section 65 (Refreshment shelters etc) of the London Passenger Transport Act 1938.

(2) Nothing in this Part of this Act shall afford a defence to a charge in respect of any offence at common law or under an enactment other than this Part of this Act.

40. Local enactments relating to street trading repealed

(1) Subject to subsection (2) below, the enactments specified in column (2) of Schedule 2 to this Act, so far as they relate to any part of Greater London, shall cease to have effect

in a borough as from the appointed day for that borough to the extent specified in column (3) of that Schedule.

(2) Notwithstanding the repeal of the enactments specified in column (2) of Schedule 2 to this Act, any licence granted by a borough council under any of those enactments which authorises street trading in the borough and which was in force immediately before the appointed day shall continue in force until three months after the appointed day or until the determination of any application made by the holder of the licence under section 25 (Application for street trading licences) of this Act, whichever is the later.

41. Savings for sales in legal markets or fairs

In the case of any market or fair held in pursuance of any statute, royal licence, royal charter or letters patent, or as of right from time immemorial, nothing in this Part of this Act shall affect the sale or exposure or offer for sale of goods in any such market or fair by any person who has paid a toll to, or is acting under the written authority of, a person holding or entitled to hold such market or fair or entitled to receive tolls in respect of sales made or stalls or stands occupied in such market or fair.

EMPLOYMENT RIGHTS ACT 1996

(Eliz II, 1996, c 18)

An Act to consolidate enactments relating to employment rights.

[22nd May 1996]

* * * * * *

PART IV

SUNDAY WORKING FOR SHOP AND BETTING WORKERS

Protected shop workers and betting workers

36. Protected shop workers and betting workers

(1) Subject to subsection (5), a shop worker or betting worker is to be regarded as 'protected' for the purposes of any provision of this Act if (and only if) subsection (2) or (3) applies to him.

(2) This subsection applies to a shop worker or betting worker if—

(a) on the day before the relevant commencement date he was employed as a shop worker or a betting worker but not to work only on Sunday,

(b) he has been continuously employed during the period beginning with that day and ending with the day which, in relation to the provision concerned, is the appropriate date, and

(c) throughout that period, or throughout every part of it during which his relations with his employer were governed by a contract of employment, he was a shop worker or a betting worker.

(3) This subsection applies to any shop worker or betting worker whose contract of employment is such that under it he—

(a) is not, and may not be, required to work on Sunday, and

(b) could not be so required even if the provisions of this Part were disregarded.

(4) Where on the day before the relevant commencement date an employee's relations with his employer had ceased to be governed by a contract of employment, he shall be regarded as satisfying subsection (2)(a) if—

(a) that day fell in a week which counts as a period of employment with that employer under section 212(2) or (3) or under regulations under section 219, and

(b) on the last day before the relevant commencement date on which his relations with his employer were governed by a contract of employment, the employee was employed as a shop worker or a betting worker but not to work only on Sunday.

(5) A shop worker is not a protected shop worker, and a betting worker is not a protected betting worker, if—

(a) he has given his employer an opting-in notice on or after the relevant commencement date, and

(b) after giving the notice, he has expressly agreed with his employer to do shop work, or betting work, on Sunday or on a particular Sunday.

(6) In this Act 'opting-in notice', in relation to a shop worker or a betting worker, means written notice, signed and dated by the shop worker or betting worker, in which the shop worker or betting worker expressly states that he wishes to work on Sunday or that he does not object to Sunday working.

(7) In this Act 'the relevant commencement date' means—
(a) in relation to a shop worker, 26th August 1994, and
(b) in relation to a betting worker, 3rd January 1995.

37. Contractual requirements relating to Sunday work

(1) Any contract of employment under which a shop worker or betting worker who satisfies section 36(2)(a) was employed on the day before the relevant commencement date is unenforceable to the extent that it—
(a) requires the shop worker to do shop work, or the betting worker to do betting work, on Sunday on or after that date, or
(b) requires the employer to provide the shop worker with shop work, or the betting worker with betting work, on Sunday on or after that date.

(2) Subject to subsection (3), any agreement entered into after the relevant commencement date between a protected shop worker, or a protected betting worker, and his employer is unenforceable to the extent that it—
(a) requires the shop worker to do shop work, or the betting worker to do betting work, on Sunday, or
(b) requires the employer to provide the shop worker with shop work, or the betting worker with betting work, on Sunday.

(3) Where, after giving an opting-in notice, a protected shop worker or a protected betting worker expressly agrees with his employer to do shop work or betting work on Sunday or on a particular Sunday (and so ceases to be protected), his contract of employment shall be taken to be varied to the extent necessary to give effect to the terms of the agreement.

(4) The reference in subsection (2) to a protected shop worker, or a protected betting worker, includes a reference to an employee who although not a protected shop worker, or protected betting worker, at the time when the agreement is entered into is a protected shop worker, or protected betting worker, on the day on which she returns to work in accordance with section 79, or in pursuance of an offer made in the circumstances described in section 96(3), after a period of absence from work occasioned wholly or partly by pregnancy or childbirth.

(5) For the purposes of section 36(2)(b), the appropriate date—
(a) in relation to subsections (2) and (3) of this section, is the day on which the agreement is entered into, and
(b) in relation to subsection (4) of this section, is the day on which the employee returns to work.

38. Contracts with guaranteed hours

(1) This section applies where—
(a) under the contract of employment under which a shop worker or betting worker who satisfies section 36(2)(a) was employed on the day before the relevant commencement date, the employer is, or may be, required to provide him with shop work, or betting work, for a specified number of hours each week,
(b) under the contract the shop worker or betting worker was, or might have been, required to work on Sunday before that date, and
(c) the shop worker has done shop work, or the betting worker betting work, on Sunday in that employment (whether or not before that day) but has, on or after that date, ceased to do so.

(2) So long as the shop worker remains a protected shop worker, or the betting worker remains a protected betting worker, the contract shall not be regarded as requiring the employer to provide him with shop work, or betting work, on weekdays in excess of the hours normally worked by the shop worker or betting worker on weekdays before he ceased to do shop work, or betting work, on Sunday.

(3) For the purposes of section 36(2)(b), the appropriate date in relation to this section is any time in relation to which the contract is to be enforced.

39. Reduction of pay etc

(1) This section applies where—

(a) under the contract of employment under which a shop worker or betting worker who satisfies section 36(2)(a) was employed on the day before the relevant commencement date, the shop worker or betting worker was, or might have been, required to work on Sunday before the relevant commencement date,

(b) the shop worker has done shop work, or the betting worker has done betting work, on Sunday in that employment (whether or not before that date) but has, on or after that date, ceased to do so, and

(c) it is not apparent from the contract what part of the remuneration payable, or of any other benefit accruing, to the shop worker or betting worker was intended to be attributable to shop work, or betting work, on Sunday.

(2) So long as the shop worker remains a protected shop worker, or the betting worker remains a protected betting worker, the contract shall be regarded as enabling the employer to reduce the amount of remuneration paid, or the extent of the other benefit provided, to the shop worker or betting worker in respect of any period by the relevant proportion.

(3) In subsection (2) 'the relevant proportion' means the proportion which the hours of shop work, or betting work, which (apart from this Part) the shop worker, or betting worker, could have been required to do on Sunday in the period ('the contractual Sunday hours') bears to the aggregate of those hours and the hours of work actually done by the shop worker, or betting worker, in the period.

(4) Where, under the contract of employment, the hours of work actually done on weekdays in any period would be taken into account determining the contractual Sunday hours, they shall be taken into account in determining the contractual Sunday hours for the purposes of subsection (3).

(5) For the purposes of section 36(2)(b), the appropriate date in relation to this section is the end of the period in respect of which the remuneration is paid or the benefit accrues.

Opting-out of Sunday work

40. Notice of objection to Sunday working

(1) A shop worker or betting worker to whom this section applies may at any time give his employer written notice, signed and dated by the shop worker or betting worker, to the effect that he objects to Sunday working.

(2) In this Act 'opting-out notice' means a notice given under subsection (1) by a shop worker or betting worker to whom this section applies.

(3) This section applies to any shop worker or betting worker who under his contract of employment—

(a) is or may be required to work on Sunday (whether or not as a result of previously giving an opting-in notice), but
(b) is not employed to work only on Sunday.

41. Opted-out shop workers and betting workers

(1) Subject to subsection (2), a shop worker or betting worker is regarded as 'opted-out' for the purposes of any provision of this Act if (and only if)—
(a) he has given his employer an opting-out notice,
(b) he has been continuously employed during the period beginning with the day on which the notice was given and ending with the day which, in relation to the provision concerned, is the appropriate date, and
(c) throughout that period, or throughout every part of it during which his relations with his employer were governed by a contract of employment, he was a shop worker or a betting worker.

(2) A shop worker is not an opted-out shop worker, and a betting worker is not an opted out betting worker, if—
(a) after giving the opting-out notice concerned, he has given his employer an opting-in notice, and
(b) after giving the opting-in notice, he has expressly agreed with his employer to do shop work, or betting work, on Sunday or on a particular Sunday.

(3) In this Act 'notice period', in relation to an opted-out shop worker or an opted-out betting worker, means, subject to section 42(2), the period of three months beginning with the day on which the opting-out notice concerned was given.

42. Explanatory statement

(1) Where a person becomes a shop worker or betting worker to whom section 40 applies, his employer shall, before the end of the period of two months beginning with the day on which that person becomes such a worker, give him a written statement in the prescribed form.

(2) If—
(a) an employer fails to comply with subsection (1) in relation to any shop worker or betting worker, and
(b) the shop worker or betting worker, on giving the employer an opting-out notice, becomes an opted-out shop worker or an opted-out betting worker,

section 41(3) has effect in relation to the shop worker or betting worker with the substitution for 'three months' of 'one month'.

(3) An employer shall not be regarded as failing to comply with subsection (1) in any case where, before the end of the period referred to that subsection, the shop worker or betting worker has given him an opting-out notice.

(4) Subject to subsection (6), the prescribed form in the case of a shop worker is as follows—

'STATUTORY RIGHTS IN RELATION TO SUNDAY SHOP WORK

You have become employed as a shop worker and are or can be required under your contract of employment to do the Sunday work your contract provides for.

However, if you wish, you can give a notice, as described in the next paragraph, to your employer and you will then have the right not to work in or about a shop on any Sunday on which the shop is open once three months have passed from the date on which you gave the notice.

Your notice must—

be in writing;

be signed and dated by you;

say that you object to Sunday working.

For three months after you give the notice, your employer can still require you to do all the Sunday work your contract provides for. After the three month period has ended, you have the right to complain to an industrial tribunal if, because of your refusal to work on Sundays on which the shop is open, your employer—

dismisses you, or

does something else detrimental to you, for example, failing to promote you.

Once you have the rights described, you can surrender them only by giving your employer a further notice, signed and dated by you, saying that you wish to work on Sunday or that you do not object to Sunday working and then agreeing with your employer to work on Sundays or on a particular Sunday.'

(5) Subject to subsection (6), the prescribed form in the case of betting worker is as follows—

'STATUTORY RIGHTS IN RELATION TO SUNDAY BETTING WORK

You have become employed under a contract of employment under which you are or can be required to do Sunday betting work, that is to say, work—

at a track on a Sunday on which your employer is taking bets at the track, or

in a licensed betting office on a Sunday on which it is open for business.

However, if you wish, you can give a notice, as described in the next paragraph, to your employer and you will then have the right not to do Sunday betting work once three months have passed from the date on which you gave the notice.

Your notice must—

be in writing;

be signed and dated by you;

say that you object to doing Sunday betting work.

For three months after you give the notice, your employer can still require you to do all the Sunday betting work your contract provides for. After the three month period has ended, you have the right to complain to an industrial tribunal if, because of your refusal to do Sunday betting work, your employer—

dismisses you, or

does something else detrimental to you, for example, failing to promote you.

Once you have the rights described, you can surrender them only by giving your employer a further notice, signed and dated by you, saying that you wish to do Sunday betting work or that you do not object to doing Sunday betting work and then agreeing with your employer to do such work on Sundays or on a particular Sunday.'

(6) The Secretary of State may by order amend the prescribed forms set out in subsections (4) and (5).

43. Contractual requirements relating to Sunday work

(1) Where a shop worker or betting worker gives his employer an opting-out notice, the contract of employment under which he was employed immediately before he gave that notice becomes unenforceable to the extent that it—

(a) requires the shop worker to do shop work, or the betting worker to do betting work, on Sunday after the end of the notice period, or

(b) requires the employer to provide the shop worker with shop work, or the betting worker with betting work, on Sunday after the end of that period.

(2) Subject to subsection (3), any agreement entered into between an opted-out shop worker, or an opted-out betting worker, and his employer is unenforceable to the extent that it—

(a) requires the shop worker to do shop work, or the betting worker to do betting work, on Sunday after the end of the notice period, or

(b) requires the employer to provide the shop worker with shop work, or the betting worker with betting work, on Sunday after the end of that period.

(3) Where, after giving an opting-in notice, an opted-out shop worker or an opted-out betting worker expressly agrees with his employer to do shop work or betting work on Sunday or on a particular Sunday (and so ceases to be opted-out), his contract of employment shall be taken to be varied to the extent necessary to give effect to the terms of the agreement.

(4) The reference in subsection (2) to an opted-out shop worker, or an opted-out betting worker, includes a reference to an employee who although not an opted-out shop worker, or an opted-out betting worker, at the time when the agreement is entered into—

(a) had given her employer an opting-out notice before that time, and

(b) is an opted-out shop worker, or an opted-out betting worker, on the day on which she returns to work in accordance with section 79, or in pursuance of an offer made in the circumstances described in section 96(3), after a period of absence from work occasioned wholly or partly by pregnancy or childbirth.

(5) For the purposes of section 41(1)(b), the appropriate date—

(a) in relation to subsections (2) and (3) of this section, is the day on which the agreement is entered into, and

(b) in relation to subsection (4) of this section, is the day on which the employee returns to work.

* * * * * *

APPENDIX A

Model Byelaws[1]

Made by the Council of in exercise of its powers under s 60 of the Food Act 1984 in respect of its open markets at , the Market Hall at and the livestock markets at[2]

Interpretation

1. In these Byelaws

(a) 'the Council' means the Council of

(b) 'open market'[3] means the open markets at respectively;

(c) 'the Market Hall' means the building known as and situate

(d) 'market place' means an open market and the Market Hall;

(e) 'livestock market' means the cattle markets maintained by the Council at respectively;

(f) 'animal' means[4] any bull, ox, cow, heifer, calf, horse, ass, mule, ram, wether, ewe, lamb, goat, kid, swine, rabbit or hare except where the context otherwise requires;

(g) 'goods' includes provisions, commodities and articles brought into the market place for the purpose of sale;

(h) 'market hours' means the hours appointed by the Council (under s 52 of the Food Act 1984) for the holding of a market;

(i) 'Market Officer' means the person appointed by the Council to exercise general management, supervision and control of a market place or livestock market or his duly authorised representative;

(j) 'poultry' means[4] turkeys, geese, ducks or any other bird or fowl both game and domesticated except where the context otherwise requires;

---

1 Based on byelaws in operation in Montgomeryshire District and confirmed by the Secretary of State for Wales in December 1981. The procedure for confirmation of byelaws is that set out in the Local Government Act 1972, s 236. It is recommended that, at draft stage, the fullest consultation with interested parties takes place. The following consultees are suggested: the highway authority; parish/community councils; the police; traders or their Association.

The courts will construe a byelaw so as to give effect, as far as reasonably possible, to the intention of the authority which made it. Cases concerning street trading and the construction of byelaws include *McQuade v Barnes* [1949] 1 All ER 154 (verbal touting); *Raymond v Cook* [1958] 1 WLR 1098 (musical ice cream van); *John v Heath* [1958] Crim LR 385 (noisy instrument).

Any provision of a local Act which confers power on a local authority to make byelaws appointing days on which or hours during which markets or fairs are to be or may be held, must be construed as conferring on the authority a power to appoint such days or hours by resolution (Local Government (Miscellaneous Provisions) Act 1976, s 36(1)).

2 The byelaws are drafted so as to have the widest possible application.

3 A local authority may, by resolution, define the physical market limits within the open market area (subject to the provision of sufficient accommodation) and also, after giving reasonable notice, remove the market to another convenient place within that area. It is better practice not to define the current market limits in the byelaws since, should the market be removed subsequently, it would no doubt be contended that the byelaws had no application in the new market place.

4 Cf definition in the Animal Health Act 1981, s 87.

(k) 'sell' and 'sale' include exposing and exposure for sale;
(l) 'stall' includes a building, shop, office, compartment, standing bench, table, place, pitch, site or space in a market place and used or intended to be used for the sale of goods;
(m) 'vehicle' includes any mechanically propelled vehicle (other than an invalid chair) and any cycle, tricycle, wheelbarrow, cart, handcart, truck, wagon or trailer.

Regulations of Traffic and Prevention of Obstruction

2. Subject to the provisions of Byelaw 5, no person in charge of a vehicle shall (a) drive or allow it to be driven onto a pavement or footway in an open market or (b) allow it to be halted in or on any avenue, passage, roadway, pavement or footway in an open market or a livestock market, or in the immediate approaches thereto for longer than is reasonably necessary for the loading or unloading of goods or animals.

3. Subject to the provisions of Byelaw 5, no person shall bring or carry to, through or from a livestock market or a market place or the immediate approaches thereto or allow to stand therein any vehicle, goods or animals in such a manner as to cause obstruction (a) in a livestock market or in a market place or in the immediate approaches thereto or (b) without prejudice to the generality of (a) above to the use of fire fighting equipment.

Provided[5] that nothing in this and the immediately preceding Byelaw shall apply to any vehicle constructed or adapted for the sale of goods therefrom and positioned in an open market with the consent of the Market Officer on a site allocated by him or at a place set apart by the Council and indicated by the display in a conspicuous place of a public notice to that effect.

4. Subject to the provisions of Byelaw 5, no person shall cause or permit any vehicle to be driven in a livestock market otherwise than in a direction indicated by signs or road surface markings erected or laid by or on behalf of the Council for the purpose of indicating the direction to be taken by vehicles in a livestock market or as directed by the Market Officer.

5. No person driving or riding any vehicle in a livestock market or in the immediate approaches thereto shall proceed at a greater speed than ten miles per hour.

Provided that nothing in this Byelaw or Byelaws 2, 3 and 4 shall apply to any vehicle being used for fire brigade, ambulance, police or refuse disposal purposes in pursuance of statutory powers or duties.

6. No person shall deposit or cause to be deposited in a market place (elsewhere than in, at or upon any stall which has been allocated to him) any goods or any receptacle for goods for a longer time or in any other manner than is reasonably necessary for the loading or unloading of the goods.

---

5 This proviso recognises the increasing use being made of such dual purpose vehicles, perhaps a trend which ought to be discouraged for reasons of visual appeal and also possible damage to the highway (where the 'stall' is removable from the vehicle and stands on legs). On the other hand, the obstruction commonly caused at times of loading and unloading is likely to be reduced if such vehicles are used. There are also obvious advantages to those traders selling meat and fish when refrigeration is required.

7. No goods nor any receptacle for goods shall be placed in or on any stall in a market place so as to project beyond the limits of such stall.

8. No part of any roof of a stall shall be less than 6ft 6in from the ground.

9. No tenant or occupier of a stall in an open market shall hang any goods on or from such stall in a manner or in a position likely to cause danger.

10. No person shall wilfully obstruct, disturb or hinder any person in the proper use of a market place or a livestock market or of the immediate approaches thereto or of any fittings trolleys or other apparatus provided for use therein and without prejudice to the generality of the foregoing no person shall without the written consent of the Market Officer pitch or occupy any stall, or place any goods, on a pavement or footway in an open market.

11. No person shall without the consent of the Market Officer or other reasonable excuse allow any animal, poultry or goods belonging to him, or in his charge, to remain in a market place or livestock market more than one hour after the market closes.

Provided that this Byelaw shall not apply to the tenants or occupiers (or their employees) of the lock-up shops or storage facilities provided by the Council within the Market Hall or a livestock market.

Authority to Use Space[6]

12. No person shall occupy or take possession of any stall or deposit or cause to be deposited any goods equipment or utensils on any stall in a market place unless and until such stall has been duly let or otherwise allocated by the Market Officer for the use of such person.

13. No person shall erect or fix or attempt to erect or fix any stall in a market place without the previous written consent of the Market Officer.

---

6 Although a local authority, or other market owner, is under no obligation to provide stalls (see, eg *Brackenborough v Spalding UDC* [1942] AC 310), this is not an uncommon practice. If traders provide their own stalls (and the byelaws have been drafted on this basis), generally they may only be erected in the market place by licence of the market owner, regardless of the ownership of the soil. It is obviously desirable that control be exercised over the size of individual stalls, but the Welsh Office has expressed the view that the powers given by s 60 of the Food Act 1984 are not sufficiently wide to allow a byelaw dealing specifically with stall size; and such a byelaw may be unreasonable. With respect, it is submitted that this interpretation is too narrow, since stall size is a factor which is important to the control and regulation of, in particular, street markets (the problem should not, of course, arise where the local authority is the owner of the soil) and for preventing nuisances and obstructions. It may also be noted that street trading licences issued under the Local Government (Miscellaneous Provisions) Act 1982, s 3 and Schedule 4 (which powers are not available in respect of a market or fair acquired or established by virtue of grant, enactment or order: *ibid*, Schedule 4, paragraph 1(2)(b)) may be made subject to a condition specifying the size and type of a stall (*ibid*, Schedule 4, paragraph 4(5)(a)). However, byelaws 12 and 13, in particular, should obviate the need for a specific byelaw restricting stall size since it will be open to the market officer to refuse consent to the erection of any stall which he reasonably considers to be too large or which is likely, by reason of size and position, to cause nuisance or obstruction. (Stall size is specified in the Model Regulations, *below*.)

14. Where the Council:
(a) appropriates any part of a market place for the sale of goods or any class of goods for sales by auction; and
(b) displays in a conspicuous place a public notice to that effect;
no person shall sell goods or hold sales by auction, except in accordance with the terms of that appropriation.

15. Every tenant or occupier of a lock-up shop in the Market Hall or a livestock market shall put up and keep up during the period of his occupation of such shop or stall his name (including a trade name, if any) and address[7] in letters of a legible size on a prominent part thereof and every occupier of a stall in an open market shall supply his name (including a trade name, if any) and address to the Market Officer who will allocate to such occupier a number which shall be painted or otherwise exhibited upon the stall in such position as shall be approved by the Market Officer and the occupier of the said stall shall maintain such number legible and undefaced.

For Maintaining Cleanliness

16. Every tenant or occupier of a stall shall—
(a) cause the stall to be properly cleansed before and after the sale of goods for the day and as often as may be necessary during the day;
(b) as often as is necessary cause all refuse from the stall, and all refuse arising from the loading or unloading of goods required in connection with the use of the stall to be removed, without creating a nuisance or obstruction.

For Preservation of Order

17. No person shall wilfully or negligently throw, drop or leave in or upon any avenue, roadway or passage in a market place or a livestock market any fruit or vegetable matter or any other litter in a manner likely to cause injury or nuisance to any person.

Provided that this Byelaw shall not apply in respect of any place in the open air to which the Litter Act 1983 or any amendment thereof applies.

18. No person other than the Market Officer shall light a fire in any part of a market place or livestock market.

19. Every light used in connection with a stall shall be extinguished not later than one hour after the market closes.

20. No person shall in any market place ring any bell or blow any horn or use any other noisy instrument or any amplifier or loudspeaker to attract the attention or custom of any person to any sale or to any goods intended for sale.

21. No person shall wilfully or improperly soil, defile, damage or destroy any part of a market place or livestock market or any ornamental trees or shrubs therein or in the approaches thereto or any of the fittings or apparatus provided by the Council for use in a market place or livestock market.

---

7 Following repeal of the Registration of Business Names Act 1916, the National Market Traders' Federation has confirmed with the Companies Registration Office that members of the Federation may display the Head Office address of the Federation instead of their private addresses.

22. No person other than an officer or servant of the Council acting in the proper execution of his duty, shall post or display any bill, placard or poster, other than a description or statement of the price of goods then or thereafter exposed or intended to be exposed for sale or the name and address of a stallholder in or on part of a market place or livestock market.

23. Unless the written consent of the Market Officer be first obtained no person in a market place or livestock market shall, except by way of sale, distribute or attempt to distribute to the public in the market place any leaflets, handbills, cards, pamphlets, booklets or other literature.

Explosives

24. No person shall to the danger of any person, keep, store or sell any gunpowder fireworks or other explosive substance or any naphtha, bottled gas, petroleum or paraffin oil or other flammable substance in a market place or a livestock market.

Provided that nothing in this Byelaw shall apply to any appliances fittings or apparatus necessary for lighting a stall so long as the same complies with the requirements of the British Standards Institute.

Use of Water Taps

25. Every person who shall use any water tap in a market place or livestock market shall cause the same to be properly turned off immediately after he shall have finished using such tap.

Animals

26. (a) No person shall bring into or allow to remain in the Market Hall any dog or animal belonging to him or in his charge and

(b) No person shall bring any dog into a livestock market or any part of a market place appropriated for the sale or exhibition of animals unless the said dog is a working dog brought into a livestock market or market place for the purpose of controlling animals.

27. No stallholder shall keep any dog or animal at his stall[8].

Provided that nothing in this and Byelaw 26 shall prevent a blind person from bringing into and keeping in a market place any guide dog belonging to him or in his charge.

Livestock Markets

28. No person shall enter or remain in any sale ring or pen in a livestock market during the time such sale ring or pen is being used for the sale of any animal or poultry.

Provided that this Byelaw shall not apply so as to prohibit the owner of the animal or poultry offered for sale or a person offering the animal or poultry for sale with the authority of the owner or a drover nominated by such owner or person from entering or remaining in such sale ring for the purpose of controlling the animal or poultry.

---

8 It is now an offence to carry on a business of selling animals as pets in any part of a street or public place or at a stall or barrow in a market (Pet Animals Act 1951 as amended by the Pet Animals Act 1951 (Amendment) Act 1983).

29. No person shall slaughter any animal or poultry in a livestock market or in the immediate approaches thereto except where it is necessary to prevent suffering by that animal or poultry.

Provided that nothing in this Byelaw shall prevent the slaughtering of an animal or poultry under the Animal Health Act 1981[9].

Penalties

30. Every person who shall offend against any of these Byelaws shall be liable on summary conviction to a fine not exceeding [level 2 on the standard scale].

Repeal of Byelaws

31. The Byelaws relating to markets which were made by the [Borough] Council and confirmed by the Secretary of State on the day of are hereby repealed.

GIVEN under the Common Seal of Council this day of One thousand nine hundred and

9 See ss 31–34 and Schedule 3.

Department of the Environment, Memo 7D

APPLICATIONS TO THE SECRETARY OF STATE FOR CONFIRMATION OF BYELAWS UNDER SECTION 236[10] OF THE LOCAL GOVERNMENT ACT 1972

---

1. The council should pass a resolution—

(a) authorising the affixing of the common seal to the byelaws and

(b) authorising the Chief Executive to carry out the necessary procedure and apply to the Secretary of State for confirmation.

2. The seal should be affixed and duly attested, and the date of sealing inserted in the attestation.

The date of sealing, and *not* the date of the resolution, is the date on which the byelaws are made, and until they are made the council have no power to carry out the rest of the statutory procedure.

3. At least one clear calendar month before applying to the Secretary of State for confirmation:—

A. Notice of the council's intention to apply for confirmation must be given in one or more local newspapers circulating in the area to which the byelaws will apply.

A suggested form of notice is appended to this memorandum. A series of byelaws should be described by giving the heading it bears on the draft informally approved by the Secretary of State. If the byelaws are to apply to part only of the council's district, the notice should explain which part will be affected.

B. A copy of the byelaws must be deposited at the council's offices and be open to public inspection without charge at all reasonable times during that month.

4. The byelaws may be submitted for confirmation any time after the month has elapsed. They should be printed, and should conform to the approved draft; and a space — at least 2½″ — should be left for the Secretary of State's endorsement. All manuscript corrections should be initialled by the persons who attested the sealing.

The application should be accompanied by—

(i) a copy of the council's resolution;

(ii) two copies of the sealed byelaws;

(iii) the approved draft;

(iv) a copy of the newspaper(s) containing the notice;

(v) the clerk's certificate as to deposit of a copy of the byelaws;

(vi) copies of objections, if any, received by the council;

(vii) the clerk's certificate that the sealed byelaws correspond exactly with the agreed draft.

---

10 This section empowers a local authority to make byelaws for the good rule and government of the whole or any part of its district, and for the prevention and suppression of nuisance; but the procedure for confirmation of byelaws contained in *ibid*, s 236 and as set out in Memo 7D applies to all local authority byelaws (including byelaws made under the Food Act 1984, s 60) for which specific provision is not otherwise made: s 236(1).

5. The Secretary of State emphasises that he has power to confirm only if the procedure laid down in s 236 of the Act and outlined above is properly carried out. He has no power to excuse deviation from this procedure.

6. The Secretary of State has power to fix the date on which the byelaws come into operation. He considers that the first day of a month will normally be most convenient; and as s 236 provides that, if he does not fix a date, byelaws shall come into operation one month after confirmation, he will normally bring byelaws into operation on the first day of the month next following the expiry of this period.

APPENDIX

BOROUGH/DISTRICT/PARISH/COMMUNITYOF ....

CONFIRMATION OF BYELAWS

'Notice is hereby given that the council of intend, after the expiry of the period mentioned below, to apply to the Secretary of State for confirmation of byelaws made by the council (insert description of byelaws and, where necessary, of the area to which they will apply — see para 3A of this memorandum).

Copies of these byelaws will be kept at the offices of the council at , and will be open to public inspection without payment on any week day, during the usual office hours, for one month from the date of the publication of this notice. Copies of the byelaws or any part thereof will be supplied at a fee not exceeding ten pence for each hundred words.

An objection to the confirmation of the byelaws should be made by letter addressed to the Secretary, Department of the Environment, 2 Marsham Street, London SW1P 3EB/Welsh Office, Cathays Park, Cardiff CF1 3NQ.

(*Signed*)

(*Insert date of signature*) *Clerk/Chief Executive of the Council*

APPENDIX B

Model Regulations

COUNCIL OF..

Open Market Regulations[1]

1. (a) 'The Council' means the Council of

(b) 'The Market' means the open markets held in respectively in the locations determined by the Council.

(c) 'The Market Officer' means the Council's Chief Public Services Officer or his duly authorised representative.

(d) 'Stall' includes a compartment, standing bench, table, place, pitch or space in the market and used or intended to be used for the sale of goods.

(e) 'Goods' includes provisions, commodities and articles brought into the Market for the purpose of sale.

2. These Regulations govern the use of stalls in the Market by stallholders.

Any stallholder who contravenes any of the Regulations of any of the Byelaws relating to the Market may be refused permission to pitch a stall in the Market[1].

Market Days and Tolls

3. The Market shall be open for trading and tolls based on the area occupied by a stall shall be payable as follows:

Market	*Fair Days*	*Market Days*[2]	*Market Hours*[2]	*Charges*[3]

1 Based on regulations in operation in respect of street markets in Powys County Council, and which, in effect, constitute the terms of a contract between the local authority as market owner and traders whereby the former agrees, on certain conditions, to permit the erection of stalls in the streets and to reserve spaces for regular (or 'registered') stallholders. An area should also be reserved within the market for the erection of stalls by 'casual' traders. As with byelaws, before implementation, regulations in draft form should be discussed and agreed with traders and other interested parties. It is suggested that the 'licence' to pitch a stall may constitute the agreed regulations (a copy should be handed to each trader) together with a written receipt (which makes specific reference to the regulations) for toll or stallage issued by the market officer to each trader on market day. In *Rickard v Forest Heath District Council*, (1 May 1991, unreported), the High Court (*per* Sir Michael Ogden QC) held that as the Council's rules and regulations had not been given to the plaintiff stallholder, their incorporation into the licence could not be implied and they were therefore unenforceable.

See also note 6 to the model byelaws (*above*), and also the discussion on the two Court of Appeal decisions, *R v Barnsley Metropolitan Borough Council ex p Hook* [1976] 1 WLR 1052 and *R v Basildon District Council ex p Brown* (1981) 79 LGR 655.

2 See the Food Act 1984, s 52.

3 See the 1984 Act, s 53. The power to determine the level of charge must be exercised in a reasonable manner, although it has been held that a local authority may impose charges which would produce an income over and above the immediate needs of the market economy and which would benefit the general rate fund: *Ricketts v Havering London Borough Council* (1981) 79 LGR 146 and see *R v Birmingham City Council, ex p Dredger* (1993) 91 LGR 532.

4. Market days may be varied by the Council by virtue of public holidays and shall not be held Christmas Day, Boxing Day or New Year's Day.

5. For the purpose of measuring the area occupied by a stall[4] there shall be included in the area of the stall the ground immediately below its roof (if any) and the ground extending for one metre in front of a stall, or where trading is from more than one side of a stall one metre in front of each side from which trading takes place. Provided that nothing in this Regulation is to be deemed to authorise the placing of goods on the ground or the hanging of goods from the stall or elsewhere so as to obstruct or prevent the passage of pedestrians between stalls.

6. Except as provided below charges shall be payable on Market and Fair Days on demand to the Market Officer.

Reservation and Allocation of Pitches

7. No person shall bring any goods into the Market for the purpose of sale more than one hour before or one hour after the Market opens (except as provided in Regulation 12 below) or allow them to remain there more than one hour after the Market closes.

8. All vehicles bringing goods into the Market must be removed immediately they have been unloaded.

9. No person shall be permitted by himself, his agent or nominee to place, erect or use more than one stall in the Market on the same day except with the consent of the Market Officer when in exceptional cases a person may be permitted to place, erect or use one additional stall in the Market.

10. The maximum frontage of a stall shall be and the maximum depth

11. Subject to these Regulations, a trader desiring to attend regularly at any of the Council's Markets may have a pitch reserved for each Market day on paying the appropriate charge four weeks in advance and by paying the appropriate charge for each Market day. So long as the Council has at least four weeks' charge in hand and the trader complies with all the Regulations a pitch will be reserved for him. Such stallholders shall be known as Registered Stallholders. The Market Officer will use his best endeavours to allocate pitches in the Market according to the length of time that the stallholders have been trading regularly in the Market.

A local authority which maintains a market in pursuance of a local Act may, notwithstanding aanything in any enactment relating to the market, make in connection with the market such charges as the authority determines from time to time (Local Government (Miscellaneous Provisions) Act 1976, s 36(2)).

4 In order to calculate the charge it may be better practice to charge on a frontage basis rather than by area: stallholders appear to consider the former to be of more importance. If charges are calculated on frontage, it should be remembered that trading may take place from three sides of the stall. The additional one metre mentioned in the regulation represents the area where buyers stand and which therefore may deemed to be part of the 'trading' area.

12. A pitch which is booked in advance shall only be held until 9.30am on Market days unless the Market Officer has been requested to reserve such pitch until a later time which shall be no later than 10.30am. After that time as the case may be the Market Officer may re-allocate the pitch to another trader who must off-load and remove any vehicle from the Market within half an hour of the allocation of the pitch.

13. If a pitch or space is not occupied for a period of three consecutive weeks in any year it will no longer be reserved unless notice in writing has been given to the Market Officer giving adequate reasons for such absence, eg prolonged illness, in which case it may, at the discretion of the Market Officer, be reserved for a longer period. Otherwise, it shall be considered vacant.

14. Registered Stallholders must, unless prevented for a good and sufficient reason, inform the Market Officer beforehand of their intention not to stand on any particular day or when annual holidays are taken.

15. In the event of non-attendance, a 50 per cent rebate of charge will be allowed providing that the Market Officer is informed by 9.30am on the day of the Market to which it relates.

16. Any Registered Stallholder wishing to give up his pitch shall give one week's notice in writing to the Market Officer and the Council reserves the right to give one week's notice to terminate[5] the arrangement between it and the Registered Stallholder. On such termination the Council will repay to the Registered Stallholder a proportionate part of any advance payment made by him.

17. Stallholders shall occupy only the position allocated to them by the Market Officer.

18. The allocation of a pitch in the Market by the Market Officer is personal[6] to a stallholder who must NOT permit anyone else to occupy that pitch or his stall.

19. Stallholders must inform the Market Officer of their names and addresses. The Market Officer will also allocate to a stallholder a number which must be displayed upon a prominent part of the stall.

Prevention of Obstruction, Nuisance and Damage

20. Stallholders shall not place goods beyond the limits of their stalls as allocated by the Market Officer either on the ground or hanging; all stallholders' goods, wares, empty crates, and refuse must be stored within the area allocated to a stallholder.

21. Stalls must be pitched so that they face in towards pavements or footways. Provided that this Regulation shall not apply in exceptional cases when stalls are pitched in spaces allocated by the Market Officer who considers it to be convenient and desirable that they should face towards the carriageway. This Regulation is subject also to the provisions in the Byelaws enabling a vehicle constructed or adapted and used for the sale of goods to be positioned in a site allocated by the Market Officer.

---

5 See *ex p Hook* and *Brown* (*above*).
6 See *ex p Brown* (*above*).

22. Vehicles, including carts, handcarts, wheelbarrows, trucks or trailers may only be brought by stallholders into the Market in such a manner as will cause no obstruction to any public road, avenue, passage, pavement or footway used by the public nor inconvenience or nuisance to other stallholders or the occupiers of any premises adjoining the Market and may not stand for longer than is reasonably necessary for loading or unloading goods other than those vehicles properly adapted for use as a Market stall; and in any event no vehicle of any type will be parked in the Market between the hours of 10.00am and 4.00pm without the express permission of the Market Officer. In particular, vehicles may not be driven or parked on a pavement or footway, or stalls or goods placed on a pavement or footway except with the consent of the Market Officer.

23. No stallholder shall hawk or carry about any article for sale or by calling or making any noise by means of any instrument or otherwise seek to attract attention or custom to any stall.

Hygiene

24. Stallholders shall keep their stalls and fittings and the space below and adjoining the stalls clean and free from litter, otherwise than in a proper receptacle.

25. Every stallholder shall as often as is necessary during any day on which the stall is used for the sale of goods and before he leaves the Market, cause all refuse from his trade or business to be removed and the area occupied by him cleansed to the satisfaction of the Market Officer. Without prejudice to any liability that there may be under the Litter Act 1983 or Market Byelaws, if a stallholder fails to comply with these Regulations the Council may remove the refuse and cleanse the area before mentioned and the stallholder shall be liable to pay the Council's costs thereby incurred.

26. The Council disclaims all liability for accidents caused by, or arising from the disrepair, condition or construction of any stall not owned by it.

27. All persons selling foodstuffs must comply with the Food Safety (General Food Hygiene) Regulations 1995 and the Food Safety (Temperature Control) Regulations 1995.

28. All stalls shall be maintained in a good state of repair and condition and to the satisfaction of the Market Officer.

Insurances

29. All stallholders shall hold a valid insurance policy for public liability for claims up to £500,000 and the Market Officer shall be at liberty to call for and inspect such policy of insurance and the receipt for the current premium.

Complaints

30. Any complaint with regard to these Regulations must be made in writing to the Chief Executive of the Council.

31. Stallholders shall comply with all directions of the Market Officer, which do not conflict with these Regulations or any Byelaws relating to the Market.

32. All allocations of pitches or stalls are made on the express understanding that they may be terminated forthwith[7] by the Market Officer in the event of any contravention by a stallholder of these Regulations or of any Byelaws relating to the Market.

Goods Offered for Sale

33. Stallholders shall sell or offer for sale from their stalls only those goods approved beforehand in writing by the Council or the Market Officer.

---

7 But, in light of the decisions in *ex p Hook* and *ex p Brown* (*above*), care must be taken to ensure that the trader concerned is not given cause to complain that he has been treated unfairly or in an arbitrary manner contrary to the rules of natural justice.

APPENDIX C

Precedents

(The Precedents set out below are taken from *Butterworths' Encyclopaedia of Forms and Precedents* (E F & P), *Markets and Fairs* (Fifth Edition, Vol 26, 1991.)

A TRANSFER OF MARKET

1

RESOLUTION of a company for the sale of its market to a local authority[1]

RESOLVED:
that the directors of (*company*) be and they hereby are empowered to sell and transfer to the (*local authority*) on [such terms as may be *or* the terms that have been] agreed on between the said directors on behalf of the company and the (*local authority*) [all the rights powers and privileges and all the markets premises and things which at the time of the sale shall be the property of the company *or* such of the rights powers and privileges and such of the markets premises and things which at the time of the sale shall be the property of the company as are specified in the annexed schedule] but subject to all liabilities attached to the same at the time of the sale

[SCHEDULE

(*give details of rights, powers, privileges etc*)]

1 See the Food Act 1984 s 51 (page 245, *above) which provides that the owner of a market undertaking or of any rights in respect of a market and of tolls, whether established under or enjoyed by virtue of statutory powers or not, may sell or lease to a local authority the whole or any part of his undertaking or rights but subject to all liabilities attaching to it. It is further provided that a sale by a company under the above power must be authorised, in the case of a company within the meaning of the Companies Act 1985, by a special resolution of the members, passed as provided by ibid* s 378, and, in the case of any other company, by a resolution passed by a three-quarters majority in number and value of members present, either personally or by proxy, at a meeting especially convened for the purpose with notice of the business to be transacted: Food Act 1984 s 51(2) as amended by the Companies Consolidation (Consequential Provisions) Act 1985 s 30, Sch 2 and the Food Safety Act 1990 s 52, Sch 2.

2

CONVEYANCE on sale of a market company's undertaking to a local authority[1]

THIS CONVEYANCE is made the .... day of .... BETWEEN (1) (*vendor*) having its registered office at (*address*) ('the Company') and (2) (*local authority*) of (*address*) ('the Council')

NOW THIS DEED WITNESSES as follows:

1 Recitals

1.1 By an Act of Parliament intituled (*short title*) the Company was incorporated and was empowered to purchase and hold lands and construct a market place with all necessary buildings and works for the sale of such commodities as are usually sold in markets to hold in it a weekly market and to take stallages rents and tolls

1.2 The Company in pursuance of such powers has purchased and now holds lands and has constructed a market place with all necessary buildings and works for the sale of such commodities as are usually sold in markets and now holds in it a weekly market and takes stallages rents and tolls

1.3 At a meeting of members of the Company specially convened with notice of the business to be transacted at the meeting a resolution was passed by a majority of three-quarters in number and value of the members present empowering the directors of the Company to sell and transfer to the Council on [the terms *or* such terms as might be] agreed on between the Company and the Council all the rights powers and privileges and all or any of the markets premises and things the property of the Company but subject to all liabilities attached to them[2]

1.4 The Company has agreed to sell and the Council has agreed to purchase the rights powers and privileges and the markets premises and things the property of the Company but subject to all the liabilities attached to them upon the terms contained in this Conveyance

2 Conveyance

In consideration of the sum of £ . . . (. . . pounds) paid by the Council to the Company (the receipt of which the Company acknowledges) the Company [with [full *or* limited] title guarantee][3] in pursuance of the powers contained in the Food Act 1984[4] and of any other powers enabling it grants and conveys to the Council ALL THAT (*describe land*) and all the market place buildings and works on it ('the Property') together with all markets tolls rights powers and privileges of the Company but subject nevertheless to all liabilities attached to them TO HOLD to the Council in fee simple

3 Indemnity covenant

The Council hereby covenants with the Company to pay and discharge all liabilities attached to the Property and to keep the Company effectually indemnified against all claims demands actions proceedings costs and expenses made or taken in respect of it

[4 Certificate of value

(*certificate of value if appropriate*)]

IN WITNESS etc

(*signatures* (*and common seal*) *of the parties*)
(*signatures of witnesses*)

1 As to stamp duty see E F & P Service: Stamp Duties (Conveyance or transfer).
2 If the company comes within the Companies Act 1985 (8 Halsbury's Statutes (4th Edn) COMPANIES) this will be a recital of the passing of a special resolution as provided by *ibid* s 378; see Form 1 note 1 *above*.
3 As to covenants for title and the words importing them generally see E F & P vol 36 SALE OF LAND Paragraphs 39 [243] *et seq* and 166.1 [1210] *et seq*.
4 See Form 1 note 1 *above*.

3

CONVEYANCE of a market and fair in fee simple, reserving the market place[1]

THIS CONVEYANCE is made the . . . . . day of . . . . BETWEEN (1) (*vendor*) of (*address*) ('the Vendor') and (2) (*purchaser*) of (*address*) ('the Purchaser')

NOW THIS DEED WITNESSES as follows:

1 Recitals

1.1 His Majesty King (*name*) in the (*specify*) year of his reign by charter granted to (*original grantee*) and his heirs that he and his heirs should have and hold for ever in the vill of (*specify*) on (*day*) in every week a market for buying and selling [all kinds of cattle and goods *or* (*specify commodities*)] ('the Market') with toll and with all liberties and free customs belonging to such a market

1.2 There has been held in the above vill from time immemorial a yearly fair known as the (*name*) Fair for buying and selling [all kinds of cattle and goods *or* (*specify commodities*)] from (*date*) to (*date*) in each year ('the Fair')

1.3 The owners of the Fair have been accustomed from time immemorial to take and receive reasonable tolls upon all (*specify commodities*) and other things sold in the Fair

1.4 The vill of (*specify*) is now included within and forms part of (*specify local authority district*)

1.5 The Vendor is now seised in fee simple of the Market and Fair and of the land on which the Market and Fair are now and have until now been held ('the Market Place')

1.6 The Vendor has agreed to sell and the Purchaser has agreed to buy at the price of £ . . . (. . . pounds) the Market and Fair and tolls and all other the market and fair rights (if any) of the Vendor in the above vill but it is not intended that the Vendor should sell or that the Purchaser should buy the Market Place

2 Conveyance

In consideration of the sum of £ . . . (. . . pounds) paid by the Purchaser to the Vendor (the receipt of which the Vendor acknowledges) the Vendor [with [full *or* limited] title guarantee][2] grants and conveys to the Purchaser the Market with the tolls and with all liberties and free customs belonging to it and all other franchises and rights of market and market tolls (if any) had enjoyed or exercised by the Vendor in the above (*specify local authority area*) or any part of it and the Fair together with its tolls and all other (if any) franchises or rights of fair and fair tolls had enjoyed or exercised by the Vendor in the above vill or any part of it TO HOLD to the Purchaser in fee simple

[3 Covenant for providing market place

The Vendor covenants with the Purchaser that he will immediately convey[3] to the Purchaser the property described in the [first] schedule ('the Property') so as to enable the Purchaser to hold the Market and Fair as freely and unrestrictedly as they have previously been and ought to be held and will immediately give all notices and do all things necessary for the removal of the Market and Fair from the Market Place to the Property and that he will not after the date of this Conveyance at any time hold or permit or cause to be held on the Market Place or any part of it the Market and Fair or either of them[4]

or

3 Covenant for removal

The Vendor covenants with the Purchaser that he will immediately give all notices and do all things necessary for the removal of the Market and Fair from the Market Place to (*describe property*) ('the Property') within the said vill provided by the Purchaser and that he will not after the date of this Conveyance at any time hold or permit or cause to be held on the Market Place or any part of it the Market and Fair or either of them]

[4 Acknowledgment and undertaking

The Vendor acknowledges the right of the Purchaser to the production of and to delivery of copies of the documents specified in the [second] schedule and undertakes with the Purchaser for the safe custody of the documents]

[5 Certificate of value

(*certificate of value if appropriate*)]

IN WITNESS etc

[FIRST] SCHEDULE

(*describe property on which market to be held*)

[SECOND SCHEDULE

(*list documents included in acknowledgment*)]

(*signatures (and seals) of the parties*)
(*signatures of witnesses*)

1 As to stamp duty see E F & P Service: Stamp Duties (Conveyance or transfer). A market or fair may be conveyed separately from the market place; see further E F & P vol 26 MARKETS AND FAIRS Paragraph 3 [460].

2 As to covenants for title and the words importing them generally see E F & P vol 36 SALE OF LAND Paragraphs 39 [243] *et seq* and 166.1 [1210] *et seq*.

3 This undertaking will be registrable as an estate contract: see the Land Charges Act 1972 s 2(4) Class C (iv) (37 Halsbury's Statutes (4th Edn) REAL PROPERTY). In the case of registered land a notice or caution should be entered: see the Land Registration Act 1925 ss 49, 54, 59(2) (37 Halsbury's Statutes (4th Edn) REAL PROPERTY).

4 This covenant will be registrable as a restrictive covenant: see the Land Charges Act 1972 s 2(5) Class D (ii). In the case of registered land, a notice or caution should be entered: see the Land Registration Act 1925 ss 49, 54, 59(2).

4

LEASE by tenant for life under the powers of the Settled Land Act 1925 of a market place and a market and tolls[1]

THIS LEASE is made the ..... day of .... BETWEEN (1) (*tenant for life*) of (*address*) ('the Lessor') which expression shall include the person[s] for the time being entitled to the immediate reversion of the property demised by this Lease and (2) (*lessee*) of (*address*) ('the Lessee') which expression shall include his successors and assigns

NOW THIS DEED WITNESSES as follows:

1 Recital

The Lessor is seised in fee simple of the property described below under a vesting deed dated (*date*) and made between (*parties*) ('the Vesting Deed')

2 Demise of market place

The Lessor in exercise of the powers vested in him by the Settled Land Act 1925 [and the additional powers mentioned or referred to in the Vesting Deed] and of every or any other power enabling him demises to the Lessee [with [full *or* limited] title guarantee][2] ALL THAT the market place of (*specify location*) ('the Market Place') TO HOLD to the Lessee for the term of ... years from (*date*) ('the Term') yielding and paying to the Lessor the yearly rent of £ ... payable on (*date*) in every year of the Term

3 Demise of market

The Lessor also demises to the Lessee [with [full *or* limited] title guarantee][3] all that market held at or on the Market Place on every (*day*) in every week in the year for the buying and selling of all manner of cattle goods and merchandise whatever ('the Market') and all and every tolls rents stallages piccages profits and emoluments whatever belonging or appertaining to or arising from the Market [the right to hold which Market and the tolls profits and emoluments arising from it were given and granted to *(name)* of *(specify)* by [royal grant *or* letters patent] dated (*date*) in the *(specify)* year of the reign of His Majesty King (*name*)][4] together with liberty for the Lessee in the name of the Lessor or otherwise to demand sue for recover and receive the above tolls rents stallages piccages profits and emoluments by all or any lawful means TO HOLD the Market to the Lessee for the Term yielding and paying to the Lessor the yearly rent of £ . . . payable on (*date*) in every year of the Term

4 Lessee's covenants

The Lessee hereby covenants with the Lessor as follows:

4.1 Rent

To pay to the Lessor during the Term in respect of the Market Place and the Market ('the Demised Premises') the above two rents of £ . . . and £ . . . respectively without any deductions on (*date*) in every year of the Term

4.2 Outgoings

To pay and discharge all taxes rates assessments and outgoings of every description for the time being imposed or assessed or payable on or in respect of the Demised Premises or either of them or any part of them

4.3 Not to demand unlawful tolls etc

Not to demand or take any unreasonable or unlawful tolls rents stallages piccages or any other payments in the Market Place or in respect of the Market

4.4 Accommodation and franchise rights

4.4.1 To provide sufficient accommodation for the Market at all times and hold the Market on all days on which it may be lawfully held taking the customary tolls stallages piccages and rents and doing all things in accordance with the usages of the Market and doing or neglecting nothing the doing or neglecting of which might lead to a forfeiture or loss of the Market or the tolls profits or emoluments of it or any of the franchises rights or privileges of the Lessor in respect of the Market

4.4.2 At all times during the Term to keep the Lessor fully indemnified against all acts omissions or defaults on his part whereby or by reason of which the Market or the tolls profits or emoluments of it or any of the franchises or privileges of the Lessor in respect of the Market might be forfeited or put in jeopardy

4.5 Lighting, cleaning etc

4.5.1 To keep the Market Place and its precincts at all times properly and sufficiently lighted and cleansed and free from nuisances

4.5.2 To keep the same and all the posts pales rails fences boundaries and erections and buildings drains sewers and watercourses belonging to it in repair and in all respects in a fit and proper state and condition

[4.6 **Insurance**

4.6.1 To insure and during the Term granted by this Lease keep insured the Market Place and all erections and buildings belonging or appertaining to it with all additions and improvements to the same against loss or damage by fire in the (*name*) Insurance Office or some other office or underwriters of repute to be approved of by the Lessor in a competent sum to cover the full value of them

4.6.2 To make all payments necessary for the above purposes within seven days after the same shall respectively become due

4.6.3 To produce the policy of insurance and the receipt for each such payment to the Lessor or to his agent on demand

4.6.4 To cause all monies which shall be received in respect of such insurance to be immediately laid out in rebuilding or reinstating such part or parts of the Market Place and premises as shall have been burned down or damaged by fire and if the same money shall be insufficient for rebuilding or reinstating the parts burned down or damaged by fire to provide out of his own money such further sums as may be required and immediately to expend the same for that purpose][5]

4.7 Enforcement of tolls

4.7.1 To demand and take all tolls rents stallages piccages and dues payable in the Market

4.7.2 If at any time so requested in writing by the Lessor and indemnified by him against all costs and consequences of so doing to enforce or seek to enforce payment of any toll rent stallage piccage or profit or emolument of which payment may be refused by taking legal proceedings or by distress or otherwise as may be necessary or proper[6]

4.8 Accounts

4.8.1 To keep proper records and books of account (to be open to the inspection at all reasonable times of the Lessor or his agents) of the tolls rents stallages piccages profits and emoluments arising from and collected or received on account or in respect of the Market or otherwise on account or in respect of the premises demised by this Lease in such manner that the accounts shall specify so far as possible the particular items of which each account is composed and the sources from which such items arose

4.8.2 At the end or sooner determination of the Term to deliver up to the Lessor on demand the above books

4.9 Indemnity

To indemnify the Lessor against all losses costs charges damages and expenses incurred by reason of any action or other proceeding brought or prosecuted by the Lessee (otherwise than at the request in writing of the Lessor) for recovering or enforcing payment of the tolls rents stallages piccages profits and emoluments or any of them or in consequence of any tolls rents stallages piccages profits or emoluments not lawfully payable being demanded or generally in consequence of the management of the Demised Premises

4.10 Yield up

At the end or sooner determination of the Term peaceably to deliver up to the Lessor the Demised Premises in good repair and condition

4.11 Alienation

Not to assign or underlet the Demised Premises or either of them or any part of them without the written consent of the Lessor PROVIDED that nothing contained in this Lease shall be construed to prevent the Lessee from letting stalls or standings in the Market Place on market days for such rents and in such manner as may be lawfully taken and done in accordance with the usages and customs of the Market

5 Lessor's covenant

The Lessor covenants with the Lessee that the Lessee paying the several rents and observing the covenants reserved and contained above shall peaceably and quietly enjoy the Demised Premises and shall not be disturbed by any lawful act of the Lessor or any person claiming under or in trust for him

6 Determination

It is hereby agreed that:

6.1 if the Lessee fails to observe or perform any of the covenants on his part contained above or

6.2 if any part of either of the rents reserved above shall remain unpaid for 21 days after the same shall become due (whether legally demanded or not)

it shall be lawful for the Lessor to give to the Lessee notice in writing determining the Term granted by this Lease and immediately upon the giving of such notice the Term shall absolutely determine and the Lessor may resume possession of the whole of the Demised Premises but without prejudice to any right or remedy which may have accrued to the Lessor in respect of any previous breach of covenant by the Lessee

Any such notice shall be construed (unless the contrary appears) to include the Market Place and the Term in it as well as the Market and the other premises and the Term in them

[7 Agreement for lease

[I *or* We] certify that there is no agreement for lease to which this lease gives effect][7]

IN WITNESS etc

(*signatures* (*or common seals*) *of the parties*)
(*signatures of witnesses*)

1 As to stamp duty see E F & P Service: Stamp Duties (Lease or Tack) and (Duplicate or Counterpart). The right of holding a market is a franchise and an incorporeal hereditament and so is included in the term 'land' within the meaning of the Settled Land Act 1925; see *ibid* s 117(1)(ix) (48 Halsbury's Statutes (4th Edn) TRUSTS AND SETTLEMENTS). The tenant for life may accordingly under *ibid* s 41(iv) grant a lease of a market for a term not exceeding 50 years, which must be made in accordance with the provisions of the Settled Land Act 1925 in relation to vesting deeds etc; see *ibid* ss 4, 5. As to regulations respecting leases of settled land generally, see *ibid* s 42. As to leases of registered land and the registration of title to leases, see E F & P vol 25(1) (1995 Reissue) LAND REGISTRATION. The compulsory registration provisions do not apply to incorporeal hereditaments: Land Registration Act 1925 s 120(1) proviso (37 Halsbury's Statutes (4th Edn) REAL PROPERTY).

If any premium is payable, as well as rent, the trustees of the settlement should be parties to the lease and should acknowledge receipt of the premium.

If the lease is for less than 21 years the provisions of the Settled Land Act 1925 in relation to the grant of leases are considerably relaxed; see *ibid* s 42(5). In effect a lease for less than 21 years can be granted by a tenant for life (a) if the rent is the best rent which can be reasonably obtained without fine (b) if the lessee is impeachable for waste (ie if there is a proper covenant to repair), notwithstanding (i) that the lessor gives no notice under the Settled Land Act 1925 of his intention to grant the lease or (ii) that there are no trustees of the settlement.

2 As to covenants for title and the words importing them generally see E F & P vol 36 SALE OF LAND Paragraphs 39 [243] *et seq* and 166.1 [1210] *et seq*.

3 See note 2 above.

4 The right to the franchise of holding a market at common law depends on a grant or patent from the Crown, or upon prescription, or the presumption of a lost grant. Where the title is derived from a grant from the Crown the words in square brackets should be added. The right to hold a market is distinguishable from the market place as the two are separable and may be vested in different persons; see E F & P vol 26 MARKETS AND FAIRS Paragraph 3 [460].

5 The insertion of this covenant must depend upon the nature of the market place. It is only applicable in the case of a covered market house or where there are substantial buildings used for market purposes.

6 Where the right to tolls is only prescriptive, it is advisable to require that they be demanded and taken, and in the case of a grant of a franchise of tolls, failure to levy tolls for a long time may lead to a presumption of surrender; see E F & P vol 26 MARKETS AND FAIRS Paragraph 7 [466]. As to the recovery of tolls, see E F & P vol 26 MARKETS AND FAIRS Paragraph 18 [496].

7 The Finance Act 1994 s 240 (42–44 Halsbury's Statutes (4th Edn) TAXATION) has introduced new provisions with regard to the stamping of leases and agreements for leases. A lease executed on or after 6 May 1994 will not be treated as duly stamped unless it is denoted with the duty paid on the agreement to which it gives effect, the lease is stamped with a stamp denoting that the agreement is not stampable or the lease contains a certificate that there is no such agreement, along the lines contained in this clause. See further E F & P Service: Guide to Stamp Duties Paragraphs 14 [17], 19 [25], 41 [52].

5

CLAUSES in contract of sale of property reserving a right to hold a market

The property is sold SUBJECT to an exception and reservation in favour of the Vendors in fee simple of all that the market and fair now and previously held by the Vendors and known as (*specify*) ('the Market') together with the use of the [Market Place and car park] for all the purposes of the Market on (*date*) in each year or where that day falls on a Sunday then on (*date*) and also the use of the [Market Place and car park] on the day and night preceding the Market for the purpose of erecting such booths stalls caravans and apparatus as may be required for or in connection with the Market and also the use of the [Market Place and car park] on the day and night succeeding the Market for removing the above booths stalls caravans and apparatus and the right for the Vendors and their successors in title to break up the surface of the [Market Place and car park] for the purpose of the Market or any purpose connected with it provided the Vendors and their successors in title shall at their sole expense restore and make good with all reasonable speed the surface of the [Market Place and car park] and any damage to them

And there shall also be excepted and reserved to the Vendors all tolls liberties free customs franchises and rights of market and fair until now belonging to or enjoyed or exercised by the Vendors in (*specify local authority area*) or any part of it including the [Market Place and car park]

If in circumstances and for reasons wholly within the control of the Vendors or their successors in title and not in any way against their wishes the Market shall be discontinued for the space of . . . years then the Vendors or their successors in title will not oppose proceedings by the Purchasers for the abolition of the Market and the conveyance shall include a covenant to this effect[1]

1 A fair may be abolished by order of the Secretary of State on a representation by the owners of the fair or the local authority; see the Fairs Act 1871 s 3 (page 189, *above*).

B NOTICE OF MARKET AND REMOVAL OF MARKET

6

NOTICE of date when a new market will be opened[1]

(*name*) MARKET

TAKE NOTICE that a market for the sale of (*insert details*) will be opened at (*specify location*) on (*date*) at (*time*) and will thereafter be held between the hours of (*specify hours*) on [(*day*) in every week *or* the first (*day*) in every month *or* (*specify*)] throughout the year

(*signature*)
(*proper officer of the local authority*)

1 The Markets and Fairs Clauses Act 1847 s 12 (page 180, *above*) (which applies to all markets and fairs created by local Acts incorporating *ibid* s 12 and to markets established under the Animal Health Act 1981 s 54(2) (page 218, *abpve*) provides that before a market or fair is opened for public use the undertakers must give not less than ten days' notice of the time when the market or fair will be opened. Such notice is to be given by the publication of the notice in a newspaper circulating within prescribed limits and by printed handbills posted in a conspicuous place within those limits. *Ibid* s 12 will apply to the time when the market is first opened, and it is advisable to state the days and hours when it will be held. No penalty for failure to give the notice is imposed, but the benefit of the protection of *ibid* s 13 (prohibition of sale outside market) may not be available unless the notice is given and proved; see *Hooper v Kenshole* (1877) 2 QBD 127 and E F & P vol 26 MARKETS AND FAIRS Paragraph 15.2 [490]. The Markets and Fairs Clauses Act 1847 s 12 has no application to markets authorised by charter or letters patent (as to which see further E F & P vol 26 MARKETS AND FAIRS Paragraph 2.1 [454]).

7

JUSTICES' CERTIFICATE of the completion of a market[1]

In the County of (*insert details*)
Petty Sessional Division of (*insert details*)
Before the Magistrates' Court sitting at (*insert details*) on (*date*)

WHEREAS

(1) Certain premises known as the [(*name*) Market Place *or* the (*name*) fair ground] are wholly within the above petty sessional division

(2) Proof has been adduced to us two of the justices of the peace for the above county assembled and acting together in and for the above petty sessional division that the above [market place *or* fairground] is completed and fit for public use as a [market place *or* place for holding a fair] as required by the [Animal Health Act 1981 *or* (*specify local Act*)] by virtue of the incorporation in that Act of the Markets and Fairs Clauses Act 1847

NOW THEREFORE we the said justices do hereby certify that the above [market place *or* fair ground] is completed and fit for the use of the persons resorting to it

(*signatures of justices*)
Two justices of the peace for the above county

1 This certificate is required by the Markets and Fairs Clauses Act 1847 ss 31, 32 (27 Halsbury's Statutes (4th Edn) MARKETS AND FAIRS). *Ibid* s 31 provides that, unless the special Act (ie the local Act under which the market is established; see *ibid* s 2) otherwise provides, the undertakers may not demand or receive any stallage, rent or toll until the market place or place for a fair is completed and fit for the use of persons resorting to it, and *ibid* s 32 provides that a certificate of two justices is conclusive evidence of completion and fitness for use. The justices must sign the certificate on proof being adduced to them that the market place or place for a fair is so completed and fit.

8

NOTICE of removal of a market or fair[1]

(*name*) [MARKET *or* FAIR]

NOTICE OF REMOVAL

TO ALL WHOM IT MAY CONCERN

TAKE NOTICE that on and after (*date*) the ancient (*name of market or fair*) now and previously held on (*day*) in every week in (*specify present location*) in the [Borough *or* City *or* (*specify*)] of (*insert details*) will be removed to (*specify new location*) in the [Borough *or* City *or* (*specify*)] of (*insert details*) and that on or after that date the (*name of market or fair*) will no longer be held at (*present location*) but will be held at (*new location*) on (*day*) in every week

The same tolls and stallages will be payable in the new [market place *or* fair ground] as are now and have previously been payable in the present [market place *or* fair ground]

On and after (*date*) the [market place *or* fair ground] at (*present location*) will cease to be a [market place *or* fair ground] and [will be closed to the public *or* no person will be permitted to expose goods for sale in the [market place *or* fair ground] at (*present location*) or to resort to it for the purpose of buying or selling][2]

Dated the . . . . . day of . . . .

(*signature of owner of market*)

1 The right of removal of a market or fair held by grant or prescription is incident to every grant, unless the grantee is tied by its terms to some particular location. Whenever a market or fair is granted to be held within an area such as a city, borough, township or manor, there is incident to such grant a right to remove it from time to time from one convenient place to another within that area. The owner ought to give public notice of the removal; see *Curwen v Salkeld* (1803) 3 East 538; *R v Starkey* (1837) 7 Ad & El 95. As to the circumstances in which a market may be removed, and the consequences of an unlawful removal, see further 29 Halsbury's Laws (4th Edn) para 681 *et seq*.

2 If the present market place is a highway, the second alternative wording within the square brackets should be used.

C OPERATION OF MARKET

9

APPLICATION to local authority for use of stall in market

To [(*local authority*) *or* the Markets and Fairs Committee]

I HEREBY MAKE APPLICATION for the use of a stall each week in (*name*) Market, particulars of which are stated below.

If my application is accepted I agree to pay the stallage of such stall as shall be allotted to me regularly in advance and to observe and carry out the provisions of the licence to use the said stall[1].

Dated the . . . . . day of . . . .

(*signature of applicant*)

PARTICULARS

Full name of applicant . . .
Postal address . . .
Particulars of stall applied for:
  Avenue . . .
  Stall number . . .
  Size . . .
  Rent . . .
  Class of goods to be sold . . .
  Days on which stall is desired . . .
Is applicant already a stallholder? . . .
If so, does applicant wish to give up present stall? . . .
Is applicant a resident in (*specify local authority's area*)? . . .
References . . .
Remarks . . .

This form when completed should be returned to [(*name*) *or* the Markets Superintendent] at (*address*).

1 For forms of licence see Forms 10, 11, 12 *below*.

10

LICENCE for use of stall in market[1]

THIS LICENCE is granted the . . . . . day of . . . . by (*local authority*) of (*address*) ('the Council') to (*applicant*) of (*address*) ('the Stallholder')

WHEREAS

(1) The Council are the market owners of the market held at (*specify location*) on each [Wednesday and Saturday] ('the Market') and as market owners are vested with the rights and duties of holding regulating and controlling the Market and the market place situate at (*specify location*) ('the Market Place')

(2) The Stallholder has requested the Council to grant him the licence to use a stall for trading in the articles mentioned below on part of the Market Place

IT IS AGREED as follows:

1 Grant

The Council hereby grants to the Stallholder the right to use on the market days for the sale of goods and articles mentioned below the portion of the Market Place known as stall No . . . or such other stall of equivalent size and position as the Council may from time to time in its absolute discretion determine and the right to the use of the stall or other stall shall continue from week to week for a period of (*specify*) from (*date*) unless determined by twenty-four hours' notice in writing by the Council at any time after the date of this Licence[2]

2 Conditions

The conditions on which the above right is granted are as follows:

2.1 Payments

The Stallholder shall pay to the Council on (*date*) the sum of £ . . . and afterwards on each succeeding (*day of week*) the sum of £ . . . until the determination of the right to use the stall under this Licence

2.2 Compliance with Byelaws

The Stallholder will comply with the Market Byelaws[2] and any other regulations or rules made by the Council with respect to the Market

2.3 Use by other persons

The Stallholder shall not permit any person other than his employees to use the stall

2.4 Alterations to stalls

No alteration or addition to the structure or fittings of any stall may be made by or on behalf of the Stallholder except with permission of the Markets Superintendent

2.5 Damage to stalls

The Stallholder may not drive or permit the driving of nails into the woodwork of any stall or otherwise damage or deface the property of the Council

2.6 Stall boundaries

The Stallholder may not place goods beyond the boundaries of the stall either on the ground or hanging except with the permission of the Markets Superintendent

2.7 Stall signs

The Stallholder must exhibit his name on the board or fascia space provided for the purpose in the uniform style of lettering and colour approved by the Markets Superintendent and projecting signs exhibited by the Stallholder must be likewise approved and must not project more than . . . metres from the stall or exceed . . . centimetres in depth

2.8 Lighting

2.8.1 The Stallholder may not add to or alter the electric wiring and fittings provided by the Council or provide any other kind of lighting except with the consent of the Markets Superintendent

2.8.2 The Stallholder must provide his own lamps and pay for the consumption of electricity on the scale prescribed by the Council

2.9 Heating

The Stallholder may not install heating apparatus of any kind except with the permission of the Markets Superintendent

2.10 Disposal of refuse

2.10.1 The Stallholder must deposit all vegetable and fish refuse offal etc in the bins provided for the purpose by the Council and dry refuse must be placed by him in suitable receptacles kept inside the stall

2.10.2 The Stallholder must keep the avenue adjoining his stall free from refuse and litter

2.11 Cleaning of stall

The Stallholder must keep his stall and fittings and the space below the stall clean and free from litter

2.12 Nature of trade

The Stallholder may sell from the stall the following goods: (*describe goods*) and he may not sell any other class of goods from the stall

2.13 Nuisance etc

The Stallholder must not do or permit to be done anything which in the opinion of the Markets Superintendent may be a nuisance or annoyance to any member of the public resorting to the Market or which may be detrimental to its efficient operation

3 Licence to be personal to the Stallholder

It is hereby agreed that this Licence is personal to the Stallholder and the parties acknowledge that nothing in this Licence shall be construed as creating the relationship of landlord and tenant

AS WITNESS etc

(*signatures of the parties*)

1 Exclusiveness of possession is one of the principal characteristics of a letting, as distinct from a mere licence for the use of premises; see *Addiscombe Garden Estates Ltd v Crabbe* [1958] 1 QB 513 at 528, [1957] 3 All ER 563 at 571, CA; *Street v Mountford* [1985] AC 809, [1985] 2 All ER 289, HL; *AG Securities v Vaughan, Antoniades v Villiers* [1990] 1 AC 417, [1988] 3 All ER 1058, HL. This form has been drafted with a view to attempting to avoid the conferring of an exclusive right to use any one stall or site and therefore the creation of a tenancy which might enable the stallholder to claim the protection given by the Landlord and Tenant Act 1954 Pt II as amended by the Law of Property Act 1969 Pt I (23 Halsbury's Statutes (4th Edn) LANDLORD AND TENANT). Alternatively, a tenancy of a stall may be granted: see further Form 14 note 1 *below*.

2 For a form of notice terminating a licence see Form 13 *below*.

11

TRADERS' LICENCE to trade from market hall[1]

THIS LICENCE is made the . . . . . day of . . . . BETWEEN (1) (*licensor*) of (*address*) ('the Licensor') (2) (*licensee*) of (*address*) ('the Licensee') [and (3) (*surety*) of (*address*) ('the Surety')]

IT IS AGREED as follows:

1 Definitions and interpretation

In this licence:

1.1 'the Hall' means (*insert details*)

1.2 'the Deposit' shall be the sum of £ . . . (being equivalent to 4 weeks' Licence Fee)

1.3 'the Licence Fee' shall be the sum of £ . . . per week

1.4 'the Allotted Space' means (*insert details*)

1.5 'the Period' shall be the period of (*insert details*) from the Commencement Date until (*date*)

1.6 'the Commencement Date' shall be (*date*)

1.7 'Normal Business Hours' shall be (*insert details*)

1.8 'the Goods' means (*insert details*)

2 Grant

In consideration of the Licensee paying to the Licensor the Licence Fee the Licensor permits the Licensee to sell the Goods from the Allocated Space in the Hall from the Commencement Date for the duration of the Period during Normal Business Hours subject to the terms and conditions below

3 Payment of Licence Fee

The Licence Fee shall be paid to the Licensor weekly in advance by midday on Friday of each week or such other day or time from time to time prescribed by the Licensor

4 Expiry of Period

The Licence shall subject to clause 12 continue on the expiry of the Period until determined by either party giving to the other not less than 12 weeks' previous notice in writing to expire at the end of a week PROVIDED that if the Licensee does not wish the Licence to continue after the Period the Licensee shall at least 12 weeks prior to the expiry of the Period give notice in writing of that fact to the Licensor

5 Charges and contributions

The Licensee shall pay to the Licensor within seven days of demand

5.1 the charge made by the Licensor for the cost of the electricity consumed by the Licensee at the Allocated Space such sum to be calculated as per the meter reading in the Allocated Space and at the rate from time to time prescribed by the Licensor

5.2 a contribution towards the cost of the provision of communal lighting and heating of the Hall and of any other communal services from time to time provided by the Licensor for the common benefit of all the Licensees in the Hall and the amount of any such contribution from time to time payable by the Licensee shall be such sum as the Licensor shall in its absolute discretion from time to time determine and notify to the Licensee

6 Deposit

On the signing of this Licence the Licensee shall pay in addition to the Licence Fee the Deposit to be held by the Licensor during the continuance of the Licence which sum shall be returnable (but without interest) on the termination of the Licence and after the deduction from it of

6.1 the cost of making good any damage existing at the termination of this Licence to the Allocated Space or to the Hall

6.2 any arrears of the Licence Fee

6.3 any other sums payable to the Licensor under the terms of this Licence and

6.4 any other valid claim of the Licensor against the Licensee

7 Storage of Goods outside Normal Business Hours

The Licensee may during the continuance of the Licence at the sole risk of the Licensee store the Goods in the Allocated Space outside Normal Business Hours

8 Promotional schemes etc

The Licensee agrees to participate in promotional schemes organised by the Licensor and agrees to co-operate at all times with schemes carried out by the Licensor for the benefit of the Hall and to abide by various requirements of the Licensor within the Hall concerning promotional displays opening hours and participation

9 Licensee's obligations

The Licensee shall during the subsistence of this Licence (and also where applicable after its termination or expiry) at all times perform and observe the following obligations and conditions:

9.1 Fitting out

Fit out and equip the Allocated Space in accordance with the requirements of the Licensor and make and keep it attractive for the display of the Goods

9.2 Display of name

Display at the Allocated Space a suitable sign stating the Licensee's name and trade such sign to be of a form previously approved in writing by the Licensor

9.3 Opening for trade

9.3.1 Keep the Allocated Space open for the sale of the Goods during Normal Business Hours

9.3.2 Promptly open it for trading at the commencement of Normal Business Hours

9.4 Attendance

Keep the Allocated Space properly attended by the Licensee or his competent employees during Normal Business Hours

9.5 Sale of other merchandise

Not to sell or display for sale any merchandise from the Allocated Space other than the Goods

9.6 Quality of merchandise

Offer for sale merchandise of good quality at reasonable prices and maintain a good selection and an adequate stock

9.7 Professional appearance

Wear suitable clothes and maintain a professional appearance

9.8 Compliance with trading regulations etc

Observe all Acts of Parliament and all regulations and byelaws of the local authority and other official bodies relating to the sale of goods and trading

9.9 Sale outside Allocated Space

Not to offer the Goods for sale from any passageway or other place outside the limits of the Allocated Space

9.10 Nuisance etc

Not to seek to attract attention or custom by shouting making undue noise or playing music of a nature which may cause a nuisance or inconvenience to other stallholders or customers in the Hall

9.11 Unseemly conduct

Refrain from abuse or unseemly language or conduct and extend normal courtesy to customers other stallholders and representatives of the Licensor

9.12 Auctions

Not to conduct any auction or mock auction in the Allocated Space or elsewhere in or near to the Hall

9.13 Alcohol

Not to bring into or consume any alcohol in the Hall

9.14 Cleaning of Allocated Space

Keep the Allocated Space and in conjunction with neighbouring stallholders the passages adjoining it clean and tidy at all times

9.15 Refuse

Place all waste and refuse which may be produced or which may accumulate in the course of trade from the Allocated Space in the receptacles provided by the Licensor as often as may be necessary to keep the Allocated Space clean and tidy

9.16 Obstruction by Goods

9.16.1 Not to suspend any merchandise from any part of a roof which projects beyond the limits of the Allocated Space

9.16.2 Not to suspend any merchandise over any passageway or beyond the limits of the Allocated Space

9.16.3 Not to suspend any merchandise from any part of any sprinkler installation nozzle

9.16.4 Not to obstruct or render the sprinkler system less effective by any material or object whatever

9.17 Damage etc

9.17.1 Not to remove or interfere with the structure or parts of any other Allocated Space or any part of the Hall outside the limits of the Allocated Space

9.17.2 Not to cause any damage to the Hall

9.17.3 Not to interfere with any person lawfully in the Hall

9.18 Access etc by Licensor's officers

9.18.1 Not to impede in any way the officers servants or agents of the Licensor in the exercise by them of the Licensor's rights of possession and control of the Allocated Space

9.18.2 Give all reasonable assistance and facilities to them for the alteration at any time of the layout or decoration of the Allocated Space

9.19 Compliance with fire regulations

Observe and comply with all fire regulations and directions in relation to fire regulations specified by the Licensor or the local fire authority or required by statute

9.20 Compliance with health and safety regulations

Observe and comply with all regulations and all requirements of the Health and Safety at Work etc Act 1974 and also any other regulations relating to employees of the Licensee so far as they relate to the Allocated Space and the business of the Licensee carried on in it

9.21 Alterations etc

9.21.1 Not to carry out any structural or electrical work in the Allocated Space nor use any materials for the fitting out or decoration of it without first obtaining the written consent of the Licensor who shall have absolute discretion in giving or withholding such consent

9.21.2 Not to erect any trellis work grill or other device for the protection of the Goods in the Allocated Space unless it is of a roll-down type or other form approved by the Licensor which in either case can be stored within the limits of the Allocated Space and so as to preserve the good appearance of the Hall when not in use

9.22 Heating

Not to use any space heater in the Allocated Space unless of a type approved by the Licensor

9.23 Compliance with local authority byelaws etc

Conform with all regulations and byelaws of the local authority and other official bodies relating to the Allocated Space and its fitting out

9.24 Obstruction, loading

9.24.1 Not at any time to block any drives passageways or other areas giving access to the Hall and

9.24.2 Use only the loading facilities at the times designated by the Licensor

9.25 Vacation of Hall

Vacate the Hall at the end of Normal Business Hours

9.26 Assignment etc

9.26.1 Not to assign or transfer the benefit of this Licence to any other person or company whatever

9.26.2 Not to suffer or permit any other person or company to have the use of the Allocated Space

9.27 Indemnity

Indemnify the Licensor against

9.27.1 all and any claims or demands (whenever made) and all costs and expenses incurred by the Licensor relating to or arising out of the use of the Allocated Space by the Licensee

9.27.2 any claims which may at any time be made against the Licensor (whether under the Occupiers' Liability Act 1957 or otherwise) in relation to the Allocated Space (including any claim made by any of the Licensee's employees) arising wholly or in part from any act or omission of the Licensee

9.28 Insurance

9.28.1 To adequately insure the Goods in the Allocated Space and the Hall and the Licensee's fixtures and fittings

9.28.2 To take out adequate third party insurance in respect of the Licensee's use and possession of the Allocated Space

9.28.3 In both cases to produce evidence of such insurance to the Licensor upon request

9.29 Compliance with Licensor's rules etc

Comply with all conditions rules and regulations for the time being prescribed by the Licensor for the management control and repair of the Hall or the Allocated Space

9.30 Removal of goods etc on termination

9.30.1 Remove all the Licensee's merchandise and fixtures and fittings of a temporary nature which may be put in or upon the Allocated Space by the Licensee during the continuance of this Licence upon the termination of this Licence however determined and

9.30.2 Leave the Allocated Space clean and in good repair and having repaired and made good any damage occasioned to it during the Licensee's occupation

9.31 Business Hours

Comply with any requirement of the Licensor with regard to Normal Business Hours and any temporary alteration to them during Bank Holidays and Christmas periods

10 Increase in Licence Fee

10.1 The Licensor may once every 12 months during the currency of this Licence upon serving at least 28 days' prior written notice on the Licensee increase the Licence Fee to such sum as may be specified in the written notice

10.2 The Licensee may within 14 days of receipt of such notice terminate this Licence by serving a counter notice in writing on the Licensor expiring at the end of the 12th week from the date of service of the counter notice upon which this Licence shall terminate without prejudice to the rights of the Licensor in respect of any antecedent breach of the Licensee's obligations contained in this Licence

10.3 In the event of such counter notice being served the Licence Fee shall remain as it was immediately before the notice served by the Licensor

11 Change of Allocated Space

It is agreed and declared as follows:

11.1 The Licensor may at any time from time to time change the Allocated Space from which the Licensee is entitled to trade under this Licence to another space of comparable size within the Hall but shall give the Licensee 28 days' (or such shorter period as may be reasonable) written notice of such change

11.2 The terms of this Licence shall take effect in relation to such other space as if it had been the Allocated Space originally designated for which this Licence was granted

12 Termination

The Licensor may by notice in writing[2] to the Licensee terminate this Licence immediately if:

12.1 The Licensee is in arrear for 14 days with any payment due under the terms of this Licence

12.2 The Licensee is in breach of any other terms and conditions of this Licence

12.3 The Licensee enters into liquidation or a receiver is appointed of the Licensee's business or the Licensee commits an act of bankruptcy or makes an arrangement or composition with the creditors of the Licensee

12.4 The Licensee is convicted of a criminal offence relating to the sale or possession of any property or merchandise or to his behaviour in the Hall

12.5 The Licensor reasonably considers that the Licensee is carrying on business in a manner prejudicial to the business of other Licensees within the Hall or of such a standard that it detracts from the character and/or quality of the Hall and the businesses of other Licensees

12.6 The Landlord or the Head Landlord of the Licensor refuses consent to the granting of this Licence or subsequently requires its termination or lawfully requires possession of the Hall

12.7 Any local authority or local market authority lawfully requires the Licensor to terminate this Licence or the sale of the Goods from the Allocated Space or the Licensor is lawfully required to close the Hall for trading

12.8 The Licensor closes the Hall or part of it on the grounds that it has been damaged by fire or some other cause or it is in need of repair or such other works which render it impracticable to keep it open or on the grounds that it is no longer economically viable to keep it open

13 Failure to make payments

If the Licensee fails to pay the Licence Fee or other sums of money payable under the terms of this Licence whether demanded or not at the time above prescribed or any sums properly payable by the Licensee to the Licensor the Licensor shall be entitled as the Licensee's agent to seize and sell any merchandise and/or fixtures and fittings belonging to the Licensee situated at the Allocated Space and to apply the proceeds of sale towards the deduction of any sums owing by the Licensee to the Licensor

14 Damage to Goods etc

14.1 No responsibility whatever shall in any circumstances fall upon the Licensor for the safety of or for any loss or damage however caused to the Goods in the Allocated Space or in the Hall or to the fixtures and fittings of the Licensee in the Hall

14.2 The Licensee shall be solely responsible for all insurance both for their safety and for all such loss or damage however caused including all direct or consequential loss or damage and notwithstanding such loss or damage may be due to or arise out of any defect in the Hall or the Allocated Space or the neglect or default of the Licensor or its servants or agents

15 Disputes

15.1 Where there is a dispute between the Licensee and another trader in the Hall concerning any merchandise sold or proposed to be sold by the Licensee from the Allocated Space the Licensor shall have power in its absolute discretion after affording to the Licensee an opportunity to make such representations as the Licensee may think fit to decide what merchandise should or should not be offered for sale from the Allocated Space and to give directions accordingly

15.2 The Licensee shall immediately observe and comply with and abide by any such directions for the remainder of the duration of this Licence

16 Permanent fixtures etc

The structure and permanent fixtures of the Allocated Space are and shall at all times remain the sole property of the Licensor

17 Terms of Licence

17.1 The terms of this Licence are complete terms agreed between the Licensor and the Licensee and there are no other terms relating to this Licence unless evidenced in writing

17.2 The Licensee acknowledges that the Licensee has not entered into this Licence by any oral representation

17.3 The terms of this Licence may only be varied in writing and any variation agreed on behalf of the Licensor shall only take effect if signed by a duly authorised officer of the Licensor

18 Normal Business Hours

The Licensor may in its absolute discretion vary the Normal Business Hours by increasing or decreasing the number of days per week or the hours in each day the Hall is open for trading

19 Prompt opening for trade

If the Licensee does not open the Allocated Space for trade promptly at the commencement of the Normal Business Hours on each day the Licensor may open it using such force as may be reasonably necessary including the forcing of any locks

20 Removal of property on termination

20.1 If after the determination of this Licence any property of the Licensee remains in the Allocated Space the Licensor may remove such property to a safe place

20.2 If the Licensee has not collected it within 14 days the Licensor may sell it as agent of the Licensee and retain the proceeds of sale

21 Failure to erect sign

If the Licensee does not comply with clause 9.2 (relating to signs) the Licensor may itself erect a suitable sign and the cost of so doing shall be borne by the Licensee and payable on demand to the Licensor

22 Interest on overdue payments

In the event of the Licence Fee or any other sums of money payable under the terms of this Licence remaining unpaid for a period of 14 days from the date when the same shall be due the Licensee shall pay interest to the Licensor on the amount outstanding at the rate of [4%] per annum above (*name*) Bank plc base lending rate from time to time in force

23 Notices

Any notices demands or other written communications required to be made by the Licensor to the Licensee will be deemed to be properly served if addressed to the Licensee and delivered to the Allocated Space

24 Licence personal to the Licensee

24.1 This Licence is personal to the Licensee and is not in any circumstances transferable by the Licensee to any other person firm or company

24.2 It does not entitle or permit any partner or other person connected with the Licensee to trade from the Allocated Space

24.3 It does not and is not intended to create or grant to the Licensee any estate or interest in the Allocated Space or any part of the Hall or to give rise to the relationship of landlord and tenant between the parties to this Licence

25 Approval of company Licensee's employees

If the Licensee is a limited company the person or persons employed by the Licensee to trade from the Allocated Space must be approved by the Licensor for that purpose

[26 Surety's obligations

The Surety in consideration of the Licence contained above having been made at the Surety's instance and request guarantees to the Licensor that:

26.1 the Licensee will at all times while this Licence is subsisting pay the sums payable on the days and in the manner provided above

26.2 the Licensee will observe and perform the obligations and conditions contained above or implied and on the part of the Licensee to be observed and performed

26.3 if the Licensee shall make default in payment of the sums to be paid or in the observance and performance of the obligations conditions or any of them and in every such case the Surety will pay and make good to the Licensor on demand all losses damages costs and expenses thereby sustained by the Licensor

PROVIDED ALWAYS that notwithstanding any forbearance by the Licensor to enforce against the Licensee the payment of the sums due or the observance or performance of the Licensee's obligations and conditions or the giving of time by the Licensor to the

Licensee in relation to them the Surety shall not thereby be discharged from liability under the above guarantee nor shall such liability be in any way lessened or affected]

27 Declarations

27.1 The conditions and obligations contained in clause 9 of this Licence shall be performed and observed at all times throughout this Licence by the Licensee and shall where the context permits extend to the employees and agents of the Licensee

27.2 In the case of the Licensee being two or more persons each and all shall be bound by the terms of this Licence and shall sign this agreement and they shall be jointly and severally liable for the performance of the conditions and obligations on behalf of the Licensee contained above

IN WITNESS etc

(*signatures of the parties*)
(*signatures of witnesses*)

1 See Form 10 note 1 *above*.
2 For a form of notice terminating a licence see Form 13 *below*.

12

LICENCE by local authority to auctioneer for use of special facilities in market[1]

THIS LICENCE is made the . . . . . day of . . . . BETWEEN (1) (*local authority*) of (*address*) ('the Council') and (2) (*auctioneer*) of (*address*) ('the Licensee')

IT IS AGREED as follows:

1 Grant

The Council hereby grants to the Licensee permission to use the sale rings pens and other works for the control of animals pending and during the sale of them by auction at the Cattle Market at (*insert details*) ('the Market') and on the terms and conditions set out below from (*date*) until (*date*) and afterwards until this Licence shall be determined by either party giving to the other . . . days' previous notice in writing expiring at any time subject nevertheless to the provision for determination in clause 3

2 Licensee's obligations

The Licensee in consideration of the Licence hereby granted agrees with the Council as follows:

2.1 Payment

To pay during the continuance of this Licence in advance the charges set out in the first schedule

2.2 Conditions of use

To comply with the conditions of use of the sale rings pens and other works set out in the second schedule

2.3 Accounts

2.3.1 To account to the Council or the proper officer of the Council at such times and in such manner as may reasonably be required for all animals brought into the market and sold by auction by the Licensee

2.3.2 To produce such books or other evidence as the Council or its proper officer may reasonably require in verification of such account

2.3.3 Upon the acceptance of the account by the Council or its proper officer to pay over to the Council the market tolls dues and charges which may be ascertained to be due and payable according to the scale set out in the third schedule

2.4 Observance of byelaws

To observe and comply with all rules regulations and byelaws in force at the time being whether made by the Council or by any government department having control over the sale and movements of animals

3 Breach of agreement

In the event of the Licensee failing to comply with the conditions set out in clause 2 or any of them the Council may in their discretion determine this Licence immediately or by serving seven days' notice in writing on the Licensee[2]

4 Notices

Any notice may be served on the Licensee either personally or by leaving it at his last known place of abode or by prepaid registered post or recorded delivery service letter addressed to him there

AS WITNESS etc

FIRST SCHEDULE

Auctioneer's Permit to use the sale rings, pens etc and office accommodation for Sale by Auction at the Weekly Cattle Market

	£
Annual	. . .
Half-yearly (26 weeks)	. . .
Quarterly (13 weeks)	. . .
Monthly (4 weeks)	. . .
Daily	. . .

SECOND SCHEDULE

Conditions of Use of sale rings, pens etc

1 The use of the sale rings, pens and other works in the cattle market by any one licensee shall be subject to the use of them by other licensees as provided below

2 Sales by the licensees shall take place in the order fixed by the Council such order being balloted for quarterly by holders of not less than quarterly licences and any licensees granted such a licence after the holding of such a ballot shall sell after the licensees in the ballot according to the priority in the date of their licences and

afterwards the holders of licences less than quarterly shall sell accordingly to the priority in the date of their licences

3 A licensee shall sell first the cattle held by him for sale and complete such sale before selling sheep pigs etc and the licensee next in order as provided under condition 2 shall begin his sale of cattle immediately after the previous licensee has completed his sales of cattle

4 A licensee who fails to begin his sales within five minutes of the time fixed for the commencement of sales by licensees or of the time of completion of sales by the previous licensee will forfeit his place in the order of sale and his right to sell will be postponed to follow the last licensee on the day's order of sale by licensees

5 A licensee must sell not less than 30 lots of cattle or other animals per hour

6 Cattle or other animals offered for sale by a licensee and not sold may not be re-offered until the other licensees have completed their sales

7 A licensee may sell by himself or by any other duly qualified auctioneer on his behalf

THIRD SCHEDULE

Tolls and Charges in respect of cattle entering or brought into the Cattle Market

	£
For every stallion	...
For every horse	...
For every yearling colt	...

(*continue list of livestock as required*)[3]

(*signature of the parties*)

1 See Form 10 note 1 *above*.
2 For a form of notice terminating a licence see Form 13 *below*.
3 The following should be included: ass or mule; bull; ox; cow, steer, yearling heifer; cow with calf; calf; pig; sow with litter; ram; sheep; lamb; goat; poultry; turkey or goose; duck or fowl; every other bird; rabbits (live); rabbits (dead).

13

NOTICE of termination of licence to sell from stall[1]

(*Name of local authority*)

To (*stallholder*) of (*address*)

The Council as the market owner hereby informs you that on (*date*) your licence to occupy a stall for the purpose of selling in the (*name*) Market was terminated and no stall will be available for your use on the next market day that is (*day and date*) or on future market days

Dated the . . . . . day of . . . .

(*signature of proper officer of the authority*)

1 For forms of licence see Forms 10, 11, 12 *above*.

14

TENANCY of a lockable stall in a market hall[1]

THIS AGREEMENT is made the . . . . . day of . . . . BETWEEN (1) (*landlord*) of (*address*) ('the Landlord') and (2) (*tenant*) of (*address*) ('the Tenant')

IT IS AGREED as follows:

1 Demise

The Landlord lets and the Tenant takes from (*date*) the stall numbered . . . in the Landlord's Market Hall at (*insert details*) ('the Stall') [together with the fixtures and fittings in the Stall described in the first schedule]

2 Term

The tenancy shall be quarterly and may be determined by either party giving to the other not less than one quarter's notice in writing expiring on any of the usual quarter days and in the case of notice given by the Landlord it will be sufficient if left at the Stall

3 Rent

The rent shall be £ . . . per quarter payable in advance on the usual quarter days the first payment or an apportioned part of it to be made on the signing of this Licence

4 Tenant's covenants

The Tenant agrees with the Landlord as follows:

4.1 Rent

To pay the rent at the above times without any deduction whatever

4.2 Outgoings

To pay the general and water rates and all other outgoings whatever now or afterwards chargeable in respect of the Stall

4.3 Compliance with regulations etc

To comply at all times with the [byelaws and] regulations in force in respect of the Landlord's markets insofar as the same do not conflict with the terms of this Agreement

4.4 Use of Stall

To use the Stall for the sole purpose of selling (*specify goods*) on the days and during the hours specified in the second schedule only

4.5 Alterations

At his/her own expense to fit up the Stall with such counter furniture and fittings as may be necessary for the business of the Tenant but otherwise not without the consent in writing of the Landlord to make any alteration whatever to the Stall

4.6 Repair

To keep the inside of the Stall in good repair

4.7 Cleaning of Stall
To keep the Stall including the floor and passage areas within and immediately surrounding it at all times in a clean and tidy condition

4.8 Access by Landlord
At any time during the term to permit the Landlord to enter the Stall for the purpose of examining its condition or doing any necessary repairs and for other purposes deemed expedient by the Landlord

4.9 Nuisance etc
Not to do or permit to be done in the Stall anything which in the opinion of the Landlord may interfere with or be a nuisance or annoyance to the Landlord the tenants of other stalls or members of the public resorting to the Market Hall

4.10 Auctions
Not to use or permit the Stall to be used for the purpose of a sale of goods by auction

4.11 Assignment etc
Not to assign underlet charge or part with or share possession of the Stall or any part of it[2]

4.12 Fixtures and fittings
At the end of the tenancy if required by the Landlord to leave all fixtures and fittings provided by the Tenant upon being paid their value in accordance with a valuation of an independent valuer agreed between the parties but otherwise to remove such fixtures and fittings immediately

4.13 Costs of the Agreement
To pay to the Landlord the costs of the preparation of this Agreement and the Counterpart together with the stamp duty on them

5 Landlord's covenants

The Landlord agrees with the Tenant as follows:

5.1 Structural repair
To keep the Stall in good structural repair

5.2 Quiet enjoyment
That provided the Tenant pays the rent and all other outgoings and observes and performs the obligations contained in this Agreement he/she may peaceably hold and enjoy the Stall during the tenancy without interruption by the Landlord

6 Termination

It is further agreed that if:

6.1 The rent or any part is in arrear and unpaid for 14 days after becoming due (whether formally demanded or not) or

6.2 the Tenant ceases to occupy the Stall or

6.3 the Tenant fails to observe or perform any of the obligations under this Agreement or

6.4 the Tenant commits an act of bankruptcy or if a limited company goes into liquidation then the Landlord may take immediate possession of the Stall and thereupon the tenancy will determine but without prejudice to any other remedy of the Landlord for any breach of the obligations under this Agreement

AS WITNESS etc

FIRST SCHEDULE

Fixtures and fittings

(*insert details*)

SECOND SCHEDULE

Days and hours of trading

(*insert details*)

(*signatures of the parties*)

1 If a periodic tenancy, the tenant under this agreement will presumably have the benefit of the protection given by the Landlord and Tenant Act 1954 Pt II as amended by the Law of Property Act 1969 Pt I (23 Halsbury's Statutes (4th Edn) LANDLORD AND TENANT). Alternatively, a tenancy for a term certain not exceeding six months may be granted, in which case the provisions as to security of tenure for business tenants would not apply (except where there is a provision in the lease for renewal or extension of the term, or the tenant has been in occupation for a period which, when added to the period when any predecessor in the same business had been in occupation, exceeds 12 months); see the Landlord and Tenant Act 1954 s 43(3) as amended by the Law of Property Act 1969 s 12 and reprinted as amended in *ibid* Sch 5.

It may be good policy to restrict tenants to one, or at most two, stalls each to ensure a wide mix of commodities on offer; it is mainly for this reason that an absolute covenant against assignment is desirable.

2 See note 1 *above*.

15

LICENCE for the use of a stall (supplied by the market owner) in a market

AN AGREEMENT made the .... day of .... BETWEEN (1) (*market owner*) of (*address*) ('the Licensor') and (2) (*stallholder*) of (*address*) ('the Licensee')

WHEREBY IT IS AGREED as follows:

1 Grant

The Licensor as owner of the market held at (*insert details*) each (*day*) ('the Market') grants to the Licensee licence to use stall numbered . . . or such other stall of equivalent size and position as the Licensor may in [his *or* her *or* its] absolute discretion decide ('the Stall')

2 Termination

2.1 Either party may determine this Licence by giving to the other not less than one week's notice in writing

2.2 The Licensor may determine this Licence forthwith in the event of a breach of any of its terms by the Licensee

3 Licence fee

During the subsistence of this Licence the Licensee shall pay to the Licensor on each market day the sum of £ .... for the use and occupation of the Stall

4 Licesee's obligations

The Licensee shall:

4.1 Use of Stall
Use the Stall only for the purpose of selling (*specify goods*)

4.2 Compliance with regulations ect
Comply at all times with the [byelaws and] regulations in force in respect of the Market

4.3 Licensor's rights
Not impede or interfere with the Licensor's rights of possession and control of the Stall

4.4 Nuisance etc
Not do or permit to be done anything which in the opinion of the Licensor may be a nuisance or annoyance to any member of the public resorting to the Market or which may be detrimental to the efficient operation of the Market

4.5 Storage of goods
Not store or display any goods or other articles outside the limits of the Stall

4.6 Cleaning of Stall
Keep the Stall and the area immediately around it clean and free from litter and use the litter receptacles provided

4.7 Alterations etc
Not alter or add to the structure of the Stall nor damage or deface any part of it

5 Licence personal to the Licensee

It is hereby agreed that this Licence is personal to the Licensee who shall not permit any persons other than his bona fide employees to use or occupy the Stall and the parties hereby acknowledge that nothing in this agreement shall be construed as creating the relationship of landlord and tenant.

AS WITNESS etc

(*signature of the parties*)
(*signatures of witnesses*)

Index

(All references are to page number)